ADVANCES IN HUMAN ECOLOGY

Volume 5 • 1996

EDITORIAL ADVISORS

ADVANCES IN
HUMAN ECOLOGY

Editor: LEE FREESE
Department of Sociology
Washington State University

VOLUME 5 • 1996

 JAI PRESS INC.

Greenwich, Connecticut   *London, England*

CONTENTS

LIST OF CONTRIBUTORS

William S. Abruzzi

Department of Anthropology
Pennsylvania State University,
     Ogontz

Bernd Baldus

Department of Sociology
University of Toronto

Eileen Crist

Center for the Philosophy and
     History of Science
Boston University

Richard Machalek

Department of Sociology
University of Wyoming

Michael Xinxiang Mao

Department of Sociology
Texas A & M University

Kari Marie Norgaard

Berkeley, CA

David Pellow

Department of Sociology
Northwestern University

Dudley L. Post, Jr.

Department of Sociology
Texas A & M University

Allan Schnaiberg

Department of Sociology
Northwestern University

Adam S. Weinberg

Department of Sociology
     and Anthropology
Colgate University

Gerald L. Young

Program in Environmental
     Sciences and Regional Planning
Washington State University

PREFACE

EDITORIAL POLICY

This series publishes original theoretical, empirical, and review papers on scientific human ecology. Human ecology is interpreted to include structural and functional patterns and changes in human social organization and sociocultural behavior as these may be affected by, interdependent with, or identical to changes in ecosystemic, evolutionary, or ethological processes, factors, or mechanisms. Three degrees of scope are included in this interpretation: (1) the adaptation of sociocultural forces to bioecological forces; (2) the interactions between sociocultural and bioecological forces; (3) and the integration of sociocultural with bioecological forces.

The goal of the series is to promote the growth of human ecology as a transdisciplinary problem solving paradigm. Contributions are solicited without regard for particular theoretical, methodological, or disciplinary orthodoxies, and may range across ecological anthropology, socioecology, evolutionary ecology, environmental sociology, ecological economics, ecological demography, ecological geography, and other relevant fields of specialization. The editor will be especially receptive to contributions that promote the growth of general scientific theory in human ecology. No single volume will represent the full range the series is intended to cover.

CONTENTS OF VOLUME 5

Volume 5 features four papers on evolution, all in a different mode. Richard Machalek continues work, begun in Volume 4, which analyzes the evolutionary foundations and dimensions of social exploitation. Machalek seeks to identify how natural selection may favor the evolution and retention of common expropriative behavioral strategies across different species. Eileen Crist, in keeping with the cross-specific attitude of Machalek, seeks to persuade that Charles Darwin's descriptions of nonhuman life forms have been mistakenly dismissed as metaphorical and subjective. Crist undertakes an extensive analysis of Darwin's writings to argue that his descriptive language derives from his concept of genealogical descent and, consistent with evolution by selection, was meant to convey a strong case for animal-human continuity.

There follow two papers that adapt biological theories to address cultural evolution and development. Bernd Baldus argues that neo-Darwinian evolutionary theory is inadequate to explain cultural complexity, but that Darwinian theory can be combined with the modern theory of complex systems to yield a theory of internal selection for cultural evolution. William S. Abruzzi, likewise concerned about the inadequacies of current theory to explain cultural complexity, proposes an ecological model, supported by data, for the differential development of complex human communities.

Paradigm concepts that provide interpretative frames for human ecology are frequently discussed in modern literature. Two such discussions, highly detailed but widely divergent in concept, are provided, respectively, by Gerald L. Young and Kari Marie Norgaard. Young explores the concept of interaction, arguing its centrality and exploring its different dimensions as a foundation for human ecological theory. Norgaard surveys and reviews concepts of ecological feminism, showing ecofeminism to be far more than a special ideological agenda but, rather, a unique theoretical perspective for observing and interpreting human environmental connections.

The volume concludes with two papers each of which represents a distinct ecological research tradition from within sociology. Adam S.

Weinberg, David Pellow, and Alan Schnaiberg, in the tradition of modern environmental sociology, use recycling practices as a case study to show the contradictions that emerge when sustainable development—a question of intergenerational equity—is pursued within a context of intragenerational power distributions among market actors having differential access to natural resources. Dudley L. Poston, Jr. and Michael Xinxiang Mao, in the classic tradition of sociological human ecology, analyze patterns of interstate migration in the United States for a recent five year period. Their data indicate that the volume of migration flows is better explained with variables of ecological context for the destinations rather than the origins of the flows.

Lee Freese
Editor

THE EVOLUTION OF
SOCIAL EXPLOITATION

Richard Machalek

ABSTRACT

While social behavior confers advantages to the many species that express it, it also imposes costs. One such cost is "social parasitism," a form of interaction from which one participant benefits at the other's expense. Biological research on social parasitism provides a basis for the development of a general sociological analysis of one form of social exploitation—"expropriation." Expropriation describes any behavior by means of which an individual or group usurps a resource from another individual or group that produced it. This paper identifies specific properties of expropriative behavioral strategies that contribute to their proliferation in a population. It also explains how other factors, such as individual traits and ecological context, influence patterns of expropriation. Finally, the paper reviews claims that expropriation may have played a role as a selection force in the evolution of the human brain.

Advances in Human Ecology, Volume 5, pages 1-32.
ISBN: 0-7623-0029-9

INTRODUCTION

In both human and nonhuman societies, stable patterns of cooperation are often imperiled by selfishness. One form of selfish social behavior is "expropriation," which I define broadly as any behavior by means of which an individual or group usurps a resource from another individual or group that produced it. Expropriative behaviors depend upon and subsist off of productive behaviors. They are literally parasitic. Behavioral biologists have documented such expropriative behavioral strategies widely in animal societies and have studied them under the rubric of "social parasitism" (Wilson 1975, pp. 361-377). Expropriation describes any social interaction from which one participant derives benefits by extracting resources (energy, information, or material items) from another without providing compensation. Because the interaction confers benefits to one participant at the other's expense, it can be said to be exploitative. This paper extends a theoretical analysis published earlier in this series on the basic dimensions and forms of social exploitation in both human and nonhuman societies (Machalek 1995).

The earlier paper contained a naturalistic conceptualization of social exploitation, a general discussion of sociality as an evolved device for the realization of interests, and an identification of the basic dimensions and forms of social exploitation. This paper expands the theoretical perspective developed in the first one by discussing the intimate and paradoxical relationship between production and expropriation, identifying seven traits of expropriative strategies that contribute to their success (proliferation and yield), explaining how traits of individual producers and expropriators contribute to expropriation, specifying how ecological factors influence patterns of expropriative behavior, and examining the possibility that expropriation has acted as a selection force instrumental in the design of the human brain.

PRODUCTION AND EXPROPRIATION

Even a casual review of biological studies on social parasitism, especially kleptoparasitism (any behavior whereby one organisms "steals" a resource from another organism that controls or produces it), suggests the following evolutionary hypothesis: Social parasitism evolves because it is a more efficient way of acquiring resources than having to produce them (Machalek 1995). Instead of having to develop the expertise and to invest the time, energy, and material resources needed to produce a "good," an expropriator can find another individual (or group of individuals) who has made the investments and produced a good, and then exploit the producer.

In the absence of group selection reasoning, the potential competitive advantage of expropriative strategies such as kleptoparasitism becomes readily apparent. A highly productive social system can present a kleptoparasite with a rich field of opportunities for acquiring resources at a lower cost than that entailed by producing them. Presumably, as Hansen (1986) documented for fish-acquisition behaviors in eagles, even when only a minority (42%) of the activities consists of diving and catching a fish, it is sufficient to support the majority (58%) of activities that consists of stealing fish caught by other eagles. Because Hansen concludes that the 42:58 fishing/stealing ratio represents an evolutionary stable state, we cannot conclude that stealing is any more efficient than fishing, but it appears no less efficient either. Should the ratio of stealing to fishing rise beyond a certain level, however, the returns from stealing may decline below those derived from fishing, even though the producers lose some of their catch to kleptoparasites. Thus, the efficiency of stealing is frequency-dependent. If there is too much "competition among thieves," then fishing, even in the face of theft, may be a better way of making a living than stealing.[1]

Yet, in a sufficiently productive social environment, expropriation may evolve as an efficient means of subsistence. For this reason, among others to be discussed, insect societies appear highly vulnerable to invasion by expropriative strategists. The most highly evolved forms of social parasitism among nonhumans are probably dulosis (slavery) and inquilinism (permanent social parasitism) among ants (Hölldobler and Wilson 1990, pp. 436-470). Almost certainly, the enormous productivity of ant societies, with populations reaching tens to hundreds of millions of individuals, creates a degree of "wealth" (in the form of food, nests, and labor) that readily invites invasion by expropriative competitors, including termites, beetles, and other ants. It is worth noting that the widespread emergence of slavery among humans was also associated with the evolution of social systems capable of surplus production—the horticultural societies—and was much rarer during the preceding hunting-gathering epoch (Lenski and Lenski 1978). Given a sufficient level of production and the development of new and effective means of expropriation, such as metal weapons and related technologies during the horticultural period, expropriative behavioral strategies are more likely to appear in social systems as efficient and effective means of resource acquisition.

Expropriative strategies are not themselves cost-free and executed without risk. Especially when it involves coercion, expropriation may be quite risky and metabolically (as well as socially and psychologically) expensive. Findings from criminology are interesting and relevant here (Hirschi and Gottfredson 1983; Greenberg 1985; Cohen and Land 1987). The so-called "age-graded crime curve" suggests that some illegal expropriative strategies, such as armed robbery, require strong, aggressive, and spry executors—qualities that seem to peak in early adulthood (around age 20) and decline thereafter. Armed robbery, even when aided by deadly modern weapons technologies, appears not to be a viable occupational choice for middle-aged women and men.

More recently, criminologists have linked the productivity of societies to variation in the rates of property crime. Criminologists have observed that certain types of crime increase as the productivity of a society increases, both in terms of the volume and value of goods produced. This perspective, known variously as routine activity theory or opportunity theory, has been used to explain the paradox whereby the property crime rate in a society can increase simultaneously with periods of economic growth, an observation that is counterintuitive to the hypothesis that property crimes should increase only when economies deteriorate, thereby creating theft motivated by desperation (Cohen and Felson 1979). Thus, in both human and nonhuman societies, expropriative behaviors may evolve and proliferate at least in part because they are effective forms of competition. In highly productive social systems, expropriation often pays.

It is possible to summarize this reasoning in the form of a general hypothesis: The greater the degree of productivity within a social system, the higher the rate and the greater the yield of expropriation in that system. This hypothesis is testable in principle in any social system, nonhuman or human, in which expropriation occurs. An entomologist, for example, could compare closely related species of social insects, contrasting those species with societies that are less productive to those with more productive societies and determine which is more likely to incur invasion by social parasites. Similar analyses could be conducted on human groups (organizations or societies) wherein production varies, to see if the expropriative behaviors proliferate where productivity is highest.

KEY TRAITS OF EXPROPRIATIVE STRATEGIES

Whatever the individual characteristics of producers and expropriators or the social and physical context in which expropriation occurs, the success or failure of any expropriative strategy also depends on attributes of the strategy itself. These attributes influence the ease or difficulty with which expropriative strategies can be detected, deterred, repelled, or avoided. By analogy, some microorganisms have traits that make them more successful than others at proliferating within populations. Like microscopic pathogens, expropriative strategies vary with regard to the traits that make them more or less "virulent," a property that is not restricted only to organic phenomena. Instead, the notion of virulence can be used also to describe patterns of expropriative behavior that vary in terms of the costs they impose on hosts and the speed and effectiveness with which they transmit themselves across populations and generations.

What sorts of properties make an expropriative strategy more or less virulent? It is possible to identify at least seven basic attributes of expropriative strategies that contribute to their proliferation. Expropriative strategies can be said to vary to the extent that they are (1) cryptic, (2) deceptive, (3) bold, (4) mutable, (5) mobile, (6) economical, and (7) satisfying. The first three of these attributes (crypsis, deception, boldness) have been analyzed earlier in order to distinguish among the basic types of expropriation found in any social system (Machalek 1995).

Cryptic Strategies

Inasmuch as they function by escaping detection by their hosts, cryptic expropriative strategies are among the most successful. In order to avoid expropriation, prospective hosts rely on various monitoring mechanisms in order to detect the threat of expropriative activity in social interaction. These mechanisms may be purely perceptual (e.g., auditory, olfactory, visual, or thermal) or they may involve more complex forms of awareness including, among humans at least, consciousness. Alternatively, they may be purely unconscious, as are autoimmune system reactions that target invasive pathogens. By escaping detection, cryptic forms of social exploitation may avoid provoking the evolution of counter-exploitative strategies, and thus they represent especially serious threats to their hosts.

Deceptive Strategies

Deceptive strategies are detected by their hosts, but they are not recognized (either consciously or unconsciously) as threatening to the host's interests. Deceptive strategies "misrepresent" themselves along a range from appearing entirely innocuous to appearing benevolent to their hosts. Brood parasites such as cuckoos, a widely known example, misrepresent themselves as the offspring of their "foster" parents, and they are cared for and fed by these surrogate parental hosts because of an error in kin recognition. Among some parasitic species, deception is achieved by means of elaborate adaptations. For example, some socially parasitic bird species produce offspring which have evolved patterns on the insides of their beaks that resemble those of their hosts, so that when the host parents cue on the stimulus that functions as an innate releasing mechanism for prompting them to feed their offspring, they erroneously subsidize a parasite.

Among humans, deceptive strategies are much more subtle and powerful. In large part, this is due to the complexity and richness of human systems of symbolic communication. Modern human societies are organized on the basis of complex and far-reaching systems of reciprocity, which helps to explain their extraordinary productivity; and these systems of production and reciprocity are mediated by the human communication system. Paradoxically, this same system of communication functions as a device that enables the emergence of subtle forms of deception that are represented by widely documented forms of expropriation in human societies, such as confidence games, fraud, and systems of exploitation such as class domination, sexism, and racism. Some symbols are particularly conducive to the evolution of deceptive expropriation, and good examples can be found in the history of religious hucksterism in the United States. The recent rise of "televangelism" has caused considerable concern about the expanded opportunities it has created for perpetrating fraud (Hadden and Shupe 1988). Similarly, occupants of high status professions, such as priests, mental health workers, and physicians are in excellent positions to employ deception toward expropriative ends. Clearly, public concern in the United States about abuses committed by people in such client-oriented occupations has elevated in recent years.

Bold Strategies

Instead of relying on the capacity to escape detection or to misrepresent themselves, bold strategies overtly display their presence.

Their success is a direct function of the threat they pose to a prospective host. They thereby dissuade the host from trying either to repel or to evade them. Because the effectiveness of a bold strategy is linked to the expropriator's ability to marshal an effective threat, such strategies are more likely to be adopted when there is a pronounced resource holding potential (RHP) asymmetry (Machalek 1995, p. 55) between the host and the parasite, an asymmetry which, of course, favors the parasite. In its simplest form, this can be seen whenever a larger predator, such as a hyena, forcibly extracts prey from a smaller predator, such as a jackal, that captured it. In the human context, bold expropriative strategies have been adopted commonly by dominant groups such as political, military, and business elites; criminals such as armed robbers, extortionists, organized crime figures, and hijackers; dominant race/ ethnic/religious groups; and males. Perhaps the most important factor implicated in the adoption and execution of a bold expropriative strategy is an RHP asymmetry between the expropriator and the host. Consistent with much conventional sociological thinking, this suggests that the incidence of bold expropriative activity is associated closely with the degree to which a social system is stratified. Thus, RHP asymmetry, whether it derives from individual differences or the structure of a society, is an important predictor of the incidence of bold expropriation within a society.

The qualities of crypsis, deceptiveness, and boldness all influence the likelihood that an expropriative strategy will be executed successfully. The ability, however, of expropriative strategies to proliferate throughout populations is influenced by qualities such as their *mutability*, *mobility*, *economy*, and their power to provide intrinsic *satisfaction*.

Mutable Strategies

The mutability of a strategy refers basically to its adaptability (not adaptedness). That is, a mutable strategy changes in response to changes in the environmental context within which it occurs. For example, a mutable strategy may be responsive to changes in the opportunity structure created by patterns of production, to changes in the intensity of competition among expropriative strategies themselves, or to changes in the characteristics of both those who produce resources and those who expropriate them from producers. Perhaps most importantly, mutable strategies change in response to the counter-expropriative strategies with which they are confronted and to which they sometimes give rise.

As expropriative strategies invade a population of producers, the "target" hosts often respond by adopting counterstrategies that enable them to evade or to repel the threat of expropriation. This may lead to an expropriation/counter-expropriation "arms race," one in which the mutability of both strategies may determine the outcome. It should be noted that the arms race can be played out either over biographical-historical time or evolutionary time. For instance, a host-expropriator coevolutionary arms race between a computer software company and a population of software "pirate" hackers may develop rapidly, over a period of weeks or months. On the other hand, the coevolutionary arms race between slave-making ants and their hosts occurs over long spans of evolutionary time as natural selection installs alternative behavioral strategies in the genomes of succeeding generations of contestants. For this reason, quite obviously, arms races between hosts and expropriators that involve behavioral strategies which are mediated by culture can evolve much more rapidly than those in which the behavioral strategies are genetically based adaptations.

Mobile Strategies

Mobility is the quality that describes the ease with which a strategy is transmitted among individuals and groups and across populations and generations. Highly mobile cultural strategies are those that are easily imitated or learned, generally by taking advantage of features of a society's communication system and the psychology of learning. Genetically transmitted expropriative strategies, on the other hand, depend on factors such as the organism's life span, its rate of reproduction, the length of its gestation period, and various factors that influence the mutation rate within the species. Given the differences between culturally and genetically mediated behavioral strategies, it is to be expected that the diversity of patterns of expropriation and the rate at which expropriation evolves will increase to the extent that social behavior is organized and regulated primarily by learning, symbolic communication, and cultural transmission. For this reason, we should expect *Homo sapiens* (the highly intelligent, symbolic interacting, rapidly learning ape) to be the premier executor of expropriative behaviors, the truly ultimate social parasite.

Economical Strategies

Some strategies are also more economical to adopt and to execute than are others. The economy of a strategy varies in relation to the time, energy, and resources needed to acquire (for example, by learning) and to execute it. Some strategies are relatively inexpensive—they can be learned quickly and easily by teaching or by imitation. Others may be much more costly, entailing long and painstaking apprenticeships. Some expropriative strategies can be executed only by those who have highly developed technical skills, such as computer hackers or money launderers. Yet other expropriative strategies consume considerable resources to execute. In an era of effective and complex surveillance technologies, bank or jewelry heists require planning, capital investments, technical skills, and often a great deal of patience. For this reason, less expensive strategies often proliferate much more quickly, especially when they first evolve in a population, than their more costly counterparts.

Satisfying Strategies

Finally, expropriative strategies may proliferate because their execution is, in some cases, intrinsically satisfying to those who adopt them. The ability to provide satisfaction implies the existence of psychological mechanisms that are activated by the expropriative activity itself, an idea that has appeared recently in discussions of risk-taking behavior among criminals. In his book *Seductions of Crime* (1988), Katz reports that the most important motivator of street crime may derive from the stimulation provided by the behavior itself. Crimes such as armed robbery, burglary, or grand larceny involve substantial risk-taking, which itself may be sufficiently stimulating that it acts as a powerful proximate motivator of risky expropriative activity, a more powerful motivator than perceptions of extrinsic rewards to be gained by adopting such behavior. Whether the intrinsic reward is learned or innately satisfying is of secondary concern here. The important point is that the strategy may spread among members of a population because its enactment is inherently rewarding, independent of any extrinsic payoff. The appeal of risky expropriative strategies is illuminated by the sort of work that has been done by psychologists on "sensation seeking" (Zuckerman et al. 1980). Their studies have implicated biological factors in sensation seeking, such as heart rate and brain wave responses to novel stimulation, the activity of monoamine oxidase, as well as the hormones estrogen and testosterone (Konner 1990, p. 133). While this should by no means be interpreted to mean that biological factors alone *cause* expropriation, it does suggest that they can influence the probability that expropriative strategies will be adopted.

Ascertaining whether expropriative strategies themselves have properties that affect their success is an important, but commonly neglected, dimension of research on social exploitation. Instead, researchers more commonly try to identify individual traits and social circumstances that are associated with expropriative behavior in a society. It is time to begin to inquire about how features of expropriative behavioral strategies themselves may contribute to the incidence of social exploitation in societies. This does not, however, exempt evolutionary-ecological theory from having to explain how individual traits help shape patterns of expropriation.

TRAITS OF PRODUCERS AND EXPROPRIATORS

"What kind of an individual could do such a thing?" Commonly posed when people commit heinous acts, this question has motivated both folk accounts as well as behavioral and social science research efforts to explain social exploitation among humans. The question is telling, because it reveals an assumption widely held both by laypersons and behavioral/social scientists: Expropriators expropriate because *they are somehow different* from nonexpropriators. They have different psychologies, biographies, or perhaps even biologies. These differences can be typified as "profiles." And, having profiled the "expropriative type," we can detect and defend ourselves against them.

Without denying that it is possible to construct analytical profiles of "typical" expropriators in terms of their experiences, motivations, or biologies, evolutionary theory provides an alternative way of conceptualizing how individual differences are relevant to understanding patterns of production and expropriation. Instead of making the individual the primary source and locus of activity (productive or expropriative), evolutionary theory suggests that patterns of production and expropriation may be analyzed with reference to the distribution of RHP traits among members of a population. Again, the RHP or resource holding potential of an individual refers to those traits that influence the probability that a person can acquire and control a contested resource, such as a food item, a residence, or a reproductive partner (Barash 1982; Parker 1974). Among nonhuman animals, attributes such as size, strength, age, and experience are important RHP traits that help determine the outcomes of competition for food, mates, territories, residences, and other resources. Among humans, the list of such traits expands to include numerous sociocultural characteristics such as education, occupation, income, religion, race and ethnicity, political affiliation, language, gender, power, and prestige. In fact, the entire area of sociological research devoted to the study of social inequality and stratification addresses what evolutionary theorists would call the influence of RHP traits on social behavior. In nonhuman societies, RHP traits are distributed variably—predominantly by the mechanisms of inheritance and development. While both of these sets of processes operate in human societies as well, the additional influence of culture can also contribute to the variable distribution of RHP traits among humans. Let us explore how the concept of RHP is valuable in explaining how individual differences contribute to the incidence of expropriation within a population.

In recent years, behavioral biologists have begun to make good use of game theory—a theoretical perspective developed in mathematics and applied to economic and social phenomena—in order to explain resource competition among organisms, including plants as well as animals (Maynard Smith 1974, 1979, 1982).[2] In this view, individual organisms are characterized as "contestants" who win or lose competitions over resources based on the behavioral strategy that they adopt. While game theory focuses analytical interest primarily on how characteristics of the strategy itself influence competition outcome, it also allows the analyst to assess the contribution of individual differences among the contestants themselves. These differences are specified as RHP traits possessed by each competitor. An example is the competition between two bull elephant seals for mating opportunities. A bull that is RHP-advantaged (older, larger, and more experienced) is likely to try to assemble a "harem" of female seals whose mating activities he tries to monopolize. On the other hand, an RHP-disadvantaged bull (younger, smaller, and less experienced) may adopt an alternative mating strategy; he may wait until the dominant bull is sufficiently far from the harem and then try to copulate with one of the females before he can be repelled by the dominant bull (Le Boeuf 1974).

In a population of competitors, RHP asymmetries are important determinants of the likelihood that expropriative strategies will appear and spread throughout these populations. RHP asymmetries among individuals increase the probability of expropriation in two ways. First, an individual that is RHP-advantaged can use this advantage to usurp resources from others by adopting a bold expropriative strategy. Among humans, examples abound—including slavery, tribute systems, extortion, male exploitation of females, and systems of class and state domination. On the other hand, individuals that are RHP-disadvantaged may resort to expropriative activity in order to acquire resources which, because of their RHP deficiency, they are incapable of producing.

Satellite strategists provide an example from nonhuman societies. Animals such as male crickets, frogs, and toads try to attract mates with vocalizations. A calling male may be parasitized by a smaller male (the satellite) who positions himself close to the caller, intercepts females attracted to the caller, and tries to mate with them. Even though these satellite males sometimes are less successful at mating than callers, their satellite strategy is a better-than-nothing alternative. As Dawkins puts it, they are "making the best of a bad job" (1980, pp. 344-346). In this case, the satellite strategy illustrates what biologists call a conditional strategy, one that is adopted under certain circumstances. This particular conditional strategy may be expressed verbally as a simple rule: "If large, call for mates; if small, position yourself close to a caller and try to mate with any females he attracts."

Among humans, the adoption of an expropriative strategy by an RHP-deficient individual in order to get a resource that he or she cannot produce is illustrated in the view that some people engage in expropriative acts such as theft because they have been denied the opportunity to produce the resource. For example, individuals who lack the education and social ties necessary to achieve gainful employment may try to "make the best of a bad job" (low socioeconomic status) by resorting to crime. This is the basic idea represented by Merton's (1949) classic description of the "innovator" in his theory of anomie. Thus, RHP asymmetries increase the probability of expropriation both because they tempt those who are dominant in RHP traits to take advantage of their trait superiority to expropriate from the less fortunate (e.g., tribute systems), and because they may leave those who are RHP-deficient with little recourse except to try to usurp resources from capable producers.

While biologists typically use the concept of RHP to characterize differences between two individuals competing for a resource, the concept can be applied to collectivities as well. It is possible to compare two groups in terms of mean RHP differences (e.g., mean income or mean years of formal education) between their populations. Thus, one can characterize the interactive dynamics between a dominant class and a subordinate class as competition in which an average RHP asymmetry favors individuals in one group over those in the other. Also, because RHP traits always describe empirical differences between individuals, this provides a way of analyzing expropriative relations between collectivities without reifying them. As a result, the concept of RHP should prove increasingly useful to social scientists seeking a naturalistic explanation of patterns of social exploitation between groups.

THE BEHAVIORAL ECOLOGY OF EXPROPRIATION

Behavioral ecology is the branch of behavioral biology that analyzes "the way in which behaviour [that] contributes to survival and reproduction depends on ecology" (Krebs and Davies 1981, p. 1). It entails the study of contextual influences on behavior. Behavioral ecologists try to ascertain the effects of factors such as competition, predation, disease, climate, and historical events (such as volcanic eruptions) on animal behavior patterns. Because the ecological context includes demographic and social structural constraints on behavior, behavioral ecology is the branch of behavioral biology most similar in its reasoning to sociology. This section identifies the various ecological factors that inhibit, permit, or promote the evolution of social exploitation in both human and nonhuman societies.

Analytically, it is convenient to describe the ecological context of social expropriation as including as many as five dimensions: (1) the physical, (2) the demographic, (3) the social structural, (4) the strategic, and, in the case of humans, (5) the cultural and historical. The manner in which each of these sets of ecological factors can influence the incidence and rate of expropriation within societies is discussed in the next section.

The Physical Dimension

Patterns of social exploitation are located in and constrained by various features of the physical environment. Consider, for example, the physical setting in which kleptoparasitism among eagles occurs (Hansen 1986). The contested food source, fish, is concentrated in bodies of water such as lakes or rivers. This in and of itself draws the eagles into close proximity of each other as they forage. By way of contrast, raptors that hunt rodents and other small mammals that are dispersed widely on plains and prairies are not, therefore, necessarily congregated into aggregations by the distribution of their prey. Second, the act of catching a fish is a distinctly public act of production that is highly visible to prospective expropriators. Third, having seized the fish in its talons, the hunter becomes vulnerable to harassment by other eagles and is encumbered by its prey from defending itself with maximum effectiveness. Therefore, the very setting in which eagles fish and the nature of their productive activities make theirs a form of production that is highly vulnerable to invasion by kleptoparasites. For this reason, kleptoparasitism is common among other birds that hunt in open, aquatic environments (such as gulls). Likewise, mammals that hunt on savannas are vulnerable to expropriative activity for similar reasons. This is illustrated by the kleptoparasitic behaviors displayed by carnivores such as lions. Occasionally, even larger predators can be driven from prey they kill by the harassing behaviors of several small predators and scavengers. Similarly, among humans, piracy became prevalent as marine societies evolved and as shipping, an activity that is also highly public and vulnerable to expropriation, became important in international commerce.

Sometimes physical features of an environment have enabled the evolution of social parasitism in an even more direct manner. Hölldobler and Wilson hypothesize that "there remains the possibility that life in certain climates and environments actually does predispose ant species toward parasitism" (1990, p. 447). They report that while dulosis is "a common phenomenon in the colder parts of Europe and Asia but rare in the warmer parts ... not a single example has ever been reported from the tropical or south temperate zones" (1990, p. 447). Hölldobler and Wilson suggest that the mechanism that promotes ant slavery in such regions involves colder weather that dulls the defense response by host colonies to the intrusion of parasitic queens into their nests. In fact, they showed experimentally that by chilling ant colonies in the laboratory, ants would be less likely to attack new queens introduced into the colony. It is possible that parasitic queens are able to insinuate themselves into host colonies by taking advantage of the chilling produced by the mountainous climates in which many slave-making species are found.

The Demographic Dimension

Various properties of population structure may either promote or inhibit the evolution of social exploitation. For example, population size, density, and migration patterns are likely to be important factors influencing the incidence of expropriation. As populations grow larger and denser, one would expect the rate of expropriation to increase simply because resources are more concentrated, thereby increasing available targets for expropriation. Similarly, migration by producers may increase the incidence of expropriation by transporting resources through regions occupied by expropriators, what might be called a "highwayman effect."

Among humans, evidence exists that the age and sex structure of a population may influence patterns of expropriation. The earlier reference to the age-graded crime curve illustrates this. If certain types of expropriative activities (such as armed robbery or burglary) are more likely to be adopted by individuals of a specific age and sex, say 20-year-old males, then a population with a large proportion of such individuals can be expected to feature higher rates of expropriative activities such as robberies and burglaries. As the population ages, it is possible that these types of individuals will gain RHP advantage (e.g., legitimate jobs and incomes) and abandon expropriation for production; or, the type of expropriative activity in which they become involved might change from street crimes to white-collar crimes, such as tax evasion and embezzlement, activities that require a level of physical prowess of which most healthy men and women of middle-age are fully capable.

In addition to population size, density, migration patterns, and age/sex structure, fertility and mortality rates may have an effect on the rate of expropriation within a society. The simplest prediction that could be made in this regard is that, to the extent that fertility and mortality patterns increase the degree and diversity of competition within a society, the rate of expropriation will increase. The effect would be understandably stronger when opportunities for adopting productive strategies for resource acquisition fail to keep pace with the increase in competition. This suggests hypotheses that can be tested by conventional sociological means, such as the familiar proposition that expropriation varies directly with both unemployment and underemployment within a community.

Finally, evolutionary theory suggests that it is plausible to hypothesize that population growth in a society may increase the incidence of expropriation simply because the larger a population of sexually reproducing individuals becomes, the lower the average degree of genetic relatedness among its members. According to sociobiological theory, the probability of cooperation among members of a group is expected to decline as the proportion of unrelated individuals in the group increases. For this reason, sociobiologists could offer a very rough prediction that, among most species, expropriation rates will increase in the populations of individuals engaged in cooperative-productive activity as population size increases. Clearly, a rule as general as this one will succumb frequently to numerous exceptions. For example, even though ant, bee, and wasp societies feature extremely large populations, their unusual genetics (haplodiploidy) maintain an atypically high degree of relatedness among the individuals who comprise these large populations. As a result, the unusual coincidence of the genetic interests of individuals in these groups is likely to reduce expropriation and to promote cooperation and (phenotypic) altruism, as seems to be the case. And, in some species such as humans, large societies are integrated primarily by reciprocity rather than kinship, so population size is likely to be related less directly to the incidence of expropriation than in societies where the primary mechanism of social cohesion is genetic kinship.

The Social-Structural Dimension

By far, sociologists have devoted more attention to analyzing how patterns of social organization and interaction contribute to the incidence of social exploitation among humans than they have to any other causal influence. While the evolutionary-ecological approach developed in this paper actually vindicates the emphasis that sociologists have placed on social structural causes of exploitation, it qualifies that emphasis by placing it in context of a broader range of causal influences. It is likely that much of the research conducted by sociologists on class, race and ethnic, gender, and other forms of social exploitation could be integrated readily into the theoretical perspective developed herein. Specifically, this tradition of sociological research should allow us to specify in considerable descriptive detail how various features of social organization and patterns of interaction help shape patterns of expropriation in human and perhaps even nonhuman societies. While sociologists have expressed little apparent interest to date in developing such cross-species analyses, recent developments in evolutionary biology make this a propitious time for efforts at just such a synthesis.

In any event, it is not difficult to hypothesize how certain forms and features of social organization may promote the evolution of social exploitation. One way to illustrate this is by looking at major changes in the structure of human societies over longer periods of evolutionary and historical time than those to which most sociologists are accustomed. That is, we can examine the sorts of fundamental social-structural changes associated with the transformation of human societies from the hunter-gatherer period to the modern (or "postmodern") period and try to determine how these changes may have influenced the incidence of expropriation within society. Inasmuch as expropriation depends ultimately on production, we shall focus our attention primarily on changes in the social relations of production.

Game-Theoretic Insights

Although it was developed in order to analyze patterns of cooperation and noncooperation (cheating) between members of a dyad, the Prisoner's Dilemma highlights factors that predispose or inhibit expropriation among members of collectivities as well. Using insights developed by scientists employing the Prisoner's Dilemma model and the general logic of game theory, we can specify how some of the structural changes associated with the transformation of human societies from the hunter-gatherer to the industrial era have influenced patterns of expropriation.

Basically, analyses of the Prisoner's Dilemma have revealed that patterns of cooperation between two interactors are inherently unstable, even though in the long run both interactors benefit more by cooperating with each other than by trying to exploit each other. Given the conditions that game theorists identify as favoring the evolution of stable patterns of cooperation in a dyad, we can speculate about why members of small hunter-gatherer bands may have been much less likely to suffer from expropriative social behaviors than have occupants of large, urban industrial societies. The political scientist Robert Axelrod (1984) has identified various factors that promote cooperation and inhibit cheating (nonreciprocity, a form of expropriation in exchange systems), and we can focus on these factors to see how they may have been altered by the social-structural changes accompanying the rise of modern, industrial societies.

One of the defining features of modern societies is the high degree of anonymity present even in cooperative interaction settings. When cooperators are anonymous to each other, they do not have access to critical information about each other that Axelrod calls "reputation" (1984, pp. 150-154). Reputation is information about another's behavioral record of cooperation or cheating. In small groups dominated by primary relationships, reputations are public knowledge because individuals have the opportunity to observe directly the behaviors of others, or they are in direct communication with those who have interacted previously with the individual in question. The prototype is what Tönnies (1957) called a *Gemeinschaft* form of social organization. In contrast, modern industrial societies and their economies are systems of social interaction involving vast numbers of strangers, few of whom have much reputational knowledge about others with whom they cooperate in productive activities such as trade. Both the size of these production systems and the extensive division of labor in the organization and processes of production exacerbate the problem of anonymity. Consequently, much cooperative interaction must be based either on trust, or on a sequence of low-cost initial interactions so that potential cheaters/expropriators can be identified and avoided before the resources at stake become significant.

Another factor that promotes stability in patterns of cooperation is iterated interactions among the same individuals. In the *Gemeinschaft* social setting, the same individuals interact repeatedly with each other day after day, month after month, year after year. This has two significant consequences. First, it maximizes reputational knowledge among potential interactors. This enables individuals to avoid being deceived into cooperating with expropriators. Second, it makes possible the exercise of an important counter-expropriative strategy, called "retaliation" (Axelrod 1984, p. 44). Having a reputation of retaliating against cheaters is important in establishing and maintaining a credible threat against potential expropriators (Axelrod 1984; Daly and Wilson 1988, pp. 221-251). Several features of the social organization of modern society, however, mitigate against effective retaliation. For example, many exchange episodes in modern society are non-iterative or episodic. One may engage in important economic interactions with an individual whom one never sees again. This sort of circumstance is highly favorable for the evolution of various sorts of "confidence game" forms of expropriation. Evolutionary game theory enables us to understand that the con artist is a successful expropriator because he or she is unlikely to have a bad reputation to live down when engaging a potential host, and because he or she never tries to exploit the same victim twice. In fact, confidence game strategies can work effectively only in rather large groups where their practitioners can capitalize on the anonymity characterizing such groups and thus "stay ahead" of their reputations. Of course, such forms of expropriation inevitably initiate cheater/cooperator "arms races" wherein cooperators try to assign reputations to cheaters by issuing alerts about them (and their scams—their expropriative strategies) through modern telecommunications media, and by engaging the resources of the state (law, the courts, and police) in order to deter, retaliate against, or extract compensation from expropriators. Inasmuch as many cooperative encounters in modern societies involve single-episode interactions, these societies are inevitably threatened by expropriators who have little to fear from retaliation or damaged reputations.

The Division of Labor

Another aspect of the social organization of modern industrial societies that predisposes expropriation is its system of an extensive and complex division of labor. The division of labor can be described as a form of "parallel processing" whereby several different tasks necessary for producing a good or providing a service are performed simultaneously, thereby enhancing the ergonomic effectiveness and efficiency of the social relations of production. Because of the extraordinary productivity enabled by the division of labor, it is one of the defining features of complex social systems, whether they involve modern humans or social insects (Machalek 1992, pp. 52-56). As the division of labor becomes more complex and extensive, it becomes more opaque to most of its participants. Their engagement in the production process becomes segmented and highly localized and, as a result, they are incapable of assessing the consequences of their involvement in the division of labor for the realization of their own interests. As a result, the opacity of their activities, especially their benefits and beneficiaries, makes them highly vulnerable to the intrusion of expropriators. As evident in modern industrial societies, this process was described perceptively first by Marx in connection with his analysis of alienated labor. Yet, the vulnerability to expropriation created by the division of labor is not restricted only to human societies. Rather, the division of labor is also implicated in the evolution of slavery (dulosis) among ants. Specifically, ant societies have evolved rather complex systems for dividing labor among specialized castes. Members of castes do not "recognize" each other as individuals; instead, they identify other colony members as representatives of one or another caste (e.g., major worker, minor worker, soldier, reproductive female, etc.). This means that social interaction among individual ants is, effectively, interaction among collectivities (castes) rather than distinct individuals. Incapable of recognizing others *as* individuals, they rely on pheromonal and tactile cues in order to "classify" appropriately other colony members and thus "know" how to interact with them. Consequently, if an alien species can "break the code" that mediates this communication among castes and imitate the cues that regulate cooperation among them, it can deceive and manipulate individuals to its own advantage. To illustrate the extraordinary nature of this phenomenon, Wilson (1975) quotes the famous myrmecologist W.M. Wheeler:

> Were we to behave in an analogous manner we should live in a truly Alice-in-the-Wonderland society. We should delight in keeping porcupines, alligators, lobsters, etc. in our homes, insist on their sitting down to table with us and feed them so solicitously with spoon victuals that our children would either perish of neglect or grow up as hopeless rhachitics (p. 377).

When the division of labor develops to the point that it involves cooperation among individuals who are ignorant of each others' activities and perhaps even existence, it amplifies significantly the threats of expropriation associated with anonymity. When one is enmeshed in a complex division of labor with anonymous others, there is often little way of determining if expropriators have insinuated themselves into the productive chain. Nor is it easy to assess the actual costs and benefits associated with production and thereby determine if the costs and benefits are distributed among producers according to legitimate norms of reciprocity and fair exchange. Thus, the division of labor in society both increases its productivity and, simultaneously, threatens its participants with elevated rates of expropriation.

Hierarchy

One final feature of modern societies will be discussed briefly to illustrate how social-structural forms can contribute to the evolution of social exploitation. This feature is most easily recognized by sociologists because of its role in promoting social exploitation in human societies: hierarchy. Hierarchies that are built into the very structure of human society did not become common until the appearance of the horticultural era (Lenski and Lenski 1978). It was during this period that new, fully-blown systems of social stratification first appeared in human societies, most notably in the forms of slavery and state-based systems of domination. Even with the decline of slavery associated with the collapse of feudalism and the rise of industrial capitalism, new forms of domination became prominent, especially class stratification. In terms of evolutionary game theory, this has far-reaching implications, perhaps the most important of which is that hierarchy generates pronounced and severe RHP asymmetries among individuals and groups. From the standpoint of evolutionary game theory, RHP asymmetry erodes stable patterns of cooperation, because it reduces the retaliatory capabilities of one interactor and increases those of the other. This, therefore, enables the RHP-dominant player to adopt a strategy of inexpensive, if not cost-free, cheating. Furthermore, RHP asymmetry may enable one player to exploit the other *and* prevent one from escaping the "game" in which he or she is being exploited and is unable to retaliate. If RHP asymmetries carry over into different social contexts (e.g., from the family, to work, to government), then the exploitation of the host is exacerbated. Among humans, this is very well illustrated by gender stratification.

While by no means complete, this discussion of certain key changes associated with the transformation of human societies from the hunter-gatherer period to modern times illustrates how various aspects of social organization and interaction shape patterns of expropriation.

The Strategy Ecology Dimension

Behaviors transpire in a "playing field" of other behavioral strategies being executed in a population of individuals. The composition and frequency distribution of these strategies constitute a context that exerts a significant influence on the chances for the success or failure of any particular strategy. Imagine, for example, a population in which every individual is producing goods (such as catching fish). Such a context of "pure production" represents an opportune environment for invasion by a thief. On average, the thief might be much more successful at foraging than the producer. If, however, the strategy context changes, then the payoff of theft might diminish. For example, if the strategy context changes such that the ratio of theft strategies to production strategies increases, competition among thieves could reduce the average returns to theft below those derived from production (fishing). Axelrod calls such a context of strategies a *strategy ecology* (1984, p. 51).

Although similar to the concept of social structure, strategy ecology isolates the influence of behavioral strategies themselves upon each other, whatever the organizational context in which they appear. More specifically, the idea of social structure is used typically by sociologists to identify relationships among those occupying various statuses, or positions in a social organization. As a social structural trait, hierarchy distributes individuals among various ranked statuses such as power or wealth. When occupying a dominant status within a hierarchy, an individual may be able to adopt any of a number of behavioral strategies. One may, for example, either cooperate with a subordinate or take advantage of his or her RHP superiority and cheat. While, in this case, a social-structural trait (hierarchy) probably influences the chances that individuals in the hierarchy will either cooperate or cheat, the distribution of various strategies within the population will influence the probability that a particular strategy will be adopted, the chances for its successful execution, and its payoff.

Stated differently, expropriation is frequency-dependent. One of the most important ways in which rates of expropriation are influenced by strategy ecology is illustrated by the simple ratio of expropriative acts to productive acts. As the ratio of expropriation to production increases, the average returns to the expropriator tend to decline. Eventually, a threshold may be reached which, when passed, means that the average yield of each act of production is greater than that provided by each act of expropriation. (It need not matter, incidentally, how these acts are distributed among individuals. The incidence of expropriation may rise and fall independently of the number of individuals behaving expropriatively.)

The notion of strategy ecology is important in analyzing patterns of expropriation, because it provides a way of assessing how a *population configuration of different types of activities* influences the likelihood that one or another type of activity will appear and spread within that population. In analyzing social exploitation, special efforts should be made to monitor the evolution of new forms of production, as well as expropriation, in order to try to determine how the strategic environment changes. This can provide clues from which it might be possible to gauge the likelihood that expropriative activity will increase or decrease within the population. The analysis of how strategy ecology inhibits or promotes expropriation is perhaps the least developed and one of the most promising areas of inquiry in the study of social exploitation.

The Cultural and Historical Dimension

The behavioral ecology of human societies consists not only of physical, demographic, and social factors, but of cultural and historical influences as well. Depending on one's definition of "culture," humans may or may not be the only cultural species. If the concept of culture denotes the use of complex symbol systems to encode information that is produced and transmitted by communicative action among individuals, then the term is sufficiently narrowly defined so as to limit culture to humans. Alternatively, if the term is defined more broadly, as "the transfer of information by behavioral means, most particularly by the process of teaching and learning," then culture can be said to be distributed much more widely in nature (Bonner 1980, pp. 10-11). By Bonner's definition, any species in which the behavior patterns of individuals can be altered by their observation and experience of the behavior of conspecifics can be said to possess culture. Thus, culture comes to be regarded as a trait that is not to be thought of as either present or absent in a species, but rather, as possessed to a greater or lesser extent. Stated differently, a species can be said to be "more cultural" to the extent that its behavioral responses to stimuli are alterable by information acquired by the observation and experience of conspecifics.

For many social scientists, Bonner's definition of culture is too inclusive. For evolutionary scientists, however, who seek to understand the evolution of the capacity for culture, a broad definition such as Bonner's is necessary for any effort to try to reconstruct the phylogeny of this trait. Nevertheless, given the indisputably important differences between human culture and that of virtually all other social species, a definitional distinction is in order. A practical convention could dictate the use of the term culture exclusively in connection with humans, and the term protoculture for what Bonner calls (nonhuman) animal culture.

Precisely because of the capacity for culture, humans are the only truly "historical" species. While all species have a past, only humans appear to use complex symbol systems to encode in their communication systems detailed information about their experiences, both individual and collective, to store this information, to transmit it across generations and through populations, and continually to revise both its form and content. In a fundamental and profound manner, the very idea of evolution means that organisms are constrained, in their bodies and their behavior, by their ancestries. They have phylogenetic histories. Human history, on the other hand, involves an essentially Lamarckian process whereby the experiences of predecessors are recorded and retrieved by successors. It is unlikely that the behavior of any other animal is shaped by communications about its predecessors and their experiences. Thus, this discussion of the cultural and historical dimensions of ecological influences on behavior will focus on humans.

A large share of the social-scientific literature devoted to the analysis of social exploitation consists of cultural and historical analyses. Marx, the first major theorist of social exploitation, insisted that patterns of class exploitation could be made intelligible only by means of historical analysis. Furthermore, Marx, Weber, Pareto, and other nineteenth-century pioneers of the sociological study of social exploitation placed great emphasis on explaining how cultural phenomena enabled and promoted the emergence and proliferation of various forms of social exploitation among humans. These thinkers introduced numerous concepts to modern social science that were devised specifically to help analyze exploitative social processes. It is possible to integrate some of the key insights associated with how culture influences patterns of social exploitation with the evolutionary perspective developed in this paper. Specifically, evolutionary game theory identifies key processes relevant to the sociological analysis of social exploitation. For example, ideology, false consciousness, and legitimation all represent cultural phenomena that facilitate social exploitation by enabling cheating or defection to occur and to persist in human societies.

Game theory explains that an individual will retaliate when one becomes aware that the norm of reciprocity has been violated by another with whom one is involved in an exchange relationship. The Prisoner's Dilemma model requires that each player is aware of the moves made by the other player in previous interactions. Thus, when one player "cheats," the other player is aware of this and is expected to respond strategically in an appropriate manner, presumably by retaliating with cheating in the next iteration of the game. When extrapolated to relations among collectivities, such as social classes, the lessons of evolutionary game theory can be applied to the evolution of cultural phenomena related to exploitation. In the vernacular of evolutionary game theory, false consciousness describes a player who fails to understand that he or she has been cheated by either a subtle or gross expropriator. False consciousness is enhanced by ideology, a cultural phenomenon that obscures the relationship among social interactions, their consequences, and the interests of social interactors. Thus, individuals (or groups) who are "cheated" fail to recognize that they are subsidizing an expropriator at real costs to themselves. If they are aware of this, the cultural process called "legitimation" may induce them to accept their victimization. Or, "reification" may prevent them from recognizing that alternative relationships are at least imaginable and perhaps even available. These and other such cultural devices are often employed by RHP-superior expropriators to exploit their hosts without suffering retaliation and, instead, even benefiting from the host's endorsement of expropriator-host interaction. In fact, even RHP superiority can be legitimated with the aid of culture. For example, a culture that advocates the idea that resources are distributed by mechanisms associated with fair and open competition provides a built-in rationale for both subtle and gross cheating, the victims of which can be typified as "losers" in a fair game.

Finally, the historical context within which human behavior occurs also helps contribute to the behavioral ecology of production and expropriation. For example, prior to the Civil Rights movement in the United States, numerous minority groups (e.g., other ethnic groups, gays, women) were victimized by expropriative patterns that disproportionately benefitted members of the dominant, expropriative group, namely, middle- to upper-class white males. A culture of entitlement had evolved in Western history that sustained, over generations, a pronounced asymmetry in relations between these segments of European and North American societies. As an historical event, the American Civil Rights movement enabled the emergence of a succession of challenges by other minority groups to this asymmetry, challenges that would not have been possible at an earlier historical moment. Consequently, many expropriative strategies that were used widely a half-century ago (such as the unchallenged exclusion of minorities from most institutions of higher learning and many of the professions for which they train students) are now simply unavailable to advantaged, white male expropriators.

Because culture transmits collective memories across generations, temporal contexts vary with regard to the extent that they inhibit or promote various forms of expropriative behavior. As the only truly cultural and historical social animal, and precisely *because* of this distinction, human beings confront the challenge of living a type of social existence that is unrivaled by any other social species in terms of the volume and varieties of expropriation to which it is vulnerable.

EXPLOITATION AND ADAPTATION

Social parasitism is surprisingly widely distributed among animal societies (Machalek 1995, pp. 43-50).[3] Similarly, expropriative behaviors have been prevalent in the history of human societies, and social exploitation has been pervasive in interpersonal relations as well as among groups divided by sex/gender, race and ethnicity, class, religion, and many other forms of affiliation. By usurping vital resources, successful expropriators can threaten the survival and reproductive chances of their hosts, thereby presenting them with an adaptive challenge. If expropriation is a recurrent and reproductively salient threat to those confronted by it, it may even function as a force of natural selection. Among humans, individual learning and cultural transmission are both crucial in equipping potential hosts to cope with expropriative threats. Some subcultures even contain specific expressions, such as "street smart," "savvy," or "not an easy mark," that designate those individuals and groups that have acquired information and experience that make them less likely to fall victim to expropriative strategists.

For the most part, social scientists have assumed that expropriative and counter-expropriative behaviors are mediated entirely by culture, individual learning, or a combination of the two. Clearly, expropriation among humans is almost certainly a facultative behavior, and most social scientists would probably contend that counter-expropriative strategies are as well. To date, most available evidence on expropriation among humans appears consistent with this interpretation. Even if expropriation is a problem as archaic as the productive strategies that first enabled it to emerge, few social scientists are prepared to argue that humans possess evolved adpations for defense against expropriative threats. Recently, however, two evolutionary-minded social scientists (an anthropologist and a psychologist) have taken exactly this position (Cosmides and Tooby 1992). Because their work is directly relevant to the type of expropriative behaviors discussed in this paper, and because it is framed in evolutionary terms, it deserves at least brief consideration here.

Cosmides and Tooby (1992) analyze "cheating," one form of expropriation that occurs in the context of social exchange situations and social contract relationships. Cheating is conceptualized in game-theoretic terms as the failure to reciprocate (cooperation with cooperation). In the Prisoner's Dilemma model, cheating is costly to its victims, and evolutionary game theorists contend that it can represent a serious adaptive threat with which its potential hosts must cope if they are to survive and reproduce. Cosmides and Tooby agree with evolutionary game theorists about the adaptive relevance of cheating, and they contend that nonreciprocity has been a sufficiently severe problem in human evolutionary history that it is plausible to hypothesize that humans have evolved psychological adaptations for coping with the threat of cheating in social exchange contexts. Cosmides and Tooby conceptualize these possible adaptations as "algorithms (specialized mechanisms) designed for reasoning about social exchange" (1992, p. 164). Using the "Wason selection task," which was developed to test people's abilities to detect violations of conditional rules, Cosmides and Tooby have generated evidence which, to their satisfaction, documents the existence of a specialized, domain-specific cognitive mechanism that enables people to detect rule violations committed in social contract situations. Furthermore, their experimental data support their claim that this "cheating detection mechanism" is not simply an artifact of the greater familiarity of some problems over others. Nor do their experiments lead them to believe that there is something about the social contract context itself that facilitates superior logical reasoning or greater clarity of thought. Instead, they conclude:

> The results showed that we do not have a general-purpose ability to detect violations of conditional rules. But human reasoning is well designed for detecting violations of conditional rules when these can be interpreted as cheating on a social contract (Cosmides and Tooby 1992, p. 205).

Their research is provocative in the context of the evolutionary analysis of social exploitation developed in this paper and its predecessor (Machalek 1995). Basically, the theory of social exploitation is consistent with the view that certain types of social facts (features of social organization and interaction) could have acted as selection forces that may have been instrumental in contributing to the evolution of key design features of the human brain. Stated differently, the evidence presented by Cosmides and Tooby implicates specific social processes (reciprocity and nonreciprocity) directly as selection forces in the evolution of functional properties of the human brain. While sociologists have long contended that "mind" and "self" are socially constructed products (e.g., Mead 1934; Berger and Luckmann 1967), Cosmides and Tooby have attributed even more "constructive" potency to social processes by claiming that certain kinds of social situations (like the iterated Prisoner's Dilemma) can act as forces of natural selection shaping the evolution of the human brain.

If evolutionary psychologists are to succeed in adducing additional evidence in support of their thesis that the functional properties of the human brain (which they term "mind") are the product of *social* forces of natural selection, then they must identify precisely those social processes that may have acted as selection forces. Cosmides and Tooby attempt this by using the Prisoner's Dilemma to identify cheating as a force of natural selection. Furthermore, any such selection forces must have been present in the "environments of history" (Alexander 1979, 1990) or the "environment of evolutionary adaptedness" (EEA) (Symons 1990) if they are to be credited with a role in shaping the evolution of the human brain. To date, work has only begun on the problem of identifying these selection forces. Reconstructing phylogenies is never easy, and reconstructing phylogenies of possible behavioral adaptations is one of the greatest challenges faced by evolutionary scientists.

Researchers can contend, as have Cosmides and Tooby, that the machinery of human behavior (the brain, central nervous system, and endocrine system) evolved to enable individuals to cope with specific constraints imposed by group life only if they are able to identify, with confidence, the precise features of social interaction and organization in the EEA that could have acted as selection forces. In Irons' (1994) phrasing, they must be able to specify those aspects of Pleistocene social life that were "adaptively relevant." And, even if one can demonstrate that certain features of group life present adaptive challenges to individuals, this does not mean that behavioral *adaptations* will necessarily evolve in response to these challenges. Humans may still depend primarily on culture rather than on evolved adaptations to cope with exprorpriative threats. Of course, such adaptations may, in fact, exist but may have escaped detection because researchers have not known how to look for and find them. In either case, it is plausible to surmise that throughout human evolutionary history, social life has both conferred benefits and posed threats to those involved in it. We have yet to establish whether humans are equipped with only the "capacity for culture" or also possess evolved adaptations for coping with these threats. Still, whether or not future research will corroborate claims about the existence of evolved "mechanisms" for coping with social problems such as cheating, sociologists are in a position to assist the efforts of those engaged in a search for such mechanisms by determining what these problems may have been (and may still be). Thus, even those social scientists unwilling to entertain the notion of evolved adaptations dedicated to coping with specific problems posed by group living can contribute to a research effort designed to identify the adaptive problems faced by ancestral humans by virtue of living socially.

CONCLUSIONS

At the very least, work done by evolutionary-minded psychologists might help build a bridge between biologists and sociologists interested in explaining social exploitation among humans. In the meantime, approaching the study of social exploitation by attempting to integrate basic insights from evolution, ecology, sociology, and psychology as well as other social and life sciences promises to open up new areas of inquiry and to stimulate new modes of analysis. By relaxing the assumptions involved in group-benefit reasoning, sociologists can reexamine patterns of expropriation as expressions of competition among individuals whose interests fail to coincide. This can free them from having to postulate, at the outset, the existence and influence of some sort of "pathogen," be it cultural, psychological, or biological, in order to try to account for expropriative activity. In addition, an evolutionary and ecological approach to the study of social exploitation reintroduces, somewhat ironically, a decidedly "sociological" approach to the study of social behavior. Specifically, the notion of behavioral patterns as strategies places emphasis on the manner in which existing patterns of behavior in a population inhibit or promote the expressions of other forms of behavior, whatever the characteristics of the individuals or groups executing these behaviors. While acknowledging that the characteristics of individuals and groups (via RHP factors) *are* important in influencing behavior, a focus on populations of behavioral strategies allows us to escape the more static views of behavioral causation associated with various "trait" theories of behavior, that is, the view that behaviors derive primarily from individual or group characteristics. Nor does the evolutionary-ecological approach to studying social exploitation narrowly delimit the types of interests and resources that may be contested between producers and expropriators. Instead, it provides the best available framework for the development of a truly general theory of social exploitation.

By its very nature, the evolutionary-ecological perspective presumes that any act or pattern of expropriation derives from a coalescence of all of the factors discussed in this analysis, thereby making this approach truly synthetic, and satisfying.

ACKNOWLEDGMENTS

I am grateful to Joseph Lopreato and John Sibley Butler for appointing me visiting scholar in the Department of Sociology at the University of Texas, Austin, where I conducted much of this research (1994-1995). I also thank Charles B. White for his assistance in securing library privileges for me at Trinity University, San Antonio. I thank Lee Freese for his suggestions pertaining to an earlier draft of this paper. This research was supported by a sabbatical leave awarded by the University of Wyoming.

NOTES

1.   The ratio of expropriation to production can remain static in a population, or it can oscillate. See Cohen and Machalek (1988, pp. 473-474) for a discussion of the various ways in which a population of "mixed" behavioral strategies can reach various kinds of equilibria.

2.   Consult Dawkins (1989, pp. 66-87) or Barash (1982, pp. 165-182) for accessible introductions to evolutionary game theory. A more sophisticated and comprehensive treatment is available in Maynard Smith (1982).

3.   Apparently, not even inorganic artificial life forms are immune to parasitism. Intriguing evidence about the incidence of parasitism "in silico" has been provided recently by an ecologist who has created an artificial ecosystem which he calls "Tierra" (Ray 1992). The artificial organisms in this system are informational in that they are "creatures consisting of computer instructions" and they "'live' inside the machine's core memory and compete for space in that silicon terrain" (Levy 1992, p. 217). As Tierra assembled itself, parasites and even "hyperparasites" evolved to usurp instructions from other artificial organisms. These information parasites usurp and alter the information

present in other artificial organisms, and they thus become important factors in the production of complexity in artificial ecosystems (Levy 1992, pp. 224-225).

REFERENCES

Alexander, R.D. 1979. *Darwinism and Human Affairs*. Seattle, WA: University of Washington Press.

―――. 1990. "Epigenetic Rules and Darwinian Algorithms: The Adaptive Study of Learning and Development." *Ethology and Sociobiology* 11: 241-303.

Axelrod, R. 1984. *The Evolution of Cooperation*. New York: Basic Books.

Barash, D.P. 1982. *Sociobiology and Behavior*, 2nd ed. New York: Elsevier.

Berger, P.L. and T. Luckmann. 1967. *The Social Construction of Reality: A Treatise in the Sociology of Knowledge*. Garden City, NY: Doubleday.

Bonner, J.T. 1980. *The Evolution of Culture in Animals*. Princeton, NJ: Princeton University Press.

Cohen, L.E. and M. Felson. 1979. "Social Change and Crime Rate Trends: A Routine Activity Approach." *American Sociological Review* 44: 588-608.

Cohen, L.E. and K.C. Land. 1987. "Age Structure and Crime: Symmetry and Asymmetry, and the Projection of Crime Rates through the 1990's." *American Sociological Review* 52: 170-183.

Cohen, L.E. and R. Machalek. 1988. "A General Theory of Expropriative Crime: An Evolutionary Ecological Approach." *American Journal of Sociology* 94: 465-501.

Cosmides, L. and J. Tooby. 1992. "Cognitive Adaptations for Social Exchange." Pp. 163-228 in *The Adapted Mind: Evolutionary Psychology and the Generation of Culture*, edited by J.H. Barkow, L. Cosmides, and J. Tooby. New York: Oxford University Press.

Daly, M. and M. Wilson. 1988. *Homicide*. New York: Aldine de Gruyter.

Dawkins, R. 1980. "Good Strategy or Evolutionary Stable Strategy?" Pp. 331-367 in *Sociobiology: Beyond Nature/Nurture*, edited by G.W. Barlow and J. Silverberg. Boulder, CO: Westview.

―――. 1989. *The Selfish Gene*, new edition. New York: Oxford University Press.

Greenberg, D. F. 1985. "Age, Crime, and Social Explanation." *American Journal of Sociology* 91: 1-21.

Hadden, J.K. and A. Shupe. 1988. *Televangelism: Power and Politics on God's Frontier*. New York: Henry Holt and Company.

Hansen, A.J. 1986. "Fighting Behavior in Bald Eagles: A Test of Game Theory." *Ecology* 67: 787-797.

Hirschi, T. and M. Gottfredson. 1983. "Age and Explanation of Crime." *American Journal of Sociology* 89: 552-584.

Hölldobler, B. and E.O. Wilson. 1990. *The Ants*. Cambridge, MA: The Belknap Press of Harvard University Press.

Irons, W. 1994. "Adaptively Relevant Environments (ARE's) versus the EEA." Paper presented at the annual meeting of the Human Behavior and Evolution Society, Ann Arbor, MI.

Katz, J. 1988. *Seductions of Crime*. New York: Basic Books.

Konner, M. 1990. *Why the Reckless Survive ... and Other Secrets of Human Nature.* New York: Viking.

Krebs, J.R. and N.B. Davies. 1981. *An Introduction to Behavioural Ecology.* Sunderland, MA: Sinauer Associates.

Le Boeuf, B.J. 1974. "Male-male Competition and Reproductive Success in Elephant Seals." *American Zoologist* 14: 163-176.

Lenski, G. and P. Lenski. 1978. *Human Societies: An Introduction to Macrosociology.* New York: McGraw-Hill.

Levy, S. 1992. *Artificial Life: A Report from the Frontier Where Computers Meet Biology.* New York: Vintage Books.

Machalek, R. 1992. "The Evolution of Macrosociety: Why Are Large Societies Rare?" Pp. 33-64 in *Advances in Human Ecology*, Vol. 1, edited by L. Freese. Greenwich, CT: JAI Press.

_____. 1995. "Basic Dimensions and Forms of Social Exploitation: A Comparative Analysis." Pp. 1-30 in *Advances in Human Ecology*, Vol. 4, edited by L. Freese. Greenwich, CT: JAI Press.

Maynard Smith, J. 1974. "The Theory of Games and The Evolution of Animal Conflicts." *Journal of Theoretical Biology* 47: 209-221.

_____. 1979. "Game Theory and the Evolution of Behavior." *Proceedings of the Royal Society of London* B. 205: 475-488.

_____. 1982. *Evolution and the Theory of Games.* Cambridge: Cambridge University Press.

Mead, G.H. 1934. *Mind, Self, and Society*, edited by C.W. Morris. Chicago: University of Chicago Press.

Merton, R.K. 1949. *Social Theory and Social Structure.* Glencoe, IL: Free Press.

Parker, G.A. 1974. "Assessment Strategy and the Evolution of Animal Conflicts." *Journal of Theoretical Biology* 47: 223-243.

Ray, T.S. 1992 "An Approach to the Synthesis of Life." Pp. 371-408 in *Artificial Life II*, Santa Fe Institute Studies in the Sciences of Complexity, Vol. 10, edited by C.G. Langton, C. Taylor, J.D. Farmer, and S. Rasmussen. Reading, MA: Addison-Wesley.

Symons, D. 1990. "Adaptiveness and Adaptation." *Ethology and Sociobiology* 11: 427-444.

Tönnies, F. 1957. *Community and Society*, translated and edited by C.P. Loomis. East Lansing, MI: Michigan State University Press.

Wilson, E.O. 1975. *Sociobiology: The New Synthesis.* Cambridge, MA: The Belknap Press of Harvard University Press.

Zuckerman, M., M.S. Buchsbaum, and D.L. Murphy. 1980. "Sensation Seeking and Its Biological Correlates." *Psychological Bulletin* 88: 187-214.

DARWIN'S ANTHROPOMORPHISM:
AN ARGUMENT FOR ANIMAL-HUMAN CONTINUITY

Eileen Crist

ABSTRACT

This paper examines Charles Darwin's portrayal of animals. With his consistent use of the ordinary language of action and mind to depict animal life, Darwin's approach is regarded as anthropomorphic from a contemporary biological perspective. In contrast to the appraisals of certain commentators, I argue that Darwin's anthropomorphic idiom is not metaphorical, erroneous, or insignificant in comparison to his major contributions. His employment of a subjective terminology with respect to animals is closely connected with his view of genealogical common descent. Darwin's anthropomorphic language reflects his understanding of evolutionary continuity, which includes behavioral and mental continuity between humans and animals.

Advances in Human Ecology, Volume 5, pages 33-83.
Copyright © 1996 by JAI Press Inc.
All rights of reproduction in any form reserved.
ISBN: 0-7623-0029-9

INTRODUCTION

Charles Darwin's work was seminal for the inception and establishment of the biological study of behavior. His arguments for evolution established the phylogenetic continuity between humans and animals, thereby irreparably undermining the credibility of the religious doctrines of the fixity of species, of creationism, and of the unique status of human beings. The link between human and animal worlds by common ancestry, accepted widely as an incontestable fact shortly after the publication of Darwin's *On The Origin of Species*, opened the twin conceptual possibilities of naturalist approaches to human behavior and of the scientific appreciation of phenomena of mind, will, and language in animal life. After Darwin, the domains of humans and animals were no longer separated by the barrier of a metaphysical-religious doctrine of essential difference (Mayr 1982). Besides the shift in worldviews heralded with the discovery of evolutionary continuity, Darwin's evolutionary perspective contributed to the study of animal behavior its most fundamental theoretical framework. The functional and adaptive understanding of behaviors—the purposes they are designed to serve—could now be conceived under the auspices of the theory of natural selection; like morphological features and physiological processes, behavioral patterns could be approached as vital for the survival and reproduction of animals (Tinbergen 1951; Gould 1982). The final seminal contribution of Charles Darwin to behavioral science was his virtual inception of the field of the biological study of natural behavior (which came to be called ethology) with his 1872 work, *The Expression of the Emotions in Man and Animals*, where Darwin inaugurated the scientific study of human and animal behavior and mind in light of an evolutionary viewpoint (Lorenz 1965; Burkhardt 1985).

Despite his crucial contribution to the study of behavior, there is a profound discrepancy between Darwin's depictions of animal life and the modes of depiction of twentieth-century biological studies. From a contemporary perspective, Darwin's explanatory and descriptive language has been regarded as anthropomorphic. For instance, the ethologist Samuel Barnett (1958) criticizes Darwin's depiction of animal life as anthropomorphic and, in this regard, in need of correction. Michael Ghiselin (1969), a Darwinian scholar, attempted to downplay Darwin's anthropomorphic style by claiming that his language was largely intended as metaphorical rather than literal representation. For the most part, however, Darwin's language of representation of animals has been greeted with silence. According to Richard Burkhardt, at least one reason for the relative neglect of Darwin's work on animal behavior on the part of contemporary scholarship has been "the anthropomorphic cast of many of [his] discussions of behavior" (1985, p. 328). Overall, it seems that Darwin's predilection for rendering animal life in what have been widely regarded as "human" terms is either dismissed as a quaint relic of a past epoch, reappraised as metaphorical, or ignored as irrelevant next to his major contributions.

This paper investigates Darwin's mode of depicting animal behavior and mentality. One of the aims is to criticize the reception of Darwin's anthropomorphism as either error, metaphor, or undeserving of serious attention. I show that Darwin intended his depictions of animal life as literal and veridical; his anthropomorphic portraiture of animals was submitted as a realistic appraisal. Moreover, against the assessment of his anthropomorphism as an error in need of correction, I argue that Darwin's understanding of animal life reflected his view of evolutionary continuity. Finally, I submit that Darwin's anthropomorphic depictions embody a defensible perspective on animal life, which is a powerful and worthy opponent of mechanomorphic and skeptical views, widespread in behavioral thought during this century.

I begin by presenting an extensive collection of characterizations of animal life from Darwin's works, in order to give an overview of Darwin's anthropomorphic language. To show that Darwin's mode of depicting animal life was intrinsically bound with his understanding of evolution, I then discuss Darwin's explicit standpoint on the continuity between all animals with respect to behavioral traits and mental qualities. In the section that follows, I focus on *The Expression of the Emotions in Man and Animals*, so as to investigate Darwin's perspective on animal mind. Then, in contrast to the views of Darwin's anthropomorphic style as either erroneous or metaphorical, I show that his approach reflects his perception of subjectivity—namely, the dimensions of experiential meaningfulness and authorship—in the animal world. Finally, I examine certain anecdotes in Darwin's behavioral writings. Hand in hand with anthrpomorphism, the "anecdotal method" has been disparaged as a reliable source of knowledge. I discuss how Darwin makes inductive use of anecdotal data in order to evidence certain otherwise intractable phenomena.

DARWIN'S LANGUAGE OF CONTINUITY

Darwin's language of representing animals makes a resounding statement for the evolutionary continuity of animals and humans. Darwin's implicit advocacy for continuity takes shape through a generous, unabashed use of the commonplace terms of (human) mind and action as resources through which to witness and understand animal life. Relying on the vernacular vocabulary of action to describe and interpret both animal and human behaviors is an additional way of arguing for evolutionary continuity. As Carl Degler puts it, "underlying Darwin's anthropomorphism was his determination to demonstrate as often and as thoroughly as possible the continuity between the so-called lower animals and human beings" (1991, p. 8). In the same vein, Ghiselin acknowledges that for Darwin "to attribute 'higher' mental processes to 'lower' animals was one way of arguing for evolution" (1969, p. 202).

Darwin's lack of predilection for the mechanistic view of animal conduct—a legacy of Descartes' philosophy[1]—is quite evident in his portrayals. A mechanistic rendering of behavior is not necessarily incompatible with evolutionary theory, nor even with a view of mental continuity, as is clear in the case of the views of Darwin's colleague and ally, T.H. Huxley (1874), who viewed animals, as well as human beings, as conscious automata. Darwin did not share Huxley's mechanistic thesis; indeed, in his last letter to his friend, with tenderness and not without irony Darwin wrote "I wish to God there were more automata in the world like you" ([1892] 1958, p. 347). Even though Darwin rarely discussed philosophical issues explicitly, he was not unfamiliar with the philosophical debates of his day, and his disinclination from a mechanistic perspective can also be seen in his favorable citation of Humboldt in *The Descent of Man*: "The muleteers in S. America say, 'I will not give you the mule whose step is easiest, but Las mas racional,—the one that reasons best;' and Humboldt adds, 'this popular expression, dictated by long experience, combats the system of animated machines better perhaps than all the arguments of speculative philosophy'" ([1871] 1981, vol. 1, p. 48).

Ghiselin attempted to defend Darwin against the charge of anthropomorphism by arguing that there "has been a confusion of his language with his real meaning: there is a world of difference between his metaphorical use of anthropomorphic terms and the propositions which he actually asserts" (1969, p. 188). But Ghiselin also acknowledges that Darwin "lapses into anecdotal evidence and genuine anthropomorphism" (p. 203). However, the ubiquity and consistency of Darwin's style of depiction of animal life does not bear the reading of an occasional lapse into anthropomorphic terminology. Darwin's writing embodies an approach, which is not only poignantly at odds with a mechanistic conception of animal behavior, but which also advances an alternative understanding of animal life. That Darwin did not doubt that animals have rich mental lives is especially evident in his work on the subject of mentality, namely, *The Expression of the Emotions in Man and Animals*. Further, Darwin's portrayals of animal life throughout his writings reveal that he regarded animals as subjects—that is, as agents that experience the world and author their actions.

In what follows I provide an extensive exposition of Darwin's depictions to show that he has a pronounced predilection in his trope of writing, one which is consistent and pervasive rather than incidental and sporadic. This collection from Darwin's writings underscores that it is impossible to downplay the ubiquity and intensity of his "anthropomorphism." This exposition may also impart an overall appreciation of his language of continuity—a language hitherto commonly demoted with the label "anthropomorphic." In this paper, rather than partaking uncritically in the negative connotation of the term, I am interested in exploring the nature and work of anthropomorphic reasoning.

In contemporary behavioral writings there is rarely reference to the emotions of love and attachment among animals. Darwin, however, uses these terms even in reference to animals that among contemporary behavioral scientists are sometimes regarded as "mindless automata"—for example, invertebrates.[2] Darwin writes that among Lamellicorn beetles "some live in pairs and show mutual affection" ([1871] 1981, vol. 1, p. 377). Regarding crustaceans, he cites an anecdote from a naturalist about a male and female of a pair that were separated. When "the male was again put into the same vessel ... he ... dashed into the crowd, and without any fighting at once took away his wife" ([1871] 1981, vol. 1, p. 334); Darwin concludes from this that "the males and females recognize each other, and are mutually attached" (p. 334). Recounting that "in many parts of the world fishes are known to make peculiar noises," he conjectures that even fishes may possibly use sounds "as a love-call or as a love-charm" ([1871] 1981, vol. 2, p. 22). With respect to birds, Darwin writes of males and females "exciting each other's love" (p. 107); parrots "become so deeply attached to each other that when one dies the other for a long time pines" (p. 108). Noting that dogs and monkeys show jealousy, he comments that "this shews that animals not only love, but have the desire to be loved" ([1871] 1981, vol. 1, p. 42). Just like "we long to clasp in our arms those whom we tenderly love," so "with the lower animals we see the same principle of pleasure derived from contact in association with love" ([1872] 1965, p. 213). Cats express affection by rubbing themselves on objects, which perhaps originated from "the young themselves loving each other" ([1872] 1965, p. 127). Moreover, in "the deep love of the dog for his master," Darwin discerns a distant evolutionary echo to "the feeling of religious devotion" ([1871] 1981, vol. 1, p. 68).

Regarding intense and passionate emotions, Darwin states that "even insects express anger, terror, jealousy, and love by their stridulation" ([1872] 1965, p. 349). The beetle Chiasognathus stridulates "in anger or defiance," while others "from distress or fear" ([1871] 1981, vol. 1, p. 384). Darwin cites Wallace on certain male beetles fighting "apparently in the greatest rage" (p. 375). The male Ateuchus beetle "stridulates to encourage the female in her work and from distress when she is removed" (p. 384); the male of a certain species of locusts "whilst coupled with the female, stridulates from anger or jealousy when approached by another male" (p. 352); and it is probable, according to Darwin, that the female cicadas, "like birds, ... are excited and allured by the male with the most attractive voice" (p. 352). "Bees express certain emotions, as of anger, by the tone of their humming, as do some dipterous insects" (p. 366); and again, "everyone who has attended to bees knows that their humming changes when they are angry" ([1872] 1965, p. 94). Further, "with birds the voice serves to express various emotions, such as distress, fear, anger, triumph, or mere happiness" ([1871] 1981, vol. 2, p. 51); male macaws use their loud voices "when they are excited by strong passions of love, jealousy and rage" (p. 61). Hummingbirds are characterized as "quarrelsome" (p. 40), and one hybrid goldfinch as having an "irascible disposition" ([1872] 1965, p. 99). With respect to frogs and toads, Darwin writes that "though cold-blooded, their passions are strong" ([1871] 1981, vol. 2, p. 26); "chameleons and some other lizards inflate themselves when angry" ([1872] 1965, p. 105); and snakes "have some reasoning power and strong passions" ([1871] 1981, vol. 2, p. 31). Darwin also writes of "the intense grief of the female monkeys for the loss of their young" (vol. 1, p. 40). Cats express "terror combined with anger," as well as "rage or anger" ([1872] 1965, p. 56). "Porcupines rattle their quills and vibrate their tails when angered";

rabbits "stamp loudly on the ground as a signal to their comrades ... [and] when made angry" (p. 93). Male stags use their voice "under the strong excitement of love, jealousy and rage" ([1871] 1981, vol. 2, p. 276).

With respect to notions encompassing what are often referred to as higher mental qualities, Darwin argues that animals have powers of imitation, attention, memory, imagination (seen in the dreaming of animals), and reason ([1871] 1981, vol. 1, pp. 44-46). He observes that where fur-bearing animals have been pursued with traps "they exhibit, according to the unanimous testimony of all observers, an almost incredible amount of sagacity, caution and cunning" (p. 50); and, quoting Swinhoe, Darwin suggests that "the victory of the common rat over the large Mus coninga [is due] to its superior cunning" (p. 50). He comments that "the mental powers of Crustacea are probably higher than ... expected," as "anyone who has tried to catch shore-crabs ... will have perceived how wary and alert they are" (p. 334). Darwin writes that "spiders ... exhibit much intelligence" (p. 338). He attributes to the worm "attention and some mental power" as well as "some degree of intelligence" ([1881] 1985, pp. 25, 35). "There can be no doubt," he writes, "that birds closely attend to each other's song" ([1871] 1981, vol. 2, p. 52). Dogs have five different kinds of barks, namely, the barks of eagerness, of anger, of despair, of joy and of demand (vol. 1, p. 54). Darwin implicates a capacity for judgment in the dog in that "a young shepherd-dog delights in driving and running round a flock of sheep, but not in worrying them" (p. 79); he also writes that "dogs possess something very like a conscience" (p. 78). Dogs and puppies also pretend to fight in play ([1871] 1965, pp. 102, 120, 249, 351). About porcupines, he claims that they are "so fully conscious of the power of their weapons, that when enraged they will charge backwards with their spines erected, yet still inclined backwards" (p. 94). Citing Bartlett, Darwin writes that when hyenas fight "they are mutually conscious of the wonderful power of each other's jaws, and are extremely cautious. They well know that if one of their legs were seized, the bone would instantly be crushed" (p. 122). With regard to monkeys and other animals, Darwin notes that "many anecdotes, probably true, have been published on [their] long-delayed and artful revenge" ([1871] 1981, vol. 1, p. 40); and, referring to Brehm's observations, he writes that monkeys "defend their master when attacked by anyone, as well as dogs to whom they are attached [and] some ... took much delight in teasing, in various ingenious ways, a certain old dog whom they disliked" (p. 41). He writes that "one horse shows another where he wants to be scratched, and they then nibble each other" ([1872] 1965, p. 45). Generally, among social animals "gestures and expressions are to a certain extent mutually intelligible ... Anyone who has watched monkeys will not doubt that they perfectly understand each other's gestures and expression" (p. 60).

Darwin makes frequent reference to animals' acting from and showing feelings of satisfaction and pleasure. He writes of "the deep grunt of satisfaction uttered by a pig, when pleased with its food" ([1872] 1965, p. 91). He notes that "even cows when they frisk about from pleasure, throw up their tails in a ridiculous fashion" (p. 116). Horses show eagerness to start on a journey by "pawing the ground [which] is universally recognized as a sign of eagerness" (p. 46). A foxhound "delights in hunting a fox" ([1871] 1981, vol. 1, p. 79); and a dog can be "cheerful" and in the "highest spirits" ([1872] 1965, pp. 120, 122). When ewes and lambs reunite "their mutual pleasure at coming together is manifest" (p. 85). Generally, Darwin writes, "under a transport of Joy or vivid Pleasure, there is a strong tendency to various purposeless movements" as seen in young children, in dogs, and in horses (p. 76). Among birds, the bower-birds create "curious structures" (bowers), "solely as halls of assemblages, where both sexes amuse themselves and pay their court" ([1871] 1981, vol. 2, p. 71). He observes that "we can plainly perceive, with some of the lower animals, that the males employ their voices to please the females, and that they themselves take pleasure in their own vocal utterances" ([1872] 1965, pp. 87-88). Further down, I discuss the consequences of Darwin's view of animals acting for the sake of pleasure.

This selective exposition illustrates that Darwin's anthropomorphic vocabulary of animal action and mind pervades and characterizes his writing. It exemplifies a use of language that differs profoundly from that of contemporary scientific writing on animal behavior. For instance, in contrast to behavioral studies in the wake of the twentieth-century schools of behaviorism and ethology, Darwin never places scare quotes around any concepts, even as much of his vocabulary refers to phenomena widely assessed as "human" or "subjective." The modern practice of enclosing mental predicates (such as, love, anger, jealousy, grief, understanding, pretending, knowing, etc.) in quotation marks is corollary to the assumption that such terms refer to processes or states that are either off-limits to animals or ostensibly unavailable for observation. Quotation marks around such terms work as skeptical markers.[3]

The twentieth-century practice of quotation placement around mental terms assumes that such terms stand for invisible, and hence unverifiable, phenomena. However, the absence of quotation marks, and of other skeptical qualifications, in Darwin's works does not reflect that he is making unfounded inferences about what goes on inside animals. Darwin's application of anthropomorphic terminology is well documented and does not amount to placing homunculi inside the animal; his deployment of mental terms is not derived from rash imputations of specifically human qualities to other animals. Rather, Darwin is concerned with the behavioral and physiological manifestations that support the ascription of subjective phenomena. For Darwin, evolutionary common descent entails that it is highly improbable that subjective phenomena would be the sole province of human beings. This approach is most fully developed in *The Expression of the Emotions in Man and Animals*, where Darwin provides detailed observations of how emotions and sensations like terror, pain, pleasure, joy, anger, love, jealousy, dejection, affection, and so on are apparent in the expressiveness of gesture and countenance and in physiological manifestations.

DARWIN'S VIEW OF EVOLUTIONARY CONTINUITY

Regarding Darwin's anthropomorphism, Ghiselin writes that

> one reason ... Darwin's psychology has not been understood is his tendency to express himself in anthropomorphic terms. A natural inference would be that he really believed in a close correspondence between animal and human mentality. There is some truth in this interpretation, but it has many pitfalls as well (1969, p. 188).

In light of numerous explicit statements and arguments in Darwin's works, the assessment that "there is some truth in the interpretation" that he believed in a close correspondence between human and animal mentality may be viewed as something of an understatement. There is abundant evidence that Darwin held such a view. His lack of skepticism regarding the attribution of what have often been regarded as specifically human qualities to animals originated from his commitment to the entailments of common descent. The evolutionary perspective compelled him to acknowledge continuity not only at the level of physiological and morphological traits, but with respect to behavioral and mental attributes as well.[4]

In *The Descent of Man* the first chapter presents physiological evidence for the common descent of humans and animals. The remainder of this work is devoted to what Darwin calls mental faculties, such as moral sense, aesthetic sensibility, reasoning, imagination, and self-consciousness. The core argument which permeates the discussion of these topics is that "there is no fundamental difference between man and the higher mammals in their mental faculties" ([1871] 1981, vol. 1, p. 35). Moreover, in agreement with his gradualist view of evolutionary change, that "natura non facit saltum" ([1859] 1964, p. 460), Darwin regards "mental powers" as represented in "numberless gradations" in the animal world ([1871] 1981, vol. 1, p. 35). For Darwin mental differences are differences of degree rather than of kind: "the difference in mind between man and the higher animals, great as it is, is certainly one of degree and not of kind" (p. 105); and again, "the mental faculties of man and the lower animals do not differ in kind, although immensely in degree" (p. 186). On Darwin's view, evolutionary continuity suggests, inexorably, that "as man possesses the same senses with the lower animals, his fundamental intuitions must be the same" (p. 36).

In his *Selection in Relation to Sex*, Darwin makes an explicit and strong link between mental faculties and sexual selection.[5] Commenting on sexual selection in general, Darwin characterizes it using mental terminology as "an extremely complex affair, depending as it does, on ardour in love, courage, and the rivalry of the males, and on the powers of perception, taste, and will of the female" ([1871] 1981, vol. 1, p. 296). In the same vein, with respect to birds in particular, he states that "their courtship is often a prolonged, delicate and troublesome affair" (vol. 2, p. 103). Darwin relies on this connection between mental qualities and sexual selection to argue that secondary sexual characters do not appear in the "lowest" classes of animals (such as protozoa, coelenterata, jellyfish, etc.), because they have "too imperfect senses and much too low mental powers to feel mutual rivalry, or to appreciate each other's beauty or other attractions" (vol. 1, p. 321). In this context, Darwin reiterates that the acquisition of secondary sexual characters "depends on the will, desires, and choice of either sex" (p. 321).

For Darwin, then, evolutionary relatedness signified an unbroken continuity between humans and animals in all respects, inclusive of behavioral patterns and mental faculties. In standing by this particular entailment of evolutionary continuity, Darwin went well beyond what his contemporaries were willing or able to accept. As the Darwinian scholar Robert Richards writes, "by detailing the intellectual heritage man shared with the lower animals Darwin set out on the final stretch of an evolutionary path, along which not even some of his strongest supporters ... could travel"(1987, pp. 195-196). Darwin's anthropomorphic appreciation of animal life and mind can be understood as a corollary of his travel along this "final stretch of the evolutionary path." Darwin's anthropomorphism was therefore neither careless science nor simply a metaphorical way of speaking, but rather reflected the breadth of his understanding of the entailments of continuity inherent in his evolutionary outlook.

Ernst Mayr has argued compellingly that the Darwinian evolutionary perspective is intrinsically inimical to essentialist and typological forms of thought and argumentation (1982, pp. 87, 407; 1984). In contrast to regarding "essential" qualities as real and important, and variations as imperfect and insignificant manifestations of stable essences, evolutionary thought emphasizes the seminal significance of inconstancies, gradations, and continuities. The shift from essentialist to evolutionary thinking depends precisely upon the recognition of the importance of variation, which is the very material basis of species-transformations over geological time.[6]

The anti-essentialist thrust in Darwin's behavioral work can be seen in his (overt and tacit) rejection of various dipolar typifications, traditionally evoked for the purposes of formulating a sharp boundary between human and animal life. An important conceptual facet of Darwin's view of mental continuity between animals and humans is that he did not accept the distinctions between instinct and reason, instinct and intelligence, invariability and plasticity of behaviors, or involuntary and willful action, as supportive of a saltus between animal and human nature. While he did not submit a full-scale criticism of the polarization of these categories, Darwin rarely treated them in contrastive or mutually exclusive terms. Because Darwin did not think in terms of typologies, but rather emphasized variation, he did not reify categories, that is, he did not conceive them as essential properties of phenomena.

Richards notes that "Darwin never hesitated to predicate of animals an ability to adjust their innate behavior" (1987, p. 130; see also pp. 108-109). In this vein, Darwin did not treat reason and instinct as discontinuous or mutually exclusive bases of action. For instance, he writes that "the anthropomorphous apes, guided probably by instinct, build for themselves temporary platforms; but as many instincts are largely controlled by reason, the simpler ones, such as this of building a platform, might easily pass into a voluntary and conscious act" ([1871] 1981, vol. 1, p. 53). He also objected to a typological, contrastive treatment of intelligence and instinct, writing that "those insects which possess the most wonderful instincts are certainly the most intelligent. In the vertebrate series, the least intelligent members, namely fish and amphibians, do not possess complex instincts" (p. 37).

To some extent Darwin accepted the distinction between "learned" and "instinctual" behavior, as characteristic of the human and animal realms, respectively (see [1859] 1964, p. 207). He maintains that "man cannot on his first trial, make, for instance, a stone hatchet or a canoe, through the power of imitation. He has to learn by practice; a beaver, on the other hand, can make its dam or canal ... as well, or nearly as well, the first time it tries, as when old and experienced" ([1871] 1981, vol. 1, p. 39). At the same time, Darwin did not view the capacity to learn as the sole criterion for intelligence, as he observes that "amongst mammals the animal most remarkable for its instincts, namely the beaver, is highly intelligent" (p. 37). Moreover, anticipating what ethologists would later call "imprinting" (Lorenz 1935), Darwin recognized that certain behaviors combine inextricable instinctive and learned components. He writes that "man has an instinctive tendency to speak as we see in the babble of our young children ... Young male [birds] continue practicing, or, as bird-catchers say, recording [their future song] for ten or eleven months. Their first essays show hardly a rudiment of the future song; but as they grow older we can perceive what they are aiming at; and at last they are said 'to sing their song round'" ([1871] 1981, vol. 1, p. 55). He concludes that "an instinctive tendency to acquire an art is not a peculiarity confined to man" (p. 56).

Donald Griffin has observed that in twentieth century behavioral science the "absence of learning is ... taken, almost universally, as proof that the animal has no conscious awareness of its instinctive behavior" (1984, p. 42). Darwin did not hold this a priori assumption of an incompatibilty between innate behavior and conscious awareness. So, for instance, he writes that "when we behold two males fighting for the possession of the female, or several male birds displaying their gorgeous plumage, and performing the strangest antics before an assembled body of females, we cannot doubt that, though led by instinct, they know what they are about, and consciously exert their mental and bodily powers" ([1871] 1981, vol. 1, p. 258). As this passage (among numerous others) shows, Darwin (unlike much contemporary behavioral science) did not regard the notion of "conscious instinct" as oxymoric.[7] However, in affinity with the evolutionary emphasis on variation and inconstancy, Darwin did not advance a stable, one-sided picture of animal behavior; thus he did not hold that all animal behavior is "consciously exerted." Elsewhere, for instance, he asserts that instinctual actions performed by "lower animals" have been "gained, step by step, through the variability of the mental organs and natural selection, without any conscious intelligence on the part of the animal during each successive generation" (p. 39).

Besides not treating instinctual behaviors in contrastive or incompatible terms with reason, learning, or conscious awareness, Darwin also objected to a polarization between voluntary and involuntary action. In particular, he opposed the idea that animal behavior is involuntary while human behavior is voluntary, arguing instead that behavioral responses combine involuntary and willful components. Thus, countering Sir C. Bell's wish "to draw as broad a distinction as possible between man and the lower animals," and in disagreement with Bell's claim that animals can express little beyond rage and fear, Darwin draws a lovely analogy between man and dog. He writes: "But man himself cannot express love and humility by external signs, so plainly as does a dog, when with drooping ears, hanging lips, flexuous body, and wagging tail, he meets his beloved master. Nor can these movements in the dog be explained by acts of volition or necessary instincts, any more than the beaming eyes and smiling cheeks of a man when he meets an old friend" ([1872] 1965, pp. 10-11). With this analogy Darwin makes his point compellingly, as it is clear that "the beaming eyes and smiling cheeks of a man when he meets an old friend" are not responses that can be neatly classified as either willful or involuntary. Implicitly criticizing a typological view of human and animal action through a priori, diptychal categories, Darwin suggests that not only are the responses of dog and man recalcitrant to an involuntary versus voluntary compartmentalization, but they afford a common conceptualization of action and feeling— in this case descriptions employing the terms love and humility.

In agreement, then, with Mayr's characterization of Darwin as an anti-essentialist thinker, I have briefly argued that Darwin resisted the typological oppositions of instinct versus reason, instinct versus intelligence, invariability versus plasticity of behavior, and involuntary versus willful action. He treated mentality as intractable to inventories of essential, insular types. Indeed, Darwin criticized thinkers who deployed such distinctions so as to "preserve the conventional distinction between animals and men" (Richards 1987, p. 108).

DARWIN'S *THE EXPRESSION OF THE EMOTIONS IN MAN AND ANIMALS*

Nowhere is Darwin's understanding of mental continuity clearer than in his 1872 work on emotions. In *The Expression of the Emotions in Man and Animals*, Darwin ([1872] 1965) establishes evolutionary common ancestry as the framework within which to analyze expressions and gestures of animal and human emotion. He claims that "he who admits on general grounds that the structure and habits of all animals have been gradually evolved, will look at the whole subject of Expression in a new and interesting light" (p. 12). Further on in the same work, Darwin describes his methodological approach in even more explicit terms. He proposes that the test of the soundness of an explanation of "the cause or origin of the several expressions" of emotion is "whether the same general principles can be applied with satisfactory results, both to man and the lower animals" (p. 18). Throughout this work, under the unifying, naturalistic framework of evolution, Darwin points out parallels and similarities of form between the expressions of certain emotions in humans and animals. The congruence of behavioral and physiological expressions of emotions among different animals becomes intelligible and explainable within the framework of phylogenetic, common descent.

In an essay critical of Darwin's generous ascription of mental qualities, particularly emotions, to animals, Samuel Barnett (1958) voices the skeptical perspective on animal mind in its typical twentieth-century form. Barnett treats Darwin's approach to emotions in animals with a certain degree of "Whiggish" condescension, as a quaint relic of a naivete which has been superseded by the more knowledgeable science of the twentieth century.

> Darwin ... took it for granted that terms like *love*, *fear* and *desire* can usefully be employed to describe the behaviour of animals—or at least of mammals[8]— generally. He accepted the colloquial use of the word emotion. In doing so he assumed (by implication) that other species have feelings like our own ... Since his time it has gradually been found more convenient to describe animal behaviour, not in terms of feelings of which we are directly aware only in ourselves, but in terms of the activities which can be seen and recorded by any observer; we may also try to describe the internal processes which bring these activities about. Thus today it is unusual for ethologists to speak of emotions, though they continue to study the various types of behaviour which Darwin described as expressive of emotion. If the word emotion were to be used in the

scientific study of animal behaviour, its meaning would have to be shifted from the familiar, subjective one: it would have to be used to refer, not to feelings, but to internal changes which could be studied physiologically (Barnett 1958, p. 210, emphasis in original).

Barnett regards the colloquial use of mental terms like emotion as problematic, in that the usage implies that animals "have feelings like our own." He calls upon an opposition between feelings and activities in terms of "subjective" and "objective." For Barnett, evidence is insufficient for love, fear, or desire to be attributed to animals, as these are feelings which "we are directly aware of only in ourselves;" on the other hand, activities "can be seen and recorded by any observer."

In contrast however to Barnett's evaluation, Darwin's ascription of emotions like love, fear, and desire to animals is authorized by evolutionary theory and based on observational evidence. Darwin's ascriptions of emotions are not unfounded imputations to animals. His strongly empirical approach undermines the unquestioned presupposition of skepticism, namely, the truncation of "subjective" feelings from "objective" activities. In *The Expression of the Emotions in Man and Animals* (which is the target of Barnett's critique), Darwin discusses the various emotions in humans and animals, detailing the physiological and behavioral expressive evidence. He describes the countenance of emotion, that is, the entire facial, gestural, and postural forms that are the grounds of recognition and ascription of different frames of mind. Darwin's method and reasoning involve the careful documentation of physiological and behavioral expressive forms. His approach to the identification of emotions in animals and humans is scientific in the twofold sense of the naturalist's attentiveness to the countenance of emotion and the evolutionist's concern for the generality of occurrence of similar (and hence possibly homologous) expressive forms in different species.

Throughout *The Expression of the Emotions* Darwin details the behavioral and expressive elements that are part and parcel of various frames of mind. Systematically, he draws out the intimate connections between body and mind. He draws attention to the affiliation of behavioral-physiological expressions with the recognition of states of mind. He thus notes that "when our minds are much affected, so are the movements of our bodies" ([1872] 1965, p. 32); "so strongly are our intentions and movements associated together, that if we wish an object to move in any direction we can hardly avoid moving our bodies" (p.

64); and again, "most of our emotions are so closely connected with their expression, that they hardly exist if the body remains passive— the nature of the expression depending in chief part on the nature of the actions which have been habitually performed under this particular state of mind" (pp. 237-238).

While these passages may be interpreted as embracing an ontological split between mind and body, Darwin's work emphasizes the recognitional basis of the connection between bodily expressiveness and the perception of mental modalities, ultimately undermining dualism. Darwin repeatedly draws attention to the instantaneous and pre-analytical character of the recognition of emotions. He writes of the expression of grief in a human face: "when observed, [it] is universally and instantly recognized as that of grief or anxiety, yet not one person out of a thousand who has never studied the subject, is able to say precisely what change passes over the sufferer's face" (p. 182). Further on, he reiterates the same idea in more general terms:

> We may actually behold the expression changing in an unmistakable manner in a man or animal, and yet be quite unable, as I know from experience, to analyze the nature of the change ... It has often struck me as a curious fact that so many shades of expression are instantly recognized without any conscious process of analysis on our part (pp. 358-359).

Thus Darwin's blow to a dualist view of body and mind is not accomplished by reducing mind to either physical movements of, or events in, the body. Rather his observationally powerful arguments have the effect of showing that behavioral comportment and mental states are a single, fused totality. The unity of body-mind is evidenced in the instantaneous, often precise recognition of the emotional states of others—by both humans and animals.

Darwin discusses the entire gamut of emotions describing expressive forms closely. In the case of very intense sensations and emotions— like pain, rage, joy, and terror—he notes how vivid their manifestations are, not only in behavior, but in physiological events as well. He describes pain, for instance, as expressed in "writhing with frightful contortions;" in "piercing cries and groans;" he observes that with pain every muscle of the body is brought into action and the teeth may be clenched or gnashed together; moreover, "perspiration bathes the entire body," and "circulation and respiration are much affected" (pp. 69-70). With respect to joy, Darwin writes:

Under a transport of Joy or of vivid Pleasure, there is a strong tendency to various purposeless movements, and to the utterance of various sounds. We see this in our young children, in their loud laughter, clapping of hands, and jumping for joy; in the bounding and barking of a dog when going out to walk with his master; and in the frisking of a horse when turned out into an open field (p. 76).

With respect to mental experiences of lesser intensity than pain or joy, Darwin retains his empirically robust method of close observation and detailed description. The manifestations of such mental attitudes and experiences as pleasure, hostile intention, discomfort, attention, affection, impatience, listlessness, and dejection are also available in facial and bodily countenance. Darwin discusses these various emotions in animals and humans detailing their physiological and behavioral expressions.

As Barnett notes, Darwin unproblematically deploys the vernacular use of "emotion" in the case of animals. Darwin also often enlists commonplace examples to illustrate the expression of emotions in the animal world. While relying upon common knowledge and language, he addends the naturalist's keen eye for detail and the evolutionist's focused concern for the origin and unity of expressions. For example, in his description of a cheerful dog Darwin depicts an illustrative scene of everyday life: "A dog in cheerful spirits, and trotting before his master with high elastic steps, generally carries his tail aloft, though it is not held nearly so stiffly as when he is angered" (p. 116). Darwin's concern here is to identify the elements of the countenance of cheerful spirits. His interest in evolutionary unity leads him to attend specifically to the position of the tail, "held aloft," noting that the same pattern is encountered in other animals, such as horses and cows, in similar states of mind (p. 116). Further, his naturalist vision is sensitive to discriminate between shades of stiffness of the tail. He marks the crucial difference between the expressions of cheerfulness and anger—a difference that may easily go unobserved by the layperson, particularly if the surrounding circumstances, implicating the appropriateness of cheerfulness or anger, are not obvious.

The naturalist's scientific method involves making inventories of the physical details of expressive and postural behaviors. Darwin's work is rich with observations about the position and movement of ears, the bristling or smoothness of hair or feathers, the holding of the tail at different heights and in different shades of rigidity, the baring of teeth, and even the expression in the eyes, and relative brightness or dullness of eyes. Evolutionary concerns make him attentive to the tendency of expressions of emotion to recur throughout the animal kingdom. Darwin notes a number of recurring behavioral patterns. For example, the pricking and directing forward of the ears is an expression of attention; the pawing of the ground—seen in creatures as diverse as wasps and horses—expresses impatience or eagerness; the raising of the eyebrows in dogs, apes, monkeys, and humans shows astonishment; the drawing back of the ears in cats, seals, dogs, and horses, among others, expresses hostile intention or savage disposition; and dullness of the eyes often manifests dejection or ill-health.

In Darwin's work on emotions the concerns of the naturalist and evolutionary thinker merge in sustained sets of observations focused on various expressions. This may be illustrated by the following passage, where he discusses the expressive character of the position of the ears in mammals:

> The ears through their movements are highly expressive in many animals ... A slight difference in position serves to express in the plainest manner a different state of mind, as we may daily see in the dog ... All the Carnivora fight with their canine teeth, and all, as far as I have observed, draw their ears back when feeling savage. This may continually be seen with dogs when fighting in earnest, and with puppies fighting in play. The movement is different from the falling down and slight drawing back of the ears, when a dog feels pleased and is caressed ... The lynx has remarkably long ears; and their retraction ... is very conspicuous, and is eminently expressive of its savage disposition. Even one of the Eared Seals ... which has very small ears, draws them backwards, when it makes a savage rush at the legs of its keeper ... Every one recognizes the vicious appearance which the drawing back of the ears gives to a horse (pp. 110-112).

The familiarity and widespread recurrence of similar expressions form the basis for the recognition of mental phenomena—even in cases where resources of knowledge and experience are limited. For instance, Darwin here remarks that "everyone recognizes the vicious appearance which the drawing back of the ears gives to a horse." Indeed this recognition is likely to occur even for people not familiar with horses, and despite the absence of other give-away signs, like growling and the baring of teeth. Thus while many of his examples are drawn from daily life and available to the recollection of his readers, his detailed knowledge and understanding of the countenance of emotion is the province of the naturalist. Moreover, Darwin's general survey of the expressive appearance of the ears in carnivores, and animals in general, is the province of the evolutionist. (He points out the common origin and adaptive function of retracting the ears, namely, protecting them from the opponent's teeth during a fight [p. 111].) The common recognitional basis of animal and human expression is the starting point of Darwin's inquiry into the connection of body and mind, yet his observational acuity and generalized scope of knowledge bring his perspective beyond the pale of commonsense knowledge.

Darwin provides close accounts of the expressive forms of the emotions and identifies the kind of recognition that is necessarily relied upon and that precedes such analysis. In one passage, for example, he first points out how plainly visible dejection is among the apes; he then proceeds to describe its expressive appearance. Darwin's attunement to animal life is so fine that he feels confident in describing the expression of eyes among the criteria for ascribing dejection:

> The appearance of dejection in young orangs and chimpanzees, when out of health, is as plain and almost as pathetic as in the case of our children. This state of mind and body is shown by the listless movements, fallen countenances, dull eyes, and changed complexion (p. 134).

Here Darwin characterizes dejection as a "state of mind and body," showing his monistic, non-reductionist approach to body-mind.

Darwin's method of identifying the emotions is clearly not technical and largely consists in descriptions which remind the reader of the countenance of emotion. He often argues from the basis of commonsense knowledge. In describing, for instance, the countenance of "a man in high spirits," Darwin writes: "I heard a child, a little under four years old, when asked what was meant by being in good spirits, answer, 'It is laughing, talking, and kissing.' It would be difficult to give a truer and more practical definition" (p. 210). Similarly, enlisting commonplace experience, he provides an illustrative drawing and describes "the movements of a cat, when feeling affectionate":

> She now stands upright, with slightly arched back, tail perpendicularly raised, and ears erected; and she rubs her cheeks and flanks against her master or mistress. The desire to rub something is so strong in cats under this state of mind, that they may often be seen rubbing themselves against the legs of chairs or tables, or against door posts (pp. 126-127).

In identifying the state of mind of feeling affectionate, Darwin offers a mundane, familiar scene of a cat's postures and behaviors. Relying upon the shared recognition of a cat's expressions, and using descriptive and visual elucidations, he recalls the countenance and demeanor of a cat in an affectionate state of mind. The emotion embodied in the cat's expressive forms is perceptually transparent: Only the mental concept of affection can deliver that perception fully.

The power of mental language to express and reassemble what is—at present or in memory—diaphanously perceived is entirely lost to the skeptical perspective. The ethologist Barnett expresses this perspective in his criticism of Darwin's generous usage of vernacular mental concepts. Barnett's skepticism regarding the warrantability of ascribing emotions to animals is so entrenched that, in his critique of Darwin, he objects to Darwin's phrasing of "cat in an affectionate frame of mind," stating that "today this behaviour might be described in terms of 'cutaneous stimulation'" (1958, p. 225). Barnett voices skepticism about what in everyday experience is taken to lie plainly before the eyes—namely, the expressive movements of an affectionate cat—and he drives a deep wedge between vernacular and technical languages, in the conceptual contrast between "affection" and "cutaneous stimulation." It is a measure of how deeply skepticism toward animal mentality has captured the Western imagination, that Barnett proposes the counterfeit terminology of "cutaneous stimulation" as though it could be sustained as lasting currency, or replace the directness and authenticity of Darwin's "cat in an affectionate frame of mind." Barnett's formulation has a contrived, disingenuous ring about it, not only because its usage is arcane, but also because it fails, in contrast to Darwin's formulation, to connect with what the audience of his discourse can recollect.

Darwin's assessment of animal life in terms of mental qualities is based on a particular perspective, implicit throughout his writings, on the recognition of such qualities in behavioral expressions. His approach undermines the reification of mind as an invisible domain by repeatedly underscoring the sensual availability of emotions in animals and humans. Emotion is something incarnate and vividly present for Darwin. His work on animal and human emotions can be read as a philosophical treatise on the availability of mind, as he documents the expressive countenance and form of the emotions. Hence Darwin's understanding is at odds with skepticism, which denies either the existence or the accessibility of animal mind. However, his approach is also at odds with the view that mental states in animals are discernible through empathic understanding.[9] In contrast to both skepticism and empathy, Darwin's descriptions and arguments are empirically rigorous, sensually vivid, and philosophically demystifying.

DARWIN'S NATURALIST VIEW OF ANIMALS AS SUBJECTS: ACTION AS MEANINGFUL AND AUTHORED

In what follows, I show that Darwin's use of so-called anthropomorphic language does not conflate human and animal qualities. Rather, his portrayals reflect an understanding of animals as subjects. I support this view by discussing how Darwin's ascriptions render animal activities as meaningful and authored.

The Language of Action

Thus far I have defended Darwin's anthropomorphism as an intentional and powerful perspective, warranted by evolutionary common descent and based on close observation of expressive form. Beyond appreciating Darwin's anthropomorphism in its own right, the examination of his portrayals of animal life may contribute a closer understanding of the nature of anthropomorphism.[10] Anthropomorphism is often vaguely identified with the unwarranted attribution of human mental experiences to animals. Yet, anthropomorphism clearly involves broader aspects of language use than the mere imputation of mental concepts to animals. A more comprehensive and, at the same time, more concrete and impartial view of anthropomorphism is the description and explanation of animal life in the ordinary language of objects and events, relations and community, action and mind. The effect of the sustained use of this broad spectrum of vocabulary and reasoning is the emergence of animals as *subjects*.

The idea of subjectivity—far from being a fuzzy or impressionistic notion—has two cardinal conceptual facets: It refers to the *meaningfulness* of experience and action as a constitutive facet of sentient life; and, it implicates the *authorship* of action (see Schutz 1962; Davidson 1980). What I argue in this section is that Darwin's anthropomorphism stems from his understanding of animals as subjects, which is reflected in his representation of animal life as meaningful and authored. In this regard, Darwin's portrayals are closely affiliated with a style broadly characteristic of the naturalist genre (see Crist 1996). Indeed, in his behavioral observations Darwin relied extensively on information gathered by his naturalist colleagues and predecessors (see Richards 1987, p. 196).

Darwin's presentation of a subjective dimension in animal life may be illustrated by a passage describing ant life. This description discloses how the consistent and varied use of ordinary vocabulary and reasoning portrays animal activity as experientially meaningful.

> [T]o describe the habits and powers of a female ant, would require, as Pierre Huber has shewn, a large volume; I may, however, briefly specify a few points. Ants communicate information to each other, and several unite for the same work, or games of play. They recognize their fellow ants after months of absence. They build great edifices, keep them clean, close the doors in the evening, and post sentries. They make roads, and even tunnels under rivers. They collect food for the community, and when an object too large for entrance is brought to the nest, they enlarge the door, and afterwards build it up again. They go out to battle in regular bands, and freely sacrifice their lives for the common weal. They emigrate in accordance with a preconcerted plan. They capture slaves. They keep Aphides as milch-cows. They move the eggs of their aphides, as well as their own eggs and cocoons, into warm parts of the nest, in order that they may be quickly hatched; and endless similar facts could be given (Darwin [1871] 1981, vol. 1, pp. 186-187).

This description of an ant community is exemplary of anthropomorphism, in its literal, etymological sense of "human alikening." The conceptual character of the account of ant life is transparently equivalent to human life: The ants could be substituted by a human community and, with only a few alterations, the intelligibility of the passage would be preserved intact.

Darwin's language is the vernacular of objects, action, communal life, and mind. Philosophers of social science have compellingly argued that the conceptual structure of this language is constitutive of, or internal to, its referents (see Winch 1958; Coulter 1979). To illustrate what this means, in observing construction workers carrying out certain activities, the characterization that they are "making a road" expresses both the intelligibility, for the observer, of what they are doing, and the coherence of how the workers themselves plan and concert their undertakings. As Peter Winch would put it, the *idea* of making a road is *embodied* in the workers' activities (1958, p. 128). The relationship then between the idea of making a road and the activities so characterized is a constitutive or internal relationship, in the sense that the conceptual rendering of the activity cannot be disentangled either from the way in which the activity is witnessed or from the ways in which it is produced. The idea of making a road—and similarly for the other descriptions in the above passage—is, simultaneously, a linguistic representation of how the observer sees the activity and of what the activity is for the actors themselves.

With these considerations in mind, we can see the work of the vernacular of action and community in Darwin's presentation of ant life. The effect of writing that ants "unite for work," "build edifices [and] keep them clean," "close doors," "post sentries," "make roads and even tunnels," and so forth, is the inexorable invitation to understand these ideas as constituting the ants' engagements: the concept of, inter alia, "making a road" is internal to the experiential world of the ants themselves. As in the case of human workers, to propose that the ants make roads is to disclose what they are doing, why they are doing it and, to a certain extent, how they are doing it. The coherence, purpose, systematics, and coordination of their actions centers purely on this: *that they are making a road.*

The perspectives of the actor and the witness—in this case of the ants and the human observer—are brought together because action is captured as embodying ideas that are, at once, experienced and lived from within and witnessed from without. The seminal conceptual peculiarity of ordinary concepts and reasoning is that it eludes a dichotomous conception of the actor's "subjective" orientation, on the one hand, and the observer's "objective" comprehension, on the other. The first- and third-person perspectives of witness and actor are confluent, in that what the witness sees and reports from "here" is overall conceptually on a par with what the actor experiences "over there" (Schutz 1962). In this sense, the ordinary language of objects, events, relations, action, and mind embeds the actors' subjective orientation, not as reference to an inferred private dimension, but as a tacit intimation that the very raison d'être and scenic forms of activities cannot be disentangled from the witnessing of activities as experientially meaningful.

The overall picture of the ants' activities here is consilient with the view that those activities embody ideas. Supervenient to this implicit portrayal of activities as embodying ideas is the reader's reception of the ants' communal life as an experientially and subjectively meaningful world. This supervenience is a significant facet of how anthropomorphism works. Thus the very reason that "anthropomorphism" appears to be a quality which is not crisply definable or identifiable is that it is an *effect* of language, rather than a specific set of features of its use.

States-of-Being

A recalcitrant problem in identifying the exact meaning of anthropomorphism in behavioral writings is that of drawing a clear line between terms that are purportedly off limits to animals and those that are not. Pamela Asquith makes this point succinctly, stating that "the selection of appropriate terms [by behavioral scientists] is based on little more than a vague apprehension of 'anthropomorphic license'" (1984, p. 142). As an example of the ad hoc, rule-of-thumb criteria applied in avoiding anthropomorphism, Asquith mentions the preference for the term "bond" over "friendship" with respect to primate relations. She maintains that "'bond' is more acceptable in that it need not imply such a complex arrangement of emotions as does 'friendship'" (p. 142).

Analogously to the preference of "bond" over "friendship," while terms referring to sensations such as pleasure and pain are not necessarily shunned in contemporary behavioral literature, the related notions of happiness and misery are distinctly absent. They are shunned, in Asquith's words, on the "vague apprehension" that they are anthropomorphic. Like happiness and misery, so terms like enjoyment, joy, excitement, or ennui are rarely encountered. Yet Darwin does not demur to use concepts like these in his descriptions, writing for instance that "happiness is never better exhibited than by young animals, such as puppies, kittens, lambs, etc., when playing together, like our own children. Even insects play together, as has been described by that excellent observer, P. Huber, who saw ants chasing and pretending to bite each other, like so many puppies" ([1871] 1981, vol. 1, p. 39). According to Darwin, in general "the lower animals, like man, manifestly feel pleasure and pain, happiness and misery" (p. 39). He also observes that "animals manifestly enjoy excitement and suffer from ennui, as may be seen with dogs, and, according to Rengger, with monkeys. All animals feel Wonder, and many exhibit Curiosity" (p. 42). Darwin also conjectures that "migratory birds are miserable if prevented from migrating, and perhaps they enjoy starting on their long flight" (p. 79). Moreover, "under the expectation of any great pleasure, dogs bound and jump about in an extravagant manner, and bark for joy" ([1872] 1965, p. 120).

What is peculiar about terms like happiness, misery, joy, ennui, wonder, and curiosity is that, unlike pleasure and pain which can be directly related to sensuous experiences, they rather allude to "states of being" which need not correlate with specifiable sensory experiences.

Thus, states of being are not witnessable on the basis of obvious or stable expressive responses. The notion of happiness, for instance, is not attributable on the basis of a single (or a few) behavioral manifestation(s) that can be pinpointed in a brief time span. For while one feels pleasure at specific moments, happiness is a compound state of being that is both more temporally extended and more subtle. The same applies to the conceptual pair, pain and misery (or suffering). In assigning concepts such as happiness and misery, Darwin implicitly acknowledges the relevance, in animal life, of the subtleties and complexities which these concepts imply; with the use of such terms in his depictions, he proposes to evidence states of being in animals. The effect of evidencing happiness and misery (as well as joy, ennui, wonder, triumph, grief, etc.) in animal conduct is the tacit admission of a fullness, complexity, and temporal extendedness of being.

Now, the view of Darwin's reference to happiness, misery, joy, and so forth, as metaphorical (Ghiselin 1969) derives from the assumption that such "subjective" or "mental" terms designate phenomena that are unavailable to direct observation—and so Darwin could not have been proposing them as literally applicable to animals. There are two responses to this proposal. First, as I have demonstrated, Darwin's general use of mental terminology is far too pervasive to be considered metaphorical; moreover, he rarely qualifies his language with caveats or quotation marks. Second, Darwin does not present subjective states of being in animal life on the basis of inferences from "observable" behavior to "unobservable" mind. As discussed in connection to his work on emotions, his view of subjective experience is based on observation of particular behavioral and physiological manifestations.

In other words, Darwin does not speculate about subjective states from behavioral expressions, but rather *witnesses* subjective states *in* behavioral expressions. This constitutive link between a conceptual characterization and the behavioral expression it predicates is often achieved by the presentation of the characterization as a description, as opposed to a hypothesis or a deduction. Consider, for example, how Darwin describes a horse's comportment in the following passage: "Animals which live in society often call to each other when separated, and *evidently* feel much joy at meeting; as *we see* with a horse, on the return of his companion, for whom he has been neighing" ([1872] 1965, pp. 84-85, emphasis added). What the perceptual terms "evidently" and "we see" accomplish is to convey the ascription of "feeling much joy at meeting" as a descriptive rather than an inferential proposition. By bonding subjective states of being with behaviors descriptively, Darwin invites his readers to perceive the scenery described in alignment with his own direct perception of behaviors in light of the understanding and atmosphere that subjective language makes witnessable. Thus, the expression "joy at meeting" delivers an icon to the reader of the horse's manner of response upon "the return of his companion for whom he has been neighing," even though the physical movements per se of that response are not provided. So through the perlocutionary effects[11] of state-of-being concepts conveyed with linguistic tropes of perception, the reader is invited to see the reunion of the horses as joyful. And this joy of reunion solicits ways to imagine the behavioral-physical comportment of the horses.

In his forms of argumentation and generous usage of subjective language, it is evident that Darwin does not heed the kind of philosophical dualism which conceives of inner subjectivity as something invisible that must be deduced from outer behavior. Rather, Darwin presents tropes of subjective being as directly witnessable in animal life. His descriptions of the "dancing-party" of the birds of paradise and of the "great magpie marriage" illustrate the sensual appreciation of subjective life that characterizes Darwin's thought:

> With Birds of Paradise a dozen or more full-plumaged males congregate in a tree to hold a dancing-party, as it is called by the natives; and here flying about, raising their wings, elevating their exquisite plumes, and making them vibrate, the whole tree seems, as Mr. Wallace remarks, to be filled with waving plumes. When thus engaged, *they become so absorbed*, that a skilful archer may shoot nearly the whole party ([1871] 1981, vol. 2, pp. 88-89, emphasis added).

> The common magpie (Corvus pica, Linn.), as I have been informed by the Rev. W. Darwin Fox, used to assemble from all parts of Delamere Forest, in order to celebrate the "great magpie marriage" ... [The birds] had the habit very early in the spring of assembling at particular spots, where they could be seen in flocks, chattering, sometimes fighting, bustling and flying about the trees. The whole affair was evidently considered by the birds as of the highest importance ([1871] 1981, vol. 2, p. 102, emphasis added).[12]

The proposition that the birds consider the courtship affair absorbing and important clearly incorporates the idea that the actions involved are meaningful from the birds' point of view. In turn, the effect of this intimation is that the reader pictures the birds' activities in light of the understanding and feeling that subjective meaningfulness invokes.

The question of particular interest in these passages is the status of the claims of the birds "becoming absorbed" and of courtship being "evidently considered by the birds as of the highest importance." Is Darwin proposing these as literal accounts? The attribution of the propositional content, as such, to the birds is one literal sense which is plainly meaningless; birds do not possess the notions of "absorption" or "importance," that is, they do not have human language. The implausible interpretation that Darwin could have intended this kind of literal sense compels critics to regard such anthropomorphic expressions (charitably) as metaphorical and (uncharitably) as naive and erroneous.

However, there is another literal meaning of these passages which is consistent with Darwin's thought—and with naturalist writing in general. For Darwin the fervor of the birds of paradise engagement in the courtship activities, coupled with an archer's ability to shoot them down without being noticed, are the basis for perceiving that the birds are absorbed in the courtship affair. With respect to the magpies, their wealth of behaviors on the particular occasion, what with the prolongedness of the affair, the chattering, bustling, fighting, and so on, are apprehended as evidencing that "the affair is considered by the birds as of the highest importance." Absorption in, and importance of, courtship activities are therefore embodied in the birds' expressive largesse: When an affair is absorbing and of the highest importance, *this* is what it looks like in action.

This is not to say that with these descriptions Darwin provides conceptual summaries, or incontestably objective representations, of the various courtship behaviors among magpies or birds of paradise. Nowhere in the birds' activities can it be documented, *specifically*, that they consider the courtship affair important or that they are absorbed. While these characterizations are warranted by the intensity of the birds' involvement and their obliviousness to other events, at the same time Darwin's wording suggests a particular perceptual angle on the birds' activities. The evidence for these characterizations is obliquely, rather than blatantly, available on the surface of behaviors; hence the characterizations themselves contribute a way of witnessing the birds' conduct.

The idea that action embodies an experiential point of view is a powerful current in Darwin's accounts of animal life. As mentioned, Darwin does not convey the experiential quality of action by drawing inferences about private states on the basis of what is observed. This received distinction between "inner" and "outer" realms is abrogated in Darwin's approach, for he conveys the subjective, experiential dimension as directly witnessable rather than speculatively deduced. Darwin's view of action as subjectively meaningful expresses *a way of seeing*. He sees birds flying easily "obviously for pleasure" and the magpie marriage as "evidently of the highest importance." With the addended evidentiary force of such expressions as "obviously," "evidently," and "manifestly" (which recur in his descriptions), Darwin intimates that his proposals are not deductions, but *observations*. With this intimation of his language he also invites his co-observer, the reader, to "virtually witness"[13] the subjective expressiveness embedded in his behavioral scenes as an inextricable component of the description of the scene. Thus the language of his report—"how often do we see birds which fly easily, gliding and sailing through the air obviously for pleasure"—assembles a way for the reader to picture the scene in alignment with Darwin's direct perception of the flying as something the birds both perform and experience.

The words that render actions can work as vehicles toward seeing actions in particular ways. The words impart not only sense, but also form and color, to their referents, molding the texture of images the reader forms. Darwin's writing, like that of naturalists in general, is replete with characterizations that consistently contribute an experiential, subjectively full, dimension. The articulation of this dimension eludes the dichotomy between "observation" and "interpretation" in that it is conveyed as an aspect that is witnessed. It involves both a way of seeing and something specifically seen.

Darwin's affinity with the naturalist perspective is evident not only in his own style, but also in his pervasive reliance on fellow naturalists' accounts. Quoting Warington, for example, he describes the male stickleback as "'mad with delight' when the female comes out of her hiding-place to survey the nest he has made for her" ([1871] 1981, vol. 2, p. 2). Citing Audobon, he writes of "the males of a heron ... as walking about on their long legs with great dignity before the females, bidding defiance to their rivals" (p. 68). What is peculiar about such characterizations as a stickleback "being mad with delight" and a heron "walking with great dignity" is that, while they are interpretations of what the animals are doing, they invite ways of envisioning their actions in particular contexts; hence, they also work as descriptions that guide the reader to imagine the stickleback's and the heron's bearings.

Darwin's depictions of animal life in the vernacular—that is, in the everyday language of human affairs—represents animals as subjects. As mentioned earlier, subjectivity embeds the dimensions of meaningfulness and authorship. Action is rendered meaningful through the direct or oblique constitution of an experiential dimension. For example, when Darwin speculates that "migratory birds perhaps enjoy starting on their long flight," he is going beyond a report about the long flight as something that migratory birds *do* to suggest that it is also an event that the birds *experience*.

Authorship: Acting for the Sake of Pleasure

I turn now to focus on the other seminal aspect of subjectivity, namely, the perspective upon animal action as authored. Darwin's undestanding of animals as acting for the sake of pleasure embeds the attribution of authorship, for this orientation is conceived as the *cause* of action rather than epiphenomenal to it. While acting for pleasure can be conceived within the Darwinian framework as an effect of evolutionary causes, in Darwin's portrayals it is also treated as an initial cause of courses of action.

Just as attributions of states of being, discussed previously, are largely absent from contemporary behavioral writings, so is providing accounts for animal activities in terms of the pleasure they afford. In contemporary behavioral thought, the notion of acting for the sake of pleasure is treated as either epiphenomenal or irrelevant and, instead, paramount emphasis is placed on the function and selective value of behaviors. To give an example, Joan Silk discusses grooming—a visibly sensuous affair—among primates in terms of "costs and benefits" (1987, p. 325). The pleasure that primates may take in grooming is not denied, but tacitly treated as irrelevant next to the proper functional, adaptive account.

The avoidance of alluding to acting for pleasure reflects the persistence of vigilance within neo-Darwinian thinking against the charge of anthropomorphism. Anthropomorphophobia, as Griffin calls it, is entirely absent in Darwin's behavioral writings, where acting for the sake of pleasure or amusement is a recurring theme—one shared with other naturalists. In his *Selection in Relation To Sex*, for example, Darwin ([1871] 1981, vol. 2) makes an extended argument that male birds sing in order "to excite or charm" female birds. He considers a counterargument and responds to it as follows:

> It has ... been argued that the song of the male cannot serve as a charm, because the males of certain species ... sing during the autumn. But nothing is more common than for animals to take pleasure in practicing whatever instinct they follow at other times for some real good. How often do we see birds which fly easily, gliding and sailing through the air obviously for pleasure ... Hence it is not at all surprising that male birds should continue singing for their own amusement after the season for courtship is over (pp. 54, 55).

While the idea of animals acting for pleasure or amusement may, at first glance, appear to be a trivial matter, it has significant consequences in the overall portrayal of animal life. In this passage, one attending feature may be briefly noted. Darwin's ideas that birds fly for pleasure and sing for their own amusement are at odds with the adaptationist proclivity of much neo-Darwinian thought, which has been criticized in a well-known paper by Gould and Lewontin (1979). Darwin draws a distinction between an instinct followed "for some real good" and one "practiced for pleasure," and thus makes an anti-adaptationist point by implicitly opposing the view that all behaviors must be accounted for in terms of an ultimate, functional explanation (see Burkhardt 1985).

Another aspect of Darwin's presentation of the animal as acting for pleasure or amusement is that it embeds an experiential viewpoint. As in the case of states of being—like happiness, joy, misery, wonder, or grief—acting for pleasure is inclusive not only of what animals do, but of what they experience as well. It is precisely this level of inclusion which allows him to report something as mundane as "birds which fly": "How often do we see birds which fly easily, gliding and sailing through the air [obviously for pleasure]." If the bracketed portion of the sentence were eliminated, the statement would simply be too trivial to state. However, with the qualification "obviously for pleasure" the act of flying becomes subjectively expressive and, hence, worth reporting. The simple qualification "obviously for pleasure" transforms an unremarkable behavior—flying—into an intentional action: sailing through the air *for pleasure*.

When Darwin's reasoning is placed in comparative perspective, the theme of pursuing pleasure can be seen to have broader ramifications for how animal life is viewed. In another passage, Darwin remarks that "the weaver bird ... when confined in a cage, amuses itself by neatly weaving blades of grass between the wires of its cage" ([1871] 1981, vol. 2, p. 54). A similar type of behavioral example is discussed by Konrad Lorenz, one of the founders of contemporary ethology. Lorenz (1937) recounts a captive starling's behaviors of hunting, capturing and eating an insect, in the complete absence of any insects in the room:

> The starling flew up onto the head of a bronze statue in our living room and steadily searched the "sky" for flying insects, although there were none on the ceiling. Suddenly its whole behavior showed that it had sighted a flying prey. With head and eyes the bird made a motion as though following a flying insect with its gaze; its posture tautened; it took off, snapped, returned to its perch, and with its bill performed the sideways lashing, tossing motions with which many insectivorous birds sley their prey against whatever they happen to be sitting upon. Then the starling swallowed several times, whereupon its closely laid plumage loosened up somewhat, and there often ensued a quivering reflex, exactly as it does after real satiation. The bird's entire behavior ... was so convincing, so deceptively like a normal process with survival value, that I climbed a chair not once, but many times, to check if some tiny insects had not after all escaped me. But there really were none (p. 143).

Lorenz recounts the starling's behavioral sequence for the theoretical purpose of illustrating what ethologists call vacuum behavior. His interpretation of the starling's behaviors is given extensively in an earlier paper (Lorenz 1935):

> It is hardly possible to point out a more impressive feature of instinctive actions than their property to "go off in vacuo" when the specific releasing stimuli are lacking. If an innate behavior pattern, for want of adequate stimulation, is never released in captivity, the threshold for this stimulation, strange to say, is lowered. This can go so far that the activity in question finally breaks through and "goes off" without any detectable releasing stimulus. It is as though the latent behavior pattern itself finally became an internal stimulus. Let me recall the instance of the starling who performed the full motor sequence of a fly-hunt without a fly ... As ... this observation proves clearly ... the bird ... follows no purpose, however obscure, but the "blind plan" ... of its instincts (p. 101).

Lorenz's "mechanomorphic" portrayal of the bird compelled to perform certain behaviors differs profoundly from Darwin's understanding of an animal acting for the sake of amusement.

For Lorenz, the starling's fly-hunt is an exemplary case of a *vacuum behavior*. Ethologists defined vacuum behavior in physiological terms as an innate behavioral pattern, whose corresponding "action-specific energy" has accumulated to such a degree that it finally "breaks through" in the absence of the appropriate external circumstances, or of what ethologists call "releasing stimuli" (see Tinbergen 1951). The full pattern of the starling's fly-hunting "goes off" in the absence of insects, because the necessary "threshold" of external "stimulation" has reached its theoretically possible limit of zero, and the accumulated energy corresponding to the behavioral pattern has become an "internal stimulus" sufficient to trigger the expression of the pattern (see Lorenz 1950, pp. 246-247). The mechanical imagery evoked in the account of the starling is made metaphorically explicit elsewhere, where Lorenz characterizes vacuum behaviors as having "an effect somewhat suggestive of the explosion of a boiler whose safety valve fails to function" (1950, p. 247).

Lorenz's theoretical interpretation precludes the possibility that the starling's mock fly-hunt is a form of amusement—akin to a game—even as the bird is aware that there are no flies in the room. This understanding is precluded by the nature of the explanation of the behavioral pattern as a vacuum behavior, which is conceptually wedded to the proposition, as Lorenz puts it, that "the bird follows no purpose but the blind plan of its instincts." In other words, the notion of a vacuum behavior is not only confluent with, but logically hinges upon, the condition that the bird's actions be disconnected from its awareness. Conversely, Darwin's account of an animal engaging in meaningless activity (like weaving grass on the wires of its cage) for the sake of amusement is consilient with the understanding of action as subjectively expressive and authored. Thus, while Darwin's weaver bird is intentionally present to the import of its own engagements, Lorenz's starling is an unwitting executor of the blind plan of its instincts. To articulate the contrast more starkly, while weaving grass or hunting nonexistent insects for amusement are voluntary actions, these same activities as "vacuum behaviors" are determined—that is, they are physiologically caused.

Darwin's focus on a subjective dimension is linked to his understanding of animals as the authors of their actions. The ascription of an action to a subject implies, as Alan White notes, that the subject is the author or the cause of what is brought about through the action (1968, p. 3). Authorship—embedded in the perception and interpretation of human action—is assembled in the case of animals through the use of the same descriptive and explanatory language of conduct. White's conception of the actor as the "cause of what is brought about" identifies the mark of authorship: When the author is the cause of action, deterministic accounts of action are logically prescinded. The conception of action as authored precludes other causal (as opposed to simply enabling) factors—such as physiological states, neurophysiological antecedents, or environmental stimuli. In other words, while bodily states and contextual features are certainly constituents, and sometimes prerequisites, of particular actions, they cannot be advanced as causes of authored actions; for, the determination of action by extrinsic factors derails authorship. Such factors are thus overidden in that they would negate or undermine the causal efficacy of the author as the cause of action. The vernacular vocabulary and reasoning of action and mentality resist the deterministic efficacy of factors extrinsic to the field of action and the purview of the actor. Thus the understanding of the author as the cause of action radically shrinks the conceptual space for deterministic causation.

Darwin's ([1872] 1965) description of a dog's treatment of a biscuit, which would be considered a vacuum behavior from a classical ethological perspective, again reveals the contrast between the two perspectives in terms of the discrepant conceptions of causation the accounts embody:

> When a piece of brown biscuit is offered to a terrier of mine and she is not hungry (and I have heard of similar instances), she first tosses it about and worries it, as if it were a rat or other prey; she then repeatedly rolls on it precisely as if it were a piece of carrion, and at last eats it. It would appear that an imaginary relish has to be given to the distasteful morsel; and to effect this the dog acts in this habitual manner, as if the biscuit was a live animal or smelt of carrion, though *he* [sic] *knows better than we do* that this is not the case (p. 45, emphasis added).

In Darwin's presentation there is conceptual affinity between "the dog worrying the biscuit as if it were a live animal or carrion" and the epistemic assessment that "he knows better than we do that this is not the case." On the other hand, if the dog's behavior is conceived as a vacuum behavior, any implication of "knowledge" on the dog's part is foreclosed; the behavior is the blind execution of an innate pattern. The ethological notion of a vacuum behavior denotes a lack of meaningful fit between action and external circumstances. Conversely, the concept of knowledge implies a meaningful connection between a subject's execution of an action and the occasion or object that is targeted by the action. On Darwin's view, the dog's rolling on the biscuit is akin to, or expressive of, an act of the imagination. Reference to knowledge is germane in that the "as if" trope ("as if it were a piece of carrion") is understood as belonging to the dog's point of reference (as well as to the human observer's). The action of rolling and the object of the action, the biscuit, are grasped as meaningfully connected from the dog's perspective. The dog's knowing guarantees she is the author (and hence the cause) of her action. On the ethological view, the action and its object are connected only from the observer's perspective with the technical concept of vacuum behavior, while the animal remains blind to the meaning of its behavioral expression. The behavior is caused by extrinsic physiological forces over which the animal has neither epistemic nor practical jurisdiction. Therefore, Darwin's view of animals acting for pleasure, or with imagination, leads down a profoundly different path of understanding than the subsumption of these activities under what ethologists call vacuum behaviors.

Darwin's view that "the weaver bird ... when confined in a cage, amuses itself by neatly weaving blades of grass between the wires of its cage," conveys a very different sense and image than the idea of a vacuum behavior released under the pressure of internal stimulation. The contrast helps to highlight particular effects of Darwin's interpretation of animal behavior. Simple statements—such as a bird weaving for pleasure or singing for its own amusement—embody assumptions and requirements that are far from simple: that animals' actions are experientially meaningful and, therefore, the observer's interpretive commitment is to identify and convey that meaning. Darwin unreservedly assumes that "there is something that it is like to be" an animal (see Nagel 1981). The notion that action is experientially meaningful is intimately tied with a view that animals author their actions. Thus Darwin's accounts systematically foster the witnessing of authorship in animal life, by representing action as *performed by* the animal, rather than happening to the animal. The consistency of this perspective throughout his writings on animals engages the imagination of the reader in such a way that she or he perceives the actions described, in light of this representation.

The Significance of Anecdotal Evidence

Darwin did not rely on anecdotes of animal life as massively as his disciple George Romanes (1882), yet he uses the anecdotal method consistently. Anecdotes are narratives of singular instances of animal behavior. They are rarely reconstructions of conspicuously observable, commonplace behaviors, but rather they make the point of narrating striking, extraordinary, or rare behavioral events. The anecdotal method has been regarded as non-credible at least since Edward

Thorndike's (1898) introduction of experimentally controlled studies of behavior with his notorious "puzzle boxes."[14] In contemporary science, as Daniel Dennett puts it, anecdotes have been "officially unusable" (1987, p. 250). The rejection of anecdotal evidence rests on the assessment that such evidence is unverifiable and hence unreliable; it is regarded as insufficiently corroborated or tested. However while the "official unusability" of anecdotal data weeds out the occasional fib or exaggeration with respect to animal capacities, exceptional or unique information is also thereby excluded from observational reports (see Dennett 1987). With respect to the question of animal mind, Griffin also notes that because of the "disparagement of anecdotal data," "field observers often fail to report evidence suggestive of conscious thinking even when they obtain it, and editors of scientific journals are reluctant to publish it" (1984, pp. 14, 15).

By examining the range of behaviors that anecdotal evidence makes admissible in Darwin's works, the kind of knowledge advanced with anecdotes may be brought to light. Darwin's use of anecdotes brings two aspects into view. First, the inclusion of singular events as behavioral evidence implicitly admits a wider ambit of variation within a species (or population). The use of such data may embody the assumption, as well as provide the evidence, of considerable individual variation in behavioral patterns or styles. Conversely, the exclusion of anecdotes can cloak the range of individual variability and heterogeneity of behaviors among members of a species. Therefore, the view of certain behavioral repertoires as homogeneously distributed and fixed may partially be an artifact of the scientific orthodoxy which has excluded the singular event as a legitimate or useful datum.

The second aspect of anecdotal evidence is that it can make perspicuous certain types of phenomena which are too complex to present in generalized or abstract form. This is especially the case with phenomena of ratiocination. Conversely, the inadmissibility of singular instances of behavior as "good data" may exclude the assessment of capacities of which the conceptual complexity requires recalling particular instances (or types of instances) that make those capacities unambiguously observable. These points will become clearer with the consideration of examples.

Variability

In general, Darwin placed paramount importance on variability, as it played a pivotal conceptual role in his arguments against the orthodoxy of his day, namely, the fixity of species.[15] With respect to mental characteristics Darwin ([1871] 1981, vol. 1) remained consistent in emphasizing individual variation:

> The variability of the faculties in the individuals of the same species is an important point for us ... I have found on frequent enquiry, that it is the unanimous opinion of all those who have long attended to animals of many kinds, including birds, that the individuals differ greatly in every mental characteristic (p. 36).

Perhaps the most pronounced contrast to this view has been that of classical ethology which characterized innate behaviors as "fixed action patterns" (Lorenz and Tinbergen 1957; Thorpe 1973, pp. 10-11; Grier 1984, p. 36). Especially early in the development of the field, ethologists emphasized the stereotypy and invariance of innate behaviors. Lorenz writes that "individual variability can be neglected when giving a general biological description of a species. This conception is not incompatible with the fact that certain instinctive actions can have a high regulative 'plasticity'. So do many organs" (1935, p. 121).[16] Elsewhere Lorenz articulates his conception of innate behavior in the following terms: "Behaviour patterns are not something which animals may do or not do, or do in different ways, according to the requirements of the occasion, but something which animals of a given species 'have got', exactly in the same manner as they 'have got' claws or teeth of a definite morphological structure" (1950, pp. 237-238). The representation of behaviors as fixed is closely connected with the ethological proclivity for "generic description." As I have argued elsewhere, ethologists' proclivity for generic description—that is, the abstract description of behavior delivered in typified form—can bolster a mechanomorphic portrait of animals (Crist forthcoming). The perceived absence of variation is connected in human understanding with a mechanical icon of behavior. Hence, the neglect of individual variation of behaviors and the disparagement of anecdotal evidence, coupled with generic description as a method of writing, contributed to the impression that the ethological theoretical *construct* of "fixed action pattern" was an ontological *property* of animal behavior in general.

The neglect or underestimation of variability goes hand in hand with the devaluation of anecdotal evidence, for there is a powerful link between recognizing the existence of individual variation in behaviors and capacities and valuing the collection and recounting of individual instances.[17] While some anecdotes related by Darwin are perhaps unreliable, it is likely that for the most part they are veridical descriptions of unique or rare behavioral occurrences. The veridicality of an anecdote does not guarantee that the occurrence it narrates is typical of the particular species. What it may attest to, however, is a wider ambit of individual variation in behavioral repertoires and capacities than has been generally assumed. In his discussion of animals' ability to sympathize, Darwin ([1871] 1981, vol. 1) uses anecdotal data:

> Many animals ... certainly sympathise with each other's distress or danger ... Mr. Blyth, as he informs me, saw Indian crows feeding two or three of their companions which were blind; and I have heard of an analogous case with the domestic cock. We may, if we choose, call these actions instinctive; but such cases are much too rare for the development of any special instinct. I have myself seen a dog, who never passed a great friend of his, a cat which lay sick in a basket, without giving her a few licks with his tongue, the surest sign of a kind feeling in a dog (p. 77).

Darwin's reliance on anecdotal information to demonstrate the capacity of animals to express sympathy is implicitly connected with his admission that "individuals differ greatly in every mental characteristic." It is also connected with his appreciation of actions that are "rare." These latter views have two consequences for his thinking. First, he does not react to extraordinary stories about animals with skepticism, but rather is willing to consider them as potentially unusual behaviors, instantiating individual variability.[18] Second, Darwin considers the individual case to be a valuable datum, even if it does not represent what happens on average or in general. The dog's show of sympathy for the cat ("a great friend of his") is thus appreciated by Darwin, without reservation, as sound evidence of the moral quality of sympathy in dogs.

Limits of Evidence

The Case of "Thinking"

One significant facet of anecdotal evidence, then, relates to the admission of a wide ambit of individual variation. Another involves the discernment of phenomena whose conceptual and ascriptional complexities require overcoming what may be referred to as limits of evidence. The attribution of ratiocination—for example, "thinking"—

to animals is difficult to evidence or justify in abstract, general terms. In the predication of a mental process like thinking (or of closely related phenomena, like reasoning, considering, deliberating, and planning), behavioral anecdotes are a most effective form of evidence.

Local evidence is the most convincing type of evidence for thinking, because there are no consistent or conspicuous behavioral expressions on the basis of which to perceive and maintain that an animal is thinking. The difficulties are twofold: first, the concept of thinking does not have a simple and uniform meaning, and second, its ascription cannot be stably paired with particular behaviors. There is one sense of thinking— namely, inner reflection or private soliloquy—which can be entirely divorced from behavioral expression.[19] This type of thinking presents perhaps insuperable difficulties, as there are no ratifiable grounds for ascribing thinking to animals which has no (obvious or necessary) connection with some action or expression. Yet it is worth underscoring Darwin's lack of skepticism in this connection, as he was willing to speculate that animals may think in this purely inward and imperceptible fashion. With his inimitable candor and directness, he writes that "no one supposes that one of the lower animals reflects whence he comes or whither he goes,—what is death or what is life, and so forth. But can we feel sure that an old dog with an excellent memory and some power of imagination, as shewn by his dreams, never reflects on his past pleasures in the chase? And this would be a form of self-consciousness" ([1871] 1981, vol. 1, p. 62).

However, the idea of thinking divorced from overt action or perceptible expression is only one class of the phenomena of "thinking" and, relatedly, only one of the senses in which the concept is used. There is another sense of thinking which is internally and locally connected with (some course of) action. By "internally," here, an emphasis is intended on the compellingly intelligible character of ascribing thinking, under the particular circumstances; and by "locally" an emphasis is intended on the necessity of concrete behaviors and events which occasion such an ascription. Yet, the phenomena of thinking are so complex and heteromorphous, that neither is this sense of thinking uniform, for there are various degrees of certainty in discerning thinking synchronously with (and in) a course of action. On one end, thinking is visibly, and always contextually, linked with action. *Hesitating just prior to acting* can be witnessed as the expressive indication of this kind of thinking.[20] Darwin identifies hesitation before action as a sign of reasoning, writing that "few persons any longer dispute that animals possess some power of reasoning. Animals may constantly be seen to pause, deliberate, and resolve" ([1871] 1981, vol. 1, p. 46).[21]

Following his general claim that "few dispute that animals possess some power of reasoning," Darwin proceeds to make his case by giving particular examples. Recounting an anecdote from Rengger, Darwin writes that "when he first gave eggs to his monkeys, they smashed them and thus lost much of their contents; afterwards they gently hit one end against some hard body, and picked off the bits of shell with their fingers" ([1871] 1981, vol. 1, p. 47). Darwin also recounts two anecdotes about retrievers as evidence that dogs are capable of dealing with contingencies by apparently reasoning out the situation:

> Mr. Colquhoun winged two wild-ducks, which fell on the opposite side of a stream; his retriever tried to bring over both at once, but could not succeed; she then, though never before known to ruffle a feather, deliberately killed one, brought over the other, and returned for the dead bird. Col. Hutchinson relates that two partridges were shot at once, one being killed, the other wounded; the latter ran away, and was caught by the retriever, who on her return came across the dead bird; "she stopped, evidently greatly puzzled, and after one or two trials, finding she could not take it up without permitting the escape of the winged bird, she considered a moment, then deliberately murdered it by giving it a severe crunch, and afterwards brought away both together." This was the only known instance of her ever having wilfully injured any game (p. 48).

Darwin concludes this anecdote with the comment:

> Here we have reason, though not quite perfect, for the retriever might have brought the wounded bird first and then returned for the dead one, as in the case of the two wild-ducks (p. 48).

The evidence for reasoning is adduced in the "deliberate killing" of the wounded birds by the retrievers to solve the practical problem of securing two game birds that have fallen at once. The use of the anecdote here is crucial, because the evidence for reasoning is quite literally *circumstantial*. What is notable in this example is how many different aspects must jointly converge to furnish evidence for reasoning. For the killing to be seen as deliberate action, first there is the exceptional or unusual circumstance of two birds having fallen at once—one dead, the other wounded. The deliberateness is then corroborated by the background information that neither of these dogs had previously ever "ruffled a feather" or "wilfully injured game"; and in the case of the one dog, it is given further support by the brief hesitation prior to action (namely, "she considered for a moment," which can only be visualized by the reader as a pause before action). The assessment of *deliberate* killing is linked with the pressing necessity of resolving the problem at hand. The solution provided by the dogs evidences reasoning, in that as a means it matches the end requirement of securing all game, with method and efficacy. So with these anecdotes, reasoning (and related phenomena like considering and deliberating) is perspicuous—indeed visible—in the specific dogs' course of action, with some reference to their background history, and under concrete and peculiar circumstances. Returning to the theme under discussion—the complexity of the phenomena of thinking and their evidencing through anecdotes—the story of these dogs instantiates a case of thinking which is scenically available, given local circumstances and prior history.

Darwin's examples disclose that phenomena of ratiocination are evidenced most effectively in concrete instances of actions which require, warrant, or strongly suggest that such phenomena are indeed at work. On a case-by-case basis, through the offering of specific instantiations (with all the necessary details of expressive-behavioral form, transpiring events, and relevant historical material), the existence of ratiocinating capacities in the animal world is made generally perspicuous. To wit, local and concrete evidence is the best (if not the only) evidence for the global and abstract claim that thinking and reasoning do exist in the animal world.

However, there is also the case of ratiocination which may be locally, but not visibly—not *evidently*—connected with action. In his discussion of reason, Darwin writes that "it is often difficult to distinguish between the power of reason and that of instinct" ([1871] 1981, vol. 1, p. 46). To show the difficulty he relates, after Hayes, that dogs generally draw sledges as a "compact body," but "they diverged and separated when they came to thin ice, so that their weight might be more evenly distributed. This was often the first warning and notice which the travellers received that the ice was becoming thin and dangerous" (pp. 46-47). Darwin goes on to state that it is "most difficult" to assess the dogs' actions in terms of reasoning or instinct: their spreading apart over thin ice may be a consequence of the "experience of each individual," of "the example of the older and wiser dogs," or of "instinct" selected for when the dogs' progenitors, the Arctic wolves, were impelled "not to attack their prey in a close pack when on thin ice" (pp. 46-47). Here, coming up against limits of evidence means that the dogs' action of parting on thin ice could be attributed to their reasoning out what needs to be done, yet such reasoning is neither necessarily nor visibly connected with the course of action they take. This shortage of evidence—coupled with the fact that there are alternative accounts for their action—warrants that, in this particular instance, there is no full-proof criterial basis for ascribing reasoning to the dogs.

So on the one end, thinking may be visible in a course of action, while on the other, thinking may be plausibly inferred, but not obvious. Yet another twist in the complexity of the phenomena of thinking is cases that are intermediate to these extremes. Darwin relates another anecdote after Gardner, "a trustworthy naturalist" who, while watching a shore-crab making its burrow, threw some shells toward its hole:

> One rolled in, and three other shells remained within a few inches of the mouth. In about five minutes the crab brought out the shell which had fallen in, and carried it away to the distance of a foot; *it then saw* the three other shells lying near, and *evidently thinking that* they might likewise roll in, carried them to the spot where it had laid the first. It would I think be difficult to distinguish this act from one performed by man by the aid of reason ([1871] 1981, vol. 1, pp. 334-335, emphasis added).

This case, again, reveals the connection between unusual events and the discernment of thinking, illustrating the role of anecdotal data in presenting evidence of thinking among crabs. While attesting to Darwin's distance from a skeptical standpoint, this case exemplifies another difficulty in evidencing reasoning in the animal world, namely, that the grounds for accepting an action as manifesting reasoning appear to corrode the more distant the animal is in relation to human beings, even if the behavioral evidence remains compelling. (Thus, in his discussion of recognition among shrimp, Griffin points out that "because mantis shrimp are crustaceans a few centimeters in length, it is assumed a priori that they cannot possibly be conscious" [1992, p. 200]). It seems that Darwin is alluding to this type of skeptical objection, when he underscores that the crab's action has the character of "one performed by a man by the aid of reason."

Overall, an abstract or comprehensive argument for the case that animals are capable of thinking is unconvincing because there are no firm or invariant expressions by which to descry thinking. This is so for two reasons: first, thinking (and cognate concepts) is not a unitary phenomenon; and, relatedly, there are no context-free criteria (such as stable behavioral patterns) on the basis of which to discern thinking. However, Darwin and other naturalists do not take the complexities of thinking, and the lack of transcontextual standards, as grounds for endorsing an in-principle skepticism, but instead advance evidence of thinking by providing local, perspicuous examples. The testimony for phenomena of ratiocination in the animal world is thus grounded in *inductive* reasoning and argumentation.

Arguably, then, anecdotes evidence the phenomena of thinking in animal life no more, but also no less, than they can possibly be evidenced. After recounting a number of examples, as though to underscore the inductive nature of the argument, Darwin remarks that "anyone who is not convinced by such facts as these, and by what he may observe with his own dogs, that animals can reason, would not be convinced by anything" ([1871] 1981, vol. 1, p. 47). In this way, Darwin explicitly bonds the narration of anecdotes (and drawing on personal knowledge, which is a special case of anecdotal evidence) with the admission that animals can reason. This is a connection that other naturalists make as well. For example, L.H. Morgan writes that "anecdotes of the intelligent conduct of animals are innumerable. They are not only constantly appearing, and arresting attention, but a sufficient number of instances to illustrate the subject are within personal knowledge of every individual" ([1868] 1966, p. 260).

The Case of Moral Qualities

As it is difficult to make a general argument for thinking in the animal world, limits of evidence are also encountered with respect to the attribution of moral qualities. Moral qualities do not have specific or recurring behavioral expressions, but are rather qualities which can only be attributed on the basis of concrete (long-term or episodic) evidence. In certain contexts Darwin characterizes animals in moral terms. He writes, for instance, that "animals manifestly feel emulation. They love approbation or praise; and a dog carrying a basket for his master exhibits in a high degree self-complacency or pride" ([1871] 1981, vol. 1, p. 42). Especially in dogs, Darwin repeatedly recognizes moral attributes:

> There can, I think, be no doubt that a dog feels shame, as distinct from fear, and something very like modesty when begging too often for food. A great dog scorns the snarling of a little dog, and this may be called magnanimity (p. 42).

The attribution of morally charged characteristics such as pride, shame, modesty, or magnanimity to animals is conspicuously absent in contemporary behavioral science.[22] Such attributions are viewed as unwarranted extensions of human moral sensibilities to animals. The question then is, what are Darwin's grounds for extending the notion of shame to dogs? Shame describes a rather intricate state of mind, experienced in one's being witnessed by another in doing wrong. The experience of shame arises in a form of life that encompasses at least three features, namely, strong social bonds, shared moral understanding, and some sense of selfhood, because shame entails losing face. When the subtlety of the behavioral manifestation of shame is addended to these features, its ascriptional complexity becomes even more transparent.

Yet Darwin judges that dogs are capable of feeling shame, and he also attributes to them qualities like pride and modesty, which are equally complex. He assesses that these qualities are present "beyond doubt," providing little explicit argumentative support to placate the skeptic. In these instances, Darwin appears to be alluding to expressive behaviors, within particular circumstances, that are recallable by people who have experience with dogs. He tacitly appeals to common knowledge as providing unequivocal grounds for the ascription of such moral qualities. Indeed, the only form of evidence that can be marshalled for the claim that dogs feel shame is narrating perspicuous anecdotes. A derivative of this form of argumentation is the appeal to the reader's recollection of having witnessed such a perspicuous instance.

The reason for the limits of evidence in discerning moral (as well as cognitive) qualities lies precisely in the combination of intricacy or contingency of circumstance with subtlety of expression. Thus shame requires a relationship, because shame is largely experienced in the presence of, or in relation to, another; it requires some kind of transgression, mutually understood as such by both transgressor and witness; and, with respect to its manifestation in dogs, it may well apply only to specific individuals, for even if the capacity for shame is characteristic of doghood, it may not be typical of the average dog.

With respect to the knowledge about animal life that anecdotes foster, I have discussed two features of the anecdotal method in Darwin's writing: one, that it implicitly recognizes a wider ambit of individual variability in admitting rare or unusual behaviors as valuable data; and, two, that it overcomes limitations of evidence for complex or subtle qualities by providing concrete cases of such qualities. In conclusion to the discussion of anecdotes about animals, it is evident that these two features—variability and complexity—often go hand in hand. For example, Darwin ([1871] 1981, vol. 2) quotes E. Layard, "an excellent observer," on a cobra's solution to capturing a toad:

> A Cobra thrust its head through a narrow hole and swallow[ed] a toad. With this incumbrance he could not withdraw himself; finding this, he reluctantly disgorged the precious morsel, which began to move off; this was too much for snake philosophy to bear, and the toad was again seized, and again was the snake, after violent efforts to escape, compelled to part with its prey. This time, however, a lesson had been learnt, and the toad was seized by one leg, withdrawn, and then swallowed in triumph (pp. 30-31).

This observation combines the two features of the anecdotal method, being a unique, rare event and evidencing that "a lesson had been learnt" by the cobra. The junction of these features of uniqueness and adaptability in behavior has recently been described by Griffin as versatility—the provision of "enterprising solutions to newly arisen problems" (1984, p. 209), or "cop[ing] with novel and unpredictable challenges in simple but apparently rational ways" (1992, p. 27). Griffin proposes that versatility can be considered "a widely applicable, if not all-inclusive, criterion of conscious awareness in animals" (1984, p. 37).

An example of versatile behavior related by Griffin is the contemporary discovery that green herons sometimes use bait to capture fish. In one pond studied, only about 10 percent of the bird population practice baiting, in which the heron will "pick up small pieces of bread, drop them onto the water, and then capture fish ... attracted to this bait" (Griffin 1984, p. 123). With contemporary technology this behavior can be, and has been, documented, even though it is exceedingly rare. It exemplifies the type of behavior that would count as "anecdotal"—and hence untrustworthy—without photographic documentation. Indeed a very similar behavioral incident is related by Morgan ([1868] 1966) in his work, *The American Beaver and His Works*,[23] and its status remains undecided in the absence of corroborative ratification. Morgan cites Herndon's (another naturalist) observation of fish baiting practiced by a mammal: "An enormous tiger ... was extended full length upon a rock level with the water ... From time to time he struck the water with his tail, and at the same moment raised one of his fore paws and seized a fish ... These last, deceived by the noise, and taking it for the fall of fruit (of which they are very fond), unsuspectingly approach, and soon fall into the claws of the traitor" ([1868] 1966, p. 261). This incident once more illustrates the unique behavioral event that the anecdotal method captures; the fact that the behavior is akin to baiting practices observed among birds supports the distinct possibility that it is a veridical account—even if rarely witnessed, or rarely practiced.

While today versatile behavior can be documented, previously the gathering of anecdotal evidence was the method for recording what Griffin calls "enterprising behavior." With the disparagement of the anecdotal method in twentieth-century behavioral science, the central, if not the sole, method of documenting versatile behavior, which Darwin utilized when necessary, was largely excluded from the outset. If it is concurred that Griffin's conception of versatility is a robust criterion for conscious awareness, then clearly the devaluation of the method of anecdotal evidence has both accompanied and reinforced the skeptical attitude of twentieth-century behaviorists and ethologists toward the existence of conscious awareness in animals.

CONCLUSION

Based on the pervasiveness of his style and on his explicit arguments, I have maintained that Darwin's anthropomorphism is not a metaphorical application of language from the human to the animal case. Darwin intends his descriptions, including those replete with a mental vocabulary, as realistic representations of animal life. Darwin's realistic approach to the transparency of animal subjectivity differs profoundly from mechanomorphic imagery, and implicitly opposes skepticism toward animal mind. I have argued that his view is neither naive nor the consequence of a category mistake of conflating human and animal qualities. In contrast to his critics, who either downplay or condemn his anthropomorphism, I have tried to show that the vantage point of Darwin on animal life—even if it came under (increasingly receding) disesteemation in twentieth-century behavioral science—is not only legitimate in its own right, it is, moreover, *lastingly powerful*.

Darwin's anthropomorphic language emanates from a commitment to evolutionary continuity which, for him, inexorably includes behavioral and mental continuity. He defends this view explicitly in providing numerous instantiations of a wide gamut of behavioral continuities and cognate mental faculties in many different species, from insects to primates and birds, with examples ranging from the commonplace to the rare and anecdotal. The breadth and character of his understanding of behavioral and mental continuity, as well as its strong empirical support, come to center stage in *The Expression of the Emotions in Man and Animals*.

While Darwin openly advocates continuity between all animal forms, his use of the vernacular of objects, events, relations, action, and mind makes the same argument in an even more resounding—in the persistence of its effects—manner. In affinity with the genre of naturalist writing, the anthropomorphic language of Darwin, the naturalist, reflects an understanding of subjectivity in animal life in terms of animals as *authors* of action, and of action as transparently embodying an *experientially* meaningful dimension. As a final illustration of the features of authorship and experience, I conclude with a passage that is, for me, one of the most memorable of Darwin's writing.

> I formerly possessed a large dog, who, like every other dog, was much pleased to go out walking. He showed his pleasure by trotting gravely before me with high steps, head much raised, moderately erected ears, and tail carried aloft but not stiffly. Not far from my house a path branches off to the right, leading to the hot-house, which I used often to visit for a few moments, to look at my experimental plants. This was always a great disappointment to the dog, as he did not know whether I should continue my walk; and the instantaneous and complete change of expression which came over him as soon as my body swerved in the least towards the path (and I sometimes tried this as an experiment) was laughable. His look of dejection was known to every member of the family, and was called his *hot-house face*. This consisted in the head drooping much, the whole body sinking a little and remaining motionless; the ears and tail falling suddenly down, but the tail was by no means wagged. With the falling of the ears and of his great chaps, the eyes became much changed in appearance, and I fancied that they looked less bright. His aspect was that of piteous, hopeless dejection; and it was, as I have said, laughable, as the cause was so slight. Every detail in his attitude was in complete opposition to his former joyful yet dignified bearing ([1872] 1965, pp. 57-60, emphasis in original).

The description of the dog's expressions, as well as that of the circumstances that occasioned those expressions, assemble the attentive reader's perceptual focus. Along with Darwin, the reader does not infer joy and dejection from the dog's bearings, but rather, by imbricating visual memories onto the described scene, sees joy and dejection in the dog's bearings. Darwin's understanding, without a moment's pause, skirts past the idea of mind as a private domain, and in this unassuming fashion delivers a serious blow to the chimerical dualism of observable body and unobservable mind.

NOTES

1. See Descartes' *Philosophical Letters* for his explicit denouncements of animal mind ([1630-1649] 1981).

2. See, for example, Gould and Gould (1982). On the a priori regard of insects (and invertebrates generally) as "mindless automata" see Donald Griffin's critical comments (1992).

3. However, scare quotes can also function as devices which, by exonerating the writer from a full commitment to the language, allow her or him to slip in certain (anthropomorphic or otherwise controversial) concepts. The reader grasps the meaning of particular behaviors under the auspices of these concepts regardless of whether or not they are enveloped in quotes (see Crist 1997).

4. The ethologist Colin Beer also criticizes Ghiselin's view that Darwin's anthropomorphism was merely metaphorical. Beer states that "this reading cannot be sustained when Darwin was expressly seeking to establish continuities between animal and human mental faculties" (1992, p. 72).

5. Darwin defines sexual selection as "depend[ing] on the advantage which certain individuals have over other individuals of the same sex and species in exclusive relation to reproduction" ([1871] 1981, vol. 1, p. 256).

6. Darwin writes that "individual differences are highly important for us, as they afford materials for natural selection to accumulate" ([1859] 1964, p. 45; see also Mayr 1982, pp. 38, 45-47).

7. See Griffin (1984, p. 41; 1992, p. 254). Griffin observes that behavioral scientists often assume that if a behavior is instinctual (or, in contemporary terminology, "genetically programmed") then it cannot also be conscious. Criticizing this view, he writes that "the customary assumption that if some behavior has been genetically programmed, it cannot be guided by conscious thinking, is not supported by any solid evidence" (1992, p. 254).

8. This is inaccurate, as Darwin did not reserve the concepts love, fear, desire, and so forth, for mammals alone.

9. This view is often associated with vitalism (see Bierens de Haan 1947).

10. For discussions of anthropomorphism and its inevitability in the understanding of animal life, see Asquith (1984) and Fisher (1990). For a criticism of the current resurgence of anthropomorphism from a neo-behaviorist perspective, see Kennedy (1992).

11. Perlocutions are consequential effects of language usage on an audience; these effects involve the emotive, cognitive, or practical import of a proposition, which is not referenced at all, or only obliquely, on the surface of the proposition (Austin 1962, p. 101). The perlocutionary effects of the language of animal life largely involve the sorts of pictures that are encouraged or elided in the reader's imagination.

12. While Darwin himself does not use terms such as marriage, which refer to human institutions, he sometimes reproduces such expressions from other naturalists

and informants. Elsewhere he writes of a "wife" among Crustaceans ([1871] 1981, vol. 1, p. 334) and of a "concubine" among canaries (p. 270).

13.   In their discussion of Boyle's "literary technology" in describing his experiments, Shapin and Schaffer write that "virtual witnessing involves the production in a *reader's* mind of such an image of an experimental scene as obviates the necessity for either direct witnessing or replication" (1985, p. 60, emphasis in original). Likewise, subjective terminology presented with observational indices guides the reader to see the activities performed in certain ways.

14.   Thorndike conceived of studying animal intelligence by placing hungry animals in "puzzle boxes" with food outside and testing whether, and how fast, the animal would learn to operate the box's particular mechanism in order to escape. Thorndike's puzzle box was the prelude to the Skinner box.

15.   The first two chapters of *The Origin* show the importance of Darwin's reassessment of variation for his argument for descent with modification. Darwin shows that variation is not a matter of insignificant deviations from some fixed type, but the very material and condition for evolution. He argues compellingly that differences found between individuals, lesser varieties, well marked varieties, subspecies, and species "blend into each other in an insensible series; and a series impresses the mind with the idea of an actual passage" ([1859] 1964, p. 51).

16.   Thus Lorenz did not deny plasticity, but regarded it as a nonessential deviation from a fixed type. For Lorenz plasticity (or variability) is not in itself an important or revealing attribute of innate behaviors, but a symptom of incidental modularity around a fixed essence.

17.   The naturalist Len Howard explicitly makes this connection, which is also reflected in the title of her wonderful work *Birds as Individuals* (1953). She describes the behaviors of individual birds, and narrates many anecdotes, repeatedly emphasizing and demonstrating how markedly individuals of the same species differ in their behaviors, capacities, and temperament.

18.   This is not to suggest that Darwin accepted any anecdote as reliable. It appears that he regarded the story of the birds feeding their blind companions as truthful, because he had three different anecdotal sources—about pelicans, crows, and a cock—corroborating this behavior.

19.   Skeptics have invoked this type of thinking (which is both inner-reflective and language-bound) to justify their doubts regarding the existence of animal mind (see Descartes [1630]-1649] 1981; Mead [1934] 1962).

20.   Of course, pausing before action is neither a necessary nor a sufficient condition of thinking, reasoning, considering, and so forth.

21.   In a similar vein, the philosopher Ludwig Wittgenstein writes of "the expression, the behavior, of considering. Of what do we say: It is considering something? Of a human being, sometimes of a beast ... One sign of considering is hesitating in what you do" (1980, para 561).

22.   Ethnographic accounts of primate life are a telling exception. See, for example, Goodall (1990), and Strum (1987).

23.   Morgan's work is today regarded as a classic of natural history (see bibliography). Darwin knew Morgan's work on the beaver and cites it as an "excellent account of this animal" ([1871] 1981, vol. 1, p. 37).

REFERENCES

Asquith, P. 1984. "The Inevitability and Utility of Anthropomorphism in Description of Primate Behaviour." Pp. 138-174 in *The Meaning of Primate Signals*, edited by R. Harré and V. Reynolds. Cambridge: Cambridge University Press.

Austin, J.L. 1962. *How to Do Things with Words*. Cambridge, MA: Harvard University Press.

Barnett, S., ed. 1958. "The Expression of Emotions." Pp. 206-230 in *A Century of Darwin*. New York: Books for Libraries Press.

Beer, C. 1992. "Conceptual Issues in Cognitive Ethology." Pp. 69-109 in *Advances in the Study of Behavior*, edited by P.J.B. Slater et al. San Diego: Academic Press.

Bekoff, M. and D. Jamieson, eds. 1990. *Interpretation and Explanation in the Study of Animal Behavior*. Boulder: Westview Press.

Bierens de Haan, J.A. 1947. "Animal Psychology and The Science of Animal Behaviour." *Behaviour* 1: 71-80.

Burkhardt, R., Jr. 1985. "Darwin on Animal Behavior and Evolution." In *The Darwinian Heritage*, edited by D. Kohn. Princeton, NJ: Princeton University Press.

Coulter, J. 1979. *The Social Construction of Mind: Studies in Ethnomethodology and Linguistic Philosophy*. London: Macmillan Press.

Crist, E. 1996. "Naturalists' Portrayals of Animal Life: Engaging the Verstehen Approach." *Social Studies of Science* (November).

_____. 1997. "The Ethnological Constitution of Animals as Natural Objects: The Writings of Konrad Lorenz and Nikolaas Tinbergen." *Biology and Philosophy* (forthcoming).

Darwin, C. (1859) 1964. *On the Origin of Species. A Facsimile of the First Edition*. Cambridge: Harvard University Press.

_____. (1872) 1965. *The Expression of Emotions in Man and Animals*. Chicago: University of Chicago Press.

_____. (1871) 1981. *The Descent of Man and Selection in Relation to Sex*. Princeton, NJ: Princeton University Press.

_____. (1881) 1985. *The Formation of Vegetable Mould through the Action of Worms with Observations on their Habits*. Chicago: Chicago University Press.

_____. (1892) 1958. *The Autobiography of Charles Darwin and Selected Letters*, edited by F. Darwin. New York: Dover.

Davidson, D. 1980. *Essays on Actions and Events*. Oxford: Clarendon Press.

Degler, C.N. 1991. *In Search of Human Nature: The Decline and Revival of Darwinism in American Social Thought*. Oxford: Oxford University Press.

Dennett, D.C. 1987. *The Intentional Stance*. Cambridge: The MIT Press.

Descartes, R. (1630-1649) 1981. *Philosophical Letters*, translated and edited by A. Kenny. Minneapolis: University of Minnesota Press.

Fisher, J.A. 1990. "The Myth of Anthropomorphism." Pp. 96-116 in *Interpretation and Explanation in the Study of Animal Behavior*, edited by M. Bekoff and D. Jamieson. Boulder, CO: Westview Press.

Ghiselin, M.T. 1969. *The Triumph of the Darwinian Method*. Berkeley: University of California Press.

Goodall, J. 1990. *Through a Window: My Thirty Years with the Chimpanzees of Gombe*. Boston: Houghton Mifflin.

Gould, J.L. 1982. *Ethology: The Mechanisms and Evolution of Behavior*. New York: Norton.

Gould, J.L. and C.G. Gould. 1982. "The Insect Mind: Physics or Metaphysics?" Pp. 269-297 in *Animal Mind–Human Mind*, edited by D.R. Griffin. Berlin: Springer-Verlag.

Gould, S.J. and R. Lewontin. 1979. "The Spandrels of San Marco and The Panglossian Paradigm: A Critique of The Adaptationist Programme." Pp. 8-23 in *Readings in Animal Behavior*, edited by J.F.A. Tranniello, M.P. Scott, and F. Wasserman. Lexington, MA: Ginn Press.

Grier, J.W. 1984. *Biology of Animal Behavior*. St. Louis: Times Mirror/Mosby College Printing.

Griffin, D. 1984. *Animal Thinking*. Cambridge: Harvard University Press.

————. 1992. *Animal Minds*. Chicago: The University of Chicago Press.

Howard, L. 1953. *Birds as Individuals*. New York: Doubleday.

Huxley, T.H.. 1874. "On the Hypothesis that Animals are Automata, and Its History." Pp. 199-250 in *The Collected Essays*, Vol. 1. London: Macmillan and Company.

Kennedy, J.S. 1992. *The New Anthropomorphism*. Cambridge: Cambridge University Press.

Lorenz, K. 1935. "Companionship in Bird Life." Pp. 83-128 in *Instinctive Behavior*, edited by C.H. Schiller and K.S. Lashley. New York: International University Press.

————. 1937. "The Nature of Instinct." Pp. 129-175 in *Instinctive Behavior*, edited by C.H. Schiller and K.S. Lashley. New York: International University Press.

————. 1950. "The Comparative Method in Studying Innate Behaviour Patterns." *Symposia of the Society of Experimental Biology* 4: 221-268.

————. 1965. "Introduction." C. Darwin, *The Expression of the Emotions in Man and Animals*. Chicago: Chicago University Press.

Lorenz, K. and N. Tinbergen. 1957. "Taxis and Instinctive Action in the Egg-Retrieving Behavior of the Greylag Goose." Pp. 176-208 in *Instinctive Behavior*, edited by C.H. Schiller and K.S. Lashley. New York: International University Press.

Mayr, E. 1982. *The Growth of Biological Thought: Diversity, Evolution and Inheritance*. Cambridge: Harvard University Press.

————. 1984. "Typological versus Population Thinking." Pp. 14-17 in *Conceptual Issues in Evolutionary Biology*, edited by E. Sober. Cambridge: The MIT Press.

Mead, G.H. (1934) 1962. *Mind, Self, and Society*. Chicago: The University of Chicago Press.

Morgan, L.H. (1868) 1966. *The American Beaver. A Classic of Natural History and Ecology*. (Original title: *The American Beaver and His Works*.) New York: Dover Publications.

Nagel, T. 1981. "What is It Like to Be a Bat?" Pp. 391-403 in *The Mind's I*, edited by R. Hofstadter and D.C. Dennett. New York: Basic Books.

Richards, R. 1987. *Darwin and the Emergence of Evolutionary Theories of Mind and Behavior*. Chicago: The University of Chicago Press.

Romanes, G.J. 1882. *Animal Intelligence*. London: Kegan Paul, Trench and Company.

Schutz, A. 1962. *The Problem of Social Reality, Collected Papers,* Vol. 1. The Hague: Martinus Nijhoff.

Shapin, S. and S. Schaffer. 1985. *Leviathan and the Air-Pump: Hobbes, Boyle, and the Experimental Life.* Princeton, NJ: Princeton University Press.

Silk, J.B. 1987. "Social Behavior in Evolutionary Perspective." Pp. 318-329 in *Primate Societies,* edited by B.B. Smuts et al. Chicago: The University of Chicago Press.

Strum, S. 1987. *Almost Human: A Journey into the World of Baboons.* New York: W.W. Norton.

Thorndike, E. 1898. "Animal Intelligence." In *The Psychological Review. Series of Monograph Supplements* II(4) (Whole No. 8): 1-109.

Thorpe, W.H. 1973. "Ethology as a New Branch of Biology." Pp. 5-23 in *Readings in Ethology and Comparative Psychology,* edited by M.W. Fox. Monterey: Brooks/Cole Publishing.

Tinbergen, N. 1951. *The Study of Instinct.* Oxford: Clarendon Press.

White, A.R. 1968. "Introduction." Pp. 1-18 in *The Philosophy of Action,* edited by A.R. White. Oxford: Oxford University Press.

Winch, P. 1958. *The Idea of a Social Science.* London: Routledge and Kegan Paul.

Wittgenstein, L. 1980. *Remarks on the Philosophy of Psychology,* Volume 1. Oxford: Basil Blackwell.

INTERNAL SELECTION
AND CULTURAL EVOLUTION

Bernd Baldus

ABSTRACT

The evolutionary study of human culture has found it difficult to deal with the complexity of human behavior, its frequently nonadaptive and dysfunctional character, and the fact that cultural selection is intentional and based on internal preferences. These problems do not result from the peculiarities of human behavior but from the limitations of the neo-Darwinian model of evolution that has been used to explain it. Darwin's own work shows an increasing preoccupation with the selective effects of internal preferences, from his early interest in habit and use to sexual selection, which is predominately internally guided. By combining Darwin's ideas with modern chaos theory and theories of self-organizing systems, this paper develops a theory of natural selection that recognizes the role of both internal selection and external constraints: The former provide the experimental, formative, direction-setting dynamics of evolution, while the latter test and genetically encode the results.

Advances in Human Ecology, Volume 5, pages 85-110.

INTRODUCTION

The use of evolutionary theory to explain human culture has been at best a very qualified success. Early hopes to find a general biological explanation of human culture and trace its descent to ancestral cultural origins have given way to a modest body of work which has begun to shed light on the evolutionary roots of specific human behaviors such as linguistic differentiation, kin and ethnic preferences, or male and female reproductive strategies. A recent overview of this research is given by Nielsen (1994).

These findings have strengthened the general case for *some* links between evolution and human behavior. But they have also shown the limitations of current evolutionary theorems in coming to grips with the complexity of cultural evolution. Even sympathetic summaries of sociobiological work such as Nielsen's read like a string of isolated findings held together by much hopeful prose. Most human behavior has remained beyond the reach of biological explanation and has forced neo-Darwinists to admit that biological constraints "seem most likely to be bypassed or superseded by humans" (Alexander 1979, p. 93; 1987), or to resort to theoretical expedients which are hard to reconcile with known principles of evolution. Barkow for example speculated that the frequent irrationality and maladaptiveness of human behavior was a strategy to deceive others through "the inclusion of contradictory data in an information-processing system" (1989, p. 98). Other efforts reduced cultural variety to six "interests" (Barkow 1989), seven traits (Buss 1988) or "epigenetic rules" (Lumsden and Wilson 1983; Ruse 1986), or twenty-three "behavioral predispositions" (Lopreato 1984) for which adaptive rationales could be construed more easily. Actual cultural behaviors could then be interpreted as "perverted" or "hypersocial" expressions of such hidden predispositions (Crippen and Machalek 1989; Reynolds and Tanner 1993). Fitness-neutral or maladaptive human cultural patterns were attributed to "runaway processes" (Boyd and Richerson 1985), "autopredation" and "culture stretch" (Barkow 1989), "cultural inertia" (Alexander 1979, p. 77), or nonadaptive effects of originally adaptive characteristics (Cavalli-Sforza and Feldman 1981), although it was obvious that with the growing number of exceptions the "entire enterprise of interpreting culture as enlarged inclusive-fitness-optimizing strategies must fall" (Barkow 1989, p. 283).

Four aspects of human culture posed particular problems for conventional evolutionary analysis. First, culture was imbued with "meaning," which made it difficult to find unambiguous units of selection. Second, the prevalence of functionally redundant and nonadaptive traits in culture interfered with the search for cultural equivalents of fitness. Third, human culture seemed to be driven by purpose and interest, and selection seemed to be internal; conventional evolutionary theory had no place for such internal events. Finally, social processes proved to be open and indeterminate to a degree that was difficult to reconcile with the more mechanistic features of evolutionary theorems.

These discrepancies between evolutionary models and cultural reality led some authors to abandon the search for a comprehensive evolutionary explanation of human behavior altogether. Cultural selection seemed to a large extent controlled by internal "guiding criteria" (Boyd and Richerson 1985), or "a system of poorly understood internal drives and rewards that direct the activity and choices of the individual ... towards maximizing self satisfaction" (Cavalli-Sforza and Feldman 1981, p. 363). Evolutionary biology was therefore not applicable to human culture. "Human culture has introduced a new style of change to our planet, a form that Lamarck mistakenly advocated for biological evolution, but that does truly apply to cultural change—inheritance of acquired characters" (Gould 1990, p. 20).

LIMITATIONS OF NEO-DARWINISM

This paper argues that the problems which the evolutionary analysis of culture experienced derive not from the nature of human behavior, but from the limitations of the neo-Darwinian model of evolution that has been used to explain it. Like much modern science, this model was shaped by Newtonian views of nature as a closed mechanical system. Such a system could be reduced to its smallest components. These components interacted in a functional or instrumental relationship. There were no "inner" unobservable dynamics in these systems; they were normally in a state of equilibrium which could be altered only by an observable and measurable external force. And their operation was governed by linear, deterministic causal dynamics; there was no provision for system-immanent change, or for any indeterminacy in the system's output.

In biology, these assumptions laid the foundations for the neo-Darwinist Modern Synthesis, which departed significantly from Darwin's theory of evolution. But they also imposed typical constraints on the study of human social behavior, whether by neo-Darwinist biology, sociological positivism and functionalism (Baldus 1990; Bryant 1992), or neoclassical economics (Khalil 1993).

The first of these constraints, *reductionism*, replaced Darwin's belief that natural selection worked on the whole organism with the gene as the proper unit of selection. Organisms were seen as aggregates of genetic components, "designed by genes simply as a means of enhancing gene survival and perpetuation" (Barnard 1983, p. 119; Ruse 1988, p. 24). Selection, strictly speaking, still worked on the phenotype, but the shift in emphasis from the somatic to the genetic aspects of selection encouraged the simplified working assumption that the phenotype was a direct reflection of the genotype. Its "meaning" was thus unambiguous and required no interpretation.

In reality, the gene-phenotype relationship is extremely complex: phenotypic traits, especially behavioral ones, are difficult to isolate, single genes frequently have multiple phenotypic effects, and single phenotypic traits may be the product of multiple genes. Moreover, such traits are often highly plastic. In the day-to-day ecological adaptation of organisms to environments their meaning is not predefined, but arises from the contexts in which they are employed. These problems are compounded in the study of human culture. Culture does not come in discrete, finite bits, and is therefore not easily understood in particulate terms. The boundaries of cultural concepts are fluid and hard to pin down, negotiated between messenger and recipient, and interwoven with other cultural components. Isolating them has much the same effect as taking words out of a sentence: it changes them beyond recognition. None of the many proposals for cultural equivalents of genes, such as "culturgens," "memes," or "concepts," have therefore found lasting acceptance.

The second constraint on the neo-Darwinist view of evolution grew from the mechanical functionalism of the Newtonian model. *Adaptationism* assumed that every morphological or behavioral trait was selected for its ability to make a "fitter" organism. Where Darwin had carefully noted both the marvelous adaptations and the many imperfections in nature, selection now appeared as a relentless and pervasive optimizer which left no redundant or nonfunctional traits. Although strictly speaking, the adaptive properties of a trait revealed themselves only in changes in the distribution of alleles in a population after many generations, neo-Darwinist efforts to "reverse engineer" selection events (Dennett 1995, pp. 212, 213) came to rely heavily on functional scenarios which assumed fitness to be an inherent technical property of a given trait in a given environment. The mostly hypothetical, ex-post factum nature of these scenarios facilitated that assumption; one could "always invent a plausible adaptive advantage for an observed or supposed trait" (McFarland 1985, p. 528).

In reality, environments are typically nested and variable (Freese 1994, p. 159); what is functional for proximate or present environments may not be functional for distant or future ones. Moreover, organisms modify environments by their own behavior. Also, in human cultures the utility of an action or artifact depends on the goals and preferences of actors. Such goals are subjective, finely layered, highly variable, self-made, and structured by social hierarchies. Objective measurements of the functional value of social behaviors are therefore impossible; welfare economics concluded long ago that only the comparative (ordinal), not the absolute (cardinal) utility of goods or services for individuals or societies could be determined.

Neo-Darwinist selection scenarios avoided these problems by introducing genetic change into highly simplified and constant environments, or by examining the effect of isolated environmental changes on given gene pools. Similarly, organisms were reduced to average types which were driven by simplified homogeneous goals or preferences—usually a narrow range of "survival" needs or instincts such as food, sex, and avoidance of predators—whose presence in all organisms could be taken for granted and required no further study.

Such simplifications allowed biologists to reach determinate conclusions regarding fitness differentials, but at the price of losing any resemblance to actual goals and environments (Freese 1994, p. 161). The conviction that there "must be an evolutionary advantage to a trait if we only look hard enough" (Barash 1982, p. 51) induced a strong bias to finding adaptive perfection in nature and to overlook imperfect or redundant traits (Wesson 1991, pp. 84-105). Adaptive redundancy was even more pronounced in human culture. Any view of culture as a mere accumulation of behaviors which maximized reproductive success quickly confronted the fact that "we do a great deal that doesn't make much biological sense" (Barash 1979, p. 226). Error, maladaptive behavior, suboptimal technologies, and dysfunctional cultural traits abounded in human societies; the "survival of the mediocre" (Hallpike

1986), not the survival of the optimal, was the hallmark of cultural selection. The complexity and variability of social environments and the infinite flexibility of human purposes made the objective allocation of adaptive benefits in sociocultural systems all but impossible (Dunnell 1988; Granovetter 1979).

A third impediment to the neo-Darwinist study of culture stemmed from its *operationalism*, first formulated for biology by Weismann around 1880, which confined evolutionary research to observable measurable facts. Darwin believed that animals could experience happiness and misery, playfulness and suspicion, and had powers of reasoning and imagination. Neo-Darwinism dismissed intangible aspects of mental processes such as consciousness, awareness, or purpose as anthropomorphic. They became a virtual taboo in neo-Darwinist research (Griffin 1984, p. 22).

As a result, the brain and mental processes in general were given only a limited instrumental role. The operationalist preference for replicable repetitive behavioral responses to the same stimulus encouraged the perception of brains as bundles of preprogrammed responses. They appeared as one more fitness-maximizing special-purpose organ, like hands and kidneys (Barash 1979, p. 200). Brains were composites of built-in goals (Barkow 1989, p. 131), and of computational "modules" of behavior (Nielsen 1994, p. 289; Tooby and Cosmides 1989; Barkow, Cosmides, and Tooby 1992) which evaluated external stimuli for their relevance to these goals (Barkow 1989, p. 132). Brains coordinated information about the living mechanism's operation with information about its environment, with selection favoring the speed and accuracy of processing that information. Both types of information were given; brains could not alter or create information on their own. In the cultural sphere they functioned as replicating vehicles for cultural traits which enhanced human reproductive success (Dawkins 1976, p. 206). Like freedom and dignity for the behaviorist, "self" and "consciousness" were illusions for neo-Darwinist biology, merely fitness-enhancing disguises of deeper biological drives (Barkow 1989, p. 98).

But human cultural selection seems to be under the control of purpose and intent, the mysterious "internal drives" and "guiding criteria" which Cavalli-Sforza and Feldman (1981) and Boyd and Richerson (1985) had encountered. The nature and functions of consciousness and awareness are hotly debated topics in the discussion of artificial intelligence (Penrose 1990; Searle 1992). Even recent studies of animal behavior have moved toward broader, more cognitive notions of animal intelligence, awareness, and consciousness (Cheney and Seyfarth 1990; de Waal 1989; Griffin 1992; Gould and Gould 1994; Dawkins 1993; Savage-Rumbaugh and Lewin 1994). These views conflict with neo-Darwinism's narrow instrumental view of the brain.

Determinism, the fourth intellectual influence to affect the neo-Darwinist view of evolution, derived from Newton's search for a divine order in nature and from the secular vision of a law-governed universe that eventually emerged from it. This universe had no degrees of freedom; individuals were agents of biological, historical, or rational choice dynamics which determined their behavior and in the long run the—usually progressive—historical evolution of society. Darwin, while occasionally under the sway of progressivism, remained keenly aware of the complex, active nature of the individual's struggle for existence, and of the unpredictability of its evolutionary results. Evolution led to much diversity, but followed no predetermined route. Any attempt to arrange species on a scale from lower to higher seemed "hopeless; who will decide whether a cuttle-fish be higher than a bee" (Darwin [1872] 1958, p. 331).

The neo-Darwinist model recognized only two forces which propelled evolution: genetic variation and natural selection. Both were purely exogenous factors, beyond the control of organisms. In combination, they produced traits with determinate fitness effects, and therefore determinate survival probabilities for the genome and its morphological reflections.

This led to two related problems. One was the inability of the neo-Darwinist model to account for any internal source of innovation. From the Newtonian perspective, nature and society were closed equilibrium systems whose states could be altered only from the outside. For neo-Darwinist biology, the only external source of evolutionary novelty was genetic mutation. Because information flowed only from gene to soma, organisms could make no independent, let alone intelligent, contribution to evolution. Ecological adaptation—the complex, and in Darwin's view, often innovative and creative interaction of organisms with their natural and social environments during their lifetime—was neglected in favor of the long-term evolutionary adaptation which was its result, although the two were not the same (Freese 1994, p. 155). Individuals were products, not causes of evolution; neo-Darwinist biology had no room for ecological adaptation as an endogenous source of evolutionary change.

For the same reason organic design could only appear as an exogenous process. Selection merely preserved genes on the basis of their differential fitness effects. Populations only registered the statistical result of *all* forces affecting evolution. Neither process provided a prima facie explanation for the *assembly* of genes into a variety of complex, functionally integrated life forms. There was, in particular, no place for any internal design-producing dynamic in a special purpose brain, no matter how complex: "There is no deliberation, no planning, no 'mind', nothing incorporating ends or goals to direct the selection. It is achieved through nothing more forward-looking than pressures of the environment" (Cronin 1991, p 19). Evolutionary design could only be conceived as additive adaptive refinements: "6 percent (vision) is better than 5, 7 percent better than 6, and so on up the gradual, continuous series" (Dawkins 1986, p. 81). Neo-Darwinist selection scenarios typically started with an already existing design and showed how it could have been improved.

As a consequence, the neo-Darwinist view of evolutionary design acquired a strong deterministic and progressionist character protestations to the contrary not withstanding (Dawkins 1982, ch. 3 Ruse 1986, p. 19). Constant and ubiquitous selection produced optimal traits which congealed into perfect organisms. Evolution produced optimal populations by progressively reducing cases of error-making and imperfection until populations filled all available natural niches There was nowhere better to evolve to; evolution came to an end until genetic or environmental variation provided an external impetus for further change (Allen 1992, p. 111). Sociologists found this idea particularly irresistible and responded with a plethora of "laws of progress" and stage theories of historical development, all of which offered felicitous predictions of societal advancement along orderly and predictable paths.

The view of innovation and design as a "mindless, motiveless mechanicity" (Dennett 1995, p. 76) is at odds with the endogenous nature of human creativity and the indeterminacy of its cultural results The few evolutionary studies of innovation (e.g., Campbell 1974 Simonton 1988; Kantorovitch 1993) have all recognized its endogenous intrapsychic basis. With regard to design, sociology has long recognized the pivotal role of values and interests in the assembly of culture. Values purposes, and interests have been shown to be important order producing selectors in cultural evolution, from technology (Basalla 1988) to table manners (Visser 1991) to everyday artifacts (Petroski

1992). The simultaneous presence of innovation and order-producing dynamics suggests in turn that cultural evolution is permanently poised between contingency and order, and therefore nonlinear and nondeterministic (Baker 1993; Manis and Meltzer 1994; Mann 1986; McCloskey 1991; Reisch 1991).

DARWIN, COGNITION, AND EVOLUTION

If the large number of seemingly nonadaptive and redundant cultural traits were the symptom of the malaise of the neo-Darwinist study of human culture, its ultimate cause was the neglect of the ecological, and the exclusive focus on the genetic, aspects of adaptation. Any effort to cure the problem must therefore reintegrate the actual process of adaptation during an organism's lifetime into the theory of evolution. Evolutionary theory must consider both the lived and the inherited side of the evolutionary process. This requires looking at selection from the point of view of the organism as well as the gene. What is adaptive is not "what selection can work on" (Cronin 1991, p. 102) but what an organism can work with. The fit "between what is of advantage and what evolved" is not "automatic" (Cronin 1991, p. 42), but often involves the internal evaluation, choice, and use of the manifest, phenotypic properties of evolutionary novelty by organisms. Such internal selection is therefore an integral element of evolution.

The role of the organism in natural selection was a central feature of Darwin's work. The retention or disappearance of traits in the course of natural selection depended on their *use to the organism as a whole*; variations were preserved and accumulated because they were "profitable to the preserved being," "beneficial to each creature," "useful to each being's own welfare" (Darwin [1872] 1958, pp. 100, 122, 128). Organisms, not traits, were the unit of selection (Darwin [1872] 1958, p. 74; Eiseley 1961, p. 335). While Darwin knew nothing about genes, he had encountered and rejected early versions of reductionism. When Huxley proposed in 1869 that the "war of nature" be extended to the struggle for survival between molecules and the parts of the organism, Darwin told him with his usual politeness that he "could not quite follow" this vision of natural selection (Eiseley 1961, p. 335).

Organisms were anything but passive carriers of particulate characteristics which were culled by external selective pressure. They were *active* participants in the struggle for survival, "partook" of the advantages of variations, and "seized" on "the many and widely diversified places in the polity of nature" (Darwin [1872] 1958, pp. 112, 117, 168). These advantages did not reveal themselves automatically. They had to be discovered through the trial-and-error exploration of inherited abilities and newly encountered environments. Any such activity had its ultimate origins in a conscious intentional effort. For Darwin, intentional use and disuse was therefore a crucial starting point of evolutionary processes:

> It is scarcely credible that the movements of a headless frog, when it wipes a drop of acid or other object from its thigh, and which movements are so well-coordinated for a special purpose, were not at first performed voluntarily, being afterwards rendered easy from long-continued habit so as at last to be performed unconsciously (Darwin [1872] 1965, p. 40; see also Smith 1978, p. 261).

The neo-Darwinist literature has generally dismissed Darwin's interest in the effects of use, disuse, and habit on evolution as a defensive lapse into a never fully abandoned Lamarckism, brought on by his ignorance of the real causes of variation (Eiseley 1961, pp. 245, 246; [Himmelfarb and Vorzimmer make similar suggestions; see Richards 1987, p. 195]). This argument is not convincing. First, Darwin never doubted that his own explanation of natural selection was superior to that of Lamarck. And although he readily admitted that, with regard to the causes of variation "our ignorance ... is profound" (Darwin [1872] 1958, p. 156), this posed neither a serious problem for his theory of evolution (Darwin [1872] 1958, pp. 157, 443) nor was it a point raised by his critics (Ruse 1979, p. 235).

What really drove Darwin to the study of the effects of habit and use/disuse on selection was his search for a crucial missing component in his theory of natural selection. Variation and excess reproduction had provided two key elements that could account for the differential survival of particular traits. But they did not explain how these traits were assembled into complex organic forms. Darwin realized very early that this was "really perhaps greatest difficulty to whole theory" (cited in Ruse 1979, p. 171). For an answer, he looked increasingly to consciousness, whether animal or human, as an internal source of guidance and organization in the assembly of natural organisms: "According to my views, habits give structure,—habits precede structure,—habitual instincts precede structure" (Darwin, cited in Ruse 1979 p. 171; see also Smith 1978, pp. 261, 262).

The question of how complex, functioning, phenotypic forms could emerge from a process as disorderly as natural selection had led to the most troubling objections to his work from friends and critics, such as Sedgwick, Whewell, Herschel, Asa Gray, and the most irksome of all, Mivart. All had difficulties with the idea that "the law of the higgledy-piggledy," guided only by the utilitarian value of a particular variation, could fashion complex organs, let alone complex organisms. Even Darwin's staunch defender, Huxley, felt this to be one point where he could not agree with Darwin. The lack of any explanation of direction in natural selection emerged as the weakest point in Darwin's theory of evolution.

The key to solving the problem lay in artificial selection, which Darwin had used as the point of departure for his theory in the *Origin*. Here, the breeder assembled from accidental variations supplied to him by nature those that conformed to his purpose, either by keeping only the "best" animals or by pursuing a detailed image of the desired characteristics of a breed. The breeder's intent added a crucial third element—direction—to the variations which provided the raw material with which evolution worked, and the competition for resources which generated the dynamics of selection.

Darwin's search for a corresponding force in nature convinced him more and more of the need to look at processes inside the organism which could aid in the assembly of variations and determine which of the variations supplied by nature would be used to the organism's advantage. As a result, natural selection was no longer an automatic fit between what variations provided and environments required, but a range of responses which involved organisms to different degrees in the process of selection. On one end stood the purely coincidental, external form of natural selection. It was exemplified by highly variable butterflies accidentally mixing with little-persecuted varieties with the result that those least similar to the latter were "generation after generation eliminated, and only the others left to propagate their kind" (Darwin [1872] 1958, p. 399). Here a changed environment alone, unaided by any change in the organism's behavior, altered the distribution of wing and body designs in the butterfly population. A second category of selective effects resulted from "internal laws of correlation of growth," in modern parlance pleiotropic effects of genetic change or allometric correlations in the development of the phenotype.

However, natural selection could also begin with an organism discovering and habitually using one of the many potential uses of a variation provided by nature. Darwin began to work on such internally initiated selection in the *Origin*. Using examples such as the flatfish or the prehensile tail of monkeys, he suggested that habit had a guiding effect on natural selection which was comparable to the intent of the breeder: The deliberate and presumably conscious habit of the young flatfish, to compensate for its shape and its relatively small fins by trying to look upward, led to the use of genetic variations which facilitated such behavior, and eventually to the inherited movement of their eyes which flatfishes undergo in their early phases of life. Here, intent (habit) preceded inheritance and set the stage for assembling variations in a particular direction. Intent came first, natural selection followed in its wake.

Sexual Selection and Internal Choice

In the *Origin*, Darwin was still in doubt about the relative impact of internal choice on evolution. Its role ranged from "subordinate" to "considerable" to "great" (Darwin [1872] 1958, pp. 57, 139, 229). But the evolutionary effects of habit, use, and disuse gained increasing weight as Darwin's work progressed, culminating in the theory of sexual selection in the *Descent of Man*, which acknowledged internal selection as a process equal in power to that of external environmental constraints.

In sexual selection, nature acted no longer as the external arbiter of survival, but as a source of options for choices the organism made. These choices were guided by internal standards of beauty and taste which affected the selection of mates with the preferred characteristics and, through inheritance, the eventual distribution of such characteristics in species. Sexual selection was not Lamarckian: tastes and preferences did not *cause* the preferred characteristics to appear. But once they did appear, mental images, not nature red in tooth and claw, led to their retention. Darwin's objective here was twofold. The first was to establish a continual evolutionary descent line from animal to human culture. Darwin thought that sexual selection initially appeared with the lowest order of arthropods and vertebrates (Darwin [1871] 1981, p. 396). The second was to find an explanation for the many nonadaptive incongruities and redundancies in nature and culture, and ultimately for the problem of design. The complexity of culture, exemplified in the coloration and display of different sexes which could have no conceivable adaptive purpose, often far exceeded what was required for survival. Darwin now admitted that in the earlier editions of my *Origin of Species* I perhaps attributed too much to the action of natural selection ... I had not formerly sufficiently considered the existence of many structures, which appear to be, as far as we can judge, neither beneficial nor injurious; and this I believe to be one of the greatest oversights as yet detected in my work ([1871] 1981, p. 125).

The reason he gave for this oversight contains a strong implicit critique of adaptationism, a point lost on such modern neo-Darwinist critics of sexual selection as Cronin (1991). Darwin said:

I was not able to annul the influence of my former belief, then widely prevalent, that each species had been purposely created; and this led to me tacitly assuming that every detail of structure, excepting rudiments, was of some special, though unrecognized, service ([1871] 1981, pp. 152-153).

Darwin was aware of the demands sexual selection made on his readers who were likely to feel "great difficulty in admitting that female mammals, birds, reptiles, and fish, could have acquired the high standards of taste which is implied by the beauty of males, and which generally coincides with our own standards" (Darwin [1871] 1981, p. 401). But he concluded the *Descent* with a statement which clearly established the primacy of the mind in assembling the products of evolution and in guiding its course:

He who admits the principle of sexual selection will be led to the remarkable conclusion that the cerebral system not only regulates most of the existing functions of the body, but has indirectly influenced the progressive development of various bodily structures and of certain mental qualities. Courage, pugnacity, perseverance, strength and size of body, weapons of all kinds, musical organs, both vocal and instrumental, bright colours, stripes and marks, and ornamental appendages, have all been indirectly gained by one sex or the other, through the influence of love and jealousy, through the appreciation of the beautiful in sound, colour or form, and through the exertion of a choice; and these powers of the mind manifestly depend on the development of the cerebral system (Darwin [1871] 1981, p. 402).

Sexual selection explained not only the evolution of traits that were of no significance in the Malthusian struggle for existence, but revealed the more general role of internal preferences in assembling living things from the undirected variations provided by nature. Darwin noted that sexual selection was "closely analogous to that which man unintentionally, yet effectually, brings to bear on his domesticated productions, when he continues for a long time choosing the most pleasing and useful individuals, without any wish to modify the breed" (Darwin [1871] 1981, p. 398). By turning to the internal, cognitive components of the evolutionary process, Darwin laid the foundations for an evolutionary explanation of human culture that could begin to deal with the problems on which modern neo-Darwinian sociobiology had foundered: the adaptive redundancy of so much human behavior, and the diversity and goal-directedness of human cultural evolution.

Evolution, Cognition, and Behavior

The only component missing in Darwin's thinking about internal selection was the criterion which distinguished his theory most clearly from Lamarck's: the fact that the initial appearance of variations was entirely independent of their eventual use and inheritance. Darwin knew he differed from Lamarck on this point; after all, "If the right variations occurred, and no others, natural selection would be superfluous" (Darwin 1887, vol. III, p. 85). But Darwin's lack of knowledge of the genetic bases of variation prevented him from understanding why variations occurred in all directions. Only in discussing artificial selection did he comprehend the full extent of the separation of variation and selection. Here "we clearly see that the two elements of change are distinct; variability is in some manner excited, but it is the will of man which accumulates the variations in certain directions; and it is this latter agency which answers to the survival of the fittest under nature" (Darwin [1872] 1958, pp. 132-133).

This gap was closed only after Darwin's death by Weismann's assertion that germ and body cells were separate. No communication could pass from the latter to the former. No inheritance of characteristics acquired during the lifetime of an organism could therefore occur. Genetic variation arose spontaneously, "blind" to the needs of the organism.

The implications of Weismann's discovery for a Darwinian theory of internal selection were recognized at about the same time by psychologists such as William James, John Dewey, Conwy L. Morgan, and James M. Baldwin, and philosophers such as Charles S. Peirce. They were the first to develop a properly Darwinian theory of cognition. Thought variations and innovations occurred continually and spontaneously in the human mind. They arose independent of their utility as truly free, random thought events, not subject to any purposive control, "accidental outbirths of spontaneous variation in the functional activity of the excessively unstable human brain" (James 1898, p. 247)— James' version of Weismann's blindness criterion with which he had become familiar (James 1890, vol. II, p. 686). These thought variations were then selectively adopted or rejected through trial and error comparison with the individual's conscious standards and purposes. The mind functioned as a central clearing agency that tested blindly emerging ideas and selectively retained those that conformed to internal selectors. But this process also provided the individual with a large range of autonomy for nonlethal error and experimentation, thus creating a buffer between environment and gene which allowed individuals to make subjective "sense" of environments and of their own abilities.

While James explored the functioning of the mind from a Darwinian perspective, Morgan and Baldwin explored its long-term effects on evolution. Like James, they were influenced by Weismann's discovery of the blind nature of variations. Their theory of *organic selection* described a process which accorded a central role to active selective choice by the organism, but also conformed strictly with Darwin's principles of natural selection. Baldwin suggested that an individual, faced with a change in its environment or some other form of stress, would initially respond to it by "overproduced movements," that is, undirected or blind random behavior modifications, until by trial and error an appropriate accommodation would be found that assured the organism's survival. This kept the organism alive while others died. It also preserved the genetic base for the plasticity which permitted the behavioral response. And since habits, thus acquired, were often transmitted through learning to subsequent generations, time was gained during which genetic variation could gradually trace the initial accommodation and eventually replace and improve it. Through organic selection "a weapon *analogous to artificial selection* is put into the hands of the organism itself, and the species profits by it" (Baldwin 1902, p. 175, emphasis in original). The behavioral choices by an individual set a course for evolution; natural selection registered their genetic results.

At roughly the same time as neo-Darwinism began to abandon the individual in favor of genes and populations, the work of James, Morgan and Baldwin advanced a view of evolution in which the life process of an organism was of equal importance as its reproductive consequences. During this process, the organism carried out activities that would be crucial for its self-preservation: the selective recognition of opportunities in the internal and environmental variations blindly supplied by nature, and their assembly into functionally integrated organic designs which could then be preserved through the auxiliary action of genetic inheritance. James and Baldwin had begun to close the only remaining gap in Darwin's theory, and evolutionary theory had reached an important junction. The modern synthesis between Darwin's theory and genetics could have been completed by an examination of the active, self-organizing contribution to evolution made by organisms during their lifetime.

But the rising star of behaviorism in psychology and the growing influence of operationalism in biology effectively terminated research on the cognitive dimensions of behavior, just as they rejected any role for cognitive factors in ontogeny or phylogeny (Richards 1987, pp. 495-503, ch. 11). Although it was occasionally revived in the work of Waddington, Popper, Toulmin, and Campbell, the idea that mental processes could affect evolution was dismissed by mainstream evolutionary theory as Lamarckian. An occasional footnote on the "Baldwin effect" as a residual factor in evolution was all that remained (Mayr 1976, p. 686; Bowler 1983, chs. 4 and 6; see also Simpson 1953; Waddington 1953). More sympathetic recent evaluations of Baldwin's work can be found in Richards (1987) and Dennett (1995, pp. 77-80).

INTERNAL SELECTION AND SELF-ORGANIZING EVOLUTION

If his incomplete knowledge of the blind nature of variations prevented Darwin from fully realizing the role of habit and use in directing evolution, Baldwin and James were hampered by their insufficient understanding of the biological foundations of the processes of internal selection they had described. As a result, their arguments for a role for mental events in evolution could be dismissed as suggestions that plants could think.

Only recently has research shed light on the biological origins of the three crucial components of internal selection: variation, goals, and learning. It allows us to reconstruct the natural bases of the lived side of life and its contribution to evolution in the same manner as the discovery of RNA/DNA casts light on the evolutionary role of genetic variation and heredity. Chaos theory has shown the extent and the functions of nonlinear variation in the natural world. Research on self-organizing systems has begun to reveal the biological bases of internally generated order. And the understanding of the feedback relationship between variation and order has shown the foundations of the ability of living systems to generate knowledge and to learn, which is the essential life-history prerequisite of all selection.

Together, they yield a paradigm of evolution that combines both the lived and the genetic side of life. *What distinguishes life from inanimate matter is its ability to produce blind variety—genetic, behavioral, and cognitive—in the face of chaotic and uncertain environments, and to select from that variety a temporary workable response that allows it to live and to reproduce. The maximal generation of blind variety is an optimal response to chaotic external conditions, because it maximizes the chance that a pragmatic fit between them will be found.* Gene variation and selection are merely a special case of this elementary process; by themselves they can therefore not serve as a general model of evolution.

The properties of this paradigm can be summed up as follows:

1. All life faces environments that are vital to the maintenance of its structural integrity, but tend to be unpredictable and beyond control because they are inherently chaotic, and because individual life forms have limited abilities to gather and process information.

All life forms also generate variations. In the face of unpredictable environments, such random or chaotic variation is an essential prerequisite for the evolution of life because it increases the survival chances of a system. By assuming more than one shape, systems are more likely to be compatible with external environmental changes and thus to continue to exist. But because these external changes are chaotic and unpredictable, internally generated variety must be nonlinear and blind. It must not be dedicated toward an expected outcome.

Chaotic variation is abundantly present in living and nonliving nature: from subatomic and atomic particles (Gutzwiller 1992) or the behavior of bacteria (Koshland 1980) to human physiological and mental processes (Goldberger, Rigney, and West 1990; Skarda and Freeman 1987). All living things are nonlinear, chaotic, oscillating systems.

2. Where such internally generated variations are ordered around attractors, that is, have the ability to maintain a stable structural state by keeping their movements within specific thresholds, systems are self-organizing or homeodynamic (Yates 1991, p. 211). Within these limits,

external change is accommodated, and the change in movement which it causes returns to a stable basin of attraction. If these thresholds are exceeded, the system can either establish a new basin of attraction or become unstable and cease to exist. These reactions are usually not proportional to the magnitude of the perturbation that caused them. No linear relationship exists between an input and the system's response. Self-organizing systems maintain, therefore, at least a partial autonomy in their response to external change (Barham 1990, pp. 199, 202). Again, self-organization is common in nature, from chemical and biochemical clocks to the physiological rhythms of the human body.

If chaotic oscillations are the biological basis for the ability of living things to generate variation, attractors are the biological precursors of internal order-inducing goal states characteristic of all life. Oscillations and attractors are complementary: Variety is meaningless without a preferential standard for selection and choice, while the latter cannot take place in the absence of novelty and change. Internally generated variation provides flexibility in the face of chaotic environments; homeodynamic stability maintains the structural integrity of a living system.

3.   While internal variation and homeodynamic stability are two important natural prerequisites of life, their presence does not yet permit evolution. Evolution is a knowledge-gaining activity which actively furthers the self-preservation of an organism. It requires, therefore, a feedback relationship which allows the evaluation of external change and internally generated responses in light of attractors such as metabolic needs, instincts, or cognitive goals, and generates "knowledge" on that basis.

Such feedback is the biological origin of "learning". Knowledge coordinates internal oscillations with environmental perturbations: The perception of an environmental change (information) leads to a change in frequency (selection) of internally generated variations in such a way that the structural integrity of the system is maintained or a new stable basin of attraction is established (adaptation). Knowledge or learning is a predictive state which causes the repetition, that is, the selection, of a variation as the appropriate workable, but not necessarily accurate or optimal, response when the same environmental change is encountered again (Barham 1990, pp. 204, 226). Variations which are "preferred" in light of the system's goals will be repeated as long as they do not interfere with self-preservation. Alternatively, the rate of oscillations will be increased (creativity, innovation) until a new level of adaptation between the system and its environment is established, or the system ceases its variations and dies. What turns out to be life-supporting or life-threatening in a particular situation is, therefore, always a composite result of external constraints and the choices which an organism makes.

The biological beginnings of knowledge and thus of life, and of evolution as a self-organizing, internally directed process, must be sought in the discriminatory bonding behavior of chemoreceptors such as enzymes or proteins that display these abilities in a rudimentary form (Boehmer and Kisielow 1991; Barham 1990, p. 207). The capacity of such oscillators to use internal preferred states or solutions as the basis for acquiring discriminating knowledge about their environment is of the same order of importance for the beginning of active life as that of DNA for the beginning of genetic variation and inheritance. The ability to learn and to know separates nonliving oscillating systems from living ones; it transforms attractors into central referents or goals that give "meaning" to environmental changes, and discriminates between variations on the basis of their past success and the resulting prediction that they will be suitable in the future (Barham 1990, p. 216). The ability to generate blind variations, to maintain structural integrity around goal states, and to learn must all be present before evolution can begin.

4. Learning is a choice-making activity. Redundancy is the natural corollary of all selection and choice. If evolution is to advance, life must and will tolerate, without detriment to the organism, a substantial margin for nonlethal error. Living and surviving are very different things (Barham 1990, p. 197). The rate of variation (genetic mutation, trial and error behavior, exploratory movement, visual scanning, neural excitations, or new ideas) that provides the raw material for selection *must* exceed what is required for the maintenance or increase of fitness. Organisms must at all times do more than what is needed for their survival; they must first be able to be right or wrong, and make successful or mistaken choices independent of their consequences for reproductive success if the conditions for eventual selection *with* such consequences are to be created.

5. Given their role in evolution, each of these components—variation, attractors, and learning—can be expected to be subjected to selective pressures which improve the ability of organisms to extract favorable returns from their environments.

Variation evolves in the direction of greater frequency and diversity, from the growing variability of gene pools and the evolution of sexual reproduction to the gradual increase of behavioral and cognitive, in proportion to genetic, variability. This process culminates in the creative, exploratory thought trials so typical of human cultural invention.

Attractors evolve along a gradient from relatively fixed, preprogrammed metabolic needs toward increasingly flexible, vicarious internal selectors (Campbell 1974, p. 146) which "stand in" for such requirements. The limited ability of enzymes or receptor molecules to assume several structural states or bonds which allow them to coordinate their response to environmental changes with their functional goals in nondeterministic ways (Barham 1990, p. 208) eventually evolves into central nervous systems and increasingly complex hard-wired goal states such as instincts. Attractors reach their most advanced form in the largely voluntary ability to imagine desired or future goals. This allows the probing of an environment from many different angles and maximizes the chances of finding system-compatible or system-supportive features.

Improvements in learning and knowledge-gathering lead to increasingly efficient methods of opportunistically exploring and evaluating environments. Campbell (1970) has outlined such an evolutionary sequence: from the probing by protozoa for noxious or favorable stimuli in their environments by means of simple trial-and-error locomotion, to the gradual evolution of vicarious exploratory tools such as vision, hearing, communication, language, and memory. These allow visual images, recollections, and semantic information to substitute for direct contacts with environments and drastically reduce the cost of scanning them for utility.

It is essential to see, however, that these evolutionary gains do not alter the fact that environments remain tendentially chaotic, and that *blind* variation remains the optimal response to such inherently unpredictable environments. *Internal selection is Darwinian, not Lamarckian.* Self-organization evolves toward a greater diversity and plasticity of variations and attractors, rather than fine-tuning them to particular environmental features.

CONCLUSIONS

Human culture is not Lamarckian. But it can also not be understood through a gene-based model of evolution. Genetic variation and inheritance are only half of the process of evolution. The other half consists of the use made of the phenotypic potential provided by the genome in the complex day-to-day interaction between organism and environment. Organisms have to solve the problem of living before they pass these solutions on to the gene pool of future generations. Evolution is an active, choice-making process that leaves a genetic trace. Ecological and genetic adaptation combined yield a more general Darwinian theory of evolution based on the "blind" production of variety—genetic, behavioral, and cultural—and its selective retention in response to environmental uncertainty.

In this evolutionary model, human actors are neither mere pawns of external causal laws, functional prerequisites or biological imperatives, nor are they in supreme rational control of their material and social environment. Instead, like all life forms, they are opportunists: They respond with creative variety to a chaotic and unpredictable environment in order to derive from it as much utility for their own ends as possible. Those variants and resources which they *deem* beneficial (as opposed to their actual and often very different consequences) are used and eventually retained through social learning in the long-term behavior patterns that constitute culture. But this selective retention remains Darwinian. It draws on *blind* sources; random thought trials leading to individual creativity and innovation (Campbell 1974), the accumulated knowledge of past generations (Pacey 1990), or the many complementary windfall advantages in everyday environments (Baldus 1977). None of these appear *because* they are useful to an individual's plans. For the most part, they are the pre-done work of others, based on goals and purposes entirely unrelated to those of the present user, a fact that is overlooked only because we tend to treat the inventor as hero, conceal the role of antecedent work, and simplify the connection between technological and socioeconomic change (Basalla 1988, p. 57).

The biological changes that separated humans from their primate ancestors were improvements in the *efficiency* of this trial and error opportunism, particularly in storing vicarious images of environments through memory, transmitting them through language, and invoking internal goals and purposes at will and largely independent of biological constraints. These gains were the last significant biological change to affect the human species. Most subsequent cultural change in human societies resulted not from its effect on fitness or reproductive success, but from purely technical advances in the efficiency of the trial-and-error exploitation of social and natural environments. These were primarily improvements in information storage and transmission in denser communication networks brought about by population growth and closer residential patterns, and by inventions such as writing, printing, and modern mass communications. They made the ideas and artifacts of others—and the opportunities they offered—more accessible and speeded up their cumulative effect.

At the same time, the human ability to make selective decisions remains far from perfect. The cognitive and technical tools at the disposal of human beings are often notoriously prone to error. Cultural evolution itself makes the social and natural environments that surround human beings less predictable; complexity breeds perplexity. Culture is the work of human tinkerers who pursue their individual or collective objectives by muddling through and making do inventively with opportunities that happen to come their way. As a result, culture often strays far from the linear or optimizing course charted for it by so many developmental sociological models, not infrequently with lethal consequences for its protagonists.

An internal selection theory of evolution is able to analyze these processes, and deal with the four problems which caused so much grief for the neo-Darwinist study of human cultural evolution. The first two, the search for cultural equivalents of genes and fitness, were generated entirely by the gene-oriented bias of neo-Darwinist theory. From an internal selection point of view, meaning and interrelatedness of cultural concepts and artifacts are to be expected, and their imprecision and changing boundaries are no surprise. It is much easier to identify the subjective, perceived goals of human actors, and to compare them with their intended and unintended results, than to be compelled to prove their effect on reproductive success. Sociologists, historians, and anthropologists have had no difficulty charting the evolution, interrelatedness, and dissemination of ideas and institutions, from the stirrup to the rise of feudal rule, from the protestant ethic to capitalism, from anomie to suicide, from the family to the state. These reconstructions are not always accurate, but the problems encountered are not conceptual but technical, namely, the lack of sufficient historical evidence.

Perhaps the most important advantage of an internal selection view of evolution is its completely different perspective of redundancy. For theories in the Newtonian tradition redundancy was an irritant, to be kept at bay in the form of constants or as yet "unexplained variance."

For internal selection theory, error and the resulting redundancy are not only a normal by-product of evolution; they are crucial prerequisites for learning from mistakes, and basic sources of novelty and change. Change is driven by the non-average (Allen 1992, p. 121). What is an error in one goal context forms the pool of uncommitted variation from which innovations are drawn for another. Because their emergence is unrelated to their eventual use, there is no way of telling which of the redundant variants will enter the draw for what purpose, when, and with what consequences.

Finally, internal selection points to the autocatalytic, self-organizing features of natural selection as an important source of evolutionary design. Evolution does not mean the diversification of life into pre-existing niches. Environments are "interpreted" by organisms in accordance with their own performance characteristics; such interpretations can be fixed through positive feedback and can direct the subsequent selection of other compatible components of the organism-environment relationship. Implicit in this view is the emergence, at some point in the evolutionary process, of a self-organizing, generative role for the mind, and with it the elimination of the mind-nature dualism which has been such a powerful obstacle to the extension of the Darwinian revolution to the understanding of human culture.

REFERENCES

Alexander, R.D. 1979. *Darwinism and Human Affairs.* Seattle: University of Washington Press.
———. 1987. *The Biology of Moral Systems.* New York: Aldine de Gruyter.
Allen, P.M. 1992. "Modelling Evolution and Creativity in Complex Systems." *World Futures* 34: 105-123.
Baker, P.L. 1993. "Chaos, Order, and Sociological Theory." *Sociological Inquiry* 63: 123-149.
Baldus, B. 1977. "Social Control in Capitalist Societies: An Examination of the 'Problem of Order' in Liberal Democracies." *Canadian Journal of Sociology* 2(3): 247-262.
———. 1990. "Positivism's Twilight?" *Canadian Journal of Sociology* 15(2): 149-163.
Baldwin, J.M. 1902. *Development and Evolution.* New York: Macmillan.
Barash, D. 1979. *The Whisperings Within.* Harmondsworth: Penguin.
———. 1982. *Sociobiology and Behavior.* New York: Elsevier.
Barham, J. 1990. "A Poincaréan Approach to Evolutionary Epistemology." *Journal of Social and Biological Structures* 13(3): 193-258.

Barkow, J.H. 1989. *Darwin, Sex, and Status.* Toronto: University of Toronto Press.
Barkow, J.H., L. Cosmides, and J. Tooby, eds. 1992. *The Adapted Mind. Evolutionary Psychology and the Generation of Culture.* New York: Oxford University Press.
Barnard, C.J. 1983. *Animal Behavior and Evolution: Ecology and Behavior.* New York: John Wiley.
Basalla, G. 1988. *The Evolution of Technology.* Cambridge: Cambridge University Press.
Boehmer, H. and P. Kisielow. 1991. "How the Immune System Learns about Self." *Scientific American* (October): 74-81.
Bowler, P.J. 1983. *The Eclipse of Darwinism.* Baltimore: Johns Hopkins University Press.
Boyd, R. and P.J. Richerson. 1985. *Culture and the Evolutionary Process.* Chicago: Chicago University Press.
Bryant, J.M. 1992. "Positivism Redivivus? A Critique of Recent Uncritical Proposals for Reforming Sociological Theory." *Canadian Journal of Sociology* 17(1): 29-53.
Buss, A.H. 1988. *Personality: Evolutionary Heritage and Human Distinctiveness.* Hillsdale, NJ: Lawrence Erlbaum Associates.
Campbell, D.T. 1970. "Natural Selection as an Epistemological Model." Pp. 51-85 in *A Handbook of Methods in Cultural Anthropology*, edited by R. Naroll and R. Cohen. Garden City, NY: Natural History Press.
_____. 1974. "Unjustified Variation and Selective Retention in Scientific Discovery." Pp. 139-161 in *Studies in the Philosophy of Biology*, edited by F.J. Ayala and T. Dobzhansky. Berkeley: University of California Press.
Cavalli-Sforza, L.L. and M.W. Feldman. 1981. *Cultural Transmission and Evolution: A Quantitative Approach.* Princeton, NJ: Princeton University Press.
Cheney, D.L. and R.M. Seyfarth. 1990. *How Monkeys See the World.* Chicago: University of Chicago Press.
Crippen, T.M. and R. Machalek. 1989. "The Evolutionary Foundations of Religious Life." *International Review of Sociology* 3: 61-84.
Cronin, H. 1991. *The Ant and the Peacock.* Cambridge: Cambridge University Press.
Darwin, C. 1887. *The Life and Letters of Charles Darwin.* London: J. Murray.
_____. (1872) 1958. *The Origin of Species*, 6th ed. New York: New American Library.
_____. (1872) 1965. *On the Expression of Emotions in Man and Animals.* Chicago: University of Chicago Press.
_____. (1871) 1981. *The Descent of Man.* Princeton, NJ: Princeton University Press.
Dawkins, R. 1976. *The Selfish Gene.* Oxford: Oxford University Press.
_____. 1982. *The Extended Phenotype: The Gene as the Unit of Selection.* Oxford: W.H. Freeman.
_____. 1986. *The Blind Watchmaker.* Burnt Mill: Longman.
Dawkins, M.S. 1993. *Through Our Eyes Only? A Search for Animal Consciousness.* Oxford: W.H. Freeman.
Dennett, D. 1995. *Darwin's Dangerous Idea.* New York: Simon and Schuster.
Dunnell, R.C. 1988. "The Concept of Progress in Cultural Evolution." Pp. 169-194 in *Evolutionary Progress*, edited by M.H. Nitecki. Chicago: University of Chicago Press.

Eiseley, L. 1961. *Darwin's Century*. Garden City, NY: Doubleday.

Freese, L. 1994. "Evolutionary Tangles for Sociocultural Systems." Pp. 139-171 in *Advances in Human Ecology*, Vol 3. Greenwich, CT: JAI Press.

Goldberger, A.L., D.R. Rigney, and B. West. 1990. "Chaos and Fractals in Human Physiology." *Scientific American* 262(2): 42-49.

Gould, J.L. and C.G. Gould. 1994. *The Animal Mind*. New York: Scientific American Library (W.H. Freeman).

Gould, S.J. 1990. "Shoemaker and Morning Star." *Natural History* 12: 14-20.

Granovetter, M. 1979. "The Idea of 'Advancement' in Theories of Social Evolution and Development." *American Journal of Sociology* 85: 489-515.

Griffin, D.R. 1984. *Animal Thinking*. Cambridge: Harvard University Press.

————. 1992. *Animal Minds*. Chicago: University of Chicago Press.

Gutzwiller, M.C. 1992. "Quantum Chaos." *Scientific American* 266(1): 78-84.

Hallpike, C.R. 1986. *The Principles of Social Evolution*. Oxford: Clarendon.

James, W. 1890. *Principles of Psychology*, 2 Vols. London: Macmillan.

————. 1898. *The Will to Believe, and Other Essays in Popular Philosophy*. New York: Longmans.

Kantorovitch, A. 1993. *Scientific Discovery. Logic and Tinkering*. Albany: State University of New York Press.

Khalil, E. 1993. "Neo-classical Economics and Neo-Darwinism: Clearing the Way for Historical Thinking." Pp. 22-72 in *Economics as Worldly Philosophy: Essays in Political and Historical Economics in Honour of R.L. Heilbroner*, edited by R. Blackwell, J. Chatha, and E.J. Nell. New York: St. Martin's Press.

Koshland, D.E. 1980. *Bacterial Chemotaxis as a Model Behavioral System*. New York: Raven.

Lopreato, J. 1984. *Human Nature and Biocultural Evolution*. Boston: Allen and Unwin.

Lumsden, C.J. and E.O. Wilson. 1983. *Promethean Fire*. Cambridge: Harvard University Press.

Manis, J.G. and B.N. Meltzer. 1994. "Chance in Human Affairs." *Sociological Theory* 12(1): 45-56.

Mann, M. 1986. *The Sources of Social Power*, Vol. 1. Cambridge: Cambridge University Press.

Mayr, E. 1976. *Evolution and the Diversity of Life*. Cambridge: Belknap.

McCloskey, D.N. 1991. "History, Differential Equations, and the Problem of Narration." *History and Theory* 30: 21-36.

McFarland, D. 1985. *Animal Behavior: Psychology, Ethology, and Evolution*. Menlo Park, CA: Benjamin Cummings.

Nielsen, F. 1994. "Sociobiology and Sociology." *Annual Review of Sociology* 20: 267-303.

Pacey, A. 1990. *Technology in World Civilization*. Cambridge: MIT Press.

Penrose, R. 1990. *The Emperor's New Mind*. London: Vintage Books.

Petroski, H. 1992. *The Evolution of Useful Things*. New York: Knopf.

Reisch, G.A. 1991. "Chaos, History, and Narrative." *History and Theory* 30: 1-20.

Reynolds, V. and R.E. Tanner. 1993. *The Social Ecology of Religion*. New York: Oxford University Press.

Richards, R.J. 1987. *Darwin and the Emergence of Evolutionary Theories of Mind and Behaviour*. Chicago: University of Chicago Press.

Ruse, M. 1979. *The Darwinian Revolution.* Chicago: University of Chicago Press.
_____. 1986. *Taking Darwin Seriously.* Oxford: Blackwell.
_____. 1988. *Philosophy of Biology Today.* Albany: State University of New York Press.
Savage-Rumbaugh, S. and R. Lewin. 1994. *Kanzi: The Ape at the Brink of the Human Mind.* New York: John Wiley.
Searle, J. 1992. *The Rediscovery of the Mind.* Cambridge, MA: MIT Press.
Simonton, D.K. 1988. *Scientific Genius—A Psychology of Science.* Cambridge: Cambridge University Press.
Simpson, G.G. 1953. "The Baldwin Effect." *Evolution* 7(2): 110-117.
Skarda, A. and W.J. Freeman. 1987. "How Brains Make Chaos in Order to Make Sense of the World." *Behavioral and Brain Sciences* 10(2): 161-195.
Smith, C.U.M. 1978. "Charles Darwin, the Origin of Consciousness, and Panpsychism." *Journal of the History of Biology* 11(2): 245-267.
Tooby, J. and L. Cosmides. 1989. "Evolutionary Psychology and the Generation of Culture." *Ethology and Sociobiology* 10: 29-49.
Visser, M. 1991. *The Rituals of Dinner: the Origins, Evolution, Eccentricities, and Meaning of Table Manners.* Toronto: Harper Collins.
de Waal, F. 1989. *Peacemaking Among Primates.* Cambridge: Harvard University Press.
Waddington, C.H. 1953. "The 'Baldwin Effect,' 'Genetic Assimilation' and 'Homeostasis'." *Evolution* 7: 386-387.
Wesson, R. 1991. *Beyond Natural Selection.* Cambridge: MIT Press.
Yates, F.E. 1991. "A Banquet at Barham's Table." *Journal of Social and Biological Structures* 14(2): 209-214.

ECOLOGICAL THEORY
AND THE EVOLUTION OF
COMPLEX HUMAN COMMUNITIES

William S. Abruzzi

ABSTRACT

Explaining social evolution has long been a central concern of anthropology. However, the discipline has yet to develop a systematic and testable model of social evolution that can effectively account for the differential development of complex human communities in diverse ethnographic contexts. This paper offers a model of community development based on the relationship between productivity, stability, and diversity in ecological systems to account for the variable evolution of complex human communities. The utility of the model is illustrated through its application to nineteenth-century Mormon settlements in the Little Colorado River Basin.

Advances in Human Ecology, Volume 5, pages 111-156.
Copyright © 1996 by JAI Press Inc.
All rights of reproduction in any form reserved.
ISBN: 0-7623-0029-9

INTRODUCTION

Anthropologists have long been concerned with explaining social evolution (cf. Maine 1861; Tylor 1871; Morgan 1877; Spencer 1876; Frazer 1890; White 1959; Sahlins and Service 1960; Fried 1967; Flannery 1972; Adams 1975; Kottak 1982). However, despite more than a century of evolutionary thinking, anthropology as a discipline has yet to achieve a systematic and testable model of social evolution that effectively explains the evolution of complex human communities. Comparing the relative success and maturity of biological versus social evolutionary theory, Robert Nisbet (1969, pp. 227-228) noted that

> The differences between contemporary biological evolutionary theory and the biological theory of Darwin are immense. The difference between contemporary social evolutionary theory and the theory of Herbert Spencer do not seem very large or very significant.

Nisbet's observation still applies, and the situation he describes has largely been given two general explanations. The more common claim is that human communities are inherently distinct from and more complex than nonhuman communities and are, therefore, not as amenable to strict scientific explanation. This argument is a variant of the more general Human Exemptionist Paradigm (HEP), which contends that human behavior is inherently different from that of all other species and demands a qualitatively different form of explanation (see Hardesty 1977; Catton and Dunlap 1980). A central problem with the HEP is that the analytical distinction between human and nonhuman behavior is proposed a priori, rather than as the result of a failure in applying comparable analytical methods to the study of human and nonhuman communities. It ultimately rests on what Leslie White (1949) called our "anthropocentric illusion" of the uniqueness of the human species. However, scientific research has increasingly undermined the empirical basis of anthropocentrism, and those individuals who claim that human behavior and the evolution of human communities must be analyzed differently from that of all other species are adopting a position that runs counter to the scientific mainstream (see Cartmill 1994).

A second line of argument used to explain the historical shortcoming of social evolutionary theories is that they constitute at best poor analogies borrowed from the biological sciences (Vayda and McCay

1975; Bennett 1976; Lees and Bates 1984; Smith 1984; Young and Broussard 1986). Eisely (1958), Harris (1968), Stocking (1968), Nisbet (1969) and others have long since exposed the fallacy of the thesis that social evolutionary theory emerged as a stepchild of Darwinian evolution. They have, in fact, demonstrated quite the opposite: that (1) evolution is a concept with deep roots in Western thought, and (2) that evolution eventually emerged as the prevailing paradigm of the biological sciences only after it had thoroughly permeated most other fields of inquiry, including the social sciences. As Harris (1968, p. 122) points out, "Darwin's principles were an application of social science concepts to biology." Both Darwin and Alfred Wallace were strategically influenced by the writings of Thomas Malthus (an economist), and it was Herbert Spencer (a sociologist) who coined the term, "survival of the fittest," which eventually became incorporated into the title of Darwin's chapter on natural selection. Indeed, Harris (1968, p. 129) suggests that the term, "Biological Spencerism ... (represents) ... an appropriate label for that period of the history of biological theory in which Darwin's ideas gained their ascendancy."

The explanatory limitations of social evolutionary theory do not, therefore, stem from the inappropriate application of a biological metaphor, although the superficial metaphorical use of biological concepts has all too frequently occurred. Rather, the deficiency results from the continuing failure of social evolutionary theory to specify the significant characteristics of evolving societies within an operational and theoretically coherent model of community development that can be applied to a variety of local empirical situations. The failure to achieve this form of explanation ultimately derives from the application of "Aristotelian" methods of explanation that have long since been abandoned in the physical and biological sciences (cf. Lewin 1935; Wilson 1969). Like outdated Aristotelian explanations in physics and biology, anthropological attempts to explain the evolution of complex human communities have generally lacked the fundamental scientific concern for applying a synthetic general theory to make testable predictions about specific empirical developments within a local spatiotemporal context. For the most part, social evolutionary theory in anthropology has largely consisted of empirical generalizations regarding the sequence of qualitatively defined developmental stages abstracted from the ethnographic record (cf. Tylor 1871; Morgan 1877; White 1959; Sahlins and Service 1960; Service 1971; Flannery 1972; Faris 1975; Rose 1981; Kottak 1982). However, empirical generalizations do not constitute explanation in science (see Hempel 1965; Nagel 1979). Rather, they result only in "imperfect laws" (see Brodbeck 1962; Wilson 1969) of social evolution, that is, laws whose efficacy is based on statistical correlations regarding the frequency of historical occurrences rather than on their ability to provide a detailed consideration of a specific empirical event. This approach is clearly illustrated by Carneiro's (1962, 1967, 1968) use of Guttman scaling to determine the "main sequence of cultural evolution," as well as by White's (1959) "Law of Cultural Evolution," Kaplan's (1960) "Law of Cultural Dominance," Service's (1960) "Law of Evolutionary Potential" and many subsequent attempts to propose laws of social evolution (cf. Flannery 1972; Faris 1975; Rose 1981; Kottak 1982). However, the concern should be to develop "perfect laws" that focus on the full concreteness of a specific situation. When this is the case, historical frequency no longer determines the validity of a law. Lawfulness exists not in the empirical association between historically connected phenomena, but rather in the theoretical relationship between variables. The historical occurrences themselves are not lawful; rather, they are explained through the application of laws.

Anthropological explanations of social evolution have also been seriously handicapped by their widespread use of synchronic or cross-sectional data. This is a direct result of the typological orientation of social evolutionary theory and its traditional reliance on such questionable analytical procedures as the "ethnographic present" and the "comparative method." It is inappropriate to infer diachronic processes from the observation of synchronic data (see Barth 1967; Graves, Graves, and Kobrin 1969; Plog 1974). Evolution is, by definition, a diachronic process and must be explained through the observation of time-structured information.

Anthropological theories of social evolution have also been severely limited by their reliance on cultures and societies as basic analytical units (cf. White 1959; Sahlins and Service 1960; Rappaport 1968; Bennett 1969, 1976; Flannery 1972; Leone 1979; Kottak 1982). Neither societies nor cultures constitute viable analytical units for investigating social evolution. To begin with, societies and cultures are nonoperational concepts; they, therefore, cannot be quantitatively linked to variations in specific environmental or material conditions. The selective forces that generate community development operate upon individual populations adapting to specific local environments and to the particular material conditions imposed upon them by encompassing regional systems (Vayda and Rappaport 1968; Ricklefs 1987). Although studies exist in which anthropologists have focused on the developmental implications of local populations adapting to specific material environments, too often in such studies the environment has been viewed qualitatively (as a "thing") rather than as a complex and dynamic multivariate system (Athens 1977; cf. Steward 1955, Sahlins 1958; Netting 1968; Rappaport 1968; Bennett 1969; Meggers 1971; Leone 1979; Kottak 1982). Consequently, from such studies general models have not emerged that (1) systematically interrelate quantifiable environmental and social variables within a predictive and testable theoretical framework; and (2) can be readily exported to a variety of distinct ethnographic situations. Such models can only be achieved when studies of social evolution concentrate on specific local populations adapting to precise measurable conditions in their material environments.

In this paper, I suggest that general ecological theory provides a useful model of community development which, because it lacks the limitations inherent in most traditional anthropological theories of social evolution, can be applied to explain the evolution of complex human communities. The proposed model is an adaptation of the general model developed by plant and animal ecologists to explain the evolution of complex multispecies communities. Before I discuss the proposed model, it will be useful if I first address some of the general issues surrounding the application of ecological concepts in human ecology.

ECOLOGY AND COMMUNITY DEVELOPMENT

Considerable controversy surrounds the application of ecological concepts in anthropological human ecology. Although numerous anthropologists have utilized ecological concepts and principles to explain human social behavior (cf. Barth 1956; Rappaport 1968; Gall and Saxe 1977; Leone 1979; Winterhalder and Smith 1981; Abruzzi 1982, 1987, 1993), others have rejected the strict application of ecological concepts and principles to human populations as naive and inappropriate uses of biological concepts (cf. Young 1974; Richerson 1977; Vayda and McCay 1975; Bennett 1976; Lees and Bates 1984; Smith 1984; Young and Broussard 1986). Disagreement over the application of ecological concepts and principles to human populations has even divided anthropologists who adopt an explicit ecological orientation (see Moran 1984). Those ecological anthropologists who view themselves as *human ecologists* generally see ecology as providing a testable framework for analyzing both human and nonhuman social behavior within a single unified theoretical perspective. By contrast, those ecological anthropologists who view themselves as *cultural ecologists* are more likely to reject the strict application of ecological concepts and principles to human communities on the ground that culture acts as a mediating force which renders human adaptation analytically distinct from that of all other species. For cultural ecologists, ecology serves as an orientation for the study of human-environmental relations rather than as a set of operational principles that can be used to explain specific human social behaviors.

Ecological concepts have, indeed, been misused in anthropology. However, their misuse has occurred not because such concepts are inherently inapplicable to human communities, but rather because they have largely been applied incorrectly. For the most part, ecological concepts have been extended to human communities wholly disconnected from the encompassing theoretical systems from which they derive both their meaning and their utility. This is nowhere more clearly illustrated than in the historical use of such concepts as *niche* and *ecosystem* in the social sciences. These two concepts have generally not been viewed in dynamic and multidimentional terms, but rather have been applied mostly as metaphors within a largely functionalist view of human-environmental relations (cf. Barth 1956; Rappaport 1968; Leone 1979; see Vayda and McCay 1975; Smith 1984; Catton 1993, 1994). In addition, the term ecology has mostly been used in the restricted *substantive* sense in social analysis to refer simply to the relationship that exists between a human population and its natural environment. It has not primarily been applied *formally* as a body of general theory leading to testable predictions regarding the organization and evolution of specific local human communities. The purpose of this paper is to supersede a metaphorical and environmentalist approach to human ecology by demonstrating that general ecology provides a meaningful and productive theoretical framework for explaining the evolution of complex human communities.

My application of ecological theory to human communities rests on several interrelated assumptions (see Abruzzi 1982, pp. 13-14; 1993, pp. 12-14): (1) that human communities are ecological communities through which energy flows and by which population-resource relationships are regulated[1] (see Margalef 1968; E. Odum 1971; H. Odum 1971; Little and Morren 1976); (2) that any system containing living organisms constitutes an ecological system (see Margalef 1968; H. Odum 1971); (3) that both human and nonhuman communities contain a high degree of functional diversity which is ultimately dependent on continuous inputs of energy from external sources (H. Odum 1971); (4) that both human and nonhuman communities contain organizational units which vary in size and composition as a result of spatiotemporal changes in the abundance and distribution of resources (see Wilson 1968; Kummer 1971; Abruzzi 1979, 1982); and (5) that those processes which underlie the division of labor (i.e., resource partitioning) are central to the evolution of both types of communities (cf. Harris 1964; Blau 1967; Levins 1968).

Furthermore, while the properties of any particular ecological community are determined by its specific biological composition, the laws or principles which determine community evolution are inherent in the energetic (not biological) relationships which exist within and between systems subject to natural selection. Consequently, the principles which determine the organization and evolution of ecological communities apply to *all* ecological communities regardless of their specific biological composition, including terrestrial and acquatic communities, single and multispecies communities, and human and nonhuman communities. An industrial city is, therefore, just as much an ecological system as is a tropical rain forest, a coral reef, or a temperate grassland community. Regulated by energy flows that determine population distribution and functional specialization, the settlement pattern and community organization that evolve in industrial-urban communities are distinct from those found in human communities based on irrigated agriculture, nomadic pastoralism, or hunting and gathering.

It is also scientifically preferable to approach human social systems as a subset of more general ecological systems, subject to the same theoretical principles, than to continue to regard human communities as analytically distinct from all other social systems. From the perspective of theory development, it matters less whether human and nonhuman communities are substantively distinct than whether general ecological concepts and principles account for comparable empirical developments in both types of systems. Just as Newton's development of the inverse square law eliminated the arbitrary Aristotelian distinction between celestial and terrestrial motion (see Greider 1973, pp. 71-77) and the advent of Darwinian evolution removed the equally artificial distinction between human and nonhuman species in explaining biological evolution, so also does a single explanation for the organization and evolution of human and nonhuman communities provide a more parsimonious and powerful explanation for the evolution of complex ecological systems than the perpetuation of two distinct explanations—one for human communities, and one for the remainder of the organic world.

However, if the application of general ecological concepts and principles to human populations is to prove useful, it must go beyond the simple relabeling of social phenomena with ecological terms or the mere use of ecological metaphors. It must be based on a recognition that similar *processes* operate in physically distinct and unrelated systems (see Ashby 1956; von Bertalanffy 1968; Day and Grove 1975; Rapport and Turner 1977; Alexander and Borgia 1978; Abruzzi 1982). Furthermore, the central goal must be to determine whether the specific concepts and principles used to explain the evolution of complex nonhuman communities can be applied to account for specific empirical developments associated with the evolution of human communities as well. Such an approach is *systemic* not reductionist. However, to achieve this goal, ecological concepts and principles must be applied within a predictive and testable theoretical framework. It is only when the processual models of general ecology are applied formally and explicitly to human communities that testable predictions can be generated and that the applicability of these models can be objectively evaluated. Consequently, in order to explain (and not merely describe or heuristically illustrate) patterns of community development, ecological theory must account for specific empirical developments as a consequence of predictions derived from general theoretical considerations, recognizing that all general theoretical concepts and principles must be modified and operationalized to fit a specific empirical problem or context.

In the next section I outline the general features of the ecological model in question. Having completed this, I will then conclude with a brief discussion of the ways in which I have used this model to account for specific historical developments associated with Mormon colonization of the Little Colorado River Basin.

THE EVOLUTION OF COMPLEX
ECOLOGICAL COMMUNITIES

An ecological community is defined as a set of interacting populations that exists within a prescribed territory. The evolution of complex ecological communities is the organizational process whereby a growing population adapts to changing conditions of resource availability created in part by its own growth (see Brookhaven National Laboratory 1969; Whittaker 1975; Cody and Diamond 1975). Based on the principles of energy maximization that apply to all living systems subject to natural selection, the ecological theory of community development provides a set of general principles from which all community organizational characteristics can potentially be explained. The specific model employed here concerns the relationship between population growth, community productivity, and functional community diversity, and systematically connects changes in these three community parameters with variations in resource availability (see Figure 1).

The concept of *niche* is central to explaining the evolution of complex ecological communities. The niche encompasses several dimensions of a population's existence that affect its contribution to the total flow of resources through a community (see Levins 1968; Vandermeer 1972), including: (1) its habitat (spatial location), (2) its functional role within the community (including both consumptive and nonconsumptive behaviors), and (3) its distribution along environmental gradients. From an energetics perspective, the niche is a function performed within an ecological community that facilitates the flow of resources among that community's constituent organisms. A population's niche may be divided into its *fundamental niche* and its *realized niche* (see Vandermeer 1972, pp. 110-111). The former comprises the exploitative position occupied by a population within a given territory in the absence of competition, whereas the latter consists of that portion of the fundamental niche actually filled by a population in a particular community containing a specific set of competing populations.

Competition is the principal agent determining niche breadth in ecological communities. Where two populations are complete competitors and one is dominant over the entire niche, the less efficient competitor will be completely eliminated from the arena of competition (see Gause 1934; Hardin 1960). Where two populations vary in their relative competitiveness in different portions of the niche, on the other hand, complete exclusion may not occur. Each population may evolve

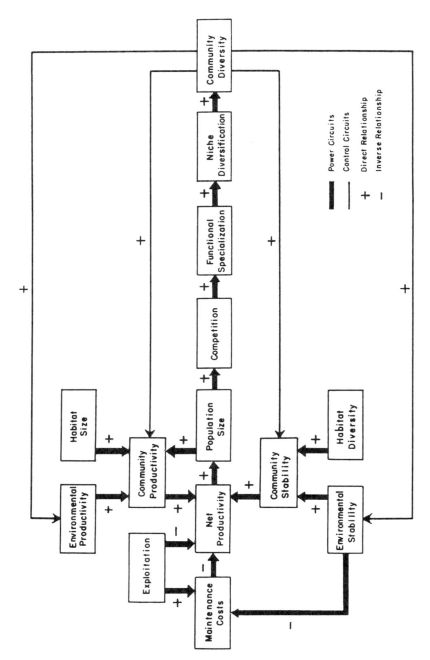

Figure 1. The Ecological Model

instead to occupy a more restricted realized niche when the two populations occur within the same community (cf. Crombie 1947; Brown and Wilson 1956). As additional populations enter the competition, species specialization and niche differentiation increase, and each population eventually comes to occupy an increasingly reduced portion of its fundamental niche (Vandermeer 1972). Such resource partitioning among competing populations is central to the evolution of complex ecological communities. An explanation of community evolution must, therefore, focus on the various conditions that either facilitate or inhibit the developmental process.

Subsidies and Drains in Community Evolution

Resource partitioning and niche differentiation in ecological communities result directly from the competitive advantage accompanying resource specialization. Species populations which exploit a limited set of resources tend to be more efficient in obtaining those resources than populations which must exploit a broad range of resources for their survival (see Levins 1968, pp. 10-38; Vandermeer 1972, pp. 114-116). Consequently, as additional species enter a community, niches are "squeezed," and the range of resources exploited by individual populations within the community is reduced. The evolution of complex multispecies communities is, thus, both an incessant and an opportunistic process through which natural selection generates the greatest functional diversity possible within the limits imposed by resource availability.

Ecological communities depend upon the existence of abundant supplies of potential energy in their environments in order to survive, and their complexity increases to the extent that this potential energy can be converted into community productivity, biomass (population) and, ultimately, functional diversity. However, only a small fraction of available potential energy can be utilized by a community. The critical factor determining how much potential energy is converted to productivity is the total cost of maintaining organisms within a community. A cumulative reduction occurs in net productivity as energy flows from one trophic level to the next, due to the cost of maintaining organisms at each trophic level. This results in the trophic pyramid that characterizes all ecological communities.

Maintenance costs are, thus, the principal factor limiting the amount of energy transferred between trophic levels. They, therefore, directly affect both the amount of biomass and the level of species diversity tha can be supported within a multispecies community. A *decrease* i maintenance costs increases (1) net productivity at each trophic leve (2) biomass and niche differentiation; and (3) the viability of mor marginal niches. Consequently, it increases community diversity. A *increase* in maintenance costs, on the other hand, decreases the tota amount of energy flowing through the system. It, therefore, decrease supportable biomass, niche differentiation, and the viability of margina niches, while increasing the likelihood of local extinction and, therefore decreasing community diversity.

Any energy source that reduces maintenance costs within community increases the total amount of energy that can be converte to community productivity. Such a source serves as an *energy subsid* to the development of that community. Conversely, any energy sourc that increases community maintenance costs diverts energy away fror a community and imposes a stress or *energy drain* upon tha community. Energy drains reduce the total amount of energy converte to community productivity and, thus, available to support nich diversification (see E. Odum 1971, pp. 43-53 for a discussion of energ subsidies and drains in ecological systems). Because the evolution c complex ecological communities ultimately depends on the availabilit of resources, all phenomena affecting productivity and energy flow i ecological systems may be viewed within an *energy subsidy/energy drai* perspective. However, research has shown that certain environmenta conditions influence the evolution of complex ecological communitie more significantly than others. These include: *environmente productivity*, *environmental stability*, *habitat diversity*, *habitat size*, an *exploitation*.

Environmental Productivity

An increase in environmental productivity raises the probability tha a sufficient abundance of resources will exist within an ecologica community to support a particular species population or adaptiv specialization. Conversely, because a reduction in environmenta productivity decreases the adaptive or competitive advantage c specialization, it reduces community diversity. For this reasor organisms and populations in less productive environments mus exploit a wider range of resources than those in more productive ones The generally high species diversity found in tropical communities an in communities at lower versus higher elevations derive in large part from the typically higher productivity associated with their encompassing ecosystems (cf. Rosenzweig 1968, 1976; Terborgh 1971).

The direct association between environmental productivity and community diversity may be compromised, however, by the existence of specific limiting factors, such as the rate of energy conversion associated with organic pollution (Odum and Pinkerton 1955) or the deficiency of oxygen that characterizes many highly productive eutrophic lakes (see Sanders 1968, p. 267). In addition, purely random perturbations in resource availability may negatively affect species diversity in highly productive communities by increasing the probability that more marginal niches will be eliminated (MacArthur 1972, p. 95; Rosenzweig 1976, pp. 129-130).

Environmental Stability

Notwithstanding the significance of environmental productivity, environmental stability is perhaps the single most important factor influencing community diversity. Unstable environmental conditions can frequently offset the positive effect that high environmental productivity has on community development (cf. Sanders, 1965, 1968; Pielou 1975; Slobodkin and Sanders 1969; MacArthur 1972; May 1973; Leigh 1975). Where environmental instability prevails to the extent that substantial resources must be expended just to maintain or replace existing organisms within a community, little energy remains to support increasing specialization and niche diversification. While resource abundance and reliability permit an increase in biomass, species specialization, and niche differentiation, fluctuations in resource availability reduce the viability of marginal adaptations and reverse the effect that competition has on niche differentiation. Species specialization, thus, serves as a reliable indicator of community stability (Leigh 1975, p. 56). The same conditions determine the diversity of social organization in single-species communities. Rapport and Turner (1977, p. 330) report, for example, that among social insects "a fluctuating environment can make a particular caste uneconomical and favor generalists over specialists even if the functions the caste performs remain as important as before" (see Wilson 1968, 1971).

Environmental fluctuations may vary in amplitude, frequency, and predictability. The extreme temperature oscillations that occur in arctic ecosystems produce high maintenance costs and result in the low species

diversity characteristic of polar communities. Similarly, an increase i
the frequency of fluctuations reduces the time available for the evolutio
of complex energy-flow networks. In his comparative examination c
species diversity in benthic communities, Sanders (1968) determine
that increased diversity was consistently associated with reduce
seasonality. The most significant aspect of environmental variatio
however, is its predictability. Slobodkin and Sanders maintain tha
even where an environment oscillates, if it

> fluctuates in a regular and predictable way and with reasonably short periodicity,
> it is possible for organisms to relate to it by adaptations of very much the same
> sort as those that occur in a constant environment.... Species diversity seems
> lower in situations with irregular fluctuations of environmental properties than
> in structures characterized by regular and predictable fluctuations of the same
> magnitude (1969, pp. 85-86).

Because a high degree of specialization can only evolve within a high
predictable environment, the most diverse multispecies communitie
occur in highly predictable environments with low variability. Thus, th
greater diversity of tropical ecosystems derives more from environmer
tal stability than from abundant productivity. Indeed, Sanders (196
determined that species diversity was not only greater in more stab
benthic communities within the same climatic zone, but also that it w
greater in communities situated in stable temperate ecosystems than i
communities located in unstable tropical ones. Notably, the mo
complex community observed by Sanders was the shallow wat
community in the Bay of Bengal, which is a productive *and* stab
tropical benthic ecosystem.

Habitat Diversity

Habitat diversity is also an important factor influencing communi
evolution. Environments differ in the degree to which resources a
evenly distributed and may vary from having resources that a
uniformly spaced (i.e., fine-grained) to those that are patchi
distributed (i.e., coarse-grained) (see Levins 1968, pp. 10-3
Vandermeer 1972, pp. 114-116). Habitat diversity (i.e., a coarse-graine
distribution of resources) increases the likelihood of niche different
ation and enhanced species diversity due to the greater efficiency c
specialized resource exploitation in coarse-grained environment

Several studies have linked species diversity to environmental heterogeneity, including Pianka's (1966) study of lizard species diversity in North America and MacArthur and MacArthur's (1961) analysis of the diversity of bird species in tropical habitats.

Habitat Size

To the extent that environmental diversity is related to the size of the physical area encompassed by an ecological community, an increase in habitat size is also related to community diversity. The adaptive advantages of resource specialization in coarse-grained environments only exist to the extent that the resources provided by differentiated habitats are sufficient to support particular populations and adaptive specializations. Such conditions are simply more likely to exist in larger habitats.

Exploitation

Exploitation occurs whenever one ecological system serves as an energy subsidy for the maintenance or growth of another system. Exploitation imposes an energy drain on the system being exploited, because the productivity upon which community evolution depends is removed from the exploited community. Human populations pose a significant source of exploitation in multispecies communities. However, wherever one draws boundaries in nature, an unequal exchange of energy flows across that boundary, which contributes to the organizational difference between the respective systems (see Margalef 1968). A predator exploits its prey, and a herbivore exploits green plants. In both situations, the energy exchanged between organisms is unequal, and one system benefits at the other's expense. The same exploitation occurs between ecological communities, and the evolution of complex communities can only proceed after their exploitation has been discontinued.

Regulation in Ecological Communities

Because stability increases the efficiency of resource exploitation, natural selection favors those mechanisms that reduce resource fluctuations within a community. A selective advantage thus exists for enhancing the control of regulating mechanisms which render ecological communities increasingly independent of immediate, short-term fluctuations in their environment. Regulating mechanisms in ecological communities may be divided into *power circuits* and *control circuits* (H. Odum 1971, p. 94). Power circuits are the major channels of energy flow which primarily determine a community's organizational structure as, for example, where oak trees process most of a forest community's energy budget. Control circuits yield only minor energy flows, but are capable of affecting the flow of energy in the substantially larger power circuits. This occurs, for example, when the gathering and planting activities of squirrels influence the size of an oak population.

Control circuits are particularly important for the work-gate functions they perform (see H. Odum 1971, pp. 38, 44-45), wherein one energy flow is enhanced by the multiplicative effect of a supplementary energy input. Agricultural practices such as weeding, plowing, and irrigation perform work-gate functions in that they augment the flow of energy that becomes stored in consumable plant material. Increasing stability in ecological systems derives largely from a greater redundancy of work-gate functions and from the potential that this redundancy offers for circumventing variable energy flows within power circuits.

The greater redundancy that exists within complex multispecies communities derives largely from the role performed by competing species populations as "compensating devices" (Whittaker and Woodwell 1972, p. 151). Interspecific competition serves to maintain community diversity, because the conditions that eliminate one species from a forest community may result in another species replacing it in the forest canopy, with the larger community retaining existing levels of productivity, biomass, and functional diversity. Interspecific competition also reduces the probability that closely related populations will exceed their resource supply, because the size of a particular species population is unlikely to increase significantly in the presence of numerous competing populations (cf. Russo 1964; Hornocker 1970).

Predation also affects species diversity. By influencing prey population size, predation regulates interspecific competition among prey species. Where predators that are capable of preventing individual prey species from monopolizing resources have either been missing or removed experimentally, the affected communities have become less diverse (see Paine 1966). Thus, while species diversity at lower trophic levels contributes to species diversity in the higher trophic categories (through the flow of energy in power circuits), species diversity at the higher trophic levels can have a regulative impact on the size and diversity of species populations in the lower trophic categories as well (through energy flow in control circuits).

However, diversity by itself does not enhance community stability. Indeed, precisely the opposite may occur. The key to maintaining community stability under variable environmental conditions lies in the degree to which *redundancy* exists in the flow of energy-resources through a community. Only where redundancy exists can one population's response to environmental variation be neutralized by the reaction of competing populations, as well as by populations occupying distinct trophic levels. Where insufficient redundancy exists, the negative consequences of environmental fluctuations are likely to ramify throughout the community and reduce community stability, even among communities containing high diversity (see May 1973; Holling 1973; Leigh 1975).

Because the evolution of endogenous rhythms requires a stable and predictable environment with the consistent selective pressures that such conditions provide, the control exerted by predators on the size and diversity of prey populations is ultimately dependent on the reliability of the same prey species as resources throughout the year. Thus, the enhanced community stability that results from the regulative effect of community diversity derives ultimately from the productivity and stability of the encompassing ecosystem, because the complex regulative functions performed within ecological communities require continuous and substantial resource flows for their maintenance. Thus, while capable of mitigating the numerous minor disturbances caused by environmental instability, complex ecological communities are especially vulnerable to major disruptions in the flow of energy. These disruptions severely undermine the selective advantage of specialization and, thus, jeopardize the niche differentiation upon which the limited regulative capacity of such communities is based.

In summation, complex multispecies communities evolve as a result of the increasing specialization and niche differentiation generated by interspecific competition. Through the increasing intensification of resource exploitation, such communities evolve the most diverse species composition possible within the energetic limits of a particular environment. Because the selective advantage of specialization depends on a resource supply that is capable of supporting increasingly marginal adaptations, community diversity is determined by community productivity. At the same time, because diversity is ultimately a function of net productivity, maintenance costs impose a major constraint on community evolution. As a result, diverse ecological communities evolve in those ecosystems that support specialized adaptations and that reduce community maintenance costs. These conditions are best met in environments that are both productive and stable, that contain numerous, large and diverse habitats, and that are free from external exploitation. With increasing diversity, ecological communities evolve a greater internal regulation of energy flow and, thus, a limited independence from minor environmental fluctuations, provided resource flows within the community possess sufficient redundancy to compensate for local fluctuations in resource availability. However, the greater energy requirements needed to maintain complex ecological communities render these systems particularly vulnerable to major disruptions in their resource supply.

THE EVOLUTION OF HUMAN COMMUNITIES

As with multispecies communities, more complex human communities evolve largely due to the opportunity costs (selective advantage) associated with greater specialization under conditions of increasing community productivity and population size. The evolution of human communities is likewise determined by resource availability, especially by those environmental conditions that present either subsidies to or drains upon the developmental process. Finally, more complex human communities also evolve endogenous rhythms that facilitate their increasing independence from local environmental variation.

Resource Partitioning in Human Communities

As previously indicated, the niche is a function that facilitates the flow of resources through an ecological community. While species diversity has most commonly been used to define the number of distinct functions within multispecies communities, *occupational categories* and *functional units* have been employed to determine the complexity of resource partitioning in human communities. Because species, occupational categories, and functional units all effectively delineate the configuration of productive functions performed within their respective communities, each represents an empirical variant of an Operational Taxonomic Unit (OTU) within niche theory (see Vandermeer 1972). Each varies in its specific dimensions as a result of the same competitive process and in relation to resource availability (cf. Clark et al. 1964).[2]

Occupational categories may be defined in terms of the type of activity performed together with the range of resources processed, and may include food production, food distribution, building construction, mining, teaching, and so forth. Each of these functions may, in turn, be divided into increasingly restricted operations. Indeed, the increasing specialization of productive functions is a central component of the evolution of complex human communities. A *functional unit* may be defined as any distinct organizational entity that participates in external exchange relations and thus facilitates the flow of resources within a community. In most recent Western communities, the functional unit has normally been a business establishment (cf. Thomas 1960; Gibson and Reeves 1970; Smith 1976). However, functional units as diverse as a communal village organization, a church, an irrigation company, and a post office operated among the early Little Colorado Mormon settlements considered here.

In order to understand the evolution of complex human communities, it is important to distinguish between "growth" and "development" (see Carneiro 1967). Growth refers simply to an increase in the number of taxonomic units within a community, whereas development denotes an increase in the kinds of units present. Thus, while an increase in the number of farms in an agricultural community constitutes growth, the emergence of new functional units and of occupations other than farming represents development. The evolution of complex human communities includes both growth and development.

Occupations and functional units (like species in multispecies communities) may be arranged into a trophic hierarchy of producers and consumers. This hierarchy is implied in the economic classification of primary, secondary, and tertiary industries, as well as in the distinction made between basic and nonbasic employment. Within any community, some resource flows may be classified as *autotrophic* in that they generate the primary resources upon which the remainder of the community depends. While farming provided the basic community productivity among Little Colorado Mormon settlements, both secondary and tertiary industries may serve as the source of basic employment within a particular community, because local communities may originate or evolve to exploit a variety of resources. The Little Colorado Mormon towns, for example, have at various times during the past century had economies that were based on farming, ranching, lumber production, tourism and/or industrial production (see Abruzzi 1985).

Heterotrophic functions, on the other hand, distribute the net productivity provided by autotrophic functions throughout the remainder of the community. They may also perform work-gate functions which regulate the productivity of primary producers. Trophic levels are, of course, abstractions, and actual functional units may operate on several trophic levels (see Ehrlich and Birch 1967). Just as phytoplankton in northern Sweden alternate seasonally between autotrophic and heterotrophic functions (Rodhe 1955), so also may a food producing unit (such as a farm) both produce and distribute the food that it grows.

Because the shifting of resources from one productive activity to another involves specific costs, individuals and functional units gain an adaptive advantage from specialization: Competition and maintenance costs are reduced. Thus, by increasing the efficiency of resource exploitation and therefore the amount of *net productivity* available for exchange, increased specialization enhances the aggregate flow of resources through a community (see Samuelson 1958, p. 653). The effect that opportunity costs have on functional specialization apply to substantively noneconomic activities and functional units as well. These must also compete for the limited resources available within a community.

Other things being equal, ecological theory suggests that an increase in community productivity leads to an increase in population size within human communities, because more resources exist upon which additional individuals can be supported. Population growth, in turn, fosters an increase in the number and diversity of occupations and functional units that derive their existence from individual allocations of resources in productive activities. Being opportunistic systems (at least with regard to resource exploitation, functional specialization and community diversification), human communities, like other ecological systems, evolve to the organizational limits imposed by available resources. Similarly, mutual causality operates in the evolution of human communities as well. While occupational and functional unit specialization and differentiation contribute to increasing community diversity, existing productive and distributive arrangements select for the viability of specific additional activities within a community, as well as for whole new avenues of community development. Moreover, because specific occupations and functional units require distinct population and resource thresholds in order to exist within a community, various functions are added to human communities at different rates during the course of community development (cf. Thomas 1960; Carneiro 1962, 1968; Haggett 1966; Gibson and Reeves 1970).

An important distinction exists between human and nonhuman ecological communities with regard to the relationship between productivity and population size. Although many human communities may, like other ecological communities, evolve in response to initial increases in productivity, more often it would appear the evolution of complex human communities occurs in response to the adaptive pressures resulting from population growth within a fixed habitat (cf. Boserup 1965; Wilkinson 1973; Cohen 1977; Simon 1977; Abruzzi 1979, 1980; Sanders and Nichols 1988). An increase in population size stimulates increases in community productivity and functional diversity by increasing both the supply of and the demand for increased resource availability within a community. However, permanent increases in population size can only occur in conjunction with concurrent increases in community productivity. Consequently, population increase within a circumscribed habitat requires an additional intensification of resource exploitation in order to raise the aggregate productivity of a given territory. Such pressure for the intensification of resource exploitation places a premium on the specialization of community functions due to the more effective resource exploitation and the enhanced net productivity that such specialization provides. Finally, population growth within a fixed habitat demands an increase in per capita energy flows (cf. Boserup 1965, pp. 41-55; Harris 1980, p. 184, *passim*), which increases aggregate community productivity even further.

Continued population growth within a fixed habitat also selects for the evolution of regulative functions that assure sufficient and stable levels of productivity. Consequently, while population growth generates a greater number and diversity of functional units through its effect on productivity, it also stimulates the diversification of functional activities and organizations that serve as control circuits directing increasing resources into channels expanding community productivity due to the increased demand for resources that such growth creates.

Thus, whether specific human communities evolve in response to initial increases in productivity or population growth, the basis of community evolution remains the same. The selective advantage of specialization and niche differentiation in either case derives from the opportunity costs associated with resource partitioning in the presence of an expanded flow of resources. In both situations, the degree to which functional specialization proceeds depends upon the ability of individuals to subsist on increasingly narrow and more marginal resource flows. Community diversity, thus, remains a function of the aggregate flow of resources in a community. However, the enhanced positive feedback that exists between productivity, population growth, and community diversity in human communities does not undermine the applicability of the ecological model to these communities. The population increase that accompanies the evolution of complex human communities is founded on a simultaneous increase in community productivity made possible through the evolution of control circuits circumventing environmental limitations. As predicted by ecological theory, increasing community diversity within human communities evolves as a function of concurrent increases in community productivity and population size within specific limits imposed by local and regional environmental conditions.

Subsidies and Drains in Human Communities

As with all ecological systems, the maintenance and survival of human communities depends ultimately on the availability of resources. Thus, the various external conditions that effect human resource exploitation may also be viewed within an *energy subsidy/energy drain* perspective. Similarly, phenomena that provide energy subsidies under one set of circumstances may impose energy drains under different circumstances, even within the same community. In addition, the rate at which conditions impose themselves relative to the adaptive capacity of local populations is as important a feature of the subsidy/drain dichotomy in human communities as it is in nonhuman ones. While rainfall and a permanent stream generally provide relatively cheap energy inputs (subsidies) into agricultural productivity, excess rainfall and flooding rivers can impose a severe drain that either reduces agricultural production or increases the cost of achieving the same level of productivity. Furthermore, just as different amounts of precipitation and stream flow can have distinct effects on the maintenance costs associated with irrigation and agricultural productivity within a farming community, so also can distinct conditions of population growth have different effects on community development. While those conditions which promote stable population growth actually stimulate the evolution of more complex human communities (Boserup 1965; Coontz

1961; Culbertson 1971; Wilkinson 1973; Simon 1977), those which yield sudden increases in the size of a population (most notably through rapid immigration) may impose a severe drain on community development by increasing the stress on local resources leading to a greater proportion of productive resources having to be channeled into strictly maintenance functions (cf. Abruzzi 1993, p. 31).[3]

Productivity and Stability in Human Communities

While large discrepancies between productivity and biomass are unlikely to occur among nonhuman communities, substantial differences in per capita productivity and standard of living occur quite frequently among human communities. This difference complicates the relationship between community productivity, population size, and functional diversity in human communities (see Culbertson 1971, pp. 35-101; Wilkinson 1973). *Per capita productivity* must, therefore, be included as a necessary supplement to aggregate productivity in human communities in order to more accurately represent the surplus resources (net productivity) available to maintain community diversity in these communities. The evolution of complex human communities, with their enhanced differentiation, interdependence, organization, and managerial functions, demands an expensive allocation of community resources and thus depends fundamentally on increases in per capita productivity (see Harris 1959, 1980, pp. 183-206; H. Odum 1971; Simon 1977). As a result, those factors that reduce per capita productivity inhibit community evolution. For the Little Colorado Mormon settlements, those specific conditions that limited agricultural productivity or that increased the size of the investment required to sustain existing levels of productivity reduced available net productivity and thus inhibited community evolution.

The same factors that limit specialization in those human communities located in unproductive environments operate in communities situated in unstable ones as well. Moreover, differences in the amplitude, frequency, and predictability of environmental fluctuations have distinct effects on the development of human communities also. Differences in both the amount of resources required to rebuild dams and the frequency of dam reconstructions yielded a disproportionate drain upon the various Little Colorado Mormon towns. One of the critical factors influencing local community development was the degree to which environmental variation could be anticipated and controlled. Where the principal limiting factor was a variable and unpredictable growing season, as was the case at higher elevations, little anticipation or control could be exerted. Where, on the other hand, agricultural productivity was limited by seasonal variation in surface water availability, a measure of anticipation and control could be gained through the construction of storage reservoirs, provided suitable dam sites were available.

Habitat Size and Diversity

Habitat size is directly related to community evolution. The amount of economically exploitable farm land, for example, directly affects the potential aggregate productivity, per capita productivity, population size, and functional diversity of an individual agricultural settlement. Habitat diversity also facilitates the evolution of complex human communities, because different portions of habitat may exhibit distinct conditions of resource availability. Habitat diversity is also likely to be at least partially a function of habitat size.

Exploitation

As previously indicated, exploitation occurs whenever resources that may be used to increase population, productivity, or stability of one community are expropriated from that community in order to enhance the development of another system. Exploitation is a common feature of the exchange that takes place between ecological systems of unequal complexity, and more complex communities generally exploit the less complex systems around them (Margalef 1968). Expanding frontiers between contiguous ecological communities result largely from the competitive advantage that more complex communities possess in relation to the less complex systems on their periphery. The expansion of the American frontier was no different (cf. Shannon 1945). As this frontier expanded into the Little Colorado River Basin, specific resources that could have contributed to the development of these indigenous communities were expropriated from local use. This loss of exploitable resources imposed a substantial drain on the indigenous Mormon population and seriously threatened the success of their colonization effort (see Abruzzi 1993, pp. 165-191, 1994).

Regulation Within Human Communities

The evolution of complex human communities has invariably been characterized by an increase in the number and specificity of regulative functions (i.e., control circuits). Two general kinds of control circuits may be distinguished in human communities: *indirect* (consumer) and *direct* (management) regulative functions. The former include those functions and functional units which, through their effect on the demand for specific resources, regulate the output of a community's producers. Consumer functions affect the opportunity costs associated with specific resource allocations among competing producers, and the proportion of consumer functions providing feedback into productivity increases with the evolution of more complex human communities.[4]

Of greater significance to the evolution of complex human communities has been the increased control exerted by direct regulative functions. More complex human communities possess a larger proportion of management functions to total community organization than do less complex systems, and direct regulative functions have evolved historically to control an increasing share of community resources. Although governmental functional units have performed the principal management functions in communities since the emergence of the state, critical management functions may be performed by functional units other than those under governmental administration. Among the early Mormon settlements in the Little Colorado River Basin, the local church organization and its affiliated institutions performed many of the management functions needed to facilitate community development (see Abruzzi 1989, 1993, pp. 143-163, 180-181).

The ecological model suggests that more complex human communities possess a greater capacity for responding to environmental disturbances than do less complex communities, and that the former systems are more likely to achieve the endogenous regulation of community parameters. Having achieved a greater independence from local habitat variability, more complex human communities possess a selective advantage in adapting to unstable environmental conditions. As with nonhuman ecological communities, however, it is the greater *redundancy* of resource flows that enables complex human communities to achieve their greater stability. Where a community depends disproportionately upon a single resource, any variation in the availability of that resource will ramify throughout the community. Increasing the number and diversity of distinct local environments that are integrated into a single system of resource redistribution, on the other hand, enhances the adaptive capacity of a complex human community because it increases the number of functionally independent resource flows available to compensate for local productive deficiencies (cf. Coe and Flannery 1964; Sanders and Price 1968). However, the regulative capacity of human communities must also be viewed hierarchically. Complex human communities can only offset deficiencies in local production to the extent that aggregate environmental conditions are productive and stable enough to maintain the specialized functions which underlie resource redistribution (see Abruzzi 1982, p. 18; 1987).

In summation, then, the extension of ecological theory to human communities suggests that these communities, like their nonhuman counterparts, evolve as a result of resource partitioning among potential competitors. Due to the non-Malthusian basis of human population ecology, however, human communities can substantially enhance the level of population, productivity, and functional diversity achieved within a particular community by intensifying resource exploitation well beyond that possible in nonhuman communities. However, the potential for positive feedback that exists between population, productivity, and functional diversity in human communities does not contradict the general ecological model; rather, human communities represent a special case operating in accordance with the general principles prescribed by that model. Continued increases in population size and community diversity depend fundamentally on increases in the abundance and reliability of community productivity. Moreover, the evolution of human communities is subject to the same environmental constraints that limit community productivity and stability and that affect the cost of maintaining community operations in nonhuman communities. Similarly, while more complex human and nonhuman communities both possess an adaptive advantage due to their greater capacity for limited self-regulation, endogenous rhythms in both types of systems depend on a redundancy of resource flows within them. Consequently, like their nonhuman counterparts, the organization of complex human communities is highly vulnerable to major disruptions in energy flow.

Applying the Model to Mormom Settlements

If the ecological model of community development outlined here is to be successfully applied to Mormon settlements in the Little Colorado

River Basin, developments accompanying the settlement process must conform to expectations derived from that model. Those settlements that were located in the most productive and stable environments and that experienced the lowest maintenance costs associated with agricultural production should have achieved the greatest aggregate productivity, per capita productivity, population size, and community stability. These same settlements should also have been the most functionally diverse. Conversely, the least functionally diverse settlements should have displayed the lowest aggregate productivity, per capita productivity, and population size. They should also have been located in the least productive and most unstable habitats, as well as those that imposed the highest maintenance costs associated with agricultural production. Finally, to the extent that the redistribution of resources among individual settlements enhanced the success of the colonization effort, it should have been based on the integration of resource flows from numerous independent habitats experiencing distinct schedules of environmental variation. Only then could resource redistribution possess the redundancy needed for effective environmental regulation.

MORMON COLONIZATION

Mormon colonization of the Little Colorado River Basin began in 1876 when some 500 Mormon pioneers established four agricultural settlements—Sunset, Brigham City, St. Joseph, and Obed—along the lower valley of the Little Colorado River (see Figure 2). These initial settlements served as bases for the founding of some two dozen additional colonies throughout the river basin, including Woodruff, St. Johns, and Eagar along the upper Little Colorado River, Snowflake and Taylor on Silver Creek, and Showlow and Alpine in the southern highlands. However, despite a considerable investment of manpower, a high degree of cooperation among local communities and continuous material support from Church headquarters in Salt Lake City, the Little Colorado colonies experienced considerable local variation in agricultural production. St. Joseph suffered complete crop failures during three of the seven years between 1876 and 1882. Sunset produced an abundant harvest in 1879, but had to be abandoned in 1883 following three years of poor harvests. Brigham City failed to produce even one successful harvest and was finally abandoned in 1881. In addition,

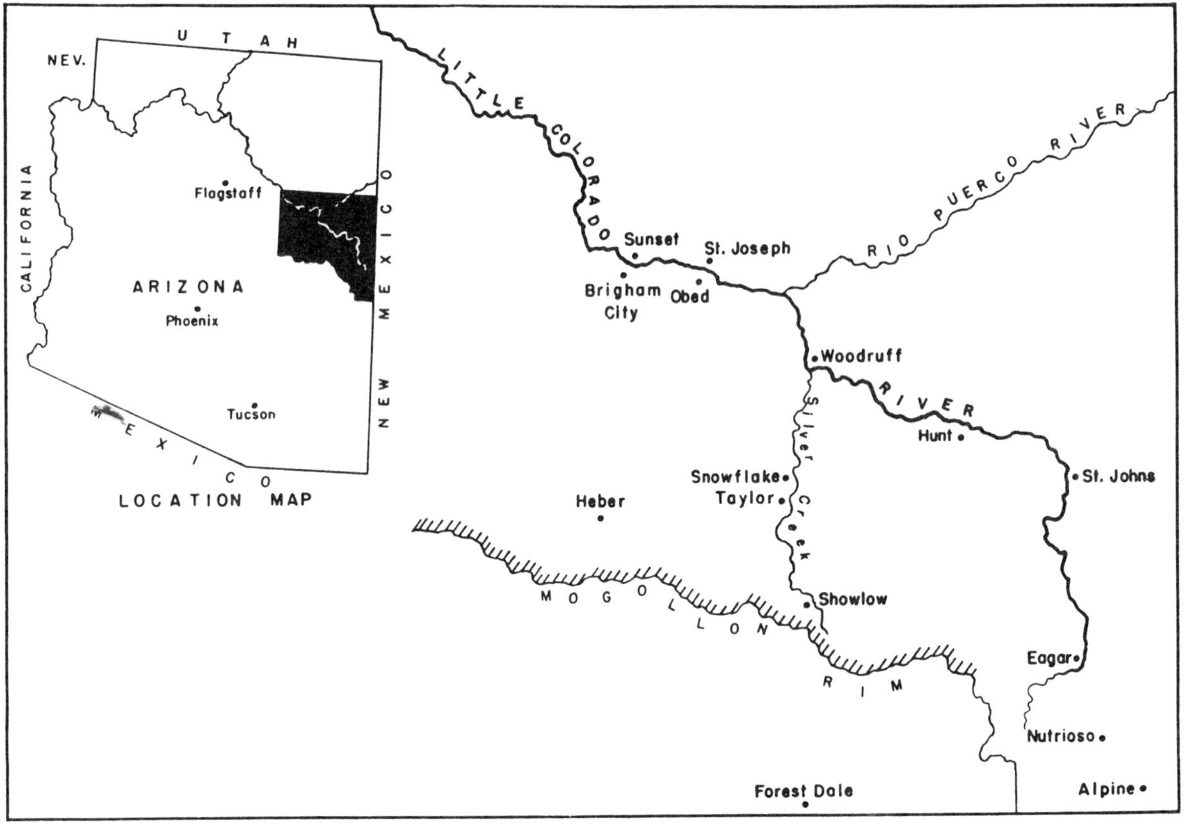

Figure 2. The Little Colorado River Basin

records indicate that either poor harvests or complete crop failures prevailed throughout the river basin during half the years between 1880 and 1900. In the end, while Snowflake, Taylor, Eagar, and St. Johns grew to several hundred inhabitants, produced relatively abundant and reliable harvests, and contained a diversity of occupations and businesses, Woodruff, St. Joseph, Showlow, and Alpine contained less than one hundred persons each and were substantially less productive and diverse. In fact, these latter towns barely survived.

The principal factor influencing community development among the Little Colorado Mormon settlements was the nature of the physical environment to which the farmers in these towns had to adapt. The Little Colorado River Basin encompasses some 5,000 square miles and increases in elevation from about 5,000 feet in the lower valley of the Little Colorado River southward to about 8,500 feet along the Mogollon Rim, a steep escarpment that defines the southern boundary over much of the region. In addition, several mountain peaks exceeding 10,000 feet exist in the eastern portion of the southern highlands. Climate throughout the region is arid to semi-arid, with annual precipitation ranging from 9 inches at lower elevations in the north to almost 25 inches in the southern highlands. As a result, northern desert vegetation predominates in the lower valley of the Little Colorado and is succeeded southward by grassland, juniper-piñon woodland, and montane forest communities. Because most of the basin receives less than 15 inches annual precipitation, the grassland and juniper-piñon woodland communities cover nearly 80 percent of the total surface area. In addition, bare soil accounts for between 55-65 percent of the total surface cover within the grassland community (Dames and Moore 1973, section 4, p. 201).

In contrast to precipitation, length of the growing season varies inversely with elevation and ranges from an average of 87 days near Alpine to 179 days at St. Joseph. Thus, both the length and the reliability of the growing season vary inversely with average annual precipitation, restricting dependable agriculture to river valleys at lower elevations. Early pioneers also had to contend regularly with early frosts, high temperatures, droughts, flooding, hailstorms, insects, and high winds. Finally, two devastating droughts ravaged the basin for nine years between 1892-1905, killing thousands of livestock and causing widespread crop failure. Such pervasive environmental variation frequently resulted in the same settlement losing crops to several causes during a single agricultural season (cf. Abruzzi 1993, pp. 23-25).

The most important environmental factor influencing community development in this arid river basin has been the availability of suitable water for irrigation (see Abruzzi 1985). The unreliability of precipitation made all early farming settlements in the region necessarily dependent on surface water for irrigation. However, because streams throughout the region flow primarily in direct response to precipitation and ambient temperature, surface water availability follows a distinct annual cycle. Runoff is generally moderate between January and March due to the melting of snowpacks at higher elevations and declines as these snowpacks disappear. Except for streams at higher elevations, most streambeds throughout the basin are dry from April to June when 45 percent of annual irrigation requirements must be applied (see Bureau of Reclamation 1947, p. 72). Stream flow increases dramatically following the onset of intense summer storms in July and subsides as these summer storms· pass. It then remains low until snow re-accumulates at higher elevations.

Although stream-flow variability is widespread, it is greatest in the lower valley of the Little Colorado River where the largest surface area is drained. Because no suitable reservoir sites exist at lower elevations, the lower valley settlements could only construct diversion dams. These settlements, therefore, remained completely vulnerable to the greatest stream-flow variability in the basin. Variation in stream flow also yielded a higher incidence of dam failures among the lower valley towns than anywhere else in the basin. St. Joseph and Woodruff suffered 13 and 10 dam failures, respectively, between 1876 and 1900, compared with only two at St. Johns, three at Snowflake and Taylor, one at Showlow, and none at Eagar and Alpine.

The direct costs imposed by dam failures and the subsequent flooding of fields included not only the time, materials, and manpower required to rebuild the dams themselves, but also those needed to repair ditches and replant fields. The indirect costs of dam failures included the labor that could not be invested in other productive activities, as well as the detrimental effect that repeated flooding had on soil fertility. The fact that only two of the six towns established in the lower valley survived strongly suggests that the cost of farming was highest in this portion of the basin.[5] No other section lost as many settlements. Furthermore, the history of dam failures at St. Joseph and Woodruff, the only two lower valley settlements to survive, demonstrates clearly that these towns would also have failed had it not been for the repeated subsidies of food, supplies, and labor they received from the other Mormon towns in the region, as well as from Church sources outside the basin (see Abruzzi 1989, 1993, pp. 123-131).

Local Differences in Community Development

For purposes of understanding local differences in community development, the Little Colorado River Basin may be conveniently divided into three subregions: (1) the lower valley of the Little Colorado River; (2) the southern highlands; and (3) the intermediate territories. The least developed of all the communities studied were those, such as Showlow and Alpine, that were located in the southern highlands. Although annual precipitation was highest in this subregion, the growing season there was both the shortest and the least reliable, considerably less than the 120 days needed for most crops. Furthermore, even though soils are deeper at higher elevations due to the greater density of vegetation in this subregion, they tend to be poorly drained, susceptible to flooding and, in many places, slightly acidic. In addition, mountain valleys tend to be small and, thus, not very conducive to the local expansion of agriculture. Communities in the southern highlands, therefore, achieved: (1) the smallest populations, (2) the lowest and most variable agricultural productivities and, consequently, (3) the least number and variety of occupations and businesses (see Table 1). They also contained the least developed Church organization (Abruzzi 1993, p. 43). By any measure of community development, the southern highlands settlements were the least developed Mormon towns in the region. Stated in ecological terms, low environmental productivity and stability resulted in a low and highly variable aggregate and net community productivity among southern highland settlements. As predicted by ecological theory, these settlements were the least functionally diverse Mormon towns in the basin.[6]

Settlements along the lower valley of the Little Colorado River, such as St. Joseph and Woodruff, enjoyed more than ample growing seasons. They therefore possessed the potential for supporting larger populations and achieving substantially greater productivity and functional diversity than settlements in the southern highlands. However, the lower valley settlements experienced high summer temperatures, frequent dust storms, and a recurring spring dry season that combined to reduce agricultural productivity and increase the frequency of crop failures. Lower valley settlements also had to contend with poor quality soils that are high in sodium and low in both phosphorus and organic matter.

Table 1. Population, Productivity, Stability, and Functional Diversity among Little Colorado Mormon Settlements, 1887-1905

Town	Total Tithing (1887-1900)		Per Capita Tithing (1887-1900)		Population Size (1807-1905)		Number of Occupations (1900)	Number of Businesses (1905)	Number of Business Categories (1905)
	X^a	V	X	V	X	V			
St. Johns	3561	.230	7.09	.179	506	.201	22	34	22
Snowflake	3025	.195	7.58	.203	404	.148	16	24	20
Eagar	1810	.180	5.15	.157	310	.231	8	20	14
Taylor	1463	.217	4.75	.169	308	.111	8	3	3
St. Joseph	1124	.435	8.49	.349	118	.269	5	3	3
Woodruff	915	.389	5.44	.358	153	.265	12	8	6
Alpine	449	.327	4.54	.419	105	.302	3	2	2
Showlow	431	.335	2.40	.323	182	.261	7	6	6

Note: [a] X = mean (in dollar values), V = coefficient of variation.
Source: Abruzzi (1987, p. 322).

In addition, due to their high clay composition, these soils possess low permeability and are highly susceptible to flooding when irrigated. The lower valley settlements also had to irrigate their relatively infertile soils with the poorest quality surface water in the region. Although the Little Colorado River originates as a clear mountain stream in the southern highlands, by the time it reaches the lower valley it has received considerable runoff throughout the grassland community, and its sediment load approaches 20 percent of stream flow (Bureau of Reclamation 1950, pp. 3, 10). Furthermore, both soil and water quality deteriorated steadily throughout the lower valley during the nineteenth century due to extensive overgrazing throughout the grassland community and to the prior appropriation of surface water upstream on both the Little Colorado River and Silver Creek (see Abruzzi 1994).

As already indicated, the lower valley settlements also suffered significantly more dam failures than any of the other Little Colorado Mormon towns, making farming in this subregion more difficult and more costly than anywhere else in the basin. Because the lower valley settlements could build only diversion dams, they also remained completely vulnerable to the intense variability displayed by the Little Colorado River at lower elevations. These environmental limitations combined to make the lower valley settlements moderately more productive, but only slightly larger than those in the southern highlands (see Table 1). With the highest incidence of dam failures occurring among some of the smallest populations, lower valley settlements also bore among the highest per capita maintenance costs in the region. Indeed, so great were the maintenance costs relative to productivity among lower valley settlements, that not only did these towns not contain substantially more occupations or businesses than those in the southern highlands, but only two of the six Mormon towns established in this subregion even survived.

In ecological terms, the lower valley settlements were situated in highly unstable habitats which possessed only moderate productivity, but which imposed especially high community maintenance costs. Moderate environmental productivity in the face of low environmental stability and high maintenance costs yielded only limited aggregate and net community productivity for these towns. As predicted by ecological theory, lower valley settlements contained among the smallest and most variable populations in the region and achieved a functional diversity that was not appreciably greater than that found among settlements in the southern highlands. Significantly, the negative effect that environmental instability had on community diversity among lower valley settlements relative to those in the southern highlands is comparable to the effect that Sanders (1968) indicates environmental variability had on the relative diversity of tropical versus temperate benthic communities. In both cases, the developmental benefits of greater productivity were negated by reduced stability.

The most successful local Mormon settlements were Snowflake, Taylor, St. Johns, and Eagar, all of which were located in river valleys at intermediate elevations. These towns all enjoyed adequate and reliable growing seasons (over 120 days per year) and were located near permanent streams whose relative abundance and reliablility were enhanced through the construction of storage reservoirs. The access of intermediate settlements to dependable water supplies and adequate growing seasons made them less vulnerable to the negative effects of climatic variability than towns located either along the lower valley of the Little Colorado River or throughout the southern highlands. Each of the intermediate towns was also located in relatively large valleys containing fertile and well-drained soils. They thus achieved the largest agricultural productivities, populations, and number and diversity of occupations and businesses of any towns in the region (see Table 1). Moreover, two of these towns—Snowflake and St. Johns—evolved the most complex Church organizations, including the two regional stake organizations that coordinated the religious and temporal affairs of all Mormon towns in the basin.[7]

From the perspective of general ecology, large valleys, good soils and abundant, superior quality surface water translated into high environmental productivity for intermediate settlements. At the same time, reliable growing seasons, together with stable surface water sources, provided high environmental stability with regard to critical agricultural resources. High environmental productivity and stability combined to produce the highest and least variable community productivities of any settlements in the region. Furthermore, because intermediate settlements did not suffer the frequency of dam failures experienced in the lower valley, and because they contained the largest populations with which to undertake dam reconstruction, they also sustained the lowest per capita maintenance costs in the region. They therefore generated the highest net productivities and were able to support the largest and most stable populations in the basin. As predicted by ecological theory, intermediate settlements evolved a greater functional community diversity than any other Mormon settlements in the region.

Table 2. Rank-Order of Mormon Settlements (1887-1905)

Settlement	Population, Productivity and Stability Rank-Order	Diversity Rank-Order
Intermediate Settlements		
Snowflake/Taylor[a]	1	1
St. Johns	2	2
Eagar	3	3
Lower Valley Settlements		
St. Joseph	4	6
Woodruff	5.5	4
Mountain Settlements		
Showlow	5.5	5
Alpine	7	7

$$r_s = .884, p < .01$$

Note: [a] Because Snowflake and Tyalor are located within three miles of each other, share a common irrigation system, and contain businesses that serve both towns, they are treated as a single community in the calculations performed (see Abruzzi 1993, pp. 194-195).
Source: Abruzzi (1987, p. 331).

Ecological theory does not only explain subregional differences in community development. It also provides an explanation for the specific variation in community development displayed by individual Mormon settlements in the region. A Rank-Order Correlation of .884 ($p < .01$) was achieved when individual Mormon settlements were compared for composite indices of population size, community productivity, and community stability, on the one hand, and functional community diversity on the other (see Table 2).

Resource Redistribution and Successful Mormon Colonization

Successful colonization of the Little Colorado River Basin was due in large part to the development of a system of resource redistribution that mitigated the negative consequences of local environmental variability (see Leone 1979; Abruzzi 1989, 1993, pp. 148-155). The region's pronounced spatial diversity provided early settlers with a unique opportunity to overcome local environmental limitations. Due largely to local differences in topography and precipitation, the basin contains numerous, widely separated local habitats that were often differentially affected by the same regional environmental influences and which, therefore, offered distinct potentials for agricultural productivity (see Abruzzi 1989). A clear adaptive advantage thus existed for these early settlements to integrate the productivities of their diverse habitats into a single multihabitat resource redistribution system. Resource redistribution among individual settlements would have enabled each town to effectively diversify its resource base and, thus, increase its ability to circumvent local environmental variability.

The Little Colorado Mormon settlements developed two distinct multihabitat resource redistribution systems during the nineteenth century. The first consisted of several productive enterprises, including a sawmill, a dairy, a tannery, and a grist mill, jointly operated by the initial settlements established in the lower valley of the Little Colorado River (see Abruzzi, 1993, pp. 143-147). These enterprises were generally located at higher elevations to the south and provided the lower valley settlements with important resources (most notably lumber, cheese, butter, meat, and certain vegetables) that could not be produced near the towns themselves. They thus supplemented the highly variable farming productivity achieved within the lower Little Colorado River Valley.

However, the conjoint enterprises were largely summer operations in the southern highlands which, due to their distance from the lower valley, required a more or less permanent resident population. These enterprises thus competed directly with farming in the lower valley for labor. As population size declined and as the number of settlements in the lower valley decreased under the strain of recurring dam failures, the conjoint enterprises could no longer be maintained and were eventually abandoned.

A second system of multihabitat resource redistribution emerged following the failure of the conjoint enterprises. This latter system operated through the redistribution of locally collected tithing resources. Tithing was mostly paid in kind to local church leaders and forwarded to regional church warehouses in Snowflake and St. Johns where it was stored and redistributed to those in need (see Leone 1979, pp. 43-85; Abruzzi 1993, pp. 148-155). Through tithing redistribution, individuals, and sometimes entire towns, were able to acquire needed resources produced elsewhere in the basin. Through the redistribution of tithing resources these early Mormon settlers used the region's spatial diversity to offset its local temporal variability. In the process, they transformed a potentially dormant surplus into a flow of resources that was ultimately responsible for the success of the colonization effort. St. Joseph and Woodruff would clearly never have survived their numerous dam failures had it not been for tithing redistribution. They would likely have become extinct, as had every other settlement in the lower valley.

The system of multihabitat exploitation based on the conjoint enterprises was not ecologically viable, because it was incompatible with local and regional environmental conditions. The small populations in the lower valley suffered intense drains on their limited resources due to the intense variability of surface water in the Little Colorado River. Flooded fields and repeated dam failures imposed a chronic labor shortage throughout the lower valley settlements and severely limited their ability to exploit distant habitats. This system thus failed as a mechanism of environmental regulation.

Tithing redistribution, on the other hand, succeeded as a mechanism of environmental regulation for the very reasons that the conjoint enterprises failed. It was able to circumvent local environmental variation in a way that the system of conjoint enterprises could not. Because it included every Little Colorado Mormon town and, therefore, integrated resource flows from every exploited habitat, the system of tithing redistribution was able to direct a substantial flow of resources at the specific times and places that resources were critically needed to counteract the destabilizing impact of environmental variation. In addition, tithing redistribution integrated the productivity and labor of over 2,000 persons in some two dozen separate settlements located within as many functionally independent habitats scattered throughout the entire river basin. The conjoint enterprises, on the other hand, integrated the material resources of only a few hundred persons inhabiting three or four neighboring settlements located in contiguous, highly unstable habitats, all of which expereinced the same schedule of variation—including the timing of dam failures. The effectiveness of tithing redistribution was also substantially enhanced by the integration of local settlements into a regional, centrally administered religious organization and by the affiliation of its primary institutions with parent organizations outside the region (see Abruzzi 1989, 1993, pp. 150-157). While the former increased the responsiveness and reliability of local tithing redistribution, the latter provided access to resources whose availability was completely independent of local and regional environmental conditions.

The differential success of Mormon attempts at multihabitat exploitation in the Little Colorado River Basin likewise conforms with expectations derived from general ecological theory. Ecological redundancy was clearly absent in the system of conjoint enterprises established by the early Mormon settlements in the lower valley of the Little Colorado River. Although these enterprises exploited resources away from the lower valley, the availability of the labor needed to operate them was directly linked to the material conditions affecting agriculture along the Little Colorado. As a result, the negative effect that environmental instability had upon farming in the lower valley ramified to the conjoint enterprises and caused their demise. The system of conjoint enterprises thus failed as a mechanism of environmental regulation despite its cooperative orientation, its communal organization, and its explicit ethnoecological foundation.

The system of tithing redistribution, on the other hand, integrated settlements throughout the entire river basin by uniting the total productivity and labor of some two dozen separate populations concentrated in the intensive and independent exploitation of a variety of distinct local habitats. Productive shortfalls at one location were generally compensated for by surplus productivity elsewhere in the region. Thus, separate resource flows originating in numerous independent habitats provided the specific redundancy needed to offset local habitat variability. Linking local tithing redistribution to encompassing Church institutions simply enhanced the redundancy already present in this system of resource redistribution. Tithing redistribution thus succeeded as a mechanism of environmental regulation despite the fact that it was based on individual profit and that its primary institutions were established for expressly nonecological purposes (see Abruzzi 1989).

CONCLUSION

I have argued here that the general model of community development used to explain the evolution of complex ecological communities provides a useful model for the evolution of complex human communities as well. I have proposed that the applicability of the general ecological model to human communities rests on the fact that human communities are ecological communities, and that the model in question applies to all ecological communities regardless of their specific biological composition. I have then applied the ecological model to explain specific historical developments associated with Mormon colonization of the Little Colorado River Basin. Specifically, I have used the model to account for local and subregional differences in community development, the role of resource redistribution in successful colonization, and the variable success of Mormon efforts to develop a viable resource redistribution system.

Ecological theory successfully explains each of these historical developments. It thus provides a more precise and parsimonious explanation of this settlement process than all previous accounts (compare, for example, Peterson 1973 and Leone 1979 with Abruzzi 1993). Moreover, it does so within an objectively verifiable explanatory framework. The relative success of the ecological model compared to earlier studies of Mormon colonization in the Little Colorado River Basin is due in large part to its application as a set of general principles from which specific local historical developments are systematically explained, rather than simply as a metaphor orienting the study of human-environmental relations in this region. The application of ecological theory to Mormon colonization of the Little Colorado River Basin suggests, therefore, that ecological theory should be applied *more* not less strictly in the study of human ecology. It is only through the explicit application of ecological theory to human populations that the validity of such applications can be objectively evaluated, and that human ecology can make a meaningful contribution to the development of ecological theory.

NOTES

1.   The term regulation refers here simply to the existence of processes through which the activity of one population influences the abundance and distribution of resources that affect the existence of other populations in a community. No equilibrium is implied.

2.   Resource distribution in both human and nonhuman communities actually results from the activities of individual organisms participating in a variety of independent exchange relations. Species and comparable functional categories in human communities comprise equivalent Operational Taxonomic Units from the perspective of niche theory in that both delineate the channeling of energy flows in their respective communities. The precise calculation of all individual productive activities would provide the optimum basis for examining functional diversity and resource partitioning in ecological communities. However, such data are unavailable for most communities. Consequently, more general categories must be used.

3.   By consuming resources which could otherwise be invested in productive activities, rapid population growth reduces the flow of net productivity available to support increasingly specialized adaptations. From this perspective, *overpopulation* may be defined as any excess of population over productivity that reduces per capita resource availability and, thus, threatens the survival of existing organisms in the community. Such overpopulation contributes to community simplification because more marginal niches become less viable as pressures mount to channel an increasing proportion of a community's resources into maintenance functions and to broaden the range of resources exploited by individuals and by specific functional units.

4.   Anthropologists have illustrated how indirect consumer functions such as the numaym and potlatch among the Kwakiutl of the American Northwest (cf. Piddocke 1965) and the "big man" and reciprocal feasting among Kaoka-speaking peoples of Guadalcanal (Hogbin 1964) enhanced local community productivity. In much the same way, a successful restaurant or restaurant chain may stimulate the production of specific food resources within a contemporary Western community.

5.   Obed was abondoned in 1877 for health reasons. Also, another town, known as "Old Taylor," was located about 6 miles downstream from St. Joseph. This town was founded and abandoned in 1878 following the failure of 5 dams.

6.   Significantly, Alpine and nearby Nutrioso, the two most highly situated settlements in the region, registered the highest proportion of nonheads of households declaring farming as their principal occupation on the 1900 census. The fact that many of these individuals were between 10-15 years of age suggests that intense demands were imposed upon farming at this altitude, resulting in the routine application of all available labor (see Abruzzi 1993, pp. 119-120).

7.   The Mormon Church is administratively divided into stakes and wards, which may be compared to dioceses and parishes, respectively, in the Roman Catholic Church. During the nineteenth century, each Little Colorado Mormon settlement comprised one ward. Wards along the lower valley of the Little Colorado River were initially organized into the Little Colorado Stake, with the remaining wards included in the Eastern Arizona Stake. In 1887, the Little Colorado wards were reorganized into the Snowflake Stake and the St. Johns Stake. These two stake organizations contained the western and eastern wards, respectively.

REFERENCES

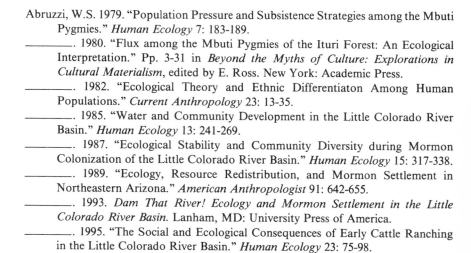

Abruzzi, W.S. 1979. "Population Pressure and Subsistence Strategies among the Mbuti Pygmies." *Human Ecology* 7: 183-189.
————. 1980. "Flux among the Mbuti Pygmies of the Ituri Forest: An Ecological Interpretation." Pp. 3-31 in *Beyond the Myths of Culture: Explorations in Cultural Materialism*, edited by E. Ross. New York: Academic Press.
————. 1982. "Ecological Theory and Ethnic Differentiaton Among Human Populations." *Current Anthropology* 23: 13-35.
————. 1985. "Water and Community Development in the Little Colorado River Basin." *Human Ecology* 13: 241-269.
————. 1987. "Ecological Stability and Community Diversity during Mormon Colonization of the Little Colorado River Basin." *Human Ecology* 15: 317-338.
————. 1989. "Ecology, Resource Redistribution, and Mormon Settlement in Northeastern Arizona." *American Anthropologist* 91: 642-655.
————. 1993. *Dam That River! Ecology and Mormon Settlement in the Little Colorado River Basin*. Lanham, MD: University Press of America.
————. 1995. "The Social and Ecological Consequences of Early Cattle Ranching in the Little Colorado River Basin." *Human Ecology* 23: 75-98.
Adams, R.N. 1975. *Energy and Structure: A Theory of Social Power*. Austin: University of Texas Press.

Alexander, R.D. and G. Borgia. 1978. "Group Selection, Altruism, and the Levels of Organization of Life." *Annual Review of Ecology and Systematics* 9: 449-474.

Ashby, W.R. 1956. *An Introduction to Cybernetics*. London: Chapman and Hall.

Athens, J.S. 1977. "Theory Building and the Study of Evolutionary Processes in Complex Societies." Pp. 353-384 in *For Theory Building in Archaeology*, edited by L.R. Binford. New York: Academic Press.

Barth, F. 1956. "Ecological Relationships of Ethnic Groups in Swat, North Pakistan." *American Anthropologist* 58: 1079-1089.

―――. 1967. "On the Study of Social Change." *American Anthropologist* 69: 661-669.

Bennett, J.W. 1969. *Northern Plainsmen: Adaptive Strategy and Agrarian Life*. Chicago: Aldine-Atherton.

―――. 1976. *The Ecological Transition: Cultural Anthropology and Human Adaptation*. New York: Pergamon.

Blau, P. 1967. *Exchange and Power in Social Life*. New York: Wiley.

Boserup, E. 1965. *The Conditions of Agricultural Growth: The Economics of Agrarian Change under Population Pressure*. Chicago: Aldine.

Brodbeck, M. 1962. "Explanation, Prediction, and 'Imperfect' Knowledge." Pp. 231-272 in *Scientific Explanation, Space and Time*, edited by H. Fiegl and G. Maxwell. Minneapolis: University of Minnesota Press.

Brookhaven National Laboratory. 1969. "Diversity and Stability in Ecological Systems." *Brookhaven Symposia in Biology*, No. 22. Springfield: U.S. Department of Commerce.

Brown, L.L. and E.O. Wilson. 1956. "Character Displacement." *Systematic Zoology* 5: 49-64.

Bureau of Reclamation. 1947. *Snowflake Project Arizona*. Project Planning Report 3-8b.2-0. Washington, DC: U.S. Department of the Interior.

―――. 1950. *Report on Joseph City Unit, Holbrook Project, Arizona*. Project Planning Report 3-8b.6-1. Washington, DC: U.S. Department of the Interior.

Carniero, R.L. 1962. "Scale Analysis as an Instrument for the Study of Cultural Evolution." *Southwestern Journal of Anthropology* 18: 149-169.

―――. 1967. "On the Relationship between Size of Population and Complexity of Social Organization." *Southwestern Journal of Anthropology* 23: 234-243.

―――. 1968. "Ascertaining, Testing and Interpreting Sequences of Cultural Development." *Southwestern Journal of Anthropology* 24: 354-374.

Cartmill, M. 1994. "Reinventing Anthropology, American Association of Physical Anthropologists Annual Luncheon Address, April 1, 1994." *Yearbook of Physical Anthropology* 37: 1-9.

Catton, W.R. 1993. "Carrying Capacity and the Death of a Culture: A Tale of Two Autopsies." *Sociological Inquiry* 63: 202-223.

―――. 1994. "Foundations of Human Ecology." *Sociological Perspectives* 37: 75-95.

Catton, W.R. and R.E. Dunlap. 1980. "A New Ecological Paradigm for Post-Exuberant Sociology." *American Behavioral Scientist* 24: 15-47.

Clark, P.J., P.T. Eckstrom, and L.D. Linden. 1964. "On the Number of Individuals Per Occupation in a Human Society." *Ecology* 45: 367-372.

Coe, M.D. and K.V. Flannery. 1964. "Microenvironments and Mesoamerica." *Science* 143: 650-654.

Cody, M.L. and J.M. Diamond, eds. 1975. *Ecology and Evolution of Communities* Cambridge, MA: Belknap Press.

Cohen, M.N. 1977. *The Food Crisis in Prehistory: Overpopulation and the Origins of Agriculture*. New Haven, CT: Yale University Press.

Coontz, S.H. 1961. *Population Theories and the Economic Interpretation*. London Routledge and Kegan Paul.

Crombie, A.C. 1947. "Interspecific Competition." *Journal of Animal Ecology* 16: 44-73.

Culbertson, J. 1971. *Economic Development: An Ecological Approach*. New York Alfred A. Knopf.

Dames & Moore, Inc. 1973. *Environmental Report, Cholla Power Project, Joseph City Arizona*. Phoenix: Arizona Public Service Company.

Day, R.H. and T. Grove, eds. 1975. *Adaptive Economic Models*. New York: Academic Press.

Eiseley, L.C. 1958. *Darwin's Century*. New York: Doubleday.

Ehrlich, P.R. and L.C. Birch. 1967. "The 'Balance of Nature' and 'Population Control'." *The American Naturalist* 101: 97-107.

Faris, J.C. 1975. "Social Evolution, Population, and Production." Pp. 235-271 in *Population, Ecology and Social Evolution*, edited by S. Polgar. The Hague Mouton.

Flannery, K.V. 1972. "The Cultural Evolution of Civilizations." *Annual Review of Ecology and Systematics* 1: 399-426.

Frazer, J.G. 1890. *The Golden Bough*. London: Macmillan.

Fried, M. 1967. *Evolution of Political Society: An Essay in Political Anthropology*. New York: Random House.

Gall, P.L. and A. Saxe. 1977. "The Ecological Evolution of Culture: The State as Predator in Prehistory." Pp. 255-268 in *Exchange Systems in Prehistory*, edited by T. Earle and J.E. Ericson. New York: Academic Press.

Gause, G.F. 1934. *The Struggle for Existence*. Baltimore: Williams and Wilkins.

Gibson, L.J. and R.W. Reeves. 1970. "Functional Bases of Small Towns: A Study of Arizona Settlements." *Arizona Review* 19: 19-26.

Graves, T.D., N.B. Graves, and M.J. Kobrin. 1969. "Historical Inferences from Guttman Scales: The Return of Age Area Magic?" *Current Anthropology* 10: 317-338.

Greider, K. 1973. *Invitation to Physics*. New York: Harcourt Brace Jovanovich.

Haggett, P. 1966. *Locational Analysis in Human Geography*. London: Halstead.

Hardesty, D.L. 1977. *Ecological Anthropology*. New York: John Wiley and Sons.

Hardin, G. 1960. "The Competitive Exclusion Principle." *Science* 131: 1292-1297.

Harris, M. 1959. "The Economy Has No Surplus?" *American Anthropologist* 61: 185-199.

———. 1964. *Patterns of Race in the Americas*. New York: Walker.

———. 1968. *The Rise of Anthropological Theory*. New York: Thomas Y. Crowell.

———. 1980. *Culture, People, Nature*, 3rd ed. New York: Harper and Row.

Hempel, C. 1965. *Aspects of Scientific Explanation: And Other Essays in the Philosophy of Science*. New York: Free Press.

Hogbin, H.I. 1964. *A Guadalcanal Society: The Kaoka Speakers.* New York: Holt, Rinehart and Winston.

Holling, C.S. 1973. "Resilience and Stability of Ecological Systems." *Annual Review of Ecology and Systematics* 4: 1-23.

Hornocker, M. 1970. *An Analysis of Mountain Lion Predation Upon Mule Deer and Elk in the Idaho Primitive Area.* Wildlife Monograph 22, The Wildlife Society.

Kaplan, D. 1960. "The Law of of Cultural Dominance." Pp. 69-92 in *Evolution and Culture*, edited by M. Sahlins and E. Service. Ann Arbor: University of Michigan Press.

Kottak, C.P. 1982. *The Past in the Present: History, Ecology, and Cultural Variation in Highland Madagascar.* Ann Arbor: University of Michigan Press.

Kummer, H. 1971. *Primate Societies: Group Techniques of Ecological Adaptation.* Chicago: Aldine.

Lees, S. and D. Bates. 1984. "Environmental Events and the Ecology of Cumulative Change." Pp. 133-159 in *The Ecosystem Concept in Anthropology*, edited by E. Moran. Boulder, CO: Westview Press.

Leigh, E.G., Jr. 1965. "On the Relation between Productivity, Biomass, Diversity and Stability of a Community." *Proceedings of the National Academy of Sciences* 53: 777-783.

————. 1975. "Population Fluctuations, Community Stability, and Environmental Variability." Pp. 51-73 in *Ecology and Evolution of Communities*, edited by M.L. Cody and J.M. Diamond. Cambridge: Belknap Press.

Leone, M. 1979. *The Roots of Modern Mormonism.* Cambridge, MA: Harvard University Press.

Levins, R. 1968. *Evolution in Changing Environments.* Princeton, NJ: Princeton University Press.

Lewin, K., ed. 1935. "The Conflict between Aristotelian and Galileian Modes of Thought in Contemporary Psychology." Pp. 1-42 in *A Dynamic Theory of Personality.* New York: McGraw-Hill.

Little, M.A. and G.E.B. Morren, Jr. 1976. *Ecology, Energetics, and Human Variability.* Dubuque, IA: Wm. C. Brown.

MacArthur, R.H. 1972. *Geographical Ecology.* New York: Harper and Row.

MacArthur, R. and J. MacArthur. 1961. "On Bird Species Diversity." *Ecology* 42: 594-598.

Margalef, R. 1968. *Perspectives in Ecological Theory.* Chicago: University of Chicago Press.

May, R.M. 1973. *Stability and Complexity in Model Ecosystems.* Princeton, NJ: Princeton University Press.

Maine, H.S. 1861. *Ancient Law.* London: J. Murray.

Meggers, B.J. 1971. *Amazonia: Man and Culture in a Counterfeit Paradise.* Chicago: Aldine-Atherton.

Moran, E., ed. 1984. *The Ecosystem Concept in Anthropology.* Boulder, CO: Westview Press.

Morgan, L.H. 1877. *Ancient Society.* New York: Holt, Rinehart and Winston.

Nagel, E. 1979. *The Structure of Science: Problems in the Logic of Scientific Explanation.* Hackett: Indianapolis.

Netting, R.M. 1968. *Hill Farmers of Nigeria: Cultural Ecology of the Kofyar of th Jos Plateau.* Seattle: University of Washington Press.

Nisbet, R.A. 1969. *Social Change and History: Aspects of the Western Theory o Development.* London: Oxford University Press.

Odum, E.P. 1971. *Fundamentals of Ecology,* 3rd ed. Philadelphia: Saunders.

Odum, H.T. 1971. *Environment, Power and Society.* New York: John Wiley and Sons

Odum, H.T. and R.C. Pinkerton. 1955. "Times Speed Regulator: the Optimum Efficiency for Maximum Output in Physical and Biological Systems." *America Scientist* 43: 331-343.

Paine, R.T. 1966. "Food Web Complexity and Species Diversity." *The America Naturalist* 100: 65-75.

Peterson, C.S. 1973. *Take Up Your Mission: Mormon Colonizing along the Littl Colorado River 1870-1900.* Tucson: University of Arizona Press.

Pianka, E.R. 1966. "Latitutinal Gradients in Species Diversity: A Review of Concepts. *The American Naturalist* 100: 33-46.

Piddocke, S. 1965. "The Potlatch System of the Southern Kwakiutl." *Southwester Journal of Anthropology* 21: 244-264.

Pielou, E.C. 1975. *Ecological Diversity.* New York: Wiley.

Plog, F.T. 1974. *The Study of Prehistoric Change.* New York: Academic Press.

Rappaport, R. 1968. *Pigs for the Ancestors: Ritual in the Ecology of a New Guine People.* New Haven, CT: Yale University Press.

Rapport, D.J. and J.E. Turner. 1977. "Economic Models in Ecology." *Science* 19! 367-373.

Richerson, P.J. 1977. "Ecology and Human Ecology: A Comparison of Theories i the Biological and Social Sciences." *American Ethnologist* 4: 1-26.

Ricklefs, R.E. 1987. "Community Diversity: Relative Roles of Local and Regiona Processes." *Science* 235: 167-171.

Rodhe, W. 1955. "Can Plankton Production Proceed during Winter Darkness i Subarctic Lakes?" *Proceedings of the International Association of Theoretic and Applied Limnologists* 12: 117-122.

Rose, D. 1981. *Energy Transition and the Local Community: A Theory of Societ Applied to Hazleton, Pennsylvania.* Philadelphia: University of Pennsylvani Press.

Rosenzweig, M.L. 1968. "Net Primary Productivity of Terrestrial Communitie Predictions from Climatological Data." *American Naturalist* 102: 67-74.

_____. 1976. "On Continental Steady States of Species Diversity." Pp. 121-140 i *Ecology and Evolution of Communities,* edited by M.L. Cody and M. Diamond Cambridge, MA: Belknap Press.

Russo, J. 1964. *The Kaibab North Deer Herd: Its History, Problems and Managemen* State of Arizona Game and Fish Department, Bulletin 7.

Sahlins, M.D. 1958. *Social Stratification in Polynesia.* Seattle: University o Washington Press.

Sahlins, M.D. and E. Service. 1960. *Evolution and Culture.* Ann Arbor: Universit of Michigan Press.

Samuelson, P. 1958. *Economics: An Introductory Analysis,* 4th ed. New York McGraw-Hill.

Sanders, H.L. 1968. "Marine Benthic Diversity: A Comparative Study." *The American Naturalist* 102: 243-282.

Sanders, W.T. and D.L. Nichols. 1988. "Ecological Theory and Cultural Evolution in the Valley of Oaxaca." *Current Anthropology* 29: 33-80.

Sanders, W.T. and B.J. Price. 1968. *Mesoamerica: The Evolution of A Civilization.* New York: Random House.

Service, E. 1960. "The Law of Evolutionary Potential." Pp. 93-122 in *Evolution and Culture,* edited by M. Sahlins and E. Service. Ann Arbor: University of Michigan Press.

————. 1971. *Primitive Social Organization: An Evolutionary Perspective,* 2nd ed. New York: Random House.

Shannon, F.A. 1945. *The Farmer's Last Frontier, Agriculture, 1960-1897.* New York: Holt, Rinehart and Winston.

Simon, J.L. 1977. *The Economics of Population Growth.* Princeton, NJ: Princeton University Press.

Slobodkin, L.B. and H.L. Sanders. 1969. "On the Contribution of Environmental Predictability to Species Diversity." *Diversity and Stability in Ecological Systems* (Brookhaven Symposia in Biology) 22: 82-95.

Smith, C.A., ed. 1976. *Regional Analysis,* Vols. I and II. New York: Academic Press.

Smith, E.A. 1984. "Anthropology, Evolutionary Ecology, and the Explanatory Limitations of the Ecosystem Concept." Pp. 51-86 in *The Ecosystem Concept in Anthropology,* edited by E. Moran. Boulder, CO: Westview Press.

Spencer, H. 1876. *Principles of Sociology.* New York: D. Appleton.

Steward, J. 1955. *Theory of Culture Change: The Methodology of Multilinear Evolution.* Urbana: University of Illinois Press.

Stocking, G.W. 1968. *Race, Culture and Evolution: Essays in the History of Anthropology.* New York: Free Press.

Terborgh, J. 1971. "Distribution on Environmental Gradients: Theory and a Preliminary Interpretation of Distributional Patterns in the Avifauna of the Cordillera Vilcabama, Peru." *Ecology* 52: 23-40.

Thomas, E.N. 1960. "Some Comments on the Functional Bases for Small Iowa Towns." *Iowa Business Digest* 31: 10-16.

Tylor, E.B. 1871. *Primitive Culture.* London: John Murray.

Vandermeer, J.H. 1972. "Niche Theory." *Annual Review of Ecology and Systematics* 3: 107-132.

Vayda, A. and B.J. McCay. 1975. "New Directions in Ecology and Ecological Anthropology." *Annual Review of Anthropology* 4: 297-306.

Vayda, A. and R. Rappaport. 1968. "Ecology: Cultural and Non-Cultural." Pp. 477-497 in *Introduction to Cultural Anthropology,* edited by J.A. Clifton. New York: Houghton-Mifflin.

von Bertalanffy, L. 1968. *General Systems Theory.* New York: Braziller.

White, L.A. 1949. *The Science of Culture.* New York: Grove Press.

————. 1959. *The Evolution of Culture.* New York: McGraw-Hill.

Whittaker, R.H. 1975. *Communities and Ecosystems,* 2nd ed. New York: Macmillan.

Whittaker, R.H. and G.M. Woodwell. 1972. "Evolution of Natural Communities." Pp. 137-159 In *Ecosystem Structure and Function,* edited by J.A. Weins. Eugene: University of Oregon Press.

Wilkinson, R. 1973. *Poverty and Progress: An Ecological Perspective on Economic Development.* New York: Praeger.

Wilson, F. 1969. "Explanation in Aristotle, Newton and Toulmin." *Philosophy of Science* 36: 291-310.

Wilson, E.O. 1968. "The Ergonomics of Caste in the Social Insects." *American Naturalist* 102: 41-66.

_____. 1971. *The Insect Societies.* Cambridge, MA: Belknap Press.

Winterhalder, B. and E. Smith, eds. 1981. *Hunter-Gatherer Foraging Strategies: Ethnographic and Archaeological Analyses.* Chicago: University of Chicago Press.

Young, G. 1974. "Human Ecology as an Interdisciplinary Concept: A Critical Inquiry." *Advances in Ecological Research* 8: 1-105.

Young, G. and C.A. Broussard. 1986. "The Species Problem in Human Ecology." Pp. 55-67 in *Human Ecology: A Gathering of Perspectives*, edited by R.J. Borden. College Park, MD: Society for Human Ecology.

INTERACTION AS A CONCEPT
BASIC TO HUMAN ECOLOGY:
AN EXPLORATION AND SYNTHESIS

Gerald L. Young

ABSTRACT

The argument in this paper is that the specific focus in ecology is not really on organisms as objects or on elements of the environment as objects, *but on the processes of interaction:* the connective processes that link all objects of ecological interest. This critical concept, however, has been insufficiently delineated as a central component in ecological theory. This paper examines the centrality and current place of the concept of interaction in general ecology, explicates it, treats it as a foundational concept, and then explores in some detail its significance for the complex and multiple interactions of the human species.

Advances in Human Ecology, Volume 5, pages 157-211.
Copyright © 1996 by JAI Press Inc.
All rights of reproduction in any form reserved.
ISBN: 0-7623-0029-9

INTRODUCTION

I had three chairs in my house; one for solitude, two for friendship, three for society.

—Thoreau (1973, p. 140)

Ecology is commonly defined as study of the interactions between an organism of some kind and its surroundings, including other organisms. Research papers seldom need to spell out ecology, so the best source for contemporary characterizations of the word and the field are recent general ecology textbooks. Consider three such texts (chosen almost at random off the shelf), in which the word interaction (italicized in each quote below for emphasis) is central to the meaning of ecology. In the third edition of Ricklefs' text (1993, p. 1), he interprets ecology as "the science by which we study how organisms (animals, plants, and microbes) *interact* in and with the natural world." Krebs (1994, p. 3), updates an earlier definition essentially by adding a phrase centered on interaction: Ecology, defined as the study of "the distribution and abundance of organisms," is recharacterized as "the scientific study of *the interactions* that determine the distribution and abundance of organisms." Finally, Brewer (1994, p. 1) states his definition in strong, simple terms: "Ecology is a study of *interactions*."

Because ecology, like the other life sciences, studies *living organisms,* that component is a given and always explicitly present in ecological research papers and in ecology textbooks. What first differentiates ecology from the other life sciences is that consideration of *environment* in some form, to some degree, is *necessarily* included in ecological texts. Ecology is also differentiated from the other life sciences in that its focus, at least implicitly, has shifted from being centered on the organism to being centered on interaction processes, or to an interaction system comprised of organisms in relation to other organisms and to the encompassing environment.

Oddly, though, that third critical component, *interaction*—the system of processes that links organisms and their surroundings, the concept so central to definition *of* the discipline and to definitions *in* the discipline, the term found so widely in so much work in ecology—is seldom explicated as a major concept in ecological texts. It does show up in specific definitions, yes, clearly and forcefully, but then is lost in the explanations and seldom shows up, for example, in the indexes of major texts in ecology. The other life sciences focus on the organism and are usually differentiated by the taxonomic group of interest. Different branches of ecology are also differentiated by taxonomic groups, with many ecologists identifying themselves first as botanists, entomologists, and so on, but ecology is also unique in that its critical focus is on the various ways in which organisms *interact* with their surrounding environment; the specific focus in ecology is not really on organisms as objects or on elements of the environment as objects, *but on the processes of interaction* that link objects of ecological interest.

It should be clearly noted here, however, that ecology is a life science, and that the interactors of interest are the organisms themselves. This means, in human ecology, that people (individuals and groups) are the interactors—and that the whole complex range of their interactions is of ecological interest.

How important is the concept of interaction and the study of interactions in ecological systems—how significant are they to ecology, and by extension to human ecology? Why is this critical concept of interaction so seldom explicated as a central component in ecological theory? This paper addresses these questions, first by examining the centrality of the concept in general ecology, and then by exploring in more detail its significance in the interdisciplinary domain of human ecology. The objective is to examine the current place of interaction in ecological theory; to *explicate* the concept; and then to explore what explicating it—as a foundational concept central to the discipline— might mean in ecology in general and, more specifically, in ecology as focused on the complex and multiple interactions of the human species. Part of the goal also is to demonstrate the strength of interaction processes as a basis for common ground linking general ecology and human ecology.

In human ecology, an initial explication of interaction as a basic concept should help move scholars toward a better understanding of how extensive human relationships really are, and of how meaningful they are. It means paying attention to, and attempting at least an initial exploration of, such changing themes as the mutating conception of self in a rapidly changing world; the role of contingency; the nature of boundaries and their permeability; and the need for mediation of interactions that are accelerating beyond those boundaries. Embodiment of accelerating interaction processes as central to ecological relationships—indeed, a rapidly quickening tangle of interactions that are reshaping all organismic relationships, including and especially, those of humans—means necessarily paying some attention as well to countervailing tendencies that emerge naturally as interactions multiply and proliferate: first, the alienation that results from peoples' attempts to withdraw from the press of constantly advancing, multiplying interactions and, second, a brief look at the stress that modern, complex edifices of multiple interactions place on humans, and on all the systems in which they operate and with which they deal.

INTERACTION: IMPLICIT IN BIOLOGICAL ECOLOGY

Central to a twentieth-century American line of thought labeled process philosophy, especially as explicated by Whitehead (1929), is the idea that nature is a structure of living processes, with *the reality in the process*. In line with this thought, contemporary biological ecology emerged in this century out of natural history and, though still concerned with "nature," has increasingly begun to focus on reality in the Whiteheadian sense, that is, more on process than on structure. That process tradition had long existed in ecology, but remained secondary and without a focus until ecologists began turning from relatively simple descriptions of the structure of ecosystems to more complex analyses of the dynamics of functional processes, particularly energy budgets and flows. That idea—of organism and environment as an interacting, dynamic, and complex web, generally acceptable in the biological sciences since Darwin's time—is now on the brink of becoming *the* central focus in ecology.

As ecology has developed in the twentieth century, a number of influential ecologists defined ecology in Whiteheadian terms. Adams (1935, pp. 319, 331), for example, early asserted that one of the distinguishing features of ecology was its major emphasis on process. Darling (1963, p. 298) agreed with Adams that "ecology deals essentially with process," and Sears suggested (1954, p. 960) that what all ecologists "have in common is an interest in process," and later (1960, p. 198) again echoing Adams, he emphasized that "ecology deals primarily with process." Bates (1956, p. 1138) claimed that organism and environment should never be thought of as discrete, definable entities but rather that scientists should "think in terms of transactions between processes."

Stephen A. Forbes, a pioneer American ecologist and a founder of the Ecological Society of America (and its second president), wrote a paper in 1880 titled "On Some Interactions of Organisms." That paper identified interaction as the process of most ecological interest; Forbes

(1880, p. 3) strongly emphasized that "the history of the lives [of living organisms] show that they are ... intimately and variously bound together by mutual interactions." Forbes' essay is now considered a classic in ecology and set an early and strong precedent for the centrality of interaction as a concept in the discipline—central but still implicit. Also, it should be added here, Forbes specifically included humans as organisms of ecological interest, for example, in his ESA presidential address (Forbes 1922).

Forbes' precedent has been followed, but too erratically and with too little explicit recognition of that essential centrality. For many ecologists, interaction as a concept has not progressed beyond the definitional stage, though its importance there is generally acknowledged. What has not been conceded, and certainly not explored, are the numerous ramifications of the central definitional concept—consequences that have committed ecology to a process way of thinking. The importance of interactions in biological ecology is still indicated only tangentially, for example, by a widespread and traditional emphasis on such relationships as predation, competition, commensalism, and so on, relationships sometimes gathered, as in Odum's classic text (1971), under the rubric of interspecies interactions. Similarly, Krebs (1994) focuses on three types of species interactions: competition, predation, and mutualism. He does discuss as well interactions with the environment in terms of factors that limit distribution, for example, temperature, moisture, and light. The term interaction is also commonly used in portrayals of the traditionally basic ecological unit, the ecosystem.

A few sample quotes from the recent literature (with emphasis added in each case) amply illustrate that the interaction concept is widely admitted in ecology, however tangential it may be in the final analysis. George Woodwell (1978, p. 138) echoes Forbes, suggesting that ecologists "have long had the thought that the biosphere is the product *of the interactions* through time of the earth's great interacting chemical and physical systems: atmosphere, oceans, continental masses, and the biota." Kormondy and McCormick (1981, p. xxiii), placing ecology in the context of rapid change in the sciences since World War II, note that "ecology has been in the midst of this change, moving from a largely organism-centered and qualitatively descriptive discourse to that of *a system of dynamically interacting and interrelated parts.*" Huston, DeAngelis, and Post (1988, p. 682) restate the obvious, but in contemporary computer terms, with their argument that "computer simulations show that many *ecological patterns can be explained by interaction* among individual organisms." Notice here that the concept of interaction is singular, but that any ecological system is of course held together by a myriad of interactions—making the concept much more formidable and challenging, but ultimately even more promising. As Thompson (1982, p. v) suggested, "species interact in a bewildering variety of ways and the evolutionary results of these interactions are stamped in their morphologies, physiologies, behaviors, and life histories. It is not only the species that change evolutionarily through interactions, however: the interactions themselves also change."

Recent ecological literature is beginning to address the linkages between multiple interactions and complexity, with Price, Gaud, and Slobodchikoff (1984, p. 2) suggesting that a new interdisciplinary, synthetic ecology is needed to address the "rich possibilities" of contemporary interactive systems. Jørgensen, Patten, and Straskraba (1992, p. 2) agree that "present-day ecology [must begin to address its failure] to produce an adequate science of large-scale, unbounded and interconnected complexity."

Leary (1976) developed what he called a "periodic coordinate system" (p. 1) that allows ecologists to make "cardinal specifications of type of interactions [as well as] quantitative statements about intensity of interaction" (p. 4). However, this work by Leary (and by others) still limits the technique to "two-dimensional groupings of interactions" and does not allow for what LaBrecque (1986, p. 2) called "the many-body problem," wherein "once the number of bodies interacting with each other grows beyond two, the problems of computing their effects on each other begin to grow out of control." The problem of complexity faced by ecologists interested in human interactions is one of many bodies indeed.

Despite such usage, interaction as an explicit concept was not deemed worthy enough to make it into the indices of either the ecologist's version of the history of ecology (McIntosh 1985) or the historian's version (Worster 1994). Like so many ecologists, both have misread the theoretical underpinnings of contemporary ecology, not recognizing or realizing the significance of the implicit "red thread" woven by interaction processes through the complex weave of contemporary ecological literature.

Forbes' early emphasis seems to have somehow allowed most subsequent writers in ecology to assume the concept of interaction (while still marginalizing its centrality and not taking advantage of its definitive power), to take process for granted, to always include interactions, but (almost always it seems) to treat them only tangentially or implicitly in ecological research and writing. This shows, for example, in a recent poll of members of the British Ecological Society, where 645 professional ecologists responded to questions about the most important concepts in ecology. Interaction is central to the delineation and development of all the basic ecological units, but three of the most widely used units were identified among the ten most important concepts, while interaction as a concept in its own right never appeared on the list (Cherrett 1989, pp. 6-7).

Interaction must eventually be admitted explicitly as a central concept by scholars in ecology, as a fundamental, foundational, inclusive concept in the discipline. This commonplace, ineluctable process has not been ignored in biological ecology (from which so many of the basic ideas in human ecology were originally drawn) but has remained implicit—a widespread but tangential, almost hidden, presence masking its importance, while at the same time confirming it. Organismic interactions are pervasive, interesting, and vital, definitive of ecological relationships and ecological systems, and offer innumerable promising avenues for research and scholarship in ecology.

Explicating interaction processes in ecology and recognizing their importance could recast ecological theory, could provide a more coherent, more inclusive framework for linking and relating concepts in ecology and in human ecology (cf. Young 1989), and could tie them more usefully and reliably into contemporary human-environmental problems. The latter is especially significant: Interaction, as a concept and as a set of processes, provides critical common ground for biological ecology and human ecology to close some of the gaps between them that have existed now for decades, and should allow better collaboration toward solutions of critical human-environmental problems. Interaction should be recognized as *the* basic concept in ecology (and in human ecology), the concept from which every other significant concept and unit in ecology is derived.

INTERACTION: EXPLICIT IN THE SOCIAL SCIENCES

The social sciences have been more successful in emphasizing and adapting the concept of interaction, but less successful than biology in providing the ecological context. McCall and Simmons (1966, p. 61), for example, claimed that interaction is not merely a school of thought in sociology or psychology but "has broadened to become a perspective in the social sciences." Shanon (1990) reiterated this with the claim that "human behavior is context-dependent" (p. 158), and that understanding behavior in the late twentieth century requires an explanation of context "which, by its very nature, is interactional" (p. 163). Here we provide just a few examples or brief illustrations from each social science, but these are persuasive, and they provide a serviceable indication of the importance of the interaction concept in these disciplines.

Shorthand Formulations of Interaction Processes

The social science literature on interaction (primarily social interaction) is large and complex. Perhaps it can be best summarized by focusing on certain convenient shorthand formulations that have been referred to and used consistently for decades, formulations that provide a clear look at the basic components of the interaction concept in the social sciences—and which slice cleanly, if perhaps too simply, through the complexity.

These shorthand formulations are what might be called "conceptual equations" rather than precise mathematical formulas. The simplest is just that, what Sells (1963, p. 696) described explicitly and straightforwardly as an *interaction equation*:

$$I = f(OE)$$

He describes I (behavior) as a function of the interactions of organisms and environment, claiming that "no one has challenged the generality of the basic equation." And, it *is* generally acceptable in human ecology if environment is defined in the broadest possible sense, without qualification, and it is acceptable beyond any narrow meaning in Sells' field of psychology. The equation is too indefinite, however, to be very meaningful beyond serving as a first-step, shorthand mental construct with interaction recognized as an absolute.

Somewhat more particularized formulations in the social sciences have been presented as "laws" of interaction, particularly Dodd's Law and Stouffer's Law. Dodd (1950, p. 245) presented what he called "the Interactance Hypothesis," essentially a gravity model claiming that "groups of people interact more as they become faster, nearer, larger and leveled up in activity." Inversely, groups of people will interact less (in proportion) if they are smaller in population, are further apart, or are more dissimilar in average activity. Dodd's Law suggests that the number of communicative acts between any two population centers will be directly proportional to the product of the populations and inversely proportional to the distance between them (see also Bassett 1946; Stern 1974):

$$C = k(P_1 \times P_2) \mathbin{/} D$$

In this "equation," C equals the number of communications and k is a proportionality constant. In a similar way, Stouffer's Law states that "the number of persons going a given distance is directly proportional to the number of opportunities at that distance and inversely proportional to the number of intervening opportunities" (see Stouffer 1940, p. 846).

The social sciences have espoused a number of such formulations of measures of "attraction," or potential attraction, between certain types of groups or centers. The most general interaction hypothesis of this type is:

$$I_{ij} = \frac{f(P_i P_j)}{f(D_{ij})}$$

where: I_{ij} = interaction between center i and center j;
P_i, P_j = population of areas i and j respectively; and
D_{ij} = distance between center i and center j.

The *gravity* notion of interaction is (again) clearly depicted in this formulation (Carrothers 1956). Distance and population become the two primary factors upon which interactions depend, still deemed true by common sense, but as Catton (1966, pp. 165-194) noted, qualified by many of the unique opportunities of contemporary life.

A further step removed from the symbolic equation formulated by Sells is the adaptation of certain simple biological interaction equations to fit the needs of human ecology. These have been adapted for use from interaction formulas devised by Spomer (1973). In the first, interaction (I) is defined in terms of an equality that relates potential differences (P) and exchange capacity (C), with (A), the effective area of exchange:

$$I = \frac{C(P)}{A}$$

The problem (even in purely biological terms) is one of evaluating capacity, so the effect of resistance on capacity is introduced in reciprocal form:

$$\frac{C(P)}{A} = \frac{k(P)}{RA}$$

where: $R =$ the total effective resistance and
$k =$ a proportionality constant relating capacity and resistance.

The problem still is to find measurable values for each variable; the assumption is that values could be formulated from present empirical data in psychology and the social sciences but that, until such data become readily available, both of the above equations also remain essentially symbolic.

Accepting them primarily for their symbolic value should do nothing to detract from the usefulness of these equations because, as conceptual tools, they still do have validity, however immeasurable. Human interactions *are* a reaction to differences; human beings *do* vary in their capacity for exchange, in their income, employment, childhood environment, religion, provincialism, and many other characteristics. It should be possible to devise a proportionality constant relating capacity for interactions with an individual's or group's resistance to interactions. One has only to think of groups such as the Amish to accept such a resistance/capacity ratio as an understandable if not measurable variable of human interactions, in the case of the Amish one based on a belief system contrary to the normative primacy of the general system of societal order (see Lennard and Bernstein 1969, p. 14). Acculturation is a by-product of increased interactions; conservative or traditional groups tend to resist the process, hoping to avoid the inevitable change that comes with it. Interestingly, though, Amish people are widely credited with close and intimate interactions with their local natural environment, farming it carefully with the intent to do little harm and to keep the land fertile and productive.

Many modifications can undoubtedly be made on these simple models, such as raising the distance factor to a variable exponent, notably as a function of the cost of traversing said distance. Complicating the issue also is the necessity to understand the role of "extensors" in the processes of human interactions—such electronic extensors of human communications capability as the telephone, the television, and lately, such innovations as the fax machine and e-mail.

These seemingly dated equations are still useful, if only because students can see immediately how important distance has been in human interactions, and how important it still is, but in different ways for different people. None of the problems posed by the equations—the impact of distance, the role of intervening variables, the questions of difference, the changes wrought by technology—have been solved. They are just different: Humans still interact in space and through units of distance, and that distance still plays a major role in the opportunity for and immediacy of human interactions, including those with all of the complexes commonly included in the term environment.

Modern Reformulations of Interaction in the Social Sciences

Unmistakably, a strong precedent for the use of the concept of interaction has been established in the social sciences. All of the social sciences have witnessed development of interaction as a basic concept. These social science uses of interaction, combined together and linked with similar uses in biology, exhibit the potential for the concept to become basic to an interdisciplinary, synthesized human ecology. It should be useful to summarize briefly the major ways in which interaction is used in each social science. This brief survey is not limited to, but emphasizes, the human ecological approach in each discipline.

The most obvious place to look in sociology is interaction as the keystone in the Parsonian approach to the study of social systems (Parsons 1968). Parsons (1968) provided what he called a paradigm of social interaction, a formulation that comes surprisingly close to presaging the effort in these pages to outline the importance of interactions in ecology and human ecology:

The broad outline of the present conceptions of interaction [focuses on] a social system generated by and composed of the interaction of units which are "behaving organisms," personalities, or various levels of collectivity. Acting units, however, are always involved in cultural systems, which express, symbolize, order, and control human orientations through patterned meaning systems consisting of both codes of meaning and specific combinations of symbols in particular contexts. At a mimimum, an interaction system in this sense involves four analytically distinguishable aspects or components: 1) a set of "units" which interact with each other; 2) a set of rules or other "code" factors, the terms of which structure both the orientations of the units and the interaction itself; 3) an ordered or patterned system or process of the interaction itself; and 4) an environment in which the system operates and with which systematic interchanges take place (p. 434).

Despite years of debate, Parsons' conception of interaction keeps showing up in the literature of sociology. Lyman (1988, p. 296), for example, closely echoes Parsons with the recent statement that "the subject matter [of sociology] is the human actor interacting with and interpreting the meaning of the objects and ideas in his environment."

Freese (1988, p. 92) points out that "the concept of interaction does not mean the same thing in social theory as it does in the natural and physical sciences. Those disciplines often speak of *interactions*, whereas sociology and social psychology do not" (emphasis added). It is critical in human ecology to recognize the necessity of dealing with interactions as plural, with a multitude of interactions—among humans and between humans and their surroundings. Another problem with utilizing interaction theory in human ecology in the way it has developed as a concept in sociology and psychology, is that in these disciplines it is usually (always?) limited to *social* interaction—and too often to micro-interactions (Kemper and Collins 1990), that is, to direct, interpersonal interactions. Turner (1988, p. vii), for example, emphasizes that "the most fundamental unit of sociological analysis [is] social interaction"—and, like so many sociologists, he never gets beyond the microlevel depiction of actor-actor relationships. Hall (1987, p. 18) makes the point clearly that "everyday behavior, interactions, and relationships cannot be understood except as contextualized," but he sharply limits that context to social organization and then only in what he calls the meso-domain, a domain which he claims transcends "the macro-micro distinction, by showing the ways societal and institutional forces mesh with human activity," a domain "characterized by the reflexive and dialectical relationship between activity and context" (p. 10). But, Freese's (1988) criticism remains true, that in most current social theory, social interaction is limited to an interpersonal process.

Sociological human ecology, especially in its recent reincarnation as "environmental sociology," goes a step further in its concern with the interactions between a social group or organization and its environment (of whatever kind). Interaction theory today, if it is to be manifested in ecological terms—in the synthesis we are here calling human ecology—must be even more incorporative, must be made more applicable, to keep up with the full range of changes in human interactions and with the full extent of their reach across all scales.

Anthropologists are also interested in the interactions between a human group and its environment, but here the focus is on the role of culture as a shaper and an intermediary in interaction processes. Ford (1990), studying a tropical montane area of Rwanda, provides a useful example of the anthropological tradition of field-based examinations of human-environment interactions. He includes interactions among the local people, interactions between those people and the physical environment (particularly in terms of changes in population and in agriculture, and the resulting changes in such environmental conditions as soil and plant cover), and also the effects (and potential effects) of interactions between local farmers and the outside world. Ironically, this text, written only six years ago, concludes that "the present politically stable Rwandese environment could change quickly, thus upsetting the delicate balance that Rwanda is seeking between stability and instability, in both political economy and agricultural systems" (p. 60). Ford wrote that before the explosive and violent interactions between Hutu and Tutsi tribes in the 1990s tore the country apart, resulting in extraordinarily negative impacts on both the humans and the land, and leaving the country unable to mediate events or to support its people.

Psychology, especially social psychology, can be interpreted specifically as a discipline working at "understanding human interaction" (Foon 1987; Beron 1994). Psychologists are interested in the interactions between and among individuals or small groups of human beings, what Goffman (1983, p. 1) called "the interaction order." Sometimes, dating back at least to Kurt Lewin's (1951) ecological psychology, the interactions with an environment of some kind are also included, more often than not the setting and influences provided by the built environment. Psychologists do tend to have an unusual sense of the concept "environment," defining it variously as natural or human-made, external, or even internal.

Geographers focus on the spatial aspects of interactions, for example, the "effects of distance on patterns of human interaction" (Hodder 1978, p. 155). Geography has one leg in the social sciences and one in the natural sciences, so ecological studies in the discipline can emerge from either tradition. Human ecological studies in geography are often defined interactionally in terms of "the human use of land and resources" (Liverman 1994, p. 67), a long tradition in the field; or in terms of planning (Nelson 1991). An interactional field in geography is defined specifically by spatial interaction—"the flows of people, goods, or other entities from place to place" (Slater 1989, p. 121; see also Ullman 1980). Numerous studies have demonstrated how this spatial interaction field has been shaped and manipulated by human actions and interests.

In a way, economics and political science are also primarily interested in humans as interactors in economic and political systems, contextual systems that influence humans and are influenced by them. John Rawls, in *A Theory of Justice* (1971), revised, restated, and breathed new life into the idea of the social contract as a basis for political structures. If the social contract is considered a derivative of interaction processes, then those processes are legitimately the concern of political science. Kemmis (1995), a state and city-level politician, insists that politics is based on civility, which originally meant "of the city," and politics is what it takes "to live next to one another, as cities, by definition, require people to do" (pp. 11-12). He goes on to suggest that "only citizenship can save politics," with real citizenship limited only to those people who are actively engaged with the place where they live, who interact in positive, balanced ways.

Economics is usually portrayed as a discipline that focuses on exchange processes and on the allocation of scarce resources. Economic interactions—the exchange of commodities, the ebb and flow of currencies, the give-and-take of labor with the community and the environment, the *quid pro quos* of business—provide much of the essential discourse of everyday life for humans around the world. Eldredge and Grene (1992) consider economic interactions more basic even than the topic as represented in the discipline of economics, arguing that economic interactions are one of two fundamental categories of interactions—the other being reproductive interactions—and that humans, more than any other species, have elaborated the differences between the two. By economic interactions, Eldredge and Grene mean all the ways in which organisms interact with each other and with their environments to get a living. They argue that Darwinian evolutionary theory is very much focused on the reproductive interactions, not just in terms of what Darwin termed sexual selection, but in terms of the whole process of intergenerational change in gene frequencies. The more effectively they conduct these economic efforts, of course, the more likely they are to pass along their genes; nevertheless, Eldredge and Grene consider the two categories of interaction as conceptually distinct. They maintain that humans do much more than any other species in the way of economic interactions that have less and less direct bearing upon their reproductive success.

Because human ecology is a field astride the still existing fence between biology and the social sciences, it should not be too difficult conceptually to comprehend the potential of the interaction concept to form a blend between the two. Eldredge and Grene (1992, title page) in fact suggest that "interactions [form] the biological context of social systems" for all organisms, including humans.

The literature has yet to produce better statements of the early importance and centrality of the interaction process in the social sciences than two matter-of-fact assertions from the late 1960s, one from a work in sociology (Lennard and Bernstein 1969) and the other from social psychology (Newcomb, Turner, and Converse 1965). Quoting two of their strongest, clearest statements emphasizes that centrality. By then paraphrasing their quoted statements slightly, it becomes possible to pose equally strong statements that clearly indicate the similarities between the concept of interaction in the social sciences and the corresponding idea in ecology, while at the same time emphasizing the centrality of the interaction process in both bioecology and human ecology. First, the original statements on interaction from the social sciences:

> Human interaction provides the medium through which societies and, indeed, all social systems perform their functions and carry out their purposes. For, unless individuals interact, no social system can continue to exist (Lennard and Bernstein 1969, p. 174).

and

> nearly every kind of social psychological problem [can be framed] in terms of psychological processes which take their particular form from the interaction context in which they occur (Newcomb, Turner, and Converse 1965, p. v).

These statements, basic to conceptions of interaction processes in the social sciences, may be paraphrased in the context of biological ecology as:

The interactions of organisms provide the medium through which (ecosystems) perform their functions. For, unless interactions take place (occur), no ecosystem can continue to exist.

and

nearly every kind of (ecological) problem can be framed in terms of (natural) processes which take their particular form from the interaction context in which they occur.

The paraphrases, as stated, are plainly exploratory in nature, and are only a beginning. But both the original statements and the paraphrases provide an initial illustration of the power and promise of the interaction concept, of how indispensable it is to derivations of other basic concepts in human ecology. Further blending is required, and it would be useful to find or attempt empirical tests of both types of statements, to further substantiate their fitness for ecological theory and systems. A comment by Parsons (1968, p. 436) can take a step in that direction: "The concept of interaction is the first-order step beyond the action concept itself toward formulating the concept of social system"—and, it might be added, perhaps the major step in formulating common ground between ecology and human ecology!

INTERACTION FIELDS AND ECOLOGICAL UNITS

Field theory has a bonafide tradition in the social sciences (cf. Lewin 1951; Yinger 1965), though often ignored and even forgotten. In biological ecology, field theory is underutilized, but is made explicit in such work as that by Wu, Sharpe, Walker, and Penridge (1985) and Walker, Sharpe, Penridge, and Wu (1989). Holtz (1967, pp. 533-534) claimed, with some justification, that "if any concept can be said to unify the attitudes of the various modern disciplines—physical, biological, social—toward the phenomena they study, it would probably be the concept of a 'field approach'."

Interactions have long been used in general ecology to establish the boundaries of certain ecological concepts, especially unit concepts such as niche, community, and ecosystem. Interaction is used as the delimiting process in even the most conventional explanations of these units. Eldredge and Grene (1992, p. 2) for example, recently stated that "we see biotic entities (populations ... species ... ecosystems) as arising from the simple activities of organisms," that is, "biotic entities (such as ecosystems) result from moment-by-moment ... interactions among component parts" (p. 3).

It may be a small step, even a self-evident one, to combine these two traditions—field theory and interaction theory—into the formation of a composite ecological unit called simply an *interaction field*. Forty years ago, the social theorist Kenneth Boulding (1956, p. 202) recognized that the two go together, but stated that "a general field theory of the dynamics of action and interaction ... is ... a long way ahead." Despite a sizeable body of literature, the situation today still remains close to the way Boulding described it. Perhaps an interactional approach to human ecology, because it is so interdisciplinary and utilizes material from so many subjects (including the biological and the social sciences), can help take another step in the path toward eventual realization of that general theory.

Toward a Concept of an Interaction Field

Research in ecology is often focused on distribution and abundance of organisms, a focus that is explicitly spatial, an approach that has been used to enscribe and delimit the discipline (Krebs 1994). The field concept in ecology and other disciplines, including human ecology, can be conceived of as a space determined by the interactions of particles or units and thus connective in an incorporative way. This suggests an interactional relationship between the properties and functions of parts or individuals and their placement within the whole-as-field. (That relationship has been described as "position" effects.) Watts (1966, p. 86) presented the interdisciplinary nature of fields specifically in ecological terms: "every scientific discipline for the study of living organisms ... must, from its own special standpoint, develop a science of ecology ... the study of organism/environment fields."

Because human interactions are so varied and occur on so many levels, realizing a vision of human ecology as the study of organism-environment fields is complex and difficult. Human interactions do take place between two or more people occupying different places, in or across space—and, obviously interactions take place as well between one or more persons and the complex of elements that make up those places (the surroundings or environment). Even in very intimate interactions, the physical bodies must occupy different spaces. A "field of play"—or a field of work, discourse, exchange, or relations—then is outlined any time an occupied space is bridged by the interaction process, what Freese (1988, p. 96) described succinctly with the comment that every "social system is a field of interactions." The extent of the interactions *defines* the extent of the field. Certainly, many other events and activities happen within any given field, but the word define is used deliberately here; because the generalized entity being addressed is an interaction field, then its shape and extent is defined *first* by the processes of interaction, despite what else may be going on. It is also recognized that this is probably a reciprocal chicken-egg sort of exegetic process: The field is characterized by interactions and the field in turn elucidates the interactions.

Through most of human history, the context of each individual's existence was marked by a limited number of composite fields. If interactions with the spirit world are not considered, then minimally, aboriginal existence was confined primarily to fields sanctioned by membership in a band and by kinship ties, and to that field bounded by the band's hunting territory or, later, zone of shifting cultivation. Individuals living in urban industrial complexes still interact—at one level and with a relatively high degree of intensity—with family and friends, colleagues at work, and neighbors made accessible by proximity. But, many of those same individuals also interact in an increasing number of other fields. Therefore, in contemporary human terms, it is possible to think in terms of a complex, multiple set of interaction fields—or for any one individual, of a composite field that incorporates the whole complex of interactions in which that person is involved.

In human ecology, then, interaction field can be conceptualized in at least two ways that should be helpful in understanding the way people relate to their surroundings. The first is a composite field for individuals, visualized if not actually constructed as an attempt to understand the dramatically changing and complex relationships of contemporary people heading into a new milennium. The second is a set of interaction fields, each one dependent on the problem to be addressed—interpersonal interactions or community interactions at various scales, or human-environment interactions on a wide range of levels. The depiction of any given field in any set would reflect an individual's or group's intensity of relationships, level of consciousness, range of influence, or extent of impact.

This means that each individual human being lives in his or her own personally specified field of interactions *and* in a complex, intertwined set of multiform fields, the spatial extent of each outlined by the nature and intensity of interactions. One field may be represented, for a particular individual, by family or kinship ties, another field by a circle of friends, another by neighborhood, the next by community, and then by regional or political ties, and so on. Individual fields are also designated by involvement with the media, by politics, by economics and consumer decisions, and by the reach of their environmental impacts. Study of the relationships of such individuals cannot be accomplished by focusing on a field of interaction of one kind or at one level: Each individual is involved in a number of networks of varying degrees of intensity. And, depending on the problem of interest, a human ecological study might focus on any one of an individual's fields of interaction—or on all of them as a composite.

At the same time, human individuals are part of group interaction fields, including those traditional to biological ecology (species, population, community, and ecosystem) as well as those more uniquely human, such as those characterized by ethnic groups, religious organizations, work groups, or the political entities of state or nation. Here the focus of a study in human ecology is not only on individuals, but on an interaction field formed through the relationships of a group, however facilitated. Each and every type of interaction field needs to be at least recognized, if the task of human ecology—which aspires to comprehend as completely as possible the complexity of the web of relationships in which modern individual human beings are enmeshed—is to be moved forward.

In ecology and human ecology, then, an interaction field can and should be considered to be *the* fundamental ecological unit, a unit that emerges from and is clarified by the nature and intensity of interactions between and among a group of organisms in a specified place. A general field concept in ecology provides a general systems term for a number of basic unit concepts, for example, niche, territory, community, and ecosystem. These may all be derived from and subordinated to a conceptual abstraction with greater incorporative utility. An interaction field traces the spatial relationships between an organism or group of organisms (such as some form of center or community) and its environment, or between that organism or group and other organisms in terms of a range of functional interactions.

Interaction fields may be delimited by their mean boundaries—those points, at varying levels, where the intensity of the interactions shows a marked change (an increase or decrease) or a significant shift of some kind. In general ecology, such boundaries may be characterized in terms of the range or territory of an organism or group of organisms. For human beings, the initial set of interaction fields may be bounded by or recognized as the local place, the neighborhood, or community However, because human interactions are accelerating, becoming ever-more complex, and spilling over boundaries at every level, ecological field theory for humans cannot be confined to traditional locales or face-to-face interactions.

A number of commonsense generalizations can be made about mean interaction fields. For example, field size may vary at any level depending on the complexity introduced by raising the distance factor to a variable exponent. The variability is a function of the mobility of an individual or group, and is complicated by such factors as access to communications technology or means of transportation. Many people in the world do not own a car, for example, or cannot afford to take advantage of commercial air transport; their interaction fields are circumscribed by that lack of access. Also, the size of any particular field may vary through time. Again, innovations in technology especially communications and transportation techniques, may change the range if not the reality of interactions. The level of education of the individual or group has an important bearing, and this may change through time. Well-educated people with good incomes are less likely to be bound by proximity, and more likely to be involved in complex interactions on many levels. And, the intensity of interactions tends to increase over time, especially as technology improves or number increase. However, the field of interactions for any particular individual can also shrink. Many elderly people, for example, retire and mix less with groups at work, and they often do not get around easily, so their fields of activity may be circumscribed.

If interaction is acknowledged as a process common to all dynamic living systems, then it can also be recognized that it is possible to sanction ecological units as derivatives of that process. The interactors are organisms, their interactions take place in space, and traditional derivations of ecological units are based on this—they are, in fact, a reflection and a measure of distribution and abundance, and of a variety of relationships. Fields, then, form the systemic interaction context in which assorted ecological units are enabled to materialize. Whether the field determines the interactions or the interactions delimit the field is once more, a chicken-and-egg thing: Each reciprocally creates and shapes the other. The field formed within that context may, in an specific instance, and depending on the types of interactions involved, be termed first a niche, a community, or an ecosystem, but any unit so specified is also, and fundamentally, one form of an interaction field. The concept of an interaction field may therefore be considered a broader, more inclusive, more facilitative unit in ecology.

Units Redefined as Field Derivatives

The British Ecological Association, in the poll of its members mentioned earlier, published a list of the "most important fifty concepts in ecology" (Cherrett 1989, pp. 6-7). Three widely used units in ecology were ranked in the top ten. Ecosystem ranked number one, far ahead of the concept (succession) in second place; niche was ranked sixth; and community, eighth. A quick scan of recent texts confirms that these three units continue to be both prominent and significant unit concepts in biological ecology. Interaction was not listed as a concept in its own right (in either the poll or the texts), but did show up, tangentially, in the poll in twentieth place, as the quite narrow and specific "predator-prey interactions," followed by twenty-first most important, "plant-herbivore interactions." No recognition was given to the fact that, in the ecological literature, interactions are widely used to detail *all* of the unit concepts considered of "top-ten" importance—and those expositions do not depend just on the three kinds of interactions specifically so identified on the list (three, because parasite-host interactions are on the list as thirty-eighth most important).

Because each unit is depicted by interactions in space, that is, is portrayed as a field construct, perhaps it would be useful to explicitly assign *interaction* more importance as an ecological concept and *interaction field* more importance as an ecological unit. The units in common use, in both ecology and human ecology—eosystem, community, niche, and others—then, in this context, each can be characterized by the general designation of interaction field, yet none of the units so considered loses its individual identity or usefulness. This is a significant generalization, because the field concept is a more useful explanatory device, for both biological and human ecology, than more specific units have been. Ecosystem, for example, as a general unit is basically descriptive only of itself, while interaction, as a process, is definitive and incorporative not only of ecosystem but of *all* of the other basic units as well. Theoretically and conceptually, interaction can be considered (actually is) the denominator common to all. It is easy to subordinate ecological units to a general field concept in biological ecology because each unit is enabled by interactions of a different kind. Species is explained by intragroup reproductive interactions, niche by competition between similar species for scarce resources, community by all of the interactions among all of the species in a given space, and ecosystem by *in-situ* organism-environment interactions. In human ecology, it is not so easy, because each individual is involved in a greater number and a greater diversity of interaction fields at several different levels. To illustrate the concept, however, it might be useful to show how the three units assigned "top-ten" importance in the survey previously noted can be, and have been, elucidated—for both biological ecology and human ecology—explicitly by the process of interaction and explicitly as interaction fields.

System and Ecosystem

Tansley (1935, p. 305), when he coined the word ecosystem, underscored the importance of interactions, declaring that all parts of such a system may be regarded as interacting factors and suggesting that the prime task of ecology is to investigate "all the components of the ecosystem and ... the ways in which they interact." Evans (1956, p. 1127) reiterating Tansley's notion, described the basic ecological unit not only as an ecosystem but pronounced it as well an "interaction system." Gates (1968, p. 1) described an ecosystem "by definition" as the total sum of organisms and environment and of the "processes of interaction between and within all parts of the system." Margalef (1968, p. 4) claimed that ecology studies "systems at a level in which individuals or whole organisms may be considered elements of interaction." Even Eugene Odum (1971, p. 4) has indicated that it is "interaction with the physical environment at each level [that] produces characteristic functional systems." The common but neglected element in all of these is *a conception of the process of interaction as definitive of the unit of ecosystem in ecology*.

The point here should be reiterated and made as explicit as possible: "The most important attributes of a system are the regular interaction[s] ... of its parts" (Lidicker 1979, p. 475). More recently, Gabriel (1995, p. 347) quite matter-of-factly reemphasizes the same point: "System research is the process by which the nature of interactions among the components of a system are discovered" (see also Takahara and Nakano 1981; Allen and Hoekstra 1992, p. 28).

Other basic units in ecology, especially community and niche, may be explicitly described from the same conceptual process-perspective, and can be formulated just as readily in terms of the interaction process. Like ecosystem, they have in fact been so formulated traditionally, though without explicit recognition of the enabling and unifying power of the interactions within such units.

Community

Community is a central concept in both biological and human ecology, and in both is commonly empowered by interaction processes (cf. Murdock and Sutton 1974, pp. 329-333; Taylor 1992, pp. 52-60). Poplin (1972, p. vii) sanctioned the community concept in biological ecology solidly in interactional terms: "Ecological communities are groups of species living closely enough together for the potential of interaction." He emphasized that most up-to-date "contemporary questions in community ecology concern the existence, importance, looseness, transience, and contingency of interactions."

In a similar way, Kaufman (1959, p. 13) early warranted the use of community in the social sciences in emphatic interactional terms, as an association formed by the interaction process, taking place in a field context:

> The community field, like other interactional complexes, may be seen in terms of actors, associations, and process or phases of action, but what is its distinctiveness? How, especially in this complex world, does one find the community? Making explicit the criteria of community action which set off community from noncommunity is a crucial problem in interactional theory.

The problem may not be quite as Kaufman stated it, but achieving a sense of community remains a major problem for humans in the modern world. Many scholars echo Cooke's (1990, p. 4) claim that "modernity destroyed community and ... created new and more fragile bases for social interaction in the teeming cities to which rural dwellers migrated." But, even in very large cities, humans seek community, often falling short, yes, but still trying to attain some satisfaction with what they can cobble together as a token semblance of it in association with specified others.

Community, as the subject of an ongoing human quest, can be considered an icon of permanence as well as an index of change. The measure of stability as well as the degree and intensity of association are determined through the processes of interaction, which provide measures of belonging. But, when interactions are as complex and far-reaching as they are for many humans today, such associations are often loose and even noncommittal. The loss of community is widely deplored in the social science literature (cf. Nishio 1985; Keller 1988). But, as Young (1994) points out, when community is recognized as a derivative of the changing interaction process, the problem is really threefold: First, the need to re-establish a place to belong, a sense of local community with other humans; second, the need—in recognition of the extended reach of human interactions and impacts today—to establish a sense of world community, a commonwealth to which all humans belong; and, third, the need to re-establish closer connections with biological communities, with which humans constantly interact, to which they really do belong, and on which they absolutely depend.

Traditional communities are formed through the process of humans interacting with each other, usually in a localized place to form a relatively stable association of some kind—a kinship group, village, town, or city. These are all forms of community. The earth itself is a locale, now recognized as such by human travel into space. And, humans interact on a global scale, creating a need for, and a rationale of, consideration of the globe itself as a human community:

> Neighbourhoods are defined by proximity. Geography rather than communal ties or shared values brings neighbours together. People may dislike their neighbours, they may distrust or fear them, and they may even try to ignore or avoid them. But they cannot escape from the effects of sharing space with them. When the neighbourhood is the planet, moving to get away from bad neighbours is not an option (Commission on Gobal Governance 1995, pp. 43-44).

Just as dysfunctional is the alienation of so many people today from the diverse biological communities of which they are, whether they acknowledge it or not, necessarily a part, and on which they depend for sustenance. The majority of people in the world today live in large urban agglomerates, which seem to them far removed from the nature in which the species grew up. But people improvise! The shortcuts people take to achieve *commun*-ity with the biological collective are admirable and genuinely satisfying. The grimmest rows of Stalinist architecture in eastern European cities are cheered by window boxes full of red geraniums; or, you can just see a small tree peaking above the rail at the top of a tall U.S. apartment building. Real sacrifices are made to keep pets of various kinds. Urban populations escape en masse to the parks that the builders of most cities wisely set aside as a "substitute" for nature.

These alternate natures may be good for the urban psyche, but they can also mask the ignorance so many people exhibit: of where food comes from, of whether agriculture is sustainable, of what clear-cut logging does to the diversity of a natural forest, of the impacts their purchases of teak furniture may have on rain forests far removed from the comfort of their urban living rooms. All people are tied in to the earth's natural systems through a multitude of interactions, but too few are tuned in to the very real impacts this accelerating press of exchanges is causing. Rapidly changing interaction patterns are transforming and qualifying the concept of community in a multitude of ways.

Niche

Niche as a unit illuminates the role, place, or fitness of an organism in relation to others in the same system. Niche relationships are established, refined, and maintained by the interactions of each organism with others and with its environment. Niche is a well established unit in biological ecology and widely used in human ecology, though there is little agreement in the latter as to how the unit should be conceptualized.

Historically, niche in bioecology was limited to what has been called the Eltonian niche—the role a given species plays in a community, usually based on trophic interactions, with *gross* Eltonian niches including producers, consumers, decomposers, and so forth, and *specific* Eltonian niches described by particular food habits, such as grass eaters, or leaf eaters, or bird parasites. Hutchinson's (1965) revolution in niche theory changed the concept to a multidimensional space spelled out by the organism's total range of interactions in a community, or at least by those interactions judged significant or that could be empirically observed or measured. Hutchinson's concept of *fundamental niche* is commonly described as pre-interactive (where a species could live in accord with environmental conditions but unrestricted by competition) and *realized niche* as post-interactive, meaning the space "on the ground" actually occupied by a species interacting with competitors and other organisms.

Because niche as developed in biological ecology is a species-specific concept, it has proven difficult to adapt to human ecology because the modern human species uses its culture and technology to live in practically any habitat on earth. The species differentiation that is used to warrant the niche concept in the study of biological communities has no serviceable equivalent in human ecology. Human individuals do of course interact with other humans, with other organisms, and with their surroundings to carve out a place for themselves in the world, but individuals are not species, and no group concept exists (except the earth-wide total population of 5.6 billion) that portrays the organism and its niche (or niches) in quite the same way that species does. Some kind of multidimensional conception of human interaction, something equivalent to niche, is needed in human ecology to describe the total aggregate of relationships at the individual or small group level, but first the species problem has to be resolved.

Other Units: Population, Territory, and Range

In addition to the three stressed in the British poll, other ecological units are enabled as well by interaction processes. In biological ecology, a population is a group of members of the same species that live as a localized subset of a specific biotic community. In taxonomy, species are usually bounded reproductively, by breeding interactions, so a population, as a species-specific unit, is more narrowly depicted as a specific group in a specific place that interacts as a tightly related group.

Territory and home range are units that can also be conceptualized as units of interaction. Territoriality, like the others, seems to be both a product of the interaction process and an influence on it, the latter to the extent that territory tends to delimit, channel, and shape the quality of interactions between individuals of the same species. Home range is traced interactionally by the areal extent within which a given species (for example, the western larch) can exist, or over which an individual (for example, a grizzly) moves through the seasons. In all these units, interaction is the essential enabling process.

All ecological units then, can be first recognized, categorized, and represented as interaction fields—as units that are derivatives of the process of interaction. Ricklefs (1990, p. vii) clearly notes the centrality of the interaction process to the derivation of ecological units: "The structure and dynamics of populations, communities, and ecosystems express the activities of, and interactions among, the organisms they comprise."

HUMAN INTERACTIONS: CHANGING CONTEXTS IN SPACE AND TIME

Rachel Carson bluntly and explicitly stated the importance and centrality that the study of interactions should have in ecology. On the first page of the main text in her 1962 classic *Silent Spring*, she states that "*The history of life on earth has been a history of interactions* between living things and their surroundings" (p. 5, emphasis added). More recently, and more explicitly in human terms, Morin, Bocchi, and Ceruti (1991, p. 187) suggest that "toute *l'histoire de l'humanite est une histoire d'interaction* entre la biosphere et l'homme" (emphasis added); translation: The entire history of humanity is a history of the interaction between humans and the biosphere. Human interactions—between actors and actors and between actors and the environment—have changed radically through time, especially in what might be called "recent" history. Perhaps no characteristic of human history has changed so profoundly.

Humans of one sort or another have lived on earth for millions of years. For the vast majority of that time, they lived in small bands, perhaps 40 to 50 or so individuals. Their daily interactions were confined mostly to their own band and to the local environment (cf. Young 1991). Their actions and exchanges had little consequence outside of that specific and bounded realm. Such small human bands did eventually become dispersed throughout most of the earth, and interactions slowly multiplied, in number, extent, and consequence: Bands became tribes, and tribes traded with and warred upon other tribes. Gradually, as their cultures and technologies changed their ways of using their environments, some tribes settled into villages, some villages then expanded into towns and, eventually, as populations increased in number and in the intensity of interactions, what are today called nations emerged.

In the last few hundred years, explorers from these nations have probed the four corners of the globe, closely followed by settlers, mostly from Europe, initiating what was to be centuries of interactions and exchanges between the old world and the new (see Crosby 1972). With the Industrial Revolution, the capability for actions and interactions, to communicate and to exchange, expanded dramatically, and then accelerated so much that now, in the late twentieth century, "all the other occupants of planet Earth are of interactive consequence to each and every individual human" (Young 1991, p. 231). Bell (1973, p. 396) described the change eloquently:

> Technology has transformed our lives in more radical, yet more subtle, forms
> ... increasing the interactions—and consequently the "moral density," to use
> Durkheim's phrase—among [people] ... the change ... is not just the increase
> in numbers, but *the quantum jump in interactions* (emphasis added).

And interactions continue to expand and accelerate: Television, the telephone, UPS, Federal Express, the fax machine, e-mail, the Internet, and interactive media of all types—not to mention long-range weapons of espionage and war—make each of us more accessible, and more vulnerable, to a multitude of other people than ever before. Human ecology today is the ecology of a species interacting—with others of its own kind, with other species, and with the environment—in ever-accelerating ways on a global scale (cf. Scott 1974).

Transcendental Change

Some social scientists distinguish only two kinds of interaction: symbolic and nonsymbolic (see Weigert 1991, p. 354). These are used to distinguish between human interactions and the interactions of other creatures, an anthropocentric distinction reflected in a variety of labels, including biologic and reflective; nonsignificant and significant; behavioral and communicative; natural and social, and so on. Weigert (p. 354) goes on to note that the "paradigmatic cases concern interaction that is face to face or in organizational settings." Joining many scholars in human ecology, he suggests that it has become necessary in today's world to recognize a third kind of human interactions, those with the natural environment—which he calls transverse interactions or interactions with the Generalized Environmental Other. It might be added here that human interactions today, the interactions we are all involved in every day in many different ways, are not just transverse, they are *transcendental*, that is, they transcend, or go far beyond, the face-to-face exchanges and the physical exchanges with the near environment that too many of us recognize as the only "real" interactions. The number and pace of interactions that each of us is engaged in are changing at precipitous rates, much faster than many of us are prepared to deal with.

Grene (1989) and, more recently, Eldredge and Grene (1992, p. 11), make a dubious distinction between replicators and interactors, dubious because they admit that "we must look to the interactions of interactors and replicators to find the patterns of evolution, including, of course, the evolution of social systems." They are forced to admit that both of their categories are interactors, so they have not provided a real or acceptable categorical distinction. But, they are certainly correct that the biological context of social systems emerges from "the multifaceted interactions that occur among organisms" and that even replicators must be viewed as "part of a larger-scale plexus of interactions" (p. 89). It is more useful to disregard the false distinction noted and instead interpret their argument as calling for two different kinds of interactions—economic and reproductive—the traditional emphasis in evolutionary theory almost exclusively on reproductive interactions— and Eldredge and Grene making a case that more attention be paid to "the characteristic, repeated patterns of economic behavior of organisms of various different species that determines the interactive nature of local ecosystems" (pp. 112-113).

Back to Weigert, who, of course, is correct. As Eldredge and Grene claim that biologists have neglected economic interactions, it can be said that social scientists have generally neglected human interactions with the natural environment, focusing heavily on human-human symbolic interactions. That can be an encompassing category, but the modern, complex world also demands recognition of other categories of interaction. Freese (1988, p. 96) urges social theorists to go beyond the limitations of their tradition and admit that "the fabric of which social systems are woven is systemic interactions." Freese and Burke (1994, p. 18) reiterate that human conditions for interaction "are twofold— situational and systemic—and the kind of interaction in which they engage is likewise twofold—symbolic and resourceful," with the latter depending on signs rather than symbols.

Physics has long used a distinction between weak and strong interactions, which in terms of the differential and often transcendental reach of human interactions today, should have utility in human ecology (cf. Smith 1992). Another possibility is to examine the gender differences in the way people interact, which some writers (cf. Aries 1976; Fishman 1983) believe achieve categorical distinctiveness.

Another obvious but consequential category of interactions is "direct- indirect," or what Turney-High (1968) called primary and secondary. These labels apply equally to human-human interactions and to human- environment interactions. We are all still involved in direct interactions, of course, but "face-to-face" does not even begin to incorporate all the different kinds of interactions in which most of us are involved every day. Even face-to-face interactions range from the intimate and personal to the cold, impersonal, and distant, too often conducted with little meaning. For one thing, the number of such interactions can far exceed the ability of any individual to assign real meaning to them. So, we pick and choose, usually engaging in what we consider meaningful interactions with a relatively small number of significant others, and with a localized, significant place or environment.

But, again, all of us are engaged in a multitude of indirect interactions—whether directly meaningful to us or not, we *are* involved—and these interactions and their consequences and impacts often span the globe through the various means available to us today. In one sense, that means we are in contact with many more people and many more places than ever before. It is easier than it used to be for each of us to "stay in touch" with people far removed from us physically. It is also easier now for us to "know" about places that we have not physically experienced. Most educated Americans, for example, have some familiarity with the characteristics of a tropical rain forest, whether or not they have interacted directly with one by visit or by being in residence. But indirect interactions, especially in great numbers, can mean less intimate knowledge of people or of places, less direct understanding of the influences or impacts created by what Plumwood (1993, p. 57) called "the complexities of the dance of interaction." As Turney-High (1968, p. 185) indicated, "It would be hard to name a phenomenon of the twentieth century of more far-reaching importance than the increasing reliance of Western Civilization on secondary interactions and relationships and the decline of one's primary interactions and relationships not only in importance and intensity but in actual bulk amounts."

Humans have transcended the limitations imposed by distance in many ways, but that creates as many problems as it has solved. Most residents of urban industrial societies have much less intimate knowledge, and much less direct knowledge, of the environments that are the real sources of the goods they need than did the aborigines who sustained themselves in often hostile environments by a daily hands-on intimacy. Perceptions are different when interactions are secondary or indirect, awareness can be lessened, and responsibility for influences and impacts is more difficult to assess or even to recognize. Interactions over distance are normally construed as *instrumental* in nature; yes, you are in close contact with people at greater distances than ever before but closeness in transmission time does not necessarily result in closeness in human terms. Accelerating interactions that have gone far beyond traditional limits suggest a need for humans to follow that transcendence with new kinds of awareness and understanding that also surmount those limits.

Contingent Relations: Levels of Interaction

Human interactions have always been contingent. Each of us has now, and has always had, as Krutch (1953, p. 100) put it, our "realm of freedom as well as [our] realm of contingency." The behavior of humans is contingent on the nature and behavior of the group(s) with which they interact. What *we* do is at least in part contingent on what *they* do. It is contingent on the character and intrusiveness of the surroundings, and on the level of technology. However, after millions of years of relative stability, all those contingencies are now in constant change. And, many people now believe accelerating interactions are resulting in a dramatic increase in the contingent nature of all human relations, accompanied by a subsequent loss of degrees of freedom.

Humans today have to deal with interactions on a complex global scale, within a context of an approaching six billion other people, with interactions that take place in contexts revealed on many levels. Each of us interacts with other individuals, with family and extended family, with neighborhood and community, with city and county, with state and nation, with other nations, with various federations, and with the globe itself. Each of us also interacts as well with a variety of environments—many different *natural* environments, most modified to some degree—as well as with a host of human created *built* environments. These multiple interactions result in a human condition now contingent on new and manifold levels of existence, with new structures, new and complex organizations, numerous and diverse hierarchical organizations of great complexity—contingencies that modern humans have to learn to deal with. Interactions across many levels create a new and richer, but far more complex, context for human individuals in today's world.

Lind (1987, p. 242) takes a traditional social science approach to ordering this variety by suggesting that "the interactions of individual actors define the *micro* level; the interactions of collective actors define the *macro* level." But interactions between humans and other humans, and between humans and a variety of environments, occur at *every* level and on many levels however depicted. Such interactions help individuals anction their own existence and identity, and require them to transcend themselves. As Rumelhart and McClelland (1985, p. 196) note, "th objects of macro theory can be viewed as *emerging from* interaction of the particles [or individuals] described at the micro level." Th interaction process works across levels and links them in elastic an almost infinite ways.

A venerable and widely accepted interdisciplinary way of dealing wit a complex of interacting levels is by recognizing that interaction inevitably create hierarchical connections. Pattee (1973, p. 132) is clea even adamant, about the importance of the interaction process in th creation of complex systems: "The most common and most concret concept we associate with hierarchical organization is *the concept c discrete but interacting levels*" (emphasis added). Gould (1983, p. 175 notes that, "in hierarchy models, levels are not independent, walled o1 by impenetrable boundaries from those above and below. *Levels lea. and interact*" (emphasis added). Grobstein (1965, p. 38) takes this ide closer to human ecology: "Life is characterized by a hierarchy c structure and of functional control that spans the range from th minuteness of atomic and molecular *interactions* to the relativel enormous communication distances achieved by human society i ordering itself." He goes on to emphasize that reality can be recovere "only in ultimate syntheses of all ... conceptions, including .. elaboration of the interaction between the levels" (p. 43). Grobstei could not be more specific: "The operative words ... are interactio and hierarchy, with successively more complex units having succesivel more complex interactions" (p. 38).

Identity and the Realization of Self

Until recently, self-identity and meaning for humans, which Evernde (1993, p. 42) described as "a field of existence designated 'self,'" wa typically realized in small groups—Cooley's (1920, pp. 23-31) primar groups of family, community, and tribe—and localized in specifi places. This was and is the face-to-face interaction already discusse and thought to be "fundamental in forming the social nature and ideal of the individual" (Cooley 1920, p. 23). From this was thought to resul a secure identity created in clearly personal terms, a process Niebuh (1955, p. 30) described as "the dialogue between the self and others, and that Hadden and Lester (1978, p. 331) could summarize as "talkin identity." But, as Evernden (1993, p. 45) suggests, humans also nee to recognize the importance of the whole complex of surroundings, eve suggesting "the extension of self into setting" and the need for people to regard "parts of [their] environment as belonging to [their] field of self."

Connections to and interactions with local groups and places still happen today, in fact in much greater numbers, but in many cases they have become less personal and often they make less of a contribution than before to the process of creating a positive identity. It is also easier today to "get out of the group," to be less totally integrated into small, immediate groups, as well as to live in a place but not to know it or to really consider oneself part of it. Many of us live in fragmented families, in communities of strangers, and in places to which we are indifferent or that are alien to us. Vidich and Bensman (1968, p. vii) in a well-known early study described "the penetration of the 'isolated' community by the agencies and culture of mass institutions." A more recent example is provided by Cerulo, Ruane, and Chayko (1992), who point out that interactions through the mass media make it all too easy for individuals to diminish regular personal contact with traditional primary groups, who connect instead with powerful media personalities and with similar but unknown media-targeted consumer groups of other individuals. Another example emerges from Etchelecou's (1991) study of 182 rural communities in the Pyrenees Occidentales in France. He concluded that location as the cornerstone of identity is giving way, even outside the cities, as people become more mobile and interact on increasingly larger scales. Krebbs (1992, p. 121), on the other hand, relates modern human interaction forms to the reality of age-old patterns to suggest that the "post-modern problem of identity" can be resolved *if only* humans remind themselves that life, as always, exists in, and must depend upon, dynamic, diverse, multilevel interactions, rather than the instrumental, mechanistic uniformity that marks so many human relationships in the modern age. That is a much too easy "if only." Conceivably, each individual human can take the responsibility for personalizing interactions to the fullest extent possible. We can each take the opportunity to enlarge our awareness, to try and retain meaning as we transcend traditional boundaries and limitations, to turn possible negatives into rewarding positives. As Piaget (1977, p. xxiv) indicated, "No issue touches the thinking person more deeply than the relation of the individual to the world."

However disposed, the community still "provides a field of interaction for the manifestation of collective involvement and the social definition of self" (Allen 1995, p. 51). Each of us as individual human beings still establishes our identity through interactions with people and place. But, the multitude of inputs has accelerated those interactions to the point that contact groups for many people may be too large and complex, and contact with place too superficial and instrumental, for identities to be unconditionally clear and persistently stable. Thayer (1972, p. 48), for example, blames the expanded, complex hierarchies of modern life, suggesting that "hierarchy compels us to impersonalize all social interaction, thus making it impossible to realize ourselves." That is far too simple because hierarchical structures can be and are interactive and connective, and should not be defined solely by the dominance hierarchies that Thayer is condemning (cf. Young 1992). The dilemma though, *is* still a question of scale: Individual human beings have difficulty relating to great complexity even when it is ordered. Order is achieved through hierarchization; once hierarchies are identified, order does become recognizable, identifiable, and more accessible, but so does recognition that each successive level is once removed, twice removed, three times removed, from the individual. Relationships may have been identified—and realized and/or maintained through various forms of interaction—but they may seem remote, even detached. The rapid increase in the number of criminal gangs in even midsize American cities, and the formation of local militias in so many parts of the United States, especially in the West, are examples of groups who are acting on feelings of remoteness and on beliefs in detachment from levels of authority any higher than their own local leaders.

Boulding (1956, p. 201) claimed that a phenomenon "of almost universal significance for all disciplines is that of the interaction of an 'individual' of some kind with its environment." Lewontin's (1990, p. 45) comment remains as true as ever, that "Every individual in every species is the unique consequence of a development process that is, at every moment, an interaction between the internal and external, between genes and environment." As Evernden (1993, p. 46) notes, "Ultimately we must all invest ourselves in the world.... the fundamental fact of our existence is our involvement with the world." That world, as Merleau-Ponty (1962, p. xi) claimed, "is the natural setting of, and field for, all my thoughts and all my explicit perceptions," so each human needs to create a self cognizant of the world of its own time. The impinging environment for humans now transcends the local and the immediate and involves interactions on complex sets of multiple scales.

The Public Interest

The idea of a *public* is closely akin to that of community: an association of all the people constituting an aggregate on some common ground. A public is delimited by the interaction process, and the resulting notion of the character and extent of that public helps to shape, and to extend or to limit, the interactions of the people included, and to decide on those to be excluded. Traditionally localized and bounded, the public is a community concept that has expanded to the national level, and is now expanding, perhaps, to the international level. Political leaders often justify their decisions, and limit them, as being for *the public good*—the public here defined as all the people within a given political boundary.

But when human interactions spill over such boundaries, as they now do continuously, then how should "public" and "public interest" be reinterpreted? Accelerated inteactions that transcend boundaries make an already nebulous concept even more vague, but perhaps also more critical, more crucial to civility and order in our time. The public interest is a concept strongly related to the ethical foundations of a society and to the idea that contemporary institutions (notably those of a decision-making nature) are externalized. Thus individuals are too often buffered from those decisions that so markedly affect their lives.

Private interest functions in human associations in which individuals or designated groups can experience and control consequences directly. When consequences of human association cannot be experienced and controlled directly, which is the case in most contemporary societies, then public interest is generated. As John Dewey (1927, p. 126) observed, in this "new age of human relationships ... conjoint and interacting behaviors" that result in "indirect, extensive, enduring and serious consequences ... call a public into existence having a common interest in controlling these consequences."

The so-called Wise Use Movement in the western United States provides a current example of the conflict between private use and public interest. Many livestock ranchers in the West not only do not want to be held accountable for environmental impacts that spill over from their own private property, but also believe that their personal and local interests should prevail over any larger public interest on federally owned lands in their area, even if that interest means only short-term gain and even if it results in degradation of the range. An interactional blueprint of the public interest demands recognition of the ways in which human interactions are changing and impinging on others, even changing what humans may do on private property, if the resulting impacts are not contained within the bounds of that property—and increasingly they are not. Such recognition may enlarge the concepts of public and public interest considerably, making them more difficult of denotation but potentially more significant, as measures of the impacts and extent of human decision making (public or private) about other people and about a myriad of environments become more apparent.

MEDIATION OF INTERACTIONS

Throughout the millenia of human existence, people have developed techniques to mediate interactions between individual humans and between groups of humans. Kinship systems are one obvious way in which mediation was accomplished and maintained among pre-modern bands of humans. In contemporary societies, kinship ties are still used to mediate interactions, but have weakened because interactions have increased so drastically, in number and in extent, and because the diverse ways in which mediation is needed far transcend the reach of most kinship groups. Arguably, the current era is different from all but the very recent past, with sustained accelerations in human interactions creating what might be called a vexatious antinomium period, one of paradox, contradiction, and widespread conflict. As exchanges (interactions) between humans become potentially even more chaotic, as human actions and behaviors increasingly impinge on other humans, as we increasingly get in each others' way, sundry forms of mediation are increasingly required—some means of effecting controlled limits on action and behavior.

The ways in which humans mediate interactions, and the changes they must make to mediate accelerating interactions, have necessarily become a central concern in human ecology (see Pratt 1992, pp. 510-511). A strong case can be made, as Allen (1995, p. 51) indicates, for using interactional field theory as a "background for understanding the mediation of environmental disputes within a community framework." Mediation of human interactions in contemporary societies is accomplished through a hodgepodge of ethical systems, through increasingly elaborate institutions, and through the various instruments of law. These will each be explored, briefly, in turn, in a human ecological context.

Ethics

Caldwell (1970, p. 247) maintained that the greatest single cause of the ecological crisis of modern society has been that humans have "thus far failed to unite science and ethics in a manner adequate to guide, restrain, and control individual and collective behavior in relation to the real world." How can such a union be achieved? The literature is large and ever-increasing on what is usually called environmental ethics, but scant indeed on what can be counted as a truly ecological approach to ethics. The recent anthology edited by Tucker and Grim (1993), for example, illustrates the difficulty ethicists in philosophy seem to have in distinguishing between "environmental" and "ecological." Further, scholarly thinking that uses a realistic conception of changing human interactions as a base for an ecological ethic is even less in evidence (for a hint of this approach, see Haan 1983).

Naturally we humans derive our sense of ethics from, and extend it to, only those with whom we interact. The more familiar the contact or association, the more intense and formal the need for an ethical (intervening) factor. Conversely, as human interaction fields become ever more global in scale, mediation (ethical?) systems to serve their essential function must follow suit. The actual process of interaction has accelerated and become global, but for many humans, perceptions of that reality remain too limited to comprehend this new complexity. Many of us continue to behave as though the number and intensity of interactions among people have not changed since the prehistoric isolation of tribal groups. In other words, our age-old systems of obligation to other humans, our tribal systems of ethics, are still critically needed, but have become too limited, almost anachronisms on the larger stage of accelerating interactions. Niebuhr (1965, pp. 84-105) stated it unequivocally: The chief source of the inhumanity of humans to humans "seems to be the tribal limits of [their] sense of obligation" to other people. We have failed to recognize the common humanity of all people or to admit the "fact of interconnection as a general principle of life" (Shepard 1969, p. 2).

All human societies seek to achieve a set of reciprocal rules by which to live, hoping to achieve an ordered association deriving from interaction as a sort of redemptive process. Accelerating interactions easily outpace such rules, especially as they are usually specific to a certain bounded group, a specificity different from neighboring groups. Evidence of that acceleration, and signs of the limitations of present rules, indicate a need for substantial expansion of what Goffman called the accommodative process: the tacit covenant by which everyone agrees to accommodate the interactions of others, to conduct themselves so as to maintain both their own "face and the faces of the other participants" (see Berman 1972, p. 2). These oaths of mutual acceptance, or miniature social contracts, are, on a limited scale, "reenacted by every one of us, unthinkingly, hundreds of times every day," a process that keeps "the forces of doubt, hate, and chaos away" (p. 2). Can we do it on a much larger scale?

In this context, interactions become the base for what may best be described as *humanistic ecology*. Humanism has always functioned as an educational tool in the creation of the human community by inculcating common ideals and by stressing the reciprocal responsibilities of humans. But it remains a constrained sort of tribalism; it cannot be considered true humanism if it does not recognize the radical changes in the nature of the human condition caused by dramatic extensions of interaction processes. Only through recognition that *all* people are human and to be respected as such, and that all life forms are unique and precious, can humanism be translated into an ethic that transcends the tribal boundaries of ethnic group, race, religion, nationality, or even species.

Increased interactions increase the potential for overlapping and subsequent conflict of interest:

> Multicultural communities are facing strains in many parts of the world. The partition of British India and the green line dividing Cyprus bear witness to the failure of the modern state to reconcile community and territory by substituting nationality for entrenched religious, ethnic, or linguistic sources of identity. But so, too, do riots in U.S. cities or the burnt-out homes of Belfast. And now many industrialized countries face the challenges of a new multiculturalism fueled by post-war migration. The more that people accept the logic of growing interdependence of human society, the more ready they will be to seek opportunities to overcome destructive notions of "otherness" and "separateness" and to find ways to work together (Commission on Global Governance 1995, p. 44).

Accepting the logic of increasing interactions that lead to growing interdependence, and finding ways to work together in this age of accelerating human interactions, demands some form of mediation or, more negatively, arbitration. If "ordered" interactions cannot be achieved through voluntary recognition of a common global humanity and an interdependent biosphere, with subsequent restraint (perhaps through a transcendent ethical system), then some sort of arbitration is more likely to be eventually imposed. The answer can be found in the original United Nations charter: "to practice tolerance and live together in peace with one another as good neighbours." It is sad that the human species may still be so immature that the United Nations, rather than viewed positively as a realization of a global human community, is seen too often as a threatening central authority with increasingly real dominion over heretofore sovereign nations. Failure by local populations to police their own actions and relationships to others, does increasingly raise that spectre of the United Nations as an enforcer, as world police, as *the* supreme central authority.

Institutions

All humans have the same basic needs—in broad terms, subsistence, reproduction, defense against negative environmental intrusions (e.g., excessive cold or heat, snow or rain, etc.), and defense against anxiety. And, to survive, all human groups must meet those needs in a dependable way; left to chance, to trial and error, the needs are less likely to be met, and the group in question is less likely to survive. Eldredge and Grene (1992, p. 143) root this firmly in the biological context of social systems: "Social fabric arises from the moment-by-moment interactions of local conspecifics in pursuit of the economic and reproductive aspects of their lives." Humans especially organize to try to ensure success in meeting their needs. They regularize—they *institutionalize*-ways of interacting with others and with their surroundings to meet those needs, ways that over time have proven successful and dependable. In this sense, "institution" is defined as a regular, recurrent behavior set developed by a particular culture, a set of socially structured behaviors (usually) developed in response to a given need. Both basic needs and the notion of an institutional response can be generalized to all humans, but each group develops culture-specific institutional responses, for example, particularized techniques of food production and distribution to meet the general need for subsistence, localized forms of marriage and kinship to meet the species-wide need for reproduction, and so on.

In pre-industrial cultures, these regular, recurrent behavior sets became part of the adaptive skills small human groups used to survive in a localized environment. All members used the behavior sets to successfully interact with their surroundings to satisfy basic needs—the institutions inhered in each individual. All individuals, with the simple exception of some division of labor by sex, knew those techniques developed by their group to best ensure success in meeting their specific needs. Each individual interacted directly with and was intimately involved with the local environment. In the complex world of modern urban, industrial societies, however, the behaviors necessary, for example, to provide food to large, dense aggregates of humans cannot be met by broad-based individual skills and hands-on knowledge in dealing, every day, with the far-flung sources, the detailed processing, and the extensive transport of enormous quantities of provisions. Instead, specialized knowledge and expertise reside in groups trained in specific skills who focus on one part of the whole. Now, the behavior sets and adaptive skills have become external to individuals. The institutions—for example, specialized food producers and wholesale and retail grocers, one-task hospitals and schools, various agencies and corporate entities—come into existence as intermediaries *between* humans and the environment (especially the natural environment) from which people do still draw sustenance and other needs. Institutions are traditionally mediators between humans and humans and between humans and their surroundings—and they retain that mediating role today. But, institutions have now also become physical presences external to human individuals, presences especially manifest between individuals and the natural environment. For many purposes and in many ways, many humans now interact with (and/or through) these large institutions rather than directly with the natural environment. This results in the mass of people in urban societies being less closely connected to, less intimate with, and less knowledgeable about, those environments on which they do yet depend. That marks a regression not an advance in the processes of mediation.

Law

Many writers have suggested, as Burton (1995, p. 4) recently did, that "people who live in proximity to one another will find themselves at times in disputes—controversies in which two or more persons claim incompatible rights," disputes that become more likely as interactions increase and accelerate. We read about such disputes in the newspaper every day, disputes of every kind and at every scale. The disputes sometimes seem as frequent and varied as the interactions, and they may often seem trivial, but even petty conflicts can assume outsize importance and thus may provide particularly good illustrations of the kinds of problems faced by interacting individuals or groups of humans. Brautigan (1994), for example, discusses the legal regulation of noise problems caused by car horns and car alarm systems, documenting the kinds of mean-spirited, even petty, vigilante action people sometimes take (spray painting offending cars, slashing tires, etc.) when such infringements become too frequent and too stressful: "Noise, or unwanted sound, is increasingly recognized as a serious and growing environmental and health problem, particularly in urban areas" (p. 392). Urban areas are where people are subject to the greatest frequency of interactions, including negative ones, but people everywhere are increasingly exposed to the negative impacts of human-human and human-environment interactions. In law (cf. Young 1976), one person's right (to freedom from unwanted intrusions, including pervasive noise) is the jural opposite of someone else's "no-right" (to incessant honking of a horn or the blaring of an untended security device).

In the United States, and in most nations, conflicts between people or over environmental impacts are or become matters of law and lead to litigation in the courts. Most laws are passed to mediate human interactions in some form, to bring balance and order to human affairs. Aristotle, in his *Politics*, stated it clearly: "Good law means good order." Burton (1995, p. 4) puts a contemporary spin on that with his statement that "laws *prescribe* human conduct: they say how people *ought* to act" and interact. The driver of a single car in a level, open and otherwise unoccupied "field," could move in any direction at will, at any speed the car could achieve. Drivers of ten thousand cars in the same field, if they are to avoid conflicts, must be restricted in numerous ways, so traffic laws are enacted to mediate interactions among the ten thousand.

The same kinds of questions arise in conflicts where the individual actor is a nation rather than a single person or group. Individual nations today are still considered sovereign; but, how far may they pursue "sovereign rights" if such pursuits result in harm or deprivation to others in the world? How is such conflict to be mediated? In a world where interactions at every level—from individual to nation—can quickly spill over traditional boundaries, how can conciliation (and reconciliation) keep pace, and even be extended to transcend those same boundaries? And the questions widen even further, because many interactions are now regional and global, the impacts transnational or earth-wide!

As an example, as this paper is being written, Canada and the United States, sovereign nations, but also long-time friendly neighbors, are embroiled in a rather bitter imbroglio over the harvest of Chinook salmon in trans-boundary Pacific waters. As the dispute seems beyond settlement by the two immediate parties, especially because of the actions of one part of the United States (the state of Alaska), the central administrations of the two countries are turning to the next level of an interactive hierarchy—they are asking for mediation by a "higher authority," the United Nations. A similar example is the question of how effective one nation's laws can be in controlling the emissions of carbon dioxide into the global commons. The problem will not be solved unless all industrial—and industrializing—nations agree, and such agreement will depend on a willing diminishment of sovereignity, on effective trans-boundary laws.

The questions are raised again and again in people/environment and in people/people disputes: How effective is the international community in mediating the conficts between Serbs and Muslims in Bosnia? Between Tutsi and Hutu in Rwanda? Between Norway or Japan and other countries and organizations seeking to preserve the diversity of whale species in the world's oceans? Between Arab and Israeli in the Middle East? Between Catholic and protestant and the British in Northern Ireland? Between Mexico and the United States on the use of the waters of the Colorado River?

Human interactions are now transcending traditional boundaries—personal, tribal, state, regional, and national—in a multitude of ways and in runaway fashion. Fuller (1969) suggests that "if we view the law as providing guideposts for human interaction ... if we ... come to accept what may be called broadly an interactional view of law, many things would become clear that are now obscured by the prevailing conception of law as a one way projection of authority" (pp. 221-222). He goes on to make the claim quite explicit: it is "the elements of [human] interaction that create and give meaning to the law" (p. 195). As we interact in increasingly complex ways, we cannot forget that legal systems constitute frameworks "within which certain common expectations about the transactions, relationships, planned happenings, and accidents of daily life can be met" (Mermin 1982, p. 6). We must also now be thinking about what happens to human rights and human order as interactions continue to accelerate, while legal systems and other processes of mediation struggle to keep pace with the speed of change.

ALIENATION FROM INTERACTION

The ecological units presented earlier as interaction fields all imply at least some measure of success in achieving association, connectivity, or attachment among organisms. They implicitly suggest enough success in ordering the multiple interactions among humans and between humans and their various environments to at least form recognizable associations, units, and systems with some stability over time. Yet, many contemporary reports suggest that, in many places, for many people, just the opposite is also happening. In fact, they explicitly document failure after failure in the maintenance of affiliations arising from evolutionary changes in human interactions, breakdowns even among groups who have lived together for generations: tribal conflicts in Africa and Latin America, religious conflicts in Ireland and the Middle East, factional conflicts in south Asia, and ethnic conflicts in the former Yugoslavia, even intense and often abusive local conflicts between smokers and nonsmokers, to cite just a few. In the United States, anarchists and local militias deny the authority of officials at the national, state, and even the county level. They reject the idea that humans, at least in urban-industrial nations, do not live in small tribal groups anymore. They cannot accept the fact that localized groups, traditionally limited in space and in extent of interactons, and which historically could contain most actions *in situ* (or in which controls and limits were imposed by circumstances) can no longer do so. They refuse to acknowledge that their actions transcend their own persons or property or locale or tribe, and thus are subject to curtailment by a higher authority in the best interests of a greater public. They are hold-outs against what Freud called "the decisive step of civilization: asserting the power of the community" (Lewis 1995). The Commission on Global Governance noted, "As people bump against each other more frequently ... even minor differences become more evident and more contentious" (1995, p. 44). Kaplan (1994, p. 44) makes a compelling case for how problems resulting from changes in human interactions, changes that portend a coming anarchy—"scarcity, crime, overpopulation, tribalism, and disease—are rapidly destroying the social fabric of our planet."

So, in a human ecology where the interaction process is the keystone concept, a contrary idea should also be advanced: Despite the connective drive implicit in the interaction process, we humans are becoming increasingly estranged from each other in critical ways, and disconnected as well from the physical environment on which we depend. As Berry (1977, p. 137) described it, the "modern urban-industrial society is based on a series of radical disconnections between body and soul, husband and wife, marriage and community, community and the earth." The word *alienation* may be most appropriate to incorporate the idea of widespread, wide-ranging, and significant disjunctions in the interactions among peoples of the world and between people and their local *and* global environments.

Alienation is a complex and controversial topic, one not usually considered within the bounds of ecology as a discipline, either biological or human. However, if interaction can be accepted as a process that enables neighborhood and community to form among organisms, as well as enables the ecosystems that materialize from the interactions between organisms and their environment, then hindrances to the process must be given consideration as well. Yinger (1965), for example, set a very clear precedent for including alienation as a part of a field theory of human behavior. Alienation can mean a withdrawal from the "field of play," as if somehow the connective game of life was at an end—a withdrawal from direct and immediate interaction and a resulting separation and detachment from that which is no longer being interacted with, whether other humans or their environment, and it can include perceived withdrawals, detachments, or separations even if they are not necessarily real. Goffman (1957), for example, explicitly describes alienation *from* interaction. The implications for human ecology should be evident.

Many contemporary problems between humans and their natural environment issue from an evolving estrangement from that environment. Functionally, the connections between many humans and the natural environment become every day more remote. Fromm's (1941, pp. 138-139) timeless comment unfortunately still holds: modern humans' feelings

> of isolation (anomie) and powerlessness [are] increased still further by the character which all ... human relationships have assumed. The concrete relationship of one individual to another has lost its direct and human character and has assumed a spirit of manipulation and instrumentality.

That phrase about all human relationships today includes the natural environment: One can argue that we increasingly approach our natural environment as well in a "spirit of manipulation and instrumentality." Humans more and more are living in conditions described over a century ago (in 1844) by Marx (1972, p. 60), conditions in which people are dominated by forces of their own creation, which confront them "as alien objects exercising power over them." He went on to claim that "in tearing away from man the object of his production," people become estranged not only from the products of their labor, but are also estranged from the self, from each other, and from nature. The functional, concrete relationships enjoyed by our ancestors, more directly involved with their local, natural environment, are no longer accessible to most of us, a disconnection that has too often made of that environment an alien force, one that many humans feel it necessary to overcome, to conquer.

If community is the essential product of human interactions—of humans connected and in association of some sort—then alienation may be considered to be the antithesis of community, and may be seen as a function of increasing interactions accompanied by decreasing meaning and identity. It has long been understood that increases or decreases in interaction are at least in part a function of distance and scale. Such changes must also be a function of a context that is increasingly complex and diverse. In the contemporary world, our "modern" world, at some point and for too many people the bombardment of accelerating stimuli, the excitement, the effectiveness of the interaction process, starts to diminish and the frustration of overload, of breakdown, of withdrawal, of identity crises, begins. Schmitt (1994, p. 15) goes so far as to claim that "only if we use the concept of alienation can we talk about the ways in which social conditions ... damage many lives."

OVERLOAD AND STRESS

The rate at which interactions are accelerating—among individual humans and human groups, and between humans and all of earth's environments—means that both individuals and groups are finding it difficult to comprehend the ever-changing fields in which they must operate or to grasp the complexity of the ever-changing relationships in which they find themselves. Dealing with fifty other members of a band could be mediated largely through kinship ties; each member of the band knew how to treat every other member and stress in relationships was minimized. Today, each of us interacts, however intimately, or however indirectly or roundabout, with close to six billion increasingly significant others, plus a critically necessary and profoundly impacted global environment. We often do not know the best mode of behavior to exhibit with most of the people with whom we interact, many of whom are strangers, or who appear as "different," or who are connected only by instruments of the media. And most of us know so little about even our local environments—interactions also too often instrumentalized by technology and distanced by modern institutional forms—that again we don't know how to behave toward even our most immediate environments and are often unaware of the impacts our interactions have on them.

The conditions created by complex, accelerated interactions result in all kinds of stress within the complex of systems in which we humans have to operate: stresses on people, relationships, means of mediation, systems of exchange, infrastructure, and critical systems in the natural environment which in various ways must support all this increased activity. Unpredictable stresses are probable, as Passmore (1975, p. 259) suggests: "When [people] act on nature, they do not simply modify a particular quality of a particular substance. What they do rather, is to interact with a system of interactions, setting in process new interactions."

Numerous and repeated studies of animal populations have undeniably demonstrated that stress in populations is often closely related to density-dependent factors in the interaction process (cf. two pioneering studies by Christian, van Flyger, and Davis 1961; and Calhoun 1962). Such interaction factors as predation, parasitism, and competition in organisms other than humans operate to decrease density, to reduce the frequency of encounters when populations grow too large; a balance of sorts is achieved and maintained, though dynamic and uneven, and subject to influences from outside the system. Humans have come to think they are exempt from such self-correcting relationships, but such exemptions are illusory. Henig's (1995) comment, describing changes in Latin America, is typical of numerous reports appearing recently that discount the illusion and describe sharp jolts of reality: "A rapid increase in population throughout Latin America, combined with increasing poverty and rapid urbanization, led to conditions that were ripe for the spread of mosquito-borne disease," with predictable results: increases in such diseases as dengue hemorrhagic fever, yellow fever, and Lacrosse encephalitis. Despite modern medical technology many diseases are becoming, or may become, a bigger threat than in the recent past because of the increasing density of host (human) populations and the increasing resistance of the parasites. With human interactions quick and easy across global spaces, diseases can readily spread across borders, even from one continent to another.

Intraspecific competition may also ultimately be a decisive factor affecting human densities and interaction processes. One such is war, another is the competition for scarce resources, especially food and energy (witness the quick rush by the United States to defend oil supplies in Kuwait). These could become more operational—more frequent, dangerous, and unsettling—as numbers, associated demands, and presumptive conflicts, continue to escalate.

Social ills of all kinds may increasingly be a by-product of the complexity and superficiality of human interactions. The alienating power of overwhelming inputs from constantly accelerating interactions with expanding and ever more complex environments is increasing. The scale of human institutions and groupings has reached almost beyond individual comprehension. The reach and seduction of technology in the communications media threaten to turn large segments of populations into isolated "couch potatoes." Individual privacy is increasingly invaded as control factors are deemed necessary (by "authorities") to offset negative interactions.

Stress and overload can lead to unforeseen breakdowns in the full range of systems of which humans are a part and on which they depend. This includes breakdowns in the complex systems of which human individuals themselves are composed, breakdowns that can result in mental disintegration of various kinds, in deviance, or even death. The natural environments of the earth, massive and diverse as they are, are not impervious either to breakdowns, deterioration, disintegration, or even collapse, which could lead to a degradation of balances and services essential to human and other life. The carbon load in the earth's atmosphere, for example, has been approximately stable for a long time, but is presently being stressed by the large amounts of CO_2 that humans are loading into the system by burning fossil fuels. The result could be a breakdown in a global system vital to the well-being of all of the organisms living on the earth, including humans. The quest for answers to such problems may form the critical outlines of the blueprint set by the interaction concept for human ecology.

CONSPECTUS: PROCESS AND CHANGE IN HUMAN AFFAIRS

Paul Stern (1993, p. 1897) recently called for the development of a "second environmental science—one focused on human-environment interactions," a new science that "has the potential to travel along a path similar to that of ecology" (p. 1898). He goes on to claim that "although the science of human-environment interactions has been developing for decades, it has progressed slowly" (p. 1898). Part of the purpose of this paper has been to demonstrate that human ecology, as a manifold field focused on human-environment interactions, already parallels biological ecology in many ways, and that it has for some time explicitly claimed interaction as "essential to an understanding" of human-environmental relationships (Young 1974, p. 66). Indeed, human ecology has long focused on interaction as a fundamental concept, a focus that preceded Stern's directive by several decades. Stern's mandate is compromised also by a long established and singular focus in the environmental sciences on the impacts *only* of human actions, whereas the critical need is for the interactional perspective already so central to ecology. The mandate should be not for a new science, but for increased recognition and strengthening of a human ecology already defined by interaction processes, an ecology that gives full consideration to the human organism in its total range of conditions and impacts.

Saying that does not suggest that there is not considerable work to be done: further explicating and better ratifying, and communicating the importance, of interaction—both process and concept—in biological and human ecology; utilizing the interaction concept to more effectively integrate biological and human ecology; and finding more ways to use the interaction concept to solve real problems in the real world. Just recognizing the importance of interaction as a process and the remarkable changes in that process will take us a long way toward better understanding, and toward eventual solutions, of contemporary human-environment problems. As Brown (1971, p. 18) suggested, "A ... precondition for solving our problems is a realization that all of them are interlocked, with the result that they cannot be solved piecemeal. They must be approached as a *set* of problems, each of which *interacts* with the others."

A comment by Bell (1976, p. 23), can be adapted slightly to provide an adept summary of the problem: Human ecological knowledge is based less on "'orders of fact,' which can never be verified, [than on] matters of relations." In this paper, necessarily more provocative than determinative, matters of relations have been examined as an outgrowth of changes (accelerations, really) in human interactions through time and over space. Those changes and accelerations are dramatically qualifying all human relations in new ways, to other humans and to the earth as an environment. The necessity to deal with those changes and accelerations in human-human and human-environment interactions, so clearly evident in today's world, should now be changing the way ecologists think about their discipline, and the way we think about the whole dynamic complex of human-human and human-environment relations. As Lewontin, Rose, and Kamin (1984, p. 268) noted, "interactionism is the beginning of wisdom." Seeking that wisdom in a complex, fast-changing world soon entering a new milennium is a major task for scholars in human ecology.

REFERENCES

Adams, C.C. 1935. "The Relation of General Ecology to Human Ecology." *Ecology* 16(July): 316-335.

Allen, J.C. 1995. "Training Environmental Mediators: A Community-Based Approach." Pp. 49-59 in *Mediating Environmental Conflicts: Theory and Practice*, edited by J.W. Blackburn and W.M. Bruce. Westport, CT: Quorum Books.

Allen, T.F.H. and T.W. Hoekstra. 1992. *Toward a Unified Ecology*. New York: Columbia University Press.

Aries, E. 1976. "Interaction Patterns and Themes of Male, Female, and Mixed Groups." *Small Group Behavior* 6: 7-14.

Bassett, R.E. 1946. "Stouffer's Law as a Measure of Intergroup Contacts." *Sociometry* 9(May/August): 134-136.

Bates, M. 1956. "Process." Pp. 1136-1140 in *Man's Role in Changing the Face of the Earth*, edited by W.L. Thomas, Jr. Chicago: University of Chicago Press.

Bell, D. 1973. "Technology, Nature and Society: The Vicissitudes of Three World Views and the Confusion of Realms." *The American Scholar* 42(Summer): 385-404.

_____. 1976. "Lévi-Strauss and the Return to Rationalism: a Review of 'Structural Anthropology' by Claude Lévi-Strauss." *The New York Times Book Review* 125(March 14): 23-24.

Berman, M. 1972. "Book Review of 'Relations in Public: Microstudies in Public Order,' by Erving Goffman." *The New York Times Book Review* 121(February 27): 1-2, 10-18.

Beron, R A. 1994. *Social Psychology: Understanding Human Interaction*. Boston: Allyn & Bacon.

Berry, W. 1977. *The Unsettling of America: Culture and Agriculture*. San Francisco, CA: Sierra Club Books.

Boulding, K. 1956. "General Systems Theory: The Skeleton of Science." *Management Science* 2(April): 197-208.

Brautigan, S.N. 1994. "Rethinking the Regulation of Car Horns and Car Alarm Noise: An Incentive-Based Proposal to Help Restore Civility to Cities." *Columbia Journal of Environmental Law* 19: 391-444.

Brewer, R. 1994. *The Science of Ecology*, 2nd ed. Fort Worth, TX: Saunders College Publishing/ Harcourt Brace College Publishers.

Brown, H. 1971. "Scenario For An American Renaissance." *Saturday Review* 54(December 25): 18-19.

Burton, S.J. 1995. *An Introduction to Law and Legal Reasoning*, 2nd ed. Boston: Little, Brown and Company.

Caldwell, L.K. 1970. *Environment: A Challenge to Modern Society*. Garden City, NY: The Natural History Press.

Calhoun, J.B. 1962. "Population Density and Social Pathology." *Scientific American* 206(February): 139-148.

Carrothers, G.A.P. 1956. "An Historical Review of the Gravity and Potential Concepts of Human Interaction." *Journal of the American Institute for Planners* 22(Spring): 94-102.

Carson, R. 1962. *Silent Spring*. Boston: Houghton Mifflin.

Catton, W.R., Jr. 1966. *From Animistic to Naturalistic Sociology*. New York: McGraw-Hill.

Cerulo, K.A., J.M. Ruane, and M. Chayko. 1992. "Technological Ties That Bind: Media-Generated Primary Groups." *Communication Research* 19(February): 109-129.

Cherrett, J.M., ed. 1989. "Key Concepts: The Results of a Survey of Our Members' Opinions." Pp.1-16 in *Ecological Concepts: The Contribution of Ecology to an Understanding of the Natural World*. Oxford: Blackwell Scientific Publications.

Christian, J., J. Van Flyger, and D.R. Davis. 1961. "Phenomena Associated With Population Density." *Proceedings, National Academy of Sciences* 47(April): 428-449.

Commission on Global Governance. 1995. *Our Global Neighbourhood*. New York: Oxford University Press.

Cooke, P. 1990. "Locality, Structure and Agency: A Theoretical Analysis." *Cultural Anthropology* 5(February): 3-15.

Cooley, C.H. 1920. *Social Organization*. New York: Charles Scribner's Sons.

Crosby, A.W. 1972. *The Columbian Exchange*. Westport, CT: Greenwood Publishing.

Darling, F.F. 1963. "The Unity of Ecology." *Advancement of Science* 20(November): 297-306.

Dewey, J. 1927. *The Public and Its Problems*. New York: Henry Holt & Company.

Dodd, S.C. 1950. "The Interactance Hypothesis: A Gravity Model Fitting Physical Masses and Human Groups." *American Sociological Review* 15(April): 245-256.

Eldredge, N. and M. Grene. 1992. *Interactions: The Biological Context of Social Systems*. New York: Columbia University Press.

Etchelecou, A. 1991. "Population, Territory, Environment: A New Challenge for Social Regulation." *Sociologia Ruralis* 31: 300-308.

Evans, F.C. 1956. "Ecosystem as a Basic Unit in Ecology." *Science* 123(June 22): 1127-1128.

Evernden, N. 1993. *The Natural Alien: Humankind and Environment*, 2nd ed. Toronto: University of Toronto Press.

Fishman, P. 1983. "Interaction: The Work Women Do." Pp. 89-102 in *Language, Gender and Society*, edited by B. Thorne, C. Kramarea, and N. Henley. Rowley, MA: Newbury House.

Foon, A.E. 1987. "The Interpretive Conception of Social Interaction and the Logic of Deductive Explanation." *Social Psychology Quarterly* 50(March): 1-6.

Forbes, S.A. 1880. "On Some Interactions of Organisms." *Bulletin, Illinois State Laboratory of Natural History* 3(November): 3-17.

———. 1922. "The Humanizing of Ecology." *Ecology* 3(April): 89-92.

Ford, R.E. 1990. "The Dynamics of Human-Environment Interactions in the Tropical Montane Agrosystems of Rwanda: Implications for Economic Development and Environmental Stability." *Mountain Research and Development* 10(February): 43-63.

Freese, L. 1988. "Evolution and Sociogenesis: Part 2: Social Continuities." Pp. 91-118 in *Advances in Group Processes*, Vol. 5, edited by E.J. Lawler and B. Markovsky. Greenwich, CT: JAI Press.

Freese, L. and P.J. Burke. 1994. "Persons, Identities, and Social Interaction." Pp. 1-24 in *Advances In Group Processes,* Vol. 11, edited by B. Markovsky, K. Heimer, J. O'Brien, and E.J. Lawler. Greenwich, CT: JAI Press.

Fromm, E. 1941. *Escape From Freedom.* New York: Farrar and Rinehart.

Fuller, L.L. 1969. *The Morality of Law.* New Haven, CT: Yale University Press.

Gabriel, C.J. 1995. "Research in Support of Sustainable Agriculture." *BioScience* 45(May): 346-351.

Gates, D. 1968. "Toward Understanding Ecosystems." Pp. 1-35 in *Advances in Ecological Research*, Vol. 5, edited by J.B. Cragg. New York: Academic Press.

Goffman, E. 1957. "Alienation From Interaction." *Human Relations* 10: 47-60.

———. 1983. "The Interaction Order." *American Sociological Review* 48(February): 1-17.

Gould, S.J. 1983. *Hen's Teeth and Horse's Toes.* New York: W.W. Norton.

Grene, M. 1989. "Interaction and Evolution." Pp. 67-73 in *What the Philosophy of Biology Is*, edited by M. Ruse. Dordrecht/Boston: Kluwer Academic Publishers.

Grobstein, C. 1965. *The Strategy of Life.* San Francisco, CA: W.H. Freeman & Company.

Haan, N. 1983. "An Interactional Morality of Everyday Life." Pp. 218-250 in *Social Science as Moral Inquiry*, edited by N. Haan, R.N. Bellah, P. Rabinow, and W.M. Sullivan. New York: Columbia University Press.

Hadden, S.C. and M. Lester. 1978. "Talking Identity: The Production of 'Self' in Interaction." *Human Studies* 1(October): 331-356.

Hall, P.M. 1987. "Interactionism and the Study of Social Organization." *The Sociological Quarterly* 28(Spring): 1-22.

Henig, R.M. 1995. "The New Mosquito Menace." *The New York Times* 144(September 13): A17.

Hodder, I., ed. 1978. "Some Effects of Distance on Patterns of Human Interaction." Pp. 155-178 in *The Spatial Organization of Culture*. Pittsburg: University of Pittsburgh Press.

Holtz, W. 1967. "Field Theory and Literature." *The Centennial Review* 11(Fall): 532-548.

Huston, M., D. DeAngelis, and W. Post. 1988. "New Computer Models Unify Ecological Theory." *BioScience* 38(November): 682-691.

Hutchinson, G.E. 1965. "The Niche: An Abstractly Inhabited Hypervolume." Pp. 26-78 in *The Ecological Theatre and the Evolutionary Play*. New Haven, CT: Yale University Press.

Jørgensen, S.E., B.C. Patten, and M. Straskraba. 1992. "Ecosystems Emerging: Toward an Ecology of Complex Systems in a Complex Future." *Ecological Modelling* 62:1-27.

Kaplan, R.D. 1994. "The Coming Anarchy." *The Atlantic Monthly* 273(February): 44-76.

Kaufman, H.F. 1959. "Toward an Interactional Conception of Community." *Social Forces* 38(October): 8-17.

Keller, S. 1988. "The American Dream of Community: An Unfinished Agenda." *Sociological Forum* 3(Spring): 167-183.

Kemmis, D. 1995. *The Good City and the Good Life: Renewing the Sense of Community*. Boston, MA: Houghton Mifflin.

Kemper, T.D. and R. Collins. 1990. "Dimensions of Microinteraction." *The American Journal of Sociology* 96(July): 32-68.

Kormondy, E.J. and J.F. McCormick, eds. 1981. "Introduction." Pp. xxiii-xxviii in *Handbook of Contemporary Developments in World Ecology*. Westport, CT: Greenwood Press.

Krebbs, R.S., Jr. 1992. "Life: A Resolution to the Post-Modern Problem of Identity and Diversity." *History of European Ideas* 15(August): 121-126.

Krebs, C.J. 1994. *Ecology*, 4th ed. New York: HarperCollins College Publishers.

Krutch, J.W. 1953. *The Measure of Man: On Freedom, Human Values, Survival and the Modern Temper*. Indianapolis, IN: The Bobbs-Merrill Company.

LaBrecque, M. 1986. "Many—Body Problems." *Mosaic* 17(Spring): 2-13.

Leary, R.A. 1976. *Interaction Geometry: An Ecological Perspective*. St. Paul, MN: North Central Forest Experiment Station, U.S. Forest Service.

Lennard, H.L. and A. Bernstein. 1969. "Interaction Process as Context and System." Pp. 8-25 in *Patterns in Human Interaction*. San Francisco, CA: Jossey-Bass.

Lewin, K. 1951. *Field Theory in Social Science: Selected Papers*, edited by D. Cartwright. Westport, CT: Greenwood Press.

Lewis, A. 1995. "Is Reality Dawning?" *The New York Times* 144(July 31): A9.

Lewontin, R.C. 1990. "Are We Robots?" *The New York Review of Books* 37(September): 45.

Lewontin, R.C., S. Rose, and L. Kamin. 1984. *Not in Our Genes: Biology, Ideology, and Human Nature*. New York: Pantheon Books.

Lidicker, W.Z., Jr. 1979. "A Clarification of Interactions in Ecological Systems." *BioScience* 29(August): 475-477.

Lind, J.D. 1987. "Exchange Processes in History: Integrating the Micro and Macro Levels of Analysis." *The Sociological Quarterly* 28(Summer): 223-246.

Liverman, D. 1994. "Modeling Social Systems and Their Interaction with the Environment: A View From Geography." Pp. 67-78 in *Integrated Regional*

Models: Interactions Between Humans and Their Environment, edited by P.M. Groffman and G.E. Likens. New York: Chapman & Hall.

Lyman, S.M. 1988. "Symbolic Interactionism and Macrosociology." *Sociological Forum* 3(Spring): 295-301.

Margalef, R. 1968. *Perspectives in Ecological Theory*. Chicago: The University of Chicago Press.

Marx, K. 1972. "Estranged Labour." Pp. 56-67 in *The Marx-Engels Reader*, edited by R.C. Tucker. New York: W.W. Norton.

McCall, G.J. and J.L. Simmons. 1966. *Identities and Interactions*. New York: The Free Press.

McIntosh, R.P. 1985. *The Background of Ecology: Concept and Theory*. New York: Cambridge University Press.

Merleau-Ponty, M. 1962. *Phenomenology of Perception*, translated by C. Smith. New York: Humanities Press.

Mermin, S. 1982. *Law and the Legal System*. Boston: Little, Brown & Company.

Morin, E., G. Bocchi, and M. Ceruti. 1991. *Un Nouveau Commencement* [A New Beginning]. Paris: Editions Du Seuil.

Murdock, S.H. and W.A. Sutton, Jr. 1974. "The New Ecology and Community Theory: Similarities, Differences and Convergencies." *Rural Sociology* 39(Fall): 319-333.

Nelson, J.G. 1991. "Research in Human Ecology and Planning: An Interactive Adaptive Approach." *Canadian Geographer* 35: 114-127.

Newcomb, T.M., R. Turner, and P.E. Converse. 1965. *Social Psychology: The Study of Human Interaction*. New York: Holt, Rinehart & Winston.

Niebuhr, R. 1955. *The Self and the Dramas of History*. New York: Charles Scribner's Sons.

————. 1965. *Man's Nature and His Communities: Essays on the Dynamics and Enigmas of Man's Personal and Social Existence*. New York: Charles Scribner's Sons.

Nishio, J. 1985. "The Increase in Farmers Holding Side Jobs and the Resulting Transformation of Rural Life." *Japanese Sociological Review* 35(March): 32-50.

Odum, E. 1971. *Fundamentals of Ecology*, 3rd ed. Philadelphia, PA: W.B. Saunders Company.

Parsons, T. 1968. "Interaction." Pp. 429-471 in *International Encyclopedia of the Social Sciences*, Vol. 7, edited by D.L. Sills. New York: Macmillan.

Passmore, J. 1975. "Attitudes to Nature." Pp. 251-264 in *Nature and Conduct*, edited by R.S. Peters. New York: St. Martin's Press.

Pattee, H. 1973. *Hierarchy Theory: The Challenge of Complex Systems*. New York: George Braziller.

Piaget, J. 1977. *The Essential Piaget*, edited by H.E. Gruber and J.J. Voneche. New York: Basic Books.

Plumwood, V. 1993. *Feminism and the Mastery of Nature*. London: Routledge.

Poplin, D.E. 1972. *Communities: A Survey of Theories and Methods of Research*. New York: Macmillan.

Pratt, J. 1992. "Young's Conceptual Framework for an Interdisciplinary Human Ecology: A Critical Review." *Journal of Human Ecology* 3: 501-519.

Price, P.W., W.S. Gaud, and C.N. Slobodchikoff, eds. 1984. *A New Ecology: Novel Approaches to Interactive Systems.* New York: John Wiley & Sons.

Rawls, J. 1971. *A Theory of Justice.* Cambridge, MA: Belknap Press of Harvard University Press.

Ricklefs, R.E. 1990. *Ecology,* 3rd ed. New York: W.H. Freeman.

_____. 1993. *The Economy of Nature: A Textbook in Basic Ecology.* New York: W.H. Freeman.

Rumelhart, D.E. and J.L. McClelland. 1985. "Levels Indeed! A Response to Broadbent." *Journal of Experimental Psychology: General* 114(June): 193-197.

Schmitt, R. 1994. "Why Is the Concept of Alienation Important?" Pp. 1-20 in *Alienation and Social Criticism,* edited by R. Schmitt and T.E. Moody. Atlantic Highlands, NJ: Humanities Press International.

Scott, A.M. 1974. "The Global System and the Implications of Interactions." *International Interactions* 1:229-236.

Sears, P.B. 1954. "Human Ecology: A Problem in Synthesis." *Science* 120(December 10): 959-963.

_____. 1960. "The Place of Ecology in Science." *The American Naturalist* 94(May-June): 193-200.

Sells, S.B. 1963. "An Interactionist Looks at Environment." *American Psychologist* 18(November): 696-702.

Shanon, B. 1990. "What is Context?" *Journal for the Theory of Social Behavior* 20(June): 157-166.

Shepard, P. 1969. "Ecology and Man—A Viewpoint." Pp. 1-10 in *The Subversive Science: Essays Toward an Ecology of Man,* edited by P. Shepard and D. McKinley. Boston: Houghton Mifflin.

Slater, P.B. 1989. "A Field Theory of Spatial Interaction." *Environment and Planning A* 21(January): 121-126.

Smith, T.S. 1992. *Strong Interactions.* Chicago: The University of Chicago Press.

Spomer, G. 1973. "The Concepts of 'Interaction' and 'Operational Environment' in Environmental Analyses." *Ecology* 54(Winter): 200-204.

Stern, G.G. 1974. "B = f(P,E)." Pp. 559-568 in *Issues in Social Ecology,* edited by R.H. Moos and P.M. Insel. Palo Alto, CA: National Press Books.

Stern, P.C. 1993. "A Second Environmental Science: Human-Environment Interactions." *Science* 260(June 25): 1897-1899.

Stouffer, S.A. 1940. "Intervening Opportunities: A Theory Relating Mobility to Distance." *American Sociological Review* 5: 845-867.

Takahara, Y. and B. Nakano. 1981. "A Characterization of Interactions." *International Journal of General Systems* 7: 109-122.

Tansley, A.G. 1935. "The Use and Abuse of Vegetational Concepts and Terms." *Ecology* 16(July): 284-307.

Taylor, P. 1992. "Community." Pp. 52-60 in *Keywords in Evolutionary Biology,* edited by E. Fox-Keller and E.A. Lloyd. Cambridge, MA: Harvard University Press.

Thayer, F.C. 1972. "General System(s) Theory: The Promise That Could Not Be Kept." *Academy of Management Journal* 15(December): 481-494.

Thompson, J.N. 1982. *Interaction and Evolution.* New York: John Wiley & Sons.

Thoreau, H.D. 1973. *Walden.* Princeton, NJ: Princeton University Press.

Tucker, M.E. and J.A. Grim, eds. 1993. *Worldviews and Ecology.* Lewisburg, PA: Bucknell University Press.

Turner, J.F. 1988. *A Theory of Social Interaction.* Stanford, CA: Stanford University Press.

Turney-High, H.H. 1968. "Interaction and Transaction." Pp. 183-198 in *Man and System: Foundations for the Study of Human Relations.* New York: Appleton-Century-Crofts.

Ullman, E.L. 1980. *Geography as Spatial Interaction,* edited by R.R. Boyce. Seattle: University of Washington Press.

Vidich, A.J. and J. Bensman. 1968. *Small Town in Mass Society,* rev. ed. Princeton, NJ: Princeton University Press.

Walker, J., P.J.H. Sharpe, L.K. Penridge, and H. Wu. 1989. "Ecological Field Theory: The Concept and Field Tests." *Vegetation* 83: 81-95.

Watts, A. 1966. *The Book On the Taboo Against Knowing Who You Are.* New York: Collier Books.

Wiegert, A.J. 1991. "Transverse Interaction: A Pragmatic Perspective on Environment as Other." *Symbolic Interaction* 14(Fall): 353-363.

Whitehead, A.N. 1929. *Process and Reality.* New York: The Free Press.

Woodwell, G.F. 1978. "Eco-Forum: Paradigms Lost." *Bulletin Ecological Society of America* 59: 136-140.

Worster, D. 1994. *Nature's Economy: A History of Ecological Ideas,* 2nd ed. New York: Cambridge University Press.

Wu, H., P.J.H. Sharpe, J. Walker, and L.K. Penridge. 1985. "Ecological Field Theory: A Spatial Analysis of Resource Interference Among Plants." *Ecological Modelling* 29: 215-243.

Yinger, J.M. 1965. *Toward a Field Theory of Behavior.* New York: McGraw-Hill.

Young, G.L. 1974. "Human Ecology as an Interdisciplinary Concept: A Critical Inquiry." Pp. 1-105 in *Advances in Ecological Research,* Vol. 8, edited by A. Macfadyen. London: Academic Press.

——. 1976. "Environmental Law: Perspectives from Human Ecology." *Environmental Law* 6(Winter): 289-307.

——. 1989. *Interdisciplinary Human Ecology: A Conceptual Framework.* Lund, Sweden: University of Lund. (No. 1, *Acta Oecologia Hominis*).

——. 1991. "The Idea of Environment in a Historical Perspective of Human Population." *International Journal of Anthropology* 6: 231-238.

——. 1992. "Between the Atom and the Void: Hierarchy Theory in Human Ecology." Pp. 119-147 in *Advances in Human Ecology,* Vol. 1, edited by L. Freese. Greenwich, CT: JAI Press.

——. 1994. "Community With Three Faces: The Paradox of Community in Postmodern Life—With Illustrations From the United States and Japan." *Human Ecology Review* 1(Winter/Spring): 137-146.

EXPLORATIONS OF CULTURE AND NATURE:

ECOLOGICAL FEMINISM AND THE ENRICHMENT OF HUMAN ECOLOGY

Kari Marie Norgaard

ABSTRACT

Ecological feminism is an interdisciplinary perspective developing from a convergence in feminist and environmental theory. The range of perspectives within each parent discipline makes ecological feminism a broad subject. I describe three key ingredients of ecological feminism: (1) the position in which women and nature have been associated throughout Western culture and history, (2) the assertion that a common ideology underlies multiple forms of oppression, and (3) an explanation of how social and environmental problems reinforce one another. I argue that ecological feminism holds great potential for enriching theory in the field of human ecology. This claim is supported by applying ecological feminism to existing understanding of economics, demography, culture, and epistemology.

Advances in Human Ecology, Volume 5, pages 213-259.
Copyright © 1996 by JAI Press Inc.
All rights of reproduction in any form reserved.
ISBN: 0-7623-0029-9

INTRODUCTION

Academic interest in the relationship between humans and nature has coevolved with an environmental movement in the United States and worldwide. The public attention given to the environment in the 1970s spurred interest in human ecology. Similarly, social movements such as socialism and feminism have changed the content and directions of research and theory within social sciences. A new perspective on human-ecological interactions is now emerging in conjunction with a current social movement known as ecological feminism. In this paper I argue that ecological feminism contributes key understanding to the field of human ecology.

Ecological feminism, or ecofeminism, developed from a convergence of ideas within the feminist and environmental movements during the 1970s and 1980s (Merchant 1980; King 1989; Warren 1987; Caldecott and Leland 1983; Plant 1989; Diamond and Orenstein 1990). Similarities between the two movements, including their timing and social critiques, suggested that underneath these different movements lay a common perspective. It was noted, for example, that "both the women's movement and ecology movement are sharply critical of the costs of competition, aggression and domination arising from the market economy's modus operandi in nature and society" (Merchant 1980, p. xx). In fact, there exists a similarity in the critiques made by feminists and environmentalists of not only economics (see also Shiva 1988; Mies and Shiva 1993; Waring 1988), but the cultural (Heller 1993, 1994; Gaard 1993), ethical (Collard with Contrucci 1989; Warren 1987, 1990; Donovan 1993; Adams 1993; Kheel 1985, 1993; Cheney 1987; Plumwood 1991), political (Seager 1993), historical (Merchant 1980, 1989; Lahar 1993), demographic (Diamond 1994; Cuomo 1994) and epistemological (Rothschild 1983; Tuana 1989; Harding 1986, 1991; Keller 1985; Haraway 1988, 1991) systems of modern western society that shape human ecology.

While many "ecofeminists" are activists involved in social movements (Lahar 1991), ecofeminist theory is playing an increasing role in academic discourse within disciplines ranging from history and philosophy to economics and political science (e.g., Zimmerman 1987, 1994; Seager 1993; Plumwood 1986, 1988, 1989, 1993; Warren 1987, 1990; Merchant 1989). As an interdisciplinary perspective addressing cultural, ethical, economic, political, epistemological, and demographic aspects of human-ecological relationships, ecofeminism contributes substantially to the topic matter of human ecology. Just as there are multiple perspectives within both feminist and ecological theory, a number of perspectives have come to be considered as ecofeminist (Merchant 1990; Carlassare 1992; Lahar 1993; Warren 1987). Rather than giving descriptions of these specific varieties in this paper, I will illustrate the contribution of three elements of ecofeminist analyses to human ecology: (1) the description of a cultural association between women and nature (Griffin 1978; Warren 1990; Merchant 1980; Gruen 1993; Lahar 1991); (2) the theory that individual forms of domination (e.g., sexism, racism, the control of nature) arise from common underlying ideologies (Warren 1990; Plumwood 1993); and (3) the description of how specific forms of domination reinforce one another (Shiva 1988; Mies and Shiva 1993; Lahar 1991).

In this paper I will first outline key elements of an ecofeminist perspective and, second, describe how the application of this perspective enlarges an understanding of specific issues within the field of human ecology. While human ecologists are accustomed to the interchange between academic literature and material from the environmental movement, I expect the contribution of feminist perspectives will be new to most readers.

ECOFEMINIST ORIGINS: A BRIEF HISTORY OF FEMINIST AND ENVIRONMENTAL THEORY

The feminist and environmental movements each have a long history within the United States. Over this time period each movement has taken on different forms, and placed emphasis on different issues. Although the two movements may have held common elements or influenced one another in their early history due to their development within the same culture, it was during the 1960s that similarities became well defined. During the 1960s both the feminist and environmental movements entered a new phase. At this time there was a shift from addressing the specific conditions of either women or nonhuman nature, to more general critiques of the social system that produced the unsatisfactory conditions.

Both feminist and ecological theories have evolved by means of an interplay between activism within social movements and academic disciplines. The present phase of the environmental movement grew out of the wilderness preservation movement as scientific studies of

pollutants and environmental hazards indicated that environmenta
degradation had become widespread (e.g., Carson 1962; Meadows
Meadows, Randers, and Behrens 1972). Once in motion, the
environmental movement in turn applied pressure upon natural and
social scientists to devote further research attention to environmenta
problems. The women's or feminist movement in the United States arose
during the 1840s from women's desire to participate fully in society
including gaining the right to vote, attending universities, and obtaining
employment. Similarly, the present phase of the feminist movement has
challenged the social sciences to address those power relationship
within society that produce and reproduce systems of sexual inequality
as well as other forms of social domination (see, e.g., England 1993a
Stacey and Thorne 1985).

As with all theoretical frameworks, both environmental and feminis
thought have undergone an evolutionary process. In the case of these
two movements, the theory that emerged from these individua
movements has been powerfully similar, leading to the emergence o
ecological feminism or "ecofeminism" in the 1970s. Since this time
ecofeminism has gained much national and international attention. To
understand ecofeminist frameworks, as well as why they developed
some history of feminist and ecological perspectives individually wil
be necessary.

Growth and Change in the Environmental Movement and Environmental Theory

Environmental literature within the United States appears by the end
of the nineteenth century, most notably with the works of writers such
as John Muir (1901), George Perkins Marsh (1864), and Gifford
Pinchot (1910). Early environmentalists are usually characterized a
preservationists or conservationists depending on their emphasis upon
the preservation of scenic lands or the management of resources fo
continued human use (Nash 1973). Government agencies such as the
National Park Service grew from the preservationist philosophy while
the National Forest Service, and later the Bureau of Land Management
arose from conservationist perspectives. Controversy between the
philosophies of conservation and preservation continues in the moder
phase of the environmental movement.

In the 1960s and 1970s concern over factors such as pesticides (Carson
1962), the energy crisis, and the rate of growth in the human population

(Ehrlich 1968) initiated a new phase of the environmental movement. With this modern phase a much broader range of concerns gained attention as environmental issues (Pepper 1984).

By the late 1970s environmental theorists had generated a full scale critique of Western society, implicating cultural values, technology (Commoner 1967), religion (White 1967), ethics (Leopold 1948), economics (Daly and Cobb 1989), social and political structures (Schnaiberg 1980), and virtually every aspect of modern society as causes of environmental problems. Although initial discussions of these factors emphasized the significance of one element over another (such as the role of population versus technology), analyses began to develop that described population, social organization, technology, and environment as part of an "ecological complex" in which multiple factors were simultaneously operative. This understanding that multiple features of modern society were problematic for human ecological interactions led to discussions of an overall failure of modern western society, or of "modernity" (Giddens 1990; Norgaard 1994).

Modernity is the ideology of the scientific worldview coupled with the complex forms of social, economic, and political organization made possible through the material conditions of the industrial revolution. According to critics of modernity, both the belief structure of the scientific worldview (along with values such as individualism and competitiveness), and the material processes of industrialization, are problematic to human ecological relationships. Thus, scientific ideology coupled with a single conception of social progress, has led to the homogenization of both landscapes and cultures and a loss of social and biological diversity as westernization moves over the globe (Norgaard 1994). Meanwhile, through the development of macrosocieties, increasingly powerful technologies and the rise in human population, the industrial revolution is thought to have led to a dramatic increase in the degree of human impact upon ecological systems (Merchant 1989). For example, the development of hybrid seeds, chemical fertilizers, and other scientific technologies together with international corporate power structures have changed agricultural practices globally. Modern agricultural techniques significantly increase yields of specific crops, while decreasing social and biological diversity. Presently, many specific structural features of modernity are understood to accelerate human impacts on ecological systems (Schnaiberg 1980).

Following these widespread critiques of modern society, a search for alternative technologies, economic systems, and belief structures led to the development of theories such as deep ecology (Naess 1974; Deval and Sessions 1984) and social ecology (Bookchin 1982, 1990). These "radical" environmental philosophies distinguished themselves from "reform" environmental philosophies that addressed human ecological relationships using the existing values and frameworks of modern western society (Dunlap and Van Liere 1978; Dunlap 1984; Merchant 1990). In contrast, radical environmental philosophies asserted the need for a "deeper ecology," a "new environmental paradigm" (Dunlap and Van Liere 1978), or "a postmodern ecological worldview."

The environmental movement continued to change through the 1980 and 1990s. While environmentalists in the 1960s and 1970s had been primarily middle and upper class and white (Bullard 1990; Buttel and Flinn 1978; Mohai 1985), the diversity of people working on environmental issues expanded during the 1980s when it became evident that environmental hazards are differentially experienced along the lines of race, class, and sex (Bullard 1990, 1993; Bryant and Mohai 1992; Hamilton 1990, 1993). Spatial segregation by race and class within cities and counties has made it possible for corporations to locate environmentally damaging activities such as factories and hazardous waste sites in locations where the poor and people of color have greater exposure (Bryant and Mohai 1992). Environmental pollution in the form of toxic wastes, pesticides, and radiation have a particular impact on women and children. Following from their social roles as caretakers in the home and community women have played key roles in grassroots organizing efforts (Hamilton 1990). From these developments, it became clear that dominant groups such as industry have been able to force less powerful people to pay the costs of "externalities," such as air and water pollutants. Thus, the presence of poverty, sexism, and racism enables social elites, corporations, and industry to maintain an appearance of progress and success while engaging in activities that are damaging not only to individual communities but to global ecological systems. An understanding of social stratification along the lines of race class and sex expanded environmental analyses considerably by illustrating how social and ecological problems are fundamentally reinforcing.

During this same time period, environmentalists in less developed countries also emphasized the impact of social inequity upon environmental degradation (Guha 1989; Leff 1995). Such perspectives described how the resource extraction occurring with western capitalism was a continuation of earlier colonial relationships that had substantial adverse social and ecological consequences (Wallerstein 1974, 1979). Furthermore, it became clear that issues such as population growth rates and tropical deforestation were exacerbated by the wealth differences between rich and poor nations.

Over the past thirty years, theoretical perspectives within the modern environmental movement have moved from attempts to resolve specific issues within existing social structures, to the generation of increasingly complex (and problematic) political, cultural and economic critiques. Furthermore, although there exists no consensus among ecologists, present understanding of human ecological relationships now includes an emphasis upon the connections between social problems such as colonialism, poverty and racism, and environmental degradation (see, e.g., Daily, Ehrlich, and Ehrlich 1995; Dasgupta 1995). These developments have taken place as the environmental movement expanded to encompass the perspectives of a diversity of people both within and beyond the United States. Interestingly, these developments in ecological theory were paralleled by changes in a seemingly different body of thought within the social sciences.

Development of Feminist Thought

Although the American Declaration of Independence proclaimed the equality of "all men" in 1776, women did not win voting rights in the United States until 1920, or enter most universities until much later. Still, large differences exist between the status and quality of lives of women and men in the United States. In the United States women make up the majority of those under the poverty line, occupy a small minority of political offices, and earn approximately two-thirds the wages of men in corresponding positions. Although domestic violence is the largest single cause of injury to American women (U.S. Senate 1991), women's shelters, where available, are staffed by volunteers and run on shoestring budgets.

Liberal Feminism: "Add Women and Stir"

American women have organized formally to improve their living conditions since the mid-1800s. As has been the case for ecological thought, feminist theory has undergone substantial change over the past century. Before the "second wave" of the feminist movement in the 1960s, most feminists focused efforts on providing women with equal access to and rights within society, a perspective known as liberal feminism (Jaggar 1983; Tong 1989). Early waves of liberal feminism focused upon attaining suffrage, and now continue to challenge female inequality by fighting for issues such as women's legal rights and equality in the workplace. This liberal perspective has been characterized as the "add women and stir" approach because it does not question existing social structures, norms, and values but simply seeks to add women to society in its present form (Jaggar 1983; Tong 1989).

Questioning the Structure: Feminist Theory in the Second Wave

Similar to the transition within the environmental movement, during the 1960s and 1970s the feminist movement developed from a position of trying to modify existing structures to "fit women in," to the production of radical social critiques that illustrated how sexual inequality was produced and reproduced by multiple features of modern society (Jaggar 1983; Tong 1989; England 1993a). In contrast to the liberal solution of "adding women to the pie," Marxist, socialist cultural, and postmodern forms of feminism have described how the lower status of women is maintained by cultural norms and values, and economic and political structures within a society that systematically oppresses women (Jaggar 1983; Tong 1989; England 1993a). Unlike liberal feminism, these theories do not find a place to fit women into existing society. Instead, they declare that "the pie itself is rotten," and call for substantial social change.

In this vein, Marxist and socialist feminists have focused on the economic exploitation of women's labor within capitalist structures describing how men benefit from women's unpaid household labor (Collins and Gimenez 1990; Ward 1993; Shelton and Agger 1993) and from the lack of competition from women in the labor force. Cultural feminists give an alternative emphasis, by describing how traditional concepts of femininity and masculinity, or gender, shape society (Eisler 1988, 1995; Connell 1987). As the contribution of cultural feminism is of particular importance to ecofeminism, I will briefly outline this position.

Cultural Feminism and the Study of Gender

While the term sex refers to biological characteristics of female and male, the term gender describes the socially learned behaviors that comprise femininity and masculinity. Cultural feminists make a number of observations about gender. First, although gender characteristics and expectations differ cross-culturally and throughout history, at any given time gender expectations structure nearly every social situation (see, e.g., Goffman 1977; West and Zimmerman 1987; West and Fenstermaker 1993). Appropriate behaviors, social roles, occupations, and styles of language and interaction are different for women and men. Violation of these gender expectations is a socially deviant act likely to damage the credibility of the individual. Furthermore, cultural feminists describe how feminine and masculine characteristics are oppositional rather than independent categories (i.e., if a role, behavior, or occupation is considered masculine it is not considered feminine and vice versa) (Bem 1974; Plumwood 1993). Most significantly, characteristics and attributes associated with masculinity are valued above those associated with femininity. Thus, traits such as independence and individualism, important characteristics of masculinity (but considered inappropriate to femininity) are highly valued in American society. For example, mental health professionals asked to characterize a healthy female, male, and adult, used the same traits to describe a healthy adult and a healthy male. In contrast, the traits given for a healthy female were different and often contradictory to the description of a healthy adult (Broverman 1970). Such research on social expectations illustrates how men are socialized to be qualified for positions of social power, such as business executives, legislators, or presidents, while women are socialized to be unqualified for these social positions. Cultural feminists argue that when women and men are expected to behave in the appropriate feminine and masculine manner within a society where masculine characteristics and activities are more highly valued, the social construction of gender serves as a system of power.

With this "gender analysis," feminists have described how the division of women and men into rigidly defined gender roles together with the placement of a higher value upon "masculine" than "feminine" traits, in turn affects not only individual members of society but culture and social institutions. Feminists have described how gender has shaped ethical systems (Gilligan 1982; Larrabee 1993; Eisler 1988, 1995), economics (Waring 1988; England 1993b; Mies and Shiva 1993), epistemology (Harding 1986; Keller 1985), and national and international politics (Eisler 1988; Enloe 1989; Seager 1993).

Thus, since the second wave of the feminist movement, feminist theory has concerned itself not only with the status and conditions of women, but with social, cultural, and economic structures that produce and reproduce sexual inequality. Many of these feminist analyses of power apply not only to sexism but to other forms of social inequity, such as racism, classism, and heterosexism. However, just as environmental thought has been largely developed by white middle-class men, nearly all early feminist theory had been developed by white middle-class women.

Oppression from Multiple Directions: Race, Class, and Gender

During the 1970s and 1980s awareness of racism and classism within the U.S. women's movement (see, e.g., Collins 1990) initiated an expansion of feminist focus and theory. Early work by feminist and other social scientists that studied race, class, and gender had conceived of these as isolated variables that were considered to have "additive effects" when combined (Andersen 1993; Cole 1986; Collins 1990). However, with the additive-variable model a black woman is either black or a woman, and the study of gender focused on the experiences of white middle-class women, while studies of race focused on black, lower-class men, leaving invisible the experiences of those individuals in multiple "categories"—such as lower-class Native American women. By perpetuating the invisibility of lower status members of society, this approach continued to employ the very patterns feminists seek to eliminate. Recent feminist theory has studied the intersection between forms of oppression based upon race, class, and gender (see, e.g., Andersen 1993; Collins 1990). This newer scholarship encourages an understanding of how racial, class and sexual discrimination, as unique forms of oppression with both similarities and differences, together reinforce one another, creating "interactive" effects and a "matrix of domination" (Collins 1990).

Crossing the Border: Addressing the Lives of Women Worldwide

A growing understanding in the 1970s that the spread of western economic development to nonindustrialized regions had resulted in unexpected consequences for the lives of women led to the U.N. Decade for Women (from 1975-1985). During this decade, there was an increase in effort by university scientists and researchers within the United Nations to understand and improve the situation of women in developing regions. At the end of the decade however, it became apparent that western economic development policies were not improving conditions for women.

Research from this time illustrated that western male-oriented definitions of "development" and "work" as that which produced wages and market products, hid the importance of women's labor to society as a whole. An emphasis on men's activities had led agencies to focus on providing men with new skills and technologies without considering how these would impact existing land uses, gender roles, and social dynamics. The result was often to enlarge existing gaps between the status of women and men. Scholars such as Ester Boserup have described how the division of labor between women and men changed with economic developments such as cash crops that led from family to market production. Changes such as these led to benefits for men while increasing the workload for women (see, e.g., Boserup 1970; Sen and Grown 1987; Tinker 1990; Buvinic, Lycette, and McGreevey 1983; Davies 1983; Boulding 1980). Such research has indicated the need for new understandings and measures of development that recognize factors beyond GNP. A recent cross-national study finds that gender equity—the relative status of women and men—is strongly related to the quality of life in a nation as a whole (Eisler, Loye, and Norgaard 1995). This finding provides an alternative approach to understanding development, contradicting the common assumptions that GNP is the most important factor in understanding quality of life, or that gender-equity is a wealth-dependent variable.

This scholarship from the study of "women in development" frequently paralleled discussions by environmentalists of failures in international development (Norgaard 1994). In each case, research challenges the view that the spread of the scientific worldview and social structure of westernized nations will automatically benefit environmental quality and the status of women. The study of women in development expanded feminist theory, contributing to feminist understanding of the lives of women globally and adding substantially to existing feminist critiques of western economic, social, and epistemological structures (Shiva 1988).

Uniting Feminism and Ecology

Environmental and feminist perspectives have each expanded during the 1970s, 1980s, and 1990s with the increasing contributions of a diversity of voices. Both perspectives have shifted from initial attempts to adjust existing social and cultural frameworks, to the formation of radical critiques of modern society. Furthermore, in the process of moving from specific issues to deeper analyses, the two movements have produced increasingly similar critiques of the cultural, economic, and social systems which produced the unsatisfactory conditions. For example, both feminist and environmental perspectives have criticized the failure of existing economic structures to incorporate the activities of women and nature (Shiva 1988; Waring 1988; Daly and Cobb 1989); have critiqued mainstream western value systems, for their emphasis on individualism, materialism, and competition (Merchant 1990); and have criticized the philosophy and practices of western development and the epistemology of science upon which it all rests (Botkin 1990; Keller 1985; Harding 1986, 1991). Finally, both feminist and environmental frameworks have developed analyses in which multiple forms of oppression are understood to reinforce one another. The environmental movement has begun to take seriously the role of social factors such as imperialism and environmental racism in environmental degradation, while feminist theorists now address the ways in which multiple forms of social inequity such as racism, classism, and sexism are mutually reinforcing.

Based upon these and other similarities, many new social movement theorists and participants now view the feminist and environmental movements as part of a common emerging ideological system (Dalton and Kuechler 1990). This is not to say that all feminists are environmentalists, or conversely. Rather, it is to say that significant elements of each movement advocate many of the same underlying values and beliefs.

Standing alone, however, feminist and environmental theories lack not only individual contributions from the other field, but the deeper social critique that emerges from the examination of the common and mutually reinforcing aspects of sexism and the domination of nature. An ecofeminist perspective expands existing environmental critiques by addressing why human social systems are viewed as separate from ecological systems, why economic models leave out both the contributions of women and nature, and how the same cultural features are responsible for social and environmental problems. An ecofeminist perspective provides a powerful synthesis of the insights in these bodies of theory. Next, I will describe the body of ecofeminist theory, and then show more specifically how ecofeminist analyses enrich an understanding of human ecology.

THE ARRIVAL OF ECOFEMINISM

The perspectives that have been called ecofeminist are widely varied. Philosophers such as Karen Warren and Val Plumwood have focused on theoretical links between sexism and environmental degradation, while ecofeminist activists have worked in communities to protest toxic waste dumps or nuclear testing. Ecofeminists Greta Gaard and Yakov Gerome Garb have written about popular cultural imagery, while Carolyn Merchant's research has focused on social and ecological history. Riane Eisler has developed two comprehensive models of human history in which she describes "partnership" and "dominator" configurations of social structure. These conceptualizations link the dynamics of human social relationships with those expressed in human ecological relationships (Eisler 1988, 1995).

I will not attempt to delineate all the forms of ecofeminism that have been articulated. Extensive discussions of the varieties can be found elsewhere (see, e.g., Carlassare 1992; Merchant 1990). Rather, I will focus on three central elements of ecofeminist analysis: the historical and cultural association of women and nature, the theoretical links between sexism and the domination of nature, and the reinforcing qualities of sexism and environmental degradation.

There exists a popular misconception that all ecofeminists believe women to be biologically closer to nature. In the many varieties of ecofeminism, probably some ecofeminists do hold this viewpoint. Indeed, ecofeminism has strong roots in cultural and radical forms of feminism, those branches of feminism where essentialist viewpoints are most expressed. However, despite the fact that ecofeminism has been heavily criticized for this point (Bhiel 1991; Jackson 1994), one is hard pressed to find ecofeminist authors who make such a claim. What is readily apparent is the large body of literature describing cultural and historical associations between women and nature (Gruen 1993; Warren 1990; Heller 1993; Gaard 1993), a philosophical structure that links women and nature in the form of dualisms (Plumwood 1986, 1988, 1993), the way in which such associations have caused the actual lives of women to be closely intertwined with nonhuman nature (Shiva 1988), and descriptions of how this social construction has facilitated the domination of both women and nature (Warren 1990). Indeed, much attention has been given the need to reject the dualism that causes us to consider women closer to nature (Merchant 1980; Plumwood 1993). Misconceptions about ecofeminist viewpoints most likely arise from ecofeminist discussion of "revaluing" the connection between women and nature. However, because a central theme of ecofeminism is showing how all human activity is part of the activity of nature, ecofeminists believe that we must "revalue" not only the real connections of individual women to nature, but those of individual men, entire cultures, and social and economic institutions. This theme of recognizing connections between humans and nature will recur throughout this paper.

Women and Nature in Western Culture

Ecofeminists describe a cultural association between women and nature underlying the western worldview (Gruen 1993; Warren 1990; Heller 1993; Gaard 1993). This association leads to the "feminization" of nature and the earth, and to the "naturalization" of women and femininity. The feminization of nature is revealed by the use of sexualized phrases in describing nature, such as "mother earth," "virgin woods," and "the rape of the land." Images of women as "intuitive," "irrational" and "wild," notions that women instinctively know how to raise and nurture children, and biblical stories of women conversing with serpents, likewise imply that women are closer to nature.

Ecofeminists describe how perceptions of women and nature in culture, history, and philosophy are reproduced in the actual lives and experiences of the people living within the culture. For example, our concept of labor is split into productive and reproductive categories. Activities of reproduction—both biological and social—have been considered the domain of women, while productive activities are viewed as masculine (Ortner 1974; Shiva 1988; Plumwood 1993). Such conceptual divisions of labor affect the social roles of women and men, keeping women out of political roles (which are designed such that child care is incompatible) in industrialized countries, and keeping women in subsistence roles (farming and forestry) in nonindustrialized countries.

Women and Nature in Western History

The perception of parallels between feminism and environmentalism was first popularized with the publication of Susan Griffin's *Woman and Nature: The Roaring Inside Her* (1978) and Carolyn Merchant's, *The Death of Nature: Women, Ecology and The Scientific Revolution*

(1980). In these texts the authors describe links between women and nature in the history of European and American thought and experience. Literary images in the writings of Shakespeare, religious imagery in Christianity and pagan traditions, the works of Greek philosophers, and writings before and after the scientific revolution in Europe, are discussed and analyzed. Merchant and Griffin illustrate how the domination of women and nature continue to be interconnected in western culture today because of these historical associations. Furthermore, Merchant describes the scientific and industrial revolutions as precipitating a cultural transformation during which the dominant European view of nature changed from that of a living organism to an inanimate machine.

Other theorists, including Riane Eisler (1988, 1995) and Rosemary Radford Reuther (1975, 1993), also describe cultural changes that affect social and ecological relationships. These historical accounts place less emphasis on the scientific and industrial revolutions. While Eisler, Merchant, and Reuther all agree that social and ecological relationships have been more egalitarian at earlier points in human history, they each emphasize different social factors and time periods for these changes.

While Eisler does not specifically discuss relationships between women and nature, her account of cultural evolution describes how relationships between women and men impact overall social structure in a manner that applies directly to ecofeminist analyses. Eisler's research proceeds from the premise that because humanity is composed of two halves—women and men—the social construction of gender roles and relations is a key variable in a society's institutions, values, and the development and allocation of economic resources. Using this perspective, Eisler identifies an underlying pattern to present society and cultural evolution. Her work describes a dominator model of social organization, in which gender inequity prevails, and a partnership model of social organization, distinguished by gender equity (Eisler 1988, 1995). Eisler's research describes the prevalence of a partnership model of social organization during the Neolithic period in western Europe, after which time a dominator model prevailed. Eisler considers the present environmental, feminist, peace, and other "new social movements" to be expressions of the partnership model.

Rosemary Radford Reuther reviews anthropological studies to conclude that the association of women and nature is widespread and occurred early in human history as an outgrowth of social roles (see, e.g., Ortner 1974). Reuther (1993) describes how,

Although there is considerable variation of these patterns cross-culturally, generally males situated themselves in work that was both more prestigious and more occasional, demanding bursts of energy, such as hunting larger animals, war and clearing fields, but allowing them more space for leisure. This is the primary social base for the male monopolization of culture (p. 15).

In *The Death of Nature: Women, Ecology and the Scientific Revolution* (1980), Merchant provides a detailed account of the imagery of women and nature before and after the scientific revolution. Merchant theorizes that nature and women have been historically associated because human life emerges from the body of a woman, while that which sustains life emerges from the body of the earth. Merchant (1983) describes human social and ecological relationships during medieval times as "organic." During these times social taboos forbade mining:

The image of the earth as a living organism and a nurturing mother has historically served as a cultural constraint restricting the actions of human beings.... As long as the earth was considered to be alive and sensitive it could be considered a breach of human ethical behavior to carry out destructive acts against it (p. 100).

According to Merchant's research, images of nature prior to the scientific revolution are of a feminine force that was alternately benevolent and unruly. Nature gave life and abundance when harvests were good, took it away when crops failed. Large scale catastrophes throughout western Europe, such as floods in the early 1300s leading to famine, and bubonic plague during the 1360s and 1370s, were physical conditions that made life difficult and uncertain. Merchant describes humans as living at the mercy of a "chaotic nature [that] needed to be controlled" (1983, p. 127).

With the beginning of the scientific revolution there developed, according to Merchant, changes in human ecological relationships. No longer so much at the mercy of soil conditions, pest outbreaks, or unseen weather patterns, humans were increasingly able to gather consistent yields from the land as the use of science expanded. With these changes, the powerful forces of women and nature were now tamed by science.

After the scientific revolution, Merchant (1980) describes how a new image replaced the old depictions of nature and women as alternately benevolent and chaotic. This new image was of an inert, passive, mechanistic system:

Two new ideas, those of mechanism and of the domination and mastery of nature, became core concepts of the modern world. An organically oriented mentality in which female principles played an important role was undermined and replaced by a mechanically oriented mentality that either eliminated or used female principles in an exploitative manner. As Western culture became increasingly mechanized in the 1600s, the female earth and the virgin earth spirit were subdued by the machine (p. 2).

Such metaphors of a mechanized nature were reflected in the writings of many of the important scientists of the times. For example, Astronomer Johannes Kepler wrote that "my aim is to show that the celestial machine is to be likened not to a divine organism but to a clockwork" (Kepler, cited in Merchant 1980, pp. 128-129).

Following the scientific revolution, control over nature and the feminine was established through the use of science; "man" was firmly in the realm of "culture," separate from and above "nature." Nature remained feminine, women remained wild, emotional, and chaotic. At this time, Merchant describes metaphors of the control of nature and feminine principles evident in the writings of Francis Bacon, Rene Descartes, and other key figures in the scientific revolution. Bacon sought a philosophy of science that would, "bind Nature to man's service and make her his slave," and promises to create, "a blessed race of heroes and supermen" who would dominate nature and society (Keller 1985, pp. 38-39). Similarly, Rene Descartes' *Discourse on Method* ([1637] 1956) described how the use of a reductionist scientific method would "render ourselves the masters and possessors of nature" (Merchant 1980, p. xv). It was thus the desire for control over both nature and the feminine that led men to define culture and science as that which is separate from nature. Lori Gruen (1993) writes:

Objective scientists rely on an epistemology that requires detachment and distance. This detachment serves as justification for the division between active pursuer of knowledge and passive object of investigation, and establishes the power of the former over the latter. By devaluing subjective experience and reducing living, spontaneous beings to machines to be studied and establishing an epistemic privilege based on detachment, reason, the mechanistic/scientific mindset firmly distinguished man from nature, women and animals (p. 64).

Belief in the powers of women to taint science was so strong that many of the founding fathers of science were uncomfortable with women in their personal lives. Both Issac Newton and Robert Boyle (founder of modern chemistry) preferred not to associate with women and took vows of celibacy.

Merchant's interpretations of a desire for science and technology to elevate humans above the constraints of nature, found in the writings of Bacon, Descartes and other early scientists, apply also to more recent theorists. For example, Karl Marx's theory of historical materialism has been interpreted to predict the "realization of the human will" and human liberation only with the domination of nature (Henderson 1989). Merchant's text is of significance to ecofeminists not only for providing a historical context for cultural associations of women and nature. This interpretation of the scientific revolution also provides a foundation for critiques of science, which will be discussed below.

Ecofeminist Philosophy: The Dualistic Worldview and the Logic of Domination

Although ecofeminism pays special attention to the position of women in society, ecofeminist philosophy describes how multiple power differences between groups, whether they are based on sex, sexuality, class, or race, are conceptually linked. In the words of Greta Gaard, "the ideology which authorizes oppression such as those based on race, class, gender, sexuality, physical abilities and species is the same ideology which sanctions the oppression of nature" (1993, p. 1). Ecofeminists such as Karen Warren and Val Plumwood describe this general pattern of thinking as characterized by a dualistic structure and a logic of domination which sanction each specific form of social inequity (Warren 1987, 1990; Plumwood 1986, 1988). Recognizing that specific forms of domination are supported by a common belief structure is a key point for ecofeminists. To strive for the equality of women, an end to the domination of nature, or the end of racial oppression, is pointless without addressing the common ideological framework underlying these individual processes. Warren explains the ecofeminist position that all forms of oppression are interrelated:

> Insofar as other systems of oppression (e.g., racism, classism, ageism, heterosexism) are also conceptually maintained by a logic of domination, appeal to the logic of traditional feminism ultimately locates the basic conceptual interconnections among *all* systems of oppression in the logic of domination. It thereby explains at a *conceptual* level why the eradication of sexist oppression requires the eradication of the other forms of oppression (Warren 1990, p. 132).

Ecofeminist theorists and feminist philosophers of science describe modern western culture as based on a series of oppositional categories or dualisms (King 1981, 1989, 1990; Plumwood 1986, 1988, 1989, 1993; Warren 1987, 1990). Of particular importance are the dualisms between culture/nature, masculine/feminine, objective/subjective, reason/emotion, public/private, production/reproduction, civilized/primitive, and order/chaos (Plumwood 1993). Because a dualistic conceptual framework both sanctions and enables the oppression of women and nature, ecofeminists argue that understanding the dualistic character of western thought is key in making visible the operation of systems of domination. In *Feminism and the Domination of Nature*, Plumwood (1993) describes the ecofeminist perspective that,

> dualisms are not just free-floating systems of ideas; they are closely associated with domination and accumulation, and are their major cultural expressions and justifications ... (dualisms) reflect the major forms of oppression in western culture. In particular, the dualisms of male/female, mental/manual (mind/body), civilized/primitive, human/nature correspond directly to and naturalize gender, class, race and nature oppression respectively, although a number of others are indirectly involved (pp. 42-43).

Unlike other distinctions, ecofeminists describe how a dualistic structure sets up a very specific arrangement between two qualities or conditions. Dualisms are characterized by an oppositional arrangement, such that one is either masculine or feminine, civilized or primitive, acting with reason or acting with emotion, part of culture or part of nature. Furthermore, within the dualism one element is always valued above the other, for example, masculine traits are considered superior to feminine, civilized is considered superior to primitive, using reason is considered superior to using emotion. Plumwood (1993) describes this oppositional and hierarchial nature of dualisms:

> In dualism the more highly valued side (males, humans) is constructed as alien to and of a different nature or order of being from the "lower" inferiorised side (women, nature) and each is treated as lacking in qualities which make possible overlap, kinship or continuity. The nature of each is constructed in polarized ways by the exclusion of qualities shared with the other (p. 32).

Items on the up or down side of the dualism are linked together to form an interlocking structure such that women and the feminine are culturally associated with the private sphere, emotion, chaos, subjectivity, and nature, while men are associated with the public sphere, reason, order, objectivity, and culture.

Ecological feminists find dualistic thinking problematic for several reasons. By valuing one element above another, a dualistic structuring of the world clearly facilitates and justifies power differences. This is an expansion of the point made by cultural feminists regarding the dualism between femininity and masculinity. Second, the either/or framework of the dualism exaggerates differences between the two groups, polarizing concepts such as emotion and reason, culture and nature, or the roles of women and men. By homogenizing elements, this polarizing framework obscures the qualities of elements within each category. Thus, association of the dualisms man/woman and strong/weak carries not only the idea that "men are strong, women are weak." Because strong and weak are understood as dualistic categories instead of qualities on a continuum, the linking of these dualisms indicates that "all men are equally strong, all women are equally weak." Plumwood (1993) describes how "Homogenization is a feature of the master's perspective. To the master residing at what he takes to be the center, differences among those of lesser status at the periphery are of little interest or importance and might undermine comfortable stereotypes of superiority" (p. 54). Consider the common social notions that women are unfit for construction work or military service because they are not physically strong. Although many women in the United States have much larger body types and are often stronger than men throughout much of the world (e.g., Latin America and Asia), such observations about differences within groups are discouraged by a conceptual structure that polarizes male/female and strong/weak into dualisms. Instead, the obvious observation that women as a group are not as strong as men as a group, is transformed into the seemingly inevitable conclusion that women are not strong enough.

The linking of elements on the same side of each dualism further facilitates systems of domination. In the above example, the linkage of the male/female and strong/weak dualisms justifies the exclusion of women from certain activities and social spheres. The associations of women and femininity with emotions, a private sphere, and reproduction are key examples of other dualisms that have served to justify the exclusion of women from "masculine" roles and institutions.

Finally, ecofeminists find dualisms problematic because they set up a simultaneous relationship of dependency and its denial between elements. Dominant elements are always dependent on subordinate ones for their self-definition, and often for their material needs. False asymmetries result. For example, masculinity has been defined as that which is not feminine, or culture or society as that which is apart from nature. With this negative construction, masculinity can only be understood given the presence of femininity and culture/society with a background of nonhuman nature. Yet, although masculinity may be conceived in terms of independence, in fact men are dependent on mothers physically and emotionally as children, and on female friends, sisters, and wives emotionally (and physically if they desire offspring themselves) throughout their lives. Similarly, although culture/society is understood as that which is uniquely human and separate from nonhuman nature, the source of all matter and energy used by humans is the "natural" world. Plumwood (1993) describes this relationship of dependency of the dominant element for both self-definition and material needs:

> The master more than the slave requires the other in order to define his boundaries and identity, since these are defined *against* the inferiorised other ... it is the slave who makes the master a master, the colonized who make the colonizer, the periphery which makes the center. Second, the master also requires the other materially, in order to survive, for the relation of complementation has made the master dependent on the slave for fulfillment of his needs (p. 49).

The denial of human dependence on both nonhuman nature and women for the provision of food, water, and shelter is evidenced by their invisibility within western economic models. Rather, material processes such as nutrient cycling and forest growth are taken for granted and ignored, while within modern western society it has been expected that women will raise and nurture children. In both cases it is assumed that these activities will naturally occur, and that they are economically unimportant. The attempt to revalue and make visible the activities of nature and women has become the project of ecological and feminist economists.

This ecofeminist analysis of dualistic thinking expands the earlier "gender analysis" of cultural feminists, describing the polarization not only of feminine and masculine, but also how multiple dualistic structures and the dualistic perspective itself is a key element of domination. Karen Warren describes a "logic of domination" that justifies the subordination of both women and nature (1987, 1990, 1993). This logic of domination is "an argumentive structure that justifies the power and privilege of those who are 'Up' over those who are 'Down'" (1993, p. 123). Elsewhere (1990) she outlines the structure of the logic of domination as follows:

(A1)   Humans do, and plants and rocks do not, have the capacity to consciously and radically change the community in which they live.

(A2)   Whatever has the capacity to consciously and radically change the community in which it lives is morally superior to whatever lacks this capacity.

(A3)   Thus, humans are morally superior to plants and rocks.

(A4)   For any X and Y, if X is morally superior to Y, then X is morally justified in subordinating Y.

(A5)   Thus, humans are morally justified in subordinating plants and rocks (p. 129).

According to Warren (1990),

A logic of domination is not just a logical structure. It also involves a substantive value system, since an ethical premise is needed to permit or sanction the "just" subordination of that which is subordinate. This justification typically is given on the grounds of some alleged characteristic (e.g., rationality) which the dominant (e.g., men) have and the subordinate (e.g., women) lack (p. 128).

Furthermore, the logic of domination is applied to women as well as nature by their mutual association:

Patriarchal conceptual frameworks that justify the domination of women also justify the domination of nonhuman nature by conceiving women and nature in terms which feminize nature, naturalize women, and position both women and nature as inferior to male-gender identified culture. Ecofeminist philosophers insist that the logic of domination used to justify sexism be recognized as also justifying naturism (Warren 1993, p. 123).

Warren (1990) gives a formal outline of this statement as follows:

(B1)   Women are identified with nature and the realm of the physical; men are identified with the "human" and the realm of the mental.

(B2)   Whatever is identified with nature and the realm of the physical is inferior to ("below") whatever is identified with the "human" and the realm of the mental; or, conversely, the latter is superior to ("above") the former.

(B3)   Thus, women are inferior to ("below") men; or conversely, men are superior to ("above") women.

(B4)   For any X and Y, if X is superior to Y, then X is justified in subordinating Y.

(B5)   Thus, men are justified in subordinating women (p. 130).

Because dualistic thinking and value-hierarchies are characterized as central organizational features of every ideology of domination, a central tenet of ecofeminism is that all forms of inequality must be addressed simultaneously.

Environmental Degradation and Social Inequality: Reinforcing Systems

Parallel to developments within feminist theory that began to link oppression on the basis of race, class, and gender (Collins 1990), ecofeminism is concerned with how race, class, and gender stratification and environmental degradation are reinforcing processes—interlocking systems that cannot be fully understood if studied in isolation. Stephanie Lahar (1991) explains how "the mutual exclusion that thinking in conceptual dichotomies engenders makes us think that violence against women, militarism and the destruction of ecosystems are issues that can be analyzed separately." In contrast, "the central theme of most versions of ecofeminism, therefore is the inter-relationship and integration of personal, social and environmental issues" (p. 30).

Ecofeminist analyses of power structures should not be considered separate from or in opposition to other frameworks addressing oppression (such as specific theories on racism, class inequity, imperialism, capitalism, or socialism). Rather, a key element of an ecofeminist perspective is to ask how seemingly specific forms of domination not only share ideological elements, but reinforce one another either symbolically or structurally (Gaard 1993). Ecofeminist perspectives lead the observer to ask: How do racism and sexism facilitate the exploitation of nature? How does the exploitation of nature reinforce sexism and racism? How do social conceptions of women and women's work shape the economic systems that presently wreak havoc on natural environments? How has the social conceptualization of femininity or masculinity shaped the international politics that make global environmental change possible on such a massive scale?

Ecofeminists Vandana Shiva (1988), Ynestra King (1989), and Karen Warren (1991) describe how the cultural association of women and nature leads to relationships between social problems such as sexism and environmental degradation. The transfer of conceptions of masculinity and femininity onto culture/society and nonhuman nature is one such example. Issues affecting nonhuman nature receive less credibility due to an association with femininity, while the perception of women's reproductive biology as closer to nature justifies women's lower status and exclusion from culture/society. For example, in a society where women have less status than men, the feminization of nature and the masculinization of culture legitimize the conversion of natural landscapes for human purposes. Within this context, the plowing of a field or the cutting of a forest are not only activities to secure food or shelter, but symbolize the taming and control of a feminine nature by a masculine culture. Similarly, within a society where motherhood and subsistence activities such as housework are not valued, neither are the reproductive and subsistence activities of a "mother earth." Likewise, in a culture where the rape of women receives marginal attention, the "rape of nature" is of minimal importance. The flip side of this association of femininity and nature serves to keep women out of powerful social roles. Who will elect a woman to the presidency when menstruation is believed to make women irrational for three out of every twenty-eight days? Thus, ecofeminists describe how multiple forms of oppression not only share theoretical roots, but are mutually reinforcing in practice (Shiva 1988).

Clearly, systems of domination are damaging to individual women, people of color, and members of the lower classes in an immediate sense. Social inequality and environmental degradation, however, are processes which ultimately impact all members of society and life forms on the planet. While specific groups suffer the immediate damage of sexism, racism, classism, and environmental degradation dispropor-tionately, maintenance of these power relationships requires the socialization of dominant groups to accept ethical, economic, political, and epistemological systems which affect society as a whole. Furthermore, activities such as the production of dangerous chemicals, the testing of nuclear weapons, and the improper disposal of nuclear wastes, affect not only individual groups in an immediate sense (such as the citizens of poor nations or Native Americans) but, ultimately, the safety and quality of life of all people.

In other words, ecofeminists have emphasized that, in a stratified society, incentives for environmentally damaging activities are built into the social system as a whole. This occurs because powerful groups or individuals can force those less powerful to pay the costs of environmental degradation. This is the case when U.S. chemical companies manufacture dangerous materials in developing countries, when toxic materials are produced and disposed of in poor communities within the United States, and when illegal farm workers in California (who have no health insurance) apply pesticides to crops. Such instances of environmental degradation are more tolerable and remain outside public view because they victimize the least powerful people. The important point here is that not only do less powerful people face environmental discrimination, their victimization makes these environmentally degrading activities—which ultimately impact the earth as a whole—economically, ethically, and politically feasible. Instead, if companies were economically accountable for how their factory emissions lowered local air or water quality and affected cancer rates, their production—and the degradation of the environment— might no longer be economically efficient.

Why Call It Ecofeminism?

Many of the ideas discussed by ecofeminists are shared by other scholars (such as world systems theorists, women in development, philosophers of science, ecological economists, and activists in racial justice movements). Why should they be considered ecofeminist? Doesn't ecofeminism prioritize a concern with the condition of women over other forms of social inequity?

Although ecofeminism takes the oppression of women and nature to be central concerns, in part because it developed from the feminist and environmental movements, ecofeminists theorize that all forms of domination are interconnected. Ecofeminism is unique in placing an emphasis on systems of domination. The resulting perspective describes seemingly unique forms of oppression as resulting from the same ideological system and as structurally interlocking in ways that reinforce one another. The ecofeminist approach is unique in its theoretical arguments regarding dualisms and a logic of domination, the nature and depth of its social and cultural critiques, and because it explicitly challenges all systems of domination.

HUMAN ECOLOGY AND ECOFEMINISM

Ecofeminism does not add new subject matter to the study of human ecology. Nor does ecofeminism fit into human ecology in just one place. Rather, as a worldview, ecofeminism adds a new lens to our understanding of many topics of interest to human ecology, allowing human ecologists deeper insight into issues they themselves have identified to be central concerns. Because it addresses basic elements of western philosophy, culture, and social structure, an ecofeminist analysis expands virtually any discussion within human ecology. Political, ethical, and economic systems that shape human-nature interactions all express values and assumptions about the nature of reality from western thought. Next I will outline how ecofeminist analyses contribute to human ecology by expanding our understanding of demography, economics, culture, and epistemology.

Population and Human Ecology

Concern with the size and growth rate of the human population experienced a reawakening during the 1960s when biologist Paul Ehrlich brought attention to the human population growth rate and its potential ecological and human consequences (Ehrlich 1968; Ehrlich and Ehrlich 1990). Following the observation of Thomas Malthus (1798) that food resources do not increase at the same rate as population, Ehrlich called attention to the fact that human population size is limited by available resources. With population size growing beyond exponential rates, Ehrlich argued that overpopulation would lead to certain social and ecological disaster. This neo-Malthusian position emphasizes the role of human population size and growth rates in leading to ecological problems when society exceeds the "natural limits" of ecosystems, and to social problems such as overcrowding, limitations in social and economic resources, and political instability.

Since the 1960s the neo-Malthusian position has contested the dominant worldview supported by capitalist economic theory. This perspective claims that as long as free markets are in operation, the economy will continue to grow and satisfy human needs. Human ingenuity will keep technological innovation flowing to solve resource shortages; as the standard of living around the world continues to rise, infant mortality rates will drop, people will have fewer children, and population will stabilize as the developing nations follow the same demographic transition that occurred in developed nations (see, e.g., Simon 1981).

Until recently most discussions of human population have taken one or the other of the above two positions. In recent years, however, the neo-Malthusian emphasis on human population numbers as the leading cause of environmental degradation has been criticized for ignoring differences in resource use and access to power within the human population (Hartman 1987; Diamond 1994). This criticism points out that while both population size and human consumption affect environmental quality, it is generally the poor who have large families and the rich who consume the most resources. The discussion concerning population has been raised and shaped by wealthy members of wealthy societies. These groups have placed an emphasis on population while giving secondary priority to the issue of their own high level of resource consumption. Furthermore, many charge that concern over human population size is a reflection of the desire of those in the "First World" to control those in poor nations. In her recent text, *Fertile Ground: Women, Earth and the Limits of Control*, Irene Diamond (1994) describes the sentiment that, "since the granting of independence to former colonies, an incessant fear has been that if too many of 'them' propagate, the ability of Western industrialized nations to maintain their levels of consumption will be severely threatened" (pp. 125-126).

In line with the ecofeminist perspective of drawing attention to the impact of power differences within society on human-environmental relationships, ecofeminists describe how a focus on population as the cause of environmental degradation is often sexist, racist, and classist (Diamond 1994). Furthermore, this focus is described as an extension of an overzealous relationship of control that has characterized our present and highly problematic human ecological relationships. Instead, because high population growth rates are linked to the status of women (Cornelius 1987), ecofeminists suggest that the best way to lower these rates is to improve the quality of the lives of women (Birkeland 1993, p. 34). This perspective has recently entered into mainstream understanding of population issues, as evidenced by its emphasis in the 1994 International Conference on Population and Development in Cairo.

Race, Class, Sex, and Population

Approaches to human population size and growth rates that focus on numbers appear biologically sound on first impression. Clearly, as with every other species on the planet, an infinite number of humans cannot survive on earth; somewhere there must be a theoretical limit or maximum human population that can be sustained by available resources. However, ecofeminists have described how, in practice, addressing human population in terms of numbers and growth rates alone is simultaneously racist, sexist, and classist. These criticisms are based on the observation that the "overpopulation perspective" reduces the behavior of certain groups (poor people, women, and people of color) to the forces of biology; while, giving complex social and economic analysis of the behaviors of other groups (wealthy, white members of industrialized nations), appeals to the sentiment that we have too many of the wrong kind of people, and narrowly blames groups with less power for situations about which they have minimal control.

Ecofeminists describe how the selective reduction of the behavior of some groups to the forces of biology is a reflection of the dualisms between female/male, nature/culture, and primitive/civilized. This association of some groups with the primitive and with biology/nature, while others are associated with culture and the civilized, leads to the consideration of overpopulation as a "simple" biological phenomenon, while high resource consumption and materialism are considered to be shaped by complex social, cultural, and economic factors. Instead, ecofeminists argue that we must understand how human population growth is always a manifestation not only of biology, but of those complex cultural, social, and economic factors as well. In particular, ecofeminism encourages an understanding of how the prevalence of male privileges in multiple social spheres affects population growth rates.

Ecofeminism further shows how the conception of overpopulation as a problem of too many poor people is closely linked to the idea of overpopulation as too many of the wrong kind of people. Irene Diamond (1994) claims that racist, sexist, and classist elements have emerged because our desire to control human population growth is an extension of the desire to control both nature and certain members of human society. Unfortunately, the connection of overpopulation and "undesirables" has been explicit worldwide (see also, Hartman 1987). The U.S eugenics movement at the turn of the twentieth century aimed to reduce the numbers of undesirable people—those who were poor, recent immigrants, or those with less than average intelligence. In the 1920s, two-thirds of American states had passed laws allowing for the sterilization of the "unfit." Forced sterilization of poor, and especially nonwhite, women has occurred throughout the world, including the United States (Hartman 1987). As late as the 1970s American Indian women of childbearing age throughout the United States were sterilized against their will (Diamond 1994, p. 37), while poor women in nonindustrialized regions have been paid amounts equivalent to one month's wages for agreeing to become sterilized (p. 56).

Ecofeminism clarifies how approaches to population that ignore differences in social power implicitly, and sometimes explicitly, blame the poor, people of color, and women, for high population growth rates. The tendency to blame women is well illustrated by a recent bumper sticker developed by Earth First! that reads, "Love your mother, don't become one." Although on the surface this appears a sensible statement, this slogan illustrates a perspective that places the responsibility for overpopulation upon women. Yet, how much power or choice do women worldwide have with regards to their fertility? Not only the actions of mothers, but the activities of fathers, the pressure of cultural practices, religious powers, or government policy, the availability of information and means of birth control, and the very real need for child labor within many present-day economic systems, contribute to fertility rates. Given the reality of male dominance worldwide, individual women are without doubt the *least* able to influence population control. A recent United Nations statistic illustrates the lack of power most women experience: "if women who wanted no more children had the choice there would be a 38% reduction in births and a 29% drop in maternal death worldwide" (Rodda 1992, p. 70).

Population Growth and the Status of Women

In societies where women have lower status than men there is a preference for sons over daughters, women's age of marriage is younger, women have fewer socially acceptable alternatives to motherhood, and women have less control over their own fertility. Each of these conditions directly increases fertility rates.

First, son preference, which predominates worldwide but varies in magnitude regionally, has a dramatic affect on human demography. Recent studies of the sex ratio in China, for example, have revealed that some 100 million women were "missing" in the late 1980s, victims of infanticide or poor childhood nutrition (UNDP 1990). Fertility rates are affected when, as is often the case, families will continue having children until they have a son. Second, in heavily male-dominated societies, such as Muslim-dominated countries where women are rigidly confined to the private sphere, the presence of a son improves female security in later life. Once women leave their father's homes, they are dependent on the protection of their husbands. When wives outlive their husbands, or husbands fail to adequately support wives while still alive, women will only have access to societal resources through their male offspring. Women with only female offspring will continue to desire more children for their own security. Circumstances such as these contribute to the positive relationship between son preference and high fertility rates (Cornelius 1987).

Second, women marry younger than men on average worldwide. These age differences are most pronounced where differences in the social status of women and men are greatest (Seager and Olson 1986). Alternately, where women have opportunities for secondary and tertiary schooling they may postpone marriage. Clearly, younger age of marriage makes possible more years of reproductive activity and more children.

Third, in societies where women have culturally acceptable alternatives to motherhood they may receive education and enter the public sphere, where they have more direct access to economic resources. In these cases, women have the option to either delay or forego raising a family. Alternately, when homemaking is the only means open for a woman to support herself, all women will be raising families.

Finally, gender stratification substantially influences population growth rates by affecting the ability of women to make decisions regarding their fertility. In heavily stratified societies, a woman's access to contraceptives may be restricted by both government policies that forbid the use of contraceptives or access to abortion, and by household politics in which men have control over women's reproduction.

Economics and Human Ecology

Economic systems are among the most powerful structural influences shaping human ecology at the end of the twentieth century. With the rise of the modern environmental movement in the past several decades, environmental theorists have developed extensive critiques of the theory and practice of present economic systems. Modern economies have been considered incapable of accurately reflecting human ecological relationships due to such factors as unsustainable assumptions of unlimited economic growth, the generation of "externalities," discounting future resources, an inability to place value on ecosystem processes, and creating competition between present and future generations (Norgaard 1994; Howarth and Norgaard 1995). In recent years, the fields of environmental and ecological economics have begun to address these issues.

Feminist economists have also criticized modern economic systems, emphasizing such factors as the lower wages paid to the positions typically held by women in the formal economy (Tong 1989, p. 59), the inability of capitalist economies to recognize the productive activities of women in the home (Benston 1969; Dalla Costa and James 1972; Berk and Berk 1979), and the assumption that improvement in the status of women in developing regions will follow automatically as GNP increases (Waring 1988; Eisler, Loye, and Norgaard 1995).

Interestingly, both feminist and ecological economists have independently engaged in similar critiques of capitalist systems. For example, both feminist and ecological economists have addressed the impacts of the expansion of capitalist systems into nonindustrialized world regions (Tinker 1990; Sen and Grown 1987). Ecological economists have drawn attention to the accelerated pace of resource extraction and loss of biological diversity as nonindustrialized countries are incorporated into the global market. Feminist economists have described how the absence of value on the subsistence activities of women in nonindustrialized sections of the economy in "developing" regions has been directly linked to the decline in the status of women as western market economics spread to these regions (Boserup 1970; Momsen and Townsend 1987; Tinker 1990).

At present, however, few environmental or feminist economists identify similarities between the criticisms generated by each field. Drawing together insights present in both feminist theory and ecological economics, ecofeminism would hold that criticisms from both fields reflect the inadequacies of the dualistic philosophy that separates humans from nature, reproduction from production, and femininity from masculinity.

The Dualisms of Economics:
Nature/Culture, Women/Men, Reproduction/Production

Vandana Shiva (1988) and Marilyn Waring (1988) describe how, within modern economic systems, that which is associated with culture (western science and technology) is visible while that which is associated with nature (ecological processes, the subsistence activities of women and indigenous people, and reproductive activities of women in the household) is invisible. According to their analyses, present-day economic science describes activities as examples of "production" when the activities of humans and nature are mediated by technologies (aspects of culture). Thus, fields become "productive" when worked with plows, forests become "productive" when transformed into tree farms water systems become "productive" when dams are constructed; yet supposedly, in the absence of the plow the field is not productive, nor the forest in the absence of modern silviculture, nor the river system in the absence of water projects. However, not all human labor or use of technology gets counted as production. Much of the work performed by women, in the raising of families and growing of subsistence crops is classified as *reproduction*. Ecofeminists claim that the reproductive labor of women is invisible for the same reason as reproduction within the ecosystem. In the words of Indian physicist Vandana Shiva (1988)

> The neglect of nature's work in renewing herself, and women's work in producing sustenance in the form of basic, vital needs is an essential part of the paradigm of maldevelopment, which sees all work that does not produce profits and capital as non or unproductive work (p. 4).

Furthermore, the invisibility of one form of production within economic science aids in keeping the other form invisible. For example, the labor of women is "naturalized" such that child care and nurturing activities are perceived as an outgrowth of women's biology. Because these caring and nurturing activities are attributed to a general nature of women to be more caring, as part of nature, they need not be compensated within an economic system. In the same vein, the feminization of nature and the productive processes of natural systems fit into a cultural blind spot of what counts as labor.

Shiva and Waring both argue that modern economic definitions of productivity are flawed not only by what they define as "reproduction," and therefore render invisible, but also by what gets defined as "production." Many so called productive activities are, in ecological terms, highly destructive. For example, activities universally understood to be environmentally degrading, such as the Exxon-Valdez oil spill generate economic growth through the creation of jobs in spill clean-up industries, which in turn increases the GNP.

Both feminist and ecological economists have attempted to impute the value of different types of reproductive processes into capitalist economic models. Household labor has been added to measures of productivity by multiplying hours per week by the wages paid to domestic workers (see, e.g., Daly and Cobb 1989) while the value of clean lakes or pristine wilderness has been measured according to what the public is willing to pay to keep from using these resources. In each case, the imputation of value must be done indirectly and is highly problematic.

Although these attempts to impute value to invisible activities may be important in drawing attention to the absence of value given to these ecological functions, the underlying problem—that modern economics does not accurately reflect human social or human ecological relationships—remains unaddressed by these efforts. Furthermore, values are associated with things, whereas it is the well being of systems of relationships about which both ecologists and feminists are really concerned. Ecofeminism holds that we must understand why our economics does not incorporate subsistence or reproductive activities and develop alternative economic systems capable of reflecting true human needs and relationships. The template of the partnership and dominator models can be used to explain how the lesser status of women has led society to place a lower priority on traditionally feminine and life sustaining activities, while exaggerating those activities that have corresponded to traditional male roles. Obviously, the invisibility of activities which sustain life within modern economics does not decrease their centrality to human survival or to human-ecological relationships. Instead, their invisibility within the present system makes humans dangerously vulnerable. Therefore, ecofeminists argue that we must distinguish between activities that are life sustaining and activities that increase GNP, and develop economic systems based on the former rather than the latter.

An ecofeminist analysis of modern economic structures describes how the global decline in environmental quality, the decline in the status of women with westernization, and the loss of social and biological diversity are each manifestations of economic systems based on a dominator model of social organization and the dualistic worldview that artificially separates humans from nature and masculinity from femininity. In order to develop adequate economic models, ecofeminists assert that we must understand not only the structure of these dualisms, but how women and nature have been connected culturally and historically, and how their association has continued the exploitation of each individually.

Culture and Human Ecology

Human ecological relationships are influenced by the cultural symbols and values that form and reinforce economic, political, and social institutions. Recent cultural discussions within the field of human ecology have addressed the influence of materialist and anthropocentric values (Devall and Sessions 1984) and the Christian teaching that God granted humans dominion over plants and animals (White 1967) upon human ecological relationships. Ecofeminism has described in detail how symbols and values that apply to the specific roles of women and men within western society are applied to the earth. The transporting of these symbols into human ecological relationships obscures our perceptions of nonhuman nature, affects the ethical frameworks humans use with respect to nonhuman nature, and transfers cultural and social tensions between women and men onto the relationship between humans and the earth.

Numerous ecofeminist analyses of culture and gender apply directly to human ecological relationships (see, e.g., Griffin 1978; Gaard 1993; Seager 1993; Diamond and Orenstein 1990). For the purposes here I will illustrate ecofeminist analyses of the influence of culture on human ecology by describing critiques of the popular symbol of the earth as "mother."

Gender Symbols: Mother Earth Imagery

Following James Lovelock's (1987) characterization of the earth as Gaia, the phrase "mother earth" has become a popular representation for the planet earth within the environmental movement, appearing on posters, t-shirts, and bumper stickers. Ecofeminists have discussed this association of nonhuman nature with a human mother, finding it to be problematic on several counts (Gaard 1993; Seager 1993; Heller 1993; Kheel 1993; Garb 1990; Murphy 1988; Vance 1993; Lahar 1991). These ecofeminists have argued that the association of the earth with a human mother not only limits our ability to know nature by placing the specific qualities of mothers in white western society on the entire earth but, within a society where women have less status than men, the feminization of the earth gives it subordinate status. Further, they describe how mother earth imagery reinforces the notion that humans are separate from nonhuman nature and contributes to environmental degradation.

Gaard (1993) describes how the image of mothers as generous and bountiful has endorsed environmentally degrading activities:

> Mother never tires of giving precisely because her supplies are limitless.... The idea that old growth forests are inexhaustible, for example, has authorized unrestrained logging for industry. Because there is always "more" in mother's

generous apron human children have not worried about dumping raw sewage or garbage in the waters (p. 303).

Applying the symbol of a human mother to the earth supports the notion that it is impossible that we will run out of forests, because a good mother always provides. It is further impossible that rivers will become polluted beyond repair because mother always cleans up.

Ecofeminists further warn that applying a feminine stereotype to the earth within a culture that does not value women will not succeed in giving value to the earth. Rather, Patrick Murphy (1988) writes that "Designating an entity female in patriarchal culture guarantees its subservient status" (p. 157). Thus, it does not make sense to argue that we must work for "mother earth" in a culture that does not value motherhood. Gaard remarks that "until Western culture changes its conception of motherhood to one in which the mother's needs are also respected, the metaphor of mother earth will only serve to perpetuate the very notion that ecofeminism seeks to eradicate" (1993, p. 302). Instead, cultural tension between women and men, mothers and children, will be played out in the relationship between humans and nonhuman nature.

Finally, Murphy (1988) describes how the use of mother earth imagery serves to perpetuate the notion that humans and nature are separate, so separate in fact that the only way we can relate to the earth is by ascribing to it human qualities:

> Sex-typing a gender free entity also reinscribes an anthropomorphism that alienates Earth by trying to render it in our image. To say that we must describe it in human terms in order to understand it is to claim that we and it are separate and other. A division that alienates male and female can hardly serve to unite Earth and humanity (p. 165).

Meanwhile, cultural conceptions of masculinity in terms of the ability to control are played out onto a feminized landscape in which "virgin" woods are to be cut and a "wild" west needs "taming." Farmers purchase herbicides with names like "Round-up" to "manage" their fields; off-road vehicles, sold to men and having names like "Bronco" are driven over fragile desert landscapes. The military, historically one of the most strictly masculine institutions, is nearly exempt from environmental regulation and damages vast land areas in routine maneuvers and the testing of weapons. Joni Seager, in her text, *Earth Follies*, describes how male soldiers spraying herbicides during the Vietnam War developed the macho slogan, "only we can prevent forests" (1993, p. 19).

Science and Human Ecology:
The Masculinist Epistemology of Modernity

The study of human ecology incorporates many sciences, using evolutionary theory from biology and thermodynamics from physics. as well as material from anthropology and sociology. These theories form a framework of natural systems within which specifically human activity can be understood and critiqued. For example, based on evolutionary theory in biology, human ecologists are able to ask questions about sociocultural evolution, while ecological theory is used to understand the impacts of species extinction upon human ecology. Using laws of thermodynamics, human ecologists point out inconsistencies and flaws in modern economic theories. The use of a scientific epistemology influences human ecology in multiple ways. Therefore, in addition to using science, science itself has been subject to reflection and critique by literature relevant to human ecology (e.g. Kuhn 1962; Botkin 1990; Norgaard 1994; Gene 1985).

The belief that the world works in a mechanized way with processes that will repeat, and is governed by laws that humans can measure, predict and know, has been the foundation for western thought since the scientific revolution (Prigogine and Stegners 1984). While this approach has obviously been quite useful, ecofeminists claim that it also has limitations. Examining and understanding the specific epistemology used by human ecologists improves not only understanding of human ecology, but the quality of science that human ecologists create.

Feminist and ecofeminist analyses of science have described how rather than being neutral and value-free as professed, scientific epistemology has corresponded to specific traditional western conceptions of masculinity (Rothschild 1983; Tuana 1989; Harding 1986, 1991; Keller 1985; Haraway 1991). Due to this bias, science can be described as an ethnosystem reflecting and perpetuating the specific social and cultural norms of the times. Furthermore, in creating totalizing systems of knowledge, science reinforces power dynamics between women and men, rich and poor, and western and nonwestern peoples. Third, feminist and ecofeminist analyses describe how, through the elevation of biased viewpoints to universal truths, the practice of science can actually reduce our understanding of human ecology (Shiva 1988; Mies and Shiva 1993).

Building on Kuhn's contention that factors above and beyond empirical evidence and theoretical necessity influence the community's choice of a "best theory," feminist philosophers of science such as Evelyn Fox Keller have asked "how the making of men and women has affected the making of science" (1985, p. 4). Such questions lead to explanations of why the scientific community has not only excluded women, but how the qualities considered appropriate to the task of scientific inquiry are the same as those for traditional masculinity in western culture (Keller 1985; Harding 1986).

Traditional western masculinity emphasizes individuality (separateness) and the ability to control. In contrast, subjectivity, a way of knowing based on contact, interaction and experience, reflects traditional western feminine stereotypes of "being-in-relationship" (Chodorow 1978; Gilligan 1982; Larrabee 1993). In accordance with roles and behaviors appropriate for traditional masculinity, science emphasizes the use of one's intellect but not one's emotions to achieve knowledge. Objectivity, the taken-to-be-correct orientation for the scientific process, is a means of gaining knowledge based on one's distance from the world. This critique does not suggest that an objective stance is inaccurate or false; to the contrary, science has shown itself to be quite useful. Rather, among the "other factors" that Kuhn describes as entering "into the community's choice of the best theory," are those that fit the masculine worldview. Einstein described scientists as being "driven to escape from personal existence to the world of objective observing and understanding" (quoted in Keller 1985, p. 10). Furthermore, Keller writes that scientists actively embrace—even choose—a picture of reality as being "as impersonal and free of human values as the rules of arithmetic;" that scientists as human actors, "find some pictures or theories more persuasive and even more self-evident than others in part because of the conformation of these pictures or theories to their prior emotional commitments, expectations and desires" (1985, p. 10).

This description of science, as based upon masculine values and experiences of the world, further explains the use of sexualized terminology such as "soft" and "hard" sciences within universities today. So-called hard sciences, such as physics and math, are those most congruent with the characteristics of traditional masculinity. These disciplines can be pursued with the greatest degree of control and distance from subject matter (i.e., objectivity), and for which exac formulas can most often be derived. Soft sciences such as anthropology and sociology on the other hand, contain fewer if any formulas, and may even include a role for subjective knowledge.

Many ecofeminists observe that the development of science occurred not only together with the construction of masculinity as separate from femininity, but from the construction of culture/society as separate from nature: "Science and masculinity were associated in domination over nature and femininity, and the ideologies of science and gender reinforced each other" (Shiva 1988, p. 18). Thus, ecofeminist theory contributes to an understanding of epistemology not only by asking *how* but *why* we do science. Science developed as men sought to use reason to control nature.

As discussed earlier, Merchant's research describes a shift in imagery of nature from that of a living organism prior to the development of science, to that of an inanimate machine following the scientific revolution. Other theorists have described this mechanistic model and its implications. Daniel Botkin (1990) describes how the human desire for a safe and orderly world has influenced the development of ecological models that unrealistically emphasize balance and harmony. Botkin's argument rests on the observation that historical conception of nature in western thought characterize nature as an alternately wild and benevolent feminine force. Botkin then argues that our desire for nature to be serene and orderly rather than wild and chaotic has led to a science of ecology that emphasizes harmony, equilibrium, and balance.

These and other accounts describe how scientific theories have not reflected objective truths, but the social, material and psychological needs of particular groups of people at given points in history. Ecofeminists then suggest that, if scientific theories are social constructions, we must ask: Whose knowledge are we using, for what purpose is this knowledge used, and how useful is it to understanding human ecology?

A further issue arises when a specific epistemology is valued to the exclusion of all others. For example, our culture's view that using science is the only acceptable way to know the world discredits indigenous knowledge of local ecology, much of which is being lost as the dominant western culture expands. A similar loss of indigenous knowledge appears to have occurred in Europe corresponding to the scientific revolution and the early development of "modern" medicine.

Rosemary Radford Reuther (1975) describes the infamous "witch trials" throughout Europe as part of a paradigm shift in which traditional women healers, representing a threat to the new scientific worldview, were targeted. As a result of this cultural genocide, present people of European descent retain little "folk knowledge" of the medicinal properties of plants. Ecofeminism holds that if we can allow that science is neither the only nor always the best way to know the world, but instead recognize the wealth of knowledge present in both the individual experience and nonscientific traditional cultures, we can only increase our understanding of human ecology.

Finally, many ecofeminists suggest that, to the extent that scientific epistemology reflects the separation of masculinity from femininity and culture/society from nature, it has limited our ability to know and understand natural systems, and has had a negative impact on human relationships with nonhuman nature. If, as many in the environmental movement and academy have asserted, the framework of human domination and control over nature has led to many environmental problems, ecofeminists want to know how these problems can be resolved using a framework which itself perpetuates this separation. None of these critiques suggest that we replace the notion of universal truth in science with relativism, rather, that we must become more honest and critical of the biases from any given perspective. Instead, by speaking in terms of "partial perspectives" and "situated knowledges" (Haraway 1988), we can articulate a more valid and hopefully more complete description of the world.

CONCLUSION

The term ecofeminism has become widely applied to theories simultaneously addressing the circumstances of both women and nature. Without outlining all the varieties of ecofeminism, I have described three key ingredients of an ecofeminist perspective. These features—the description of a cultural and historical association of women and nature, the assertion that a common ideology underlies multiple forms of oppression, and an explanation of how social and environmental problems reinforce one another—can be applied to specific issues within the field of human ecology.

In each case, using an ecofeminist analysis can extend understanding of human ecological relationships. When applied to the issue of human population growth, ecofeminism describes how racist, sexist, and classist assumptions in the traditional perspective limit our understanding of population problems and their solutions, reducing the behavior of some groups to a biological phenomenon and ignoring the role of sexual inequality in high fertility rates. Ecofeminism warns that an emphasis on population control (rather than reduction of consumption or other strategies) is an extension of a general and problematic emphasis on control over nature and humans within western culture.

An ecofeminist analysis of culture describes the role of gender in shaping social institutions, human relationships to nonhuman nature and the symbols used in the environmental movement. In particular ecofeminists describe how the application of feminine stereotypes to the earth places cultural tension between the sexes onto the relationship between humans and nature. Furthermore, within a sexist society, such feminine stereotypes encourage a relationship of domination and control over the earth, which in turn negatively impacts human ecological relationships.

When applied to economics, ecofeminism unites the efforts of feminist and ecological economists by explaining how the split between reproductive and productive forms of labor has led to the invisibility of much of the activity both of women and natural systems. An ecofeminist understanding of modern economics warns against attempts to impute value to processes of ecological or social reproduction describing how their exclusion is an expression of deeper problems within the modern western worldview. Ecofeminism holds that we must address this dualistic and dominator worldview before we can develop a system of economics that accurately reflects relationships within society and between humans and the nonhuman world.

Finally, ecofeminism describes how the use of science, for all its merits, is still an ethnosystem shaped by the experiences and values of a particular group of people. Ecofeminism encourages those using a scientific perspective to be aware that science is not value free, to recognize and make a place for indigenous and nonscientific forms of knowledge, and to acknowledge that raising biased perspectives to the level of a universal truth cannot increase knowledge overall.

With the use of an ecofeminist perspective, human ecologists should be able to expand their understanding of the factors shaping culture, science, and social institutions, and the interrelationship of social and environmental systems, both theoretically and practically. These tools give anyone studying human ecological relationships a new perspective on human population dynamics, modern economics, culture, and the use of science. As an interdisciplinary approach which adds dramatically to the subject matter of the field, ecofeminism is a perspective that human ecologists cannot afford to ignore.

ACKNOWLEDGMENTS

My thanks to Lee Freese for encouraging me to synthesize and expand these ideas from a graduate seminar, and to Wendi Grasseschi, Richard Norgaard, and Sam Stroich for invaluable comments on early drafts. Address correspondence to: Kari Marie Norgaard, 1198 Keith Avenue, Berkeley, CA 94708.

REFERENCES

Adams, C., ed. 1993. *Ecofeminism and the Sacred.* New York: Orbis Books.

Andersen, M. 1993. "From the Editor." *Gender and Society* 7: 157-161.

Bem, S.L. 1974. "The Measurement of Psychological Androgyny." *Journal of Counseling and Clinical Psychology* 42: 155-162.

Benston, M. 1969. "The Political Economy of Women's Liberation." *Monthly Review* 21: 13-27.

Berk R. and S. Berk. 1979. *Labor and Leisure at Home: Content and Organization of the Household Day.* Beverly Hills, CA: Sage.

Bhiel, J. 1991. *Rethinking Ecofeminist Politics.* Boston: South End Press.

Birkeland, J. 1993. "Ecofeminism: Linking Theory and Practice." Pp. 13-60 in *Ecofeminism: Women, Animals, Nature,* edited by G. Gaard. Philadelphia: Temple University Press.

Bookchin, M. 1982. *The Ecology of Freedom.* Palo Alto, CA: Cheshire Books.

————. 1990. *Remaking Society: Pathways to a Green Future.* Boston: South End Press.

Boserup, E. 1970. *Women's Role in Economic Development.* New York: St. Martin's.

Botkin, D. 1990. *Discordant Harmonies: A New Ecology for the Twenty-first Century.* New York: Oxford University Press.

Boulding, E. 1980. *Women: The Fifth World.* New York: The Foreign Policy Association.

Broverman, I. 1970. "Sex Role Stereotypes and Clinical Judgements of Mental Health." *Journal of Counseling and Clinical Philosophy* 34: 1-7.

Bryant B. and P. Mohai. 1992. *Race and the Incidence of Environmental Hazard: A Time for Discourse.* Boulder, CO: Westview Press.

Bullard, R. 1990. *Dumping in Dixie: Race, Class and Environmental Quality.* Boulder, CO: Westview Press.

————. 1993. "Anatomy of Environmental Racism and the Environmental Justice Movement." Pp. 15-40 in *Confronting Environmental Racism: Voices from the Grassroots,* edited by R. Bullard and Chavis. Boston: South End Press.

Buttel, F. and W. Flinn. 1978. "Social Class and Mass Environmental Beliefs." *Environment and Behavior* 10: 433-450.

Buvinic, M., M. Lycette, and W. McGreevey. 1983. *Women and Poverty in the Third World.* Baltimore: John Hopkins University Press.

Caldecott, L. and S. Leland. 1983. eds. *Reclaim the Earth: Women Speak Out for Life on Earth.* London: The Women's Press.

Carlassare, E. 1992. "An Exploration of Ecofeminism." Unpublished M.A. thesis, Energy and Resources Group, University of California, Berkeley.

Carson, R. 1962. *Silent Spring.* Boston: Houghton Mifflin.

Cheney, J. 1987. "Ecofeminism and Deep Ecology." *Environmental Ethics* 9: 115-145.

Chodorow, N. 1978. *The Reproduction of Mothering: Psychoanalysis and the Sociology of Gender.* Berkeley: University of California Press.

Cole, J. 1986. "Commonalities and Differences." Pp. 1-6 in *All American Women: Lines that Divide, Ties that Bind,* edited by J. Cole. New York: The Free Press.

Collard A. with J. Contrucci. 1989. *Rape of the Wild: Man's Violence Against Animals and the Earth.* Bloomington: Indiana University Press.

Collins J.L. and M. Gimenez, eds. 1990. *Work Without Wages: Domestic Labor and Self-Employment Within Capitalism.* Albany: State University of New York Press.

Collins, P.H. 1990. *Black Feminist Thought: Knowledge, Consciousness, Empowerment.* New York: Routledge.

Commoner, B. 1971. *The Closing Circle.* New York: Knopf.

Connell, R. W. 1987. *Gender and Power.* Stanford: Stanford University Press.

Cornelius, D. L. 1987. "Patriarchal Structure, Women's Status and Fertility in Jordan." Unpublished M.A. thesis, Department of Sociology, Washington State University, Pullman.

Cuomo, C. 1994. "Ecofeminism, Deep Ecology and Human Population." Pp. 88-105 in *Ecological Feminism,* edited by K.J. Warren. New York: Routledge.

Daily, G.C., A.H. Ehrlich, and P.R. Ehrlich. 1995. "Socioeconomic Equity—A critical Element in Sustainability." *Ambio* 24: 58-59.

Dalla Costa, M. and S. James. 1972. *The Power of Women and the Subversion of the Community.* Bristol: Falling Wall Press.

Dalton, R.J. and M. Kuechler, eds. 1990. "The Challenge of New Movements." Pp. 3-22 in *Challenging the Political Order: New Social and Political Movements in Western Democracies.* New York: Oxford University Press.

Daly, H. and J. Cobb. 1989. *For The Common Good.* Boston: Beacon Press.

Dasgupta, P.S. 1995. "Population, Poverty and the Local Environment." *Scientific American* 272: 40-45.

Davies, M. 1983. *Third World, Second Sex.* London: Zed Press.

Descartes, R. (1637) 1956. *Discourse on Method.* Translated by L.J. Lafleur. Indianapolis: Bobbs-Merrill.

Devall, B. and G. Sessions. 1984. *Deep Ecology: Living as if Nature Mattered.* Salt Lake City: Peregrine Smith Books.

Diamond, I. 1994. *Fertile Ground: Women, Earth and the Limits of Control.* Boston: Beacon Press.

Diamond, I. and G.F. Orenstein, eds. 1990. *Reweaving the World: The Emergence of Ecofeminism.* San Francisco: Sierra Club.

Donovan, J. 1993. "Animal Rights and Feminist Theory." Pp. 167-193 in *Ecofeminism: Women, Animals, Nature*, edited by G. Gaard. Philadelphia: Temple University Press.

Dunlap, R. 1984. "Commitment to the Dominant Social Paradigm and Concern for Environmental Quality." *Social Science Quarterly* 65: 1013-1028.

Dunlap, R. and K. Van Liere. 1978. "The New Environmental Paradigm." *The Journal of Environmental Education* 9: 10-19.

Ehrlich, P. 1968. *The Population Bomb*. New York: Ballantine.

Ehrlich, P. and A. Ehrlich. 1990. *The Population Explosion*. New York: Simon and Schuster.

Eisler, R. 1988. *The Chalice and the Blade*. San Francisco: Harper San Francisco.

————. 1995. *Sacred Pleasure: Sex, Myth and the Politics of the Body*. San Francisco: Harper San Francisco.

Eisler, R., D. Loye, and K. Norgaard. 1995. *Women, Men and the Global Quality of Life*. Carmel: Center for Partnership Studies.

England, P., ed. 1993a. *Theory on Gender, Feminism on Theory*. New York: Walter de Gruyter.

————, ed. 1993b. *Beyond Economic Man: Feminist Theory and Economics*. Chicago: The University of Chicago Press.

Enloe, C. 1989. *Bananas, Beaches and Bases: Making Feminist Sense of International Politics*. Berkeley: University of California Press.

Gaard, G., ed. 1993. "Living Interconnections With Animals and Nature." Pp. 1-12 in *Ecofeminism: Women/Animals/Nature*. Philadelphia: Temple University Press.

Garb, Y.J. "Perspective or Escape? Ecofeminist Musings on Contemporary Earth Imagery." Pp. 264-278 in *Reweaving the World: The Emergence of Ecofeminism*, edited by I. Diamond and G.F. Orenstein. San Francisco: Sierra Club.

Gene, M. 1985. "Perception, Interpretation, and the Sciences: Toward a New Philosophy of Science." In *Evolution at a Crossroads: The New Biology and the New Philosophy of Science*, edited by D.J. Depew and B.H. Weber. Cambridge: MIT Press.

Giddens, A. 1990. *The Consequences of Modernity*. Stanford: Stanford University Press.

Gilligan, C. 1982. *In A Different Voice*. Cambridge: Harvard University Press.

Goffman, E. 1977. "The Arrangement Between the Sexes." *Theory and Society* 4: 301-331.

Griffin, S. 1978. *Woman and Nature: The Roaring Inside Her*. New York: Harper and Row.

Gruen, L. 1993. "Dismantling Oppression: An Analysis of the Connection Between Women and Animals." Pp. 60-90 in *Ecofeminism: Women/Animals/Nature*, edited by G. Gaard. Philadelphia: Temple University Press.

Guha, R. 1989. *The Unquiet Woods: Ecological Change and Peasant Resistance in the Himalaya*. Berkeley: University of California Press.

Hamilton, C. 1990. "Women, Home and Community: The Struggle in an Urban Environment." Pp. 215-222 in *Reweaving the World: The Emergence of Ecofeminism*, edited by I. Diamond and G.F. Orenstein. San Francisco: Sierra Club.

_____. 1993. "Coping With Industrial Exploitation." Pp. 63-78 in *Confronting Environmental Racism: Voices from the Grassroots*, edited by R. Bullard and Chavis. Boston: South End Press.

Haraway, D. 1988. "Situated Knowledges: The Science Question in Feminism and the Privilege of Partial Perspective." *Feminist Studies* 14: 575-599.

_____. 1991. *Simians, Cyborgs, and Women: The Reinvention of Nature*. New York: Routledge.

Harding, S. 1986. *The Science Question in Feminism*. Ithaca: Cornell University Press.

_____. 1991. *Whose Science? Whose Knowledge: Thinking from Women's Lives*. Ithaca: Cornell University Press.

Hartman, B. 1987. *Reproductive Rights and Wrongs: The Global Politics of Population Control and Contraceptive Choice*. New York: Harper and Row.

Heller, C. 1993. "For the Love of Nature: Ecology and the Cult of the Romantic." Pp. 219-242 in *Ecofeminism: Women/Animals/Nature*, edited by G. Gaard. Philadelphia: Temple University Press.

Henderson, J. 1989. "An Ecofeminist Critique of Marx." *Dialogue* 31: 58-64.

Howarth, R. and R. Norgaard. 1995. "Intergenerational Choices Under Global Environmental Change." Pp. 111-138 in *Handbook of Environmental Economics*, edited by D.W. Bromley. Oxford: Basil Blackwell.

Jackson, C. 1994. "Gender Analysis and Environmentalisms." Pp. 113-149 in *Social Theory and the Global Environment*, edited by M. Redclift and T. Benton. London: Routledge.

Jagger, A. 1983. *Feminist Politics and Human Nature*. Otowa, NJ: Rowman and Allenheld.

Keller, E.F. 1985. *Reflections on Gender and Science*. New Haven, CT: Yale University Press.

Kheel, M. 1985. "The Liberation of Nature: A Circular Affair." *Environmental Ethics* 7: 135-149.

_____. 1993. "From Heros to Holistic Ethics: The Ecofeminist Challenge." Pp. 243-271 in *Ecofeminism: Women/Animals/Nature*, edited by G. Gaard. Philadelphia: Temple University Press.

King, Y. 1981. "Feminism and the Revolt of Nature." *Heresies* 13: 12-16.

_____. 1989. "The Ecology of Feminism and the Feminism of Ecology," Pp. 18-28 in *Healing the Wounds: The Promise of Ecofeminism*, edited by J. Plant. Philadelphia: New Society.

_____. 1990. "Healing the Wounds: Feminism, Ecology and the Nature/Culture Dualism." Pp. 106-111 in *Reweaving the World: The Promise of Ecofeminism*, edited by I. Diamond and G.F. Orenstein. San Francisco: Sierra Club Books.

Kuhn, T.S. 1962. *The Structure of Scientific Revolutions*. Chicago: University of Chicago Press.

Lahar, S. 1991. "Ecofeminist Theory and Grassroots Politics." *Hypatia* 6: 28-45.

_____. 1993. "Roots: Rejoining Natural and Social History." Pp. 91-117 in *Ecofeminism: Women/Animals/Nature*, edited by G. Gaard. Philadelphia: Temple University Press.

Larrabee, M.J., ed. 1993. *An Ethic of Care*. New York: Routledge.

Leff, E. 1995. *Green Production: Toward and Environmental Rationality*. Translated by M. Vilanueva. New York: Guilford Press.

Leopold, A. 1948. *A Sand County Almanac*. New York: Oxford University Press.

Lovelock, J. 1987. *Gaia: A New Look At Life On Earth*. Oxford: Oxford University Press.

Malthus, T. 1798. *An Essay on the Principle of Population*. London: J. Johnson.

Marsh, G.P. 1864. *Man and Nature: Or, Physical Geography as Modified by Human Action*. New York: Charles Scribner.

Meadows, D.H., D.L. Meadows, J. Randers, and W.W. Behrens, III. 1972. *The Limits to Growth*. New York: Universe.

Merchant, C. 1980. *The Death of Nature*. New York: Harper and Row.

————. 1983. "Mining the Earth's Womb." Pp. 99-117 in *Machina Ex Dea: Feminist Perspectives on Technology*, edited by J. Rothschild. New York: Pergamon Press.

————. 1989. *Ecological Revolutions: Nature, Gender and Science in New England*. Chapel Hill: University of North Carolina Press.

————. 1990. *Radical Ecology: The Search for a Livable World*. London: Routledge.

Mies, M. and V. Shiva. 1993. *Ecofeminism*. London: Zed Books.

Mohai, P. 1985. "Public Concern and Elite Involvement in Environmental-Conservation Issues." *Social Science Quarterly* 66: 820-838.

Momsen, J. and J. Townsend. 1987. *Geography of Gender in the Third World*. Albany: SUNY Press.

Muir, J. 1901. *Our National Parks*. Boston: Houghton, Mifflin.

Murphy, P. 1988. "Sex-Typing the Planet: Gaia Imagery and the Problem of Subverting Patriarchy." *Environmental Ethics* 10: 155-168.

Naess, A. 1974. "The Shallow and Deep Ecology Movement." *Inquiry* 16: 95-100.

Nash, R. 1973. *Wilderness and the American Mind*. New Haven, CT: Yale University Press.

Norgaard, R. 1994. *Development Betrayed: Progress and a Coevolutionary Revisioning of the Future*. London: Routledge.

Ortner, S. 1974. "Is Female to Male as Nature is to Culture?" Pp. 67-87 in *Women, Culture and Society*, edited by M. Rosaldo and L. Lamphere. Stanford: Stanford University Press.

Pepper, D. 1984. *The Roots of Modern Environmentalism*. London: Routledge.

Pinchot, G. 1910. *The Fight for Conservation*. New York: Doubleday, Page and Company.

Plant, J., ed. 1989. *Healing the Wounds: The Promise of Ecofeminism*. Philadelphia: New Society.

Plumwood, V. 1986. "Ecofeminism: An Overview and Discussion of Positions and Arguments." *Australian Journal of Philosophy* 64: 120-138.

————. 1988. "Women, Humanity and Nature." *Radical Philosophy* 48: 16-24.

————. 1989. "Do We Need a Sex/Gender Distinction?" *Radical Philosophy* 51: 2-11.

————. 1991. "Nature, Self and Gender: Feminism Environmental Philosophy and the Critique of Rationalism." *Hypatia* 6: 3-27.

————. 1993. *Feminism and the Domination of Nature*. London: Routledge.

Prigogine, I. and I. Stengers. 1984. *Order Out of Chaos: Man's New Dialogue With Nature*. New York: Bantam Books.

Reuther, R.R. 1975. *New Woman/New Earth: Sexist Ideologies and Human Liberation*. New York: Seabury Press.

_____. 1993. "Symbolic and Social Connections of the Oppression of Women and the Domination of Nature." Pp. 13-23 in *Ecofeminism and the Sacred*, edited by C. Adams. New York: Orbis Books.

Rodda, A. 1992. *Women and the Environment*. London: Zed Books Ltd.

Rothschild, J., ed. 1983. *Machina Ex Dea: Feminist Perspectives on Technology*. New York: Pergamon Press.

Schnaiberg, A. 1980. *The Environment: From Surplus to Scarcity*. New York: Oxford University Press.

Seager, J. 1993. *Earth Follies: Coming to Feminist Terms With the Global Environmental Crisis*. New York: Routledge.

Seager, J. and A. Olson. 1986. *Women in the World an International Atlas*. New York: Simon and Schuster.

Sen, G. and C. Grown. 1987. *Development, Crisis and Alternative Visions*. New York: New Feminist Library.

Shelton B.A. and B. Agger. 1993. "Shotgun Wedding, Unhappy Marriage, No-fault Divorce? Rethinking the Feminism-Marxism Relationship." Pp. 25-42 in *Theory on Gender, Feminism on Theory*, edited by P. England. New York: Walter de Gruyter.

Shiva, V. 1988. *Staying Alive: Women, Ecology and Development*. London: Zed Books.

Simon, J. 1981. *The Ultimate Resource*. Princeton, NJ: Princeton University Press.

Stacey J. and B. Thorne. 1985. "The Missing Feminist Revolution in Sociology." *Social Problems* 32: 301-316.

Tinker, I. 1990. *Persistent Inequalities: Women and World Development*. New York: Oxford University Press.

Tong, R. 1989. *Feminist Thought*. Boulder, CO: Westview Press.

Tuana, N. 1989. *Feminism and Science*. Indianapolis: Indiana University Press.

U.S. Senate Judiciary Committee Fact Sheet. 1991.

United Nations Development Program (UNDP). 1990. *1990 Human Development Report*. Washington, DC: Author.

Vance, L. 1993. "Ecofeminism and the Politics of Reality." Pp. 118-145 in *Ecofeminism: Women/Animals/Nature*, edited by G. Gaard. Philadelphia: Temple University Press.

Wallerstein, I. 1974. *The Modern World System*. New York: Academic Press.

_____. 1979. *The Capitalist World System*. Cambridge: Cambridge University Press.

Ward, K.B. 1993. "Reconceptualzing World System Theory to Include Women." Pp. 43-68 in *Theory on Gender, Feminism on Theory*, edited by P. England. New York: Walter de Gruyter.

Warren, K.J. 1987. "Feminism and Ecology: Making Connections." *Environmental Ethics* 9: 3-20.

_____. 1988. "Toward an Ecofeminist Ethic." *Studies in the Humanities* 140-156.

_____. 1990. "The Power and Promise of Ecological Feminism." *Environmental Ethics* 12: 125-146.

_____. 1991. "Ecological Feminism." *Hypatia* 6: 1-2.

————. 1993. "A Feminist Philosophical Perspective on Ecofeminist Spiritualities." Pp. 119-132 in *Ecofeminism and the Sacred*, edited by C. Adams. New York: Orbis Books.

————, ed. 1994. "Toward an Ecofeminist Peace Politics." Pp. 179-200 in *Ecological Feminism*, edited by K.S. Warren. New York: Routledge.

Waring, M. 1988. *If Women Counted: A New Feminist Economics*. San Francisco: Harper and Row.

West, C. and S. Fenstermaker. 1993. "Power, Inequality and the Accomplishment of Gender: An Ethnomethodological View." Pp. 151-174 in *Theory on Gender, Feminism on Theory*, edited by P. England. New York: Walter de Gruyter.

West, C. and D. Zimmerman. 1987. "Doing Gender." *Gender and Society* 1: 125-151.

White, L. 1967. "The Historical Roots of Our Ecological Crisis." *Science* 155: 1203-1207.

Zimmerman, M. E. 1987. "Feminism, Deep Ecology and Environmental Ethics." *Environmental Ethics* 9: 21-44.

————. 1994. *Contesting Earth's Future: Radical Ecology and Modernity*. Berkeley: University of California Press.

SUSTAINABLE DEVELOPMENT AS A SOCIOLOGICALLY DEFENSIBLE CONCEPT:
FROM FOXES AND ROVERS TO CITIZEN WORKERS

Adam S. Weinberg, David Pellow, and Allan Schnaiberg

ABSTRACT

We evaluate the utility of the dominant symbols and theories that revolve around current ideas of sustainable development. Using the case of recycling, we stress the role of intragenerational power distributions for future intergenerational allocations of natural resources. Sustainability requires a new type of politicized marketplace, changing where competition takes place between major social segments and operating principles under which actors compete in the marketplace. Recycling exemplifies this need, because it currently operates within an historically skewed, transactionally based market. Decision-making capacity is

Advances in Human Ecology, Volume 5, pages 261-302.
Copyright © 1996 by JAI Press Inc.
All rights of reproduction in any form reserved.
ISBN: 0-7623-0029-9

heavily influenced by major economic actors. They have every incentive to avoid accurate estimation of environmental and social costs of production, and to maintain their ability to resist competition from other social groups. Unlike citizen-workers, these market actors also lack the "knowledge-as-lived-experience" required for ensuring that a socially and environmentally benign market for recycled goods will be attained and sustained.

SUSTAINABLE DEVELOPMENT AS PROBLEM AND OUTCOME: THE VIEWS OF FOXES AND ROVERS

At a recent conference, we noted the following adjectives used to talk about sustainable development: vague, vacuous, sweeping, and meaningless. Andrew Blowers and Pieter Glasbergen wrote, "The concept of sustainable development can easily be dismissed as all things to all people, a concept so vague as to be almost meaningless. Indeed, it has been described as a cliché, a passing fashion, even as an oxymoron" (1994, p. 8). In this paper, we argue that the concept of sustainable development is worth saving from "the dustbin of history," and can properly be viewed as a sociologically defensible concept.

Using the case of recycling, we refine the concept of sustainable development, offering alternative images, explanations, and arguments. We probe the utility of the dominant symbols and theories that revolve around current ideas about sustainability. We do not develop here a fully operationalized concept. Rather, we draw from a variety of social science literatures to reconstruct *sustainable development* as a concept that challenges currently accepted social constructions. Our goal is to contextualize a current practice in order to offer a new interpretation that raises issues, reorders research, and opens room for debate. It is our contention that a strong literature on sustainable development is starting to emerge in the social sciences (Daly and Cobb 1989; Hawken 1993; Norgaard 1995). In this paper, we offer a missing and important narrative for this literature. Elsewhere, we have referred to this approach as creating sociological narratives (Weinberg 1994; Gould, Weinberg, and Schnaiberg 1993).[1]

The narrative that we present highlights the importance of *intra*generational power distributions. Sustainable development is predicated on *inter*generational equity, defined as meeting the needs of the present without compromising the ability of future generations to meet their own needs. But in few of the proposals for sustainable development is there also a focus on *intra*generational differences in contemporary citizens' access to ecosystems. These discussions ignore a major feature of the present difficulties of attaining a sustainable political economy in the indeterminate future: the historical growth of inequalities in citizens' direct access to natural resources.

We start with the observation that sustainable development is worth developing as a sociologically defensible concept. Rhetorically, it has become a public sphere for conversation between industry leaders, activists, planners, technicians, and politicians. Yet this process is, alas, one where people are often talking past one another. Despite such skepticism, though, the Rio Conference, the Brundtland Report, and the European and the U.S. Presidential Commissions on Sustainable Development all stand as countervailing evidence for the public legitimacy of the concept as a social goal.

Angela Liberatore (1994), the European Commission Directorate General for Science, Research, and Development Unit on Socio-Economic Environmental Research, herself describes the limited outcomes of these conferences, reports, and commissions. However, she notes that there now exists an *institutionalized* recognition of the need to integrate economic and environmental needs into European Commission policy (Liberatore 1994). Moreover, as Herman Daly and John Cobb state, "In legitimating the concept of sustainable development they [the Bruntland Commission] have made it easier for others to press the issue further" (1989, p. 76). Simply, much of the relatively small space for public discourse around the "need to do things differently" has emerged around the term sustainable development.[2] In many ways, this space is now relatively more important for those opposed to the current structure of transnational capitalism. The decline of socialist or other communal forms of economic organization has led to a decline in organized opposition to current forms of late capitalism, following the collapse of the USSR and many Third World alternatives to the treadmill of production (Schnaiberg and Gould 1994, ch. 9; Barnet and Cavanagh 1994).

This brings us to our second point. To be sociologically defensible, a concept must be deployable "as a coherent and useful category of social analysis, in looking concretely at life as it is lived" (Williams 1994, p. 777). A concept must help explain social action. To meet this criterion, concepts link problems and outcomes through process. A concept must outline a problem and a "more favored consequence." It must also create a process which serves as a backdrop to illuminate the problem. Finally, it must logically and theoretically undergird a course toward this more desirable consequence.

Importantly, we are two-thirds of the way towards a concept of sustainable development that meets this criterion. Dense literatures exist on both the problem of having a nonsustainable political economy, and on what a sustainably developed future would look like. Among European social scientists, Michael Redclift is the best known theorist on the problem of sustainable development (1984, 1987). For Redclift, the political economy of advanced capitalism is driven by

> a concentration of control in fewer hands for short-term gain, at the expense of longer-term benefit to the environment and the largely poor, rural populations, whose livelihoods depend upon better resource conservation (1984, p. 38).

From this set of arrangements, Redclift traces growing ecological and social disruption. Similarly, in the United States, the subfield of environmental sociology can be traced to a similar critique that emerged in the 1970s (Anderson 1976; Stretton 1976; Schnaiberg 1973, 1975; Tanzer 1974). In our own work, we have developed the model of the treadmill of production as a way of describing why current practices are *un*sustainable. Through the treadmill concept, we link unsustainability to current political and economic arrangements (Schnaiberg 1980, 1986a, 1994; Schnaiberg and Gould 1994; Gould, Weinberg, and Schnaiberg 1993; Weinberg 1995; Weinberg and Gould 1993; Gould, Schnaiberg, and Weinberg 1996; Pellow 1994).

The economic component of this political-economic system has the publicly stated goal of expanding industrial production and economic development, as well as concomitantly increasing citizens' consumption. The political component of this system has a public confluence of private capital, organized labor, and all levels of governmental bodies, jointly promoting the goal of private-sector development. This confluence of interests is based on the increasingly widespread social belief that advances in public welfare are achieved primarily through economic growth. Materially, such interests are manifested in private investments in fixed capital, in public institutions developed by the state, and in the orientation of organized (and nonorganized) labor toward these investments and institutions.

Our basic model of the treadmill starts with the observation that all production processes include additions to (pollution)[3] and withdrawals from (resource depletion)[4] the ecosystem. Thus, all production processes are, to some extent, associated with incipient ecosystem disorganization. Within the political economy of a treadmill of production, producers are organized around trying to ensure profit margins from social production practices, in part through transforming natural resources into commodities. Generally, producers believe that market exchanges and productive physical capital are the economically "efficient" ways to transform natural resources into profits. Thus, producers continually seek to replace "inefficient" labor with "efficient" capital.[5] As this occurs, continual or increased ecosystem access is needed to "efficiently" operate the more productive physical capital. This occurs through two processes. First, technological change raises the capital-intensification of production. Second, over time, expanded ecosystem use is required, as production of each enterprise must generate enough private economic surplus to:

1. support outlays to capital owners,
2. provide enough additional profits to supply an adequate level of wages,
3. maintain consumer demand, and
4. generate enough tax revenue to cover social expenditures of the state.

Important for our discussion are four features of the treadmill:

1. More decisions become transactionally based, rather than built around social relationships;
2. Growth through efficiency and rationalization (and thus capital intensification) becomes the dominant goal;
3. As the treadmill expands, it draws more participants from other political-economic systems into treadmill relationships; and
4. Over time, most treadmill participants become increasingly locked into an accelerating treadmill, thus making it extremely difficult for any one party to reject the treadmill.

Dramatic recent increases in economic competitiveness on a transnational scale have generated corresponding increases in pressures to maximize profit margins in national and transnational firms, in part through minimizing their labor costs (Barnet and Cavanagh 1994). In recent years, for example, we have witnessed increases in the routine downsizing, outsourcing, and benefit rollbacks in institutions, organizations, governments, and individual businesses (Harrison 1994). Western societies have become intent on reducing social welfare expenditures during a period in which inequalities in each of these societies has increased. New wealthy classes have been created and/or expanded, through the "lean and mean" road of squeezing labor to increase profits for owners. Similarly, this trend has increasingly moved to previously underdeveloped Pacific Rim societies, ranging from China to Indonesia and Thailand, with similar promises for Vietnam and other less developed societies, as well as Latin American societies (Barnet and Cavanagh 1994).

In this increasingly transnational diffusion of the treadmill growth model, for most managers and investors the capacity to imagine—let alone to behave—in a socially and/or environmentally responsible manner has become a veritable pie in the sky.

The problem for sustainable development is that the core logic of the treadmill is antisocial and anti-ecological: It is a logic of unsustainable development. Often, the labor cutbacks noted above are associated with substituting "improved" technology for labor. These new technologies are designed to generate higher profits per unit production, often through accelerating the transformation of natural resources into commodities. Some of these newer technologies are touted as environmentally benign, requiring fewer natural resource inputs (ecological withdrawals) and/or generating lower polluting by-products (ecological additions). Yet most of these new technologies are associated with expanding corporate production and profits, to amortize the new physical capital investment outlays (Schnaiberg and Gould 1994, ch. 10). Such expansion often entails higher aggregate withdrawals and additions, to "rationalize" these technological investments.

Paradoxically, as natural resources are continually extracted by more investors for expanded production, such resources eventually become scarcer, even though "new" sources are often made more accessible ("discovered") with new technologies. This has become more subtly apparent with regard to major ecological components such as land, water, and clean air, than with the more dramatic arguments in the 1970s about minerals and some fossil fuels. Meanwhile, both the state and major producers become increasingly committed to increasing their practices of natural resource extraction. Producers become committed in order to maintain profits needed to refinance past capital outlays, as well as to attract investors for future expansion. The state becomes dependent upon producer-driven growth to finance the social welfare needs. Such needs emerge as negative externalities of producer-driven growth, as citizen-workers become ejected from the treadmill (Gould, Schnaiberg, and Weinberg 1996). Producers and the state often collaborate to extend both corporate trade networks and political influence, as has been the case in the North American Free Trade Agreement (NAFTA) and the General Agreement on Tarriffs and Trade (GATT) (Gould et al. 1995).

As social science critiques of the treadmill's political economy have become diffused and accepted, a cottage industry of more recent texts has emerged. The latter posit what a "more favorable consequence of political economy" might be. From this discourse emerged a model for a different outcome: "sustainable development." These texts accept the Brundtland Commission definition of sustainable development as "meeting the needs of the present without compromising the ability of future generations to meet their own needs" (World Commission 1987, p. 5). But they suggest more detailed or grounded notions of what this would actually mean. These end points range from creating a restorative economy driven by true cost accounting (Hawken 1993), to a more communally based capitalism (Daly and Cobb 1989), and communal institutions to support intergenerational rights (Norgaard 1995). We note that each of these texts are embedded in some notion of sustainable development becoming a preferred outcome. Within each, the following are balanced:

1. individual and community needs,
2. short- and long-term interests, and
3. economic and ecological criteria.

However, what is still missing from this literature is a process to move from the treadmill organization toward sustainability, in a fashion outlined most clearly by Stretton (1976). We do not have a social, political, or economic *program* that can link these political economy critiques with the "better futures outcome." Creating such a program entails confronting a number of conceptual issues. The first of these is what we could refer to as "the fox in the chicken coop" problem. A typical account of sustainable development is that it arose as a way for environmentalists and producers to find common ground.

Actually, though, sustainable development arose as private producers and state actors tried to *capture* the social construction process and the label of *sustainable development* to push their own agendas. Richardson (1994) and Carter (1994) have both referred to this as the anthropocentric/biocentric tension. Producers have sought to develop an anthropocentric concept of sustainable development that repackages treadmill growth in the language of sustainable development (Richardson 1994). Likewise, environmentalists have tried to develop a biocentric approach that operationalizes sustainable development as an environmental agenda, regardless of economic and social costs (Carter 1994). Producers have tried to argue (against environmentalists) that only producers have the production expertise needed to locate the "balances." In other words, the foxes want to guard the chickens, arguing that they are the most experienced when it comes to these matters. In contrast, the only expertise that environmentalists can claim is that only they can articulate the real needs of the chickens.

The problem of foxes is a by-product of how social segments and their stakes emerge within a treadmill. At its simplest, we can contrast the major conflicts between producers and environmentalists, and the role of the state as "mediator" of these conflicts. Producers, whether capitalist or socialist (Stretton 1976; Feshbach and Friendly 1991), are largely organized around environmental resources. They attempt to capture the exchange values of such resources through the producers' operations in various economic markets. Exchange-value orientations to ecosystems involve the transformation of ecosystem elements (trees, minerals, and animals). Industrial processes generate goods, which may be exchanged for money or other goods in an open market. Producers are structurally bound to these interests, as a by-product of their need for routinized calculation of monetary profits. This high degree of consciousness around material interests to natural resource access locks producers into mobilizing all forms of control capacity to capture the exchange values in markets. In addition, they use social, political, and economic assets to influence the modern state, which partly regulates social access to ecosystems. Such controls also include the hijacking of social discourses around natural resource use (Weinberg 1995; Gould, Weinberg, and Schnaiberg 1993).

In contrast, local and national environmental movement organizations develop use-value interests in ecosystems. Use values refer here to the utilization of ecosystems by individuals, families, and communities, without substantial alteration or transformation of those ecosystems. Ecosystems may be used for recreation, physical and psychological health, and aesthetic needs without substantial ecosystem disruption, depending on the quantity and quality of such activities. These range from biological sustenance (from air, water, and agricultural land) to recreational or aesthetic interests in these systems viewed as natural habitats. For environmentalists, natural resource use is conceived as being a zero-sum game. If an ecosystem element is acted upon by treadmill participants with exchange-value interests, it destroys the use-value quality of that unit. Movement organizations will use all their available social, political, and economic discourses to stem the tide of what they perceive as rampant (or hegemonic) exchange-value actions by treadmill agents.

Importantly here, producers and environmentalists have clear and specific constructions of their respective interests, which are thought to be essential to meeting their present and future needs. For each constituency, sustainable development then is seen as an arena, a place to act on these differing interests. The goal of sustainable development is viewed as problematic and dangerous by both groups. Producers fear that any adjustments will decrease their productivity through tightening market controls, while environmentalists interpret compromise merely as business as usual by any other name. Capturing the discourse, definition, and construction of sustainable development is the only plausible option for each of these contending groups. Furthermore, both sides fear that if they do not control the construction, the other side will do so. Thus, the disparity is both a product of vested interest— the respective positions of the two social sides supporting or opposing the political-economic treadmill—rather than merely a "tragedy of the commons," that is, of the ecosystems themselves. This is a political-economic conflict between more "commons" groups (collective use-value interests) and more "anti-commons" groups (privatized exchange-value interests).

The other conceptual issue is what we could call the problem of "rovers." Here we take our cue from a Gary Larson cartoon (*The Far Side*) of a man instructing a dog, who of course does not understand human language. The man yells "Good dog, Rover, go fetch the stick, Rover"—but the dog only hears "…... Rover …...Rover." Unlike foxes, the problem with rovers is not one of their goals or intentions. Rather, rovers lack the understanding of how natural resource usage is deeply embedded in existing social, political, and economic structures. Thus, for example, well-intentioned urban planners (Pakarinen 1994; Howe

1994) and industrial technocrats (Tibbs 1993a, 1993b) seek to create spaces for and operating systems of sustainable development. But their proposals fail to appreciate how their proposed new practices will actually challenge old practices and powerful practitioners within the existing transnational treadmill. In turn, this lack of appreciation of political-economic embeddedness leads such proponents to underestimate the resistances to their proposals arising from treadmill institutions (Schnaiberg and Gould 1994, ch. 5).

An example is the newly emerged literature on industrial ecology (Tibbs 1993a, 1993b). Following some of the earlier work of Ayres (1989), Harden Tibbs outlines a model of industrial ecology that starts with the assumption that

> [d]esigns that meet, say, only basic technical criteria may well be effective over the short run. It is only when such partial solutions are deployed extensively for long periods that their environmental and other shortcomings threaten unsustainability (1993b, p. 13).

Industrial ecologists talk about producers moving (and producers being moved by their ideas) toward a Maslow-type hierarchy of: (4) personal actualization, (3) social functioning, (2) ecological fitness, (1) technical operation (Tibbs 1993b, figure 7). Tibbs notes,

> [t]he levels form a hierarchy in that in the long run systematic effectiveness of decisions made at any one level will depend on the criteria of the next highest level also being met simultaneously (1993b, p. 13).

Tibbs and other industrial ecologists offer a number of examples of the recent greening of corporations. They view this as testimony of the socioeconomic *potential* for a future industrial ecology, as well as for the immanence of a socio-environmental decision hierarchy (1993b). In each instance, a case is premised on (1) evidence of a widespread historical turnabout, representing a new corporate interest in longer term ecological protection, and/or (2) evidence that, under certain favorable conditions, corporations can and will adopt a "green" perspective.

While we are certainly aware of a diversity of corporate positions and action on "greening," we have found that upon close examination the "greening" of corporations such as those cited by Tibbs is more a *social construction* put upon disparate activities and motives. It is, so to speak, an *epidemic of local economic reports* rather than a *report of a green epidemic* (Schnaiberg 1994; Schnaiberg and Gould 1994). "Greening" is not a viable option for most organizations within the treadmill's political economy. This is amplified by the recent period of mergers and acquisitions in which producers have come to face:

1. growing indebtedness;
2. rising degrees of global liquidity leading hostile takeovers, which strip companies' assets and displace managerial and nonmanagerial labor through plant shutdowns (Anders 1992);
3. "downsizing" and "outsourcing" (Harrison 1994); and
4. globalizing trade, such as with GATT and NAFTA agreements, creating more opportunities for expansion of transnational corporations (Gould et al. 1995).

This tension is well articulated in Walley and Whitehead's (1994, p. 47) cautions about the U.S. producers trying to go "green":

> Companies should seek to minimize the destruction of shareholder value that is likely to be caused by environmental costs rather than attempt to create value through environmental enhancements.... In an area like the environment, which requires long-term commitment and cooperation, untempered idealism is a luxury. By focusing on the laudable but illusory goal of win-win solutions, corporations and policy makers are setting themselves up for a fall with shareholders and the public at large. Both constituencies will become cynical, disappointed, and uncooperative when the true costs of being green come to light. Companies are already beginning to question their public commitment to the environment, especially since such costly obligations often come at a time when many companies are undergoing dramatic expense restructuring and layoffs.

Most problematic for us is that efforts to green production practices fly in the face of a transnationally competitive market system. Managers' fates are increasingly meted out based on their short-term performance, as dictated by the "bottom line." Research on the practices, values, and tactics of major American producers find them reacting to the transnational political economy by adopting those values that are antithetical to sustainable development (Hampden-Turner and Trompenaars 1993; Harrison 1994; Barnet and Cavanagh 1994; Reich 1991). They seek short-term achievements for individual firms, as defined by growth, acquisition, and profitability. Producers internalize and manage the challenges of the treadmill by thinking about themselves as individual players in an economy without nations, while, in Reich's words, "the very idea of an American economy is becoming meaningless" (1991, p. 8).

One way to merge the problem of foxes and rovers is to think about the model for future sustainable development as sharply antithetical to the operations of the present treadmill of production. The ethical argument for sustainable development is built around needs of future generations driving social change in national and transnational production technologies. The European Community outlines the elements of such an approach to sustainable development:

> (i) it focuses on the agents and activities which deplete natural resources and otherwise damage the environment, rather than waiting for problems to emerge;

> (ii) it endeavors to initiate changes in current trends and practices which are detrimental to the environment, so as to provide optimal conditions for socioeconomic well-being and growth for the present and future generations;

> (iii) it aims to achieve such changes in society's pattern of behavior through the optimum involvement of all sectors of society in a spirit of shared responsibility, including public administration, public and private enterprise, and the general public (as both citizens and consumers);

> (iv) responsibility will be shared through a significant broadening of the range of instruments to be applied contemporaneously to the resolution of particular issues or problems (1993, p. 39).

Two phrases are expecially noteworthy in this agenda. First, "agents and activities which deplete natural resources and otherwise damage the environment" refers primarily to organizations that dominate the treadmill of production. Second, "to initate changes in current trends and practices which are detrimental to the environment, so as to provide optimal conditions for socioeconomic well-being" is a proposal to change treadmill behaviors.

In sharp contrast to this need-based approach, theoretical work on decision making argues that organizational capacities are far more significant in actually shaping these decisions (e.g., March 1987). For each component of the European Commission's agenda for sustainable development, we have the theoretical possibility of new rights/needs/values that have been articulated by some agency within the Commission. But for each dimension of socio-environmental change toward sustainability, the historical record indicates that the operations of the treadmill have recently produced regressions as well as progressions in actually achieving these socio-environmental rights, values, or goals. Examples include the abrogation of earlier minority rights, the political overruling of the Endangered Species Act and other legislation for pollution control in the name of increasing economic competitiveness, and rising unemployment and declining wages (Galbraith 1992; Goodwin 1992). Additionally, in at least the United States, since 1960 there has also been a dramatic expansion of the work week for full-time employees (Schor 1991). Taken together, these historical trends reflect a decrease in the time, money, and personal energy available to most citizen-workers in the current generation within our own societies, for supporting their leisure *and* their family life (Coontz 1992).

One interpretation of these realities is that economic development has been and continues to be the primary criterion for transnational managers and investors as well as national and local governments. When we turn to the EC agenda for expanding and sustaining social and environmental functioning and review changes in the past several decades, we find almost as many examples that contract and diminish these functions. They include mass starvation, artificial ecological disasters, and accelerated genocidal practices, despite heightened awareness of these social realities through the "electronic highway." The reality is that transnational production and capital flows, which theoretically have the capacity to reduce major social inequalities, have largely circumvented (if not worsened) them for at least the past decade or two. Empirically, we can observe a greater "unsustainability" of the lives of impoverished people all around the globe. But when exactly will their "long-run" impact alter conditions of transnational decision makers, and make their current and recent actions "unsustainable?"

We argue that the missing component of the discourse on sustainable development is the importance of citizenship (see Somers 1993, 1994; Turner 1986, 1993; Harrison 1991). We define citizenship as "participation in public life." For sociologists, the concept of citizenship draws attention to the relationship of the citizen with society as a whole (Weinberg 1995). When we talk about the process of creating more citizenship, we mean shifting the distribution of power to the citizen, giving him or her the ability to make allocative decisions about natural resources. Here we use the term *citizen-workers* to highlight the fact that most often this redistribution of power would not entail just a shift in the context in which people make decisions—from their role as managers to their role as community members—but it would shift power to a wider array of people. In contrast to producers and state actors, we believe that citizen-workers have the enduring capacity *and* motive to seek this balance of use and exchange values, over the short and long term, for both individuals' and communities' needs.

In the rest of the paper we explore the emerging U.S. recycling industry to demonstrate the above ideas. Recycling was chosen because it is the closest economic practice we have that approaches some aspects of sustainable development. In its ideal form, recycling should use natural resources more wisely, create more jobs, and reduce municipal expenditures. Furthermore, the recent rise of this industry in the mid-1980s provides a 10-year history of practice, and it allows some documentation of experiences, which may be treated as data, on progress toward achieving sustainability. We conclude by discussing how the linkage between economic outcome and sociopolitical action provides for a richer notion of sustainable development.

RECYCLING AS SUSTAINABLE DEVELOPMENT

A Brief History of an Emerging Industry

Recycling policies emerged in an historical context in which there was high and continual dependency upon discarding most producer and post-consumer wastes.[6] Incineration, landfill, and other modes necessary to deal with growing waste volumes produced growing ecological problems in terms of water and air pollution. Furthermore, these modes of waste disposal took productive land out of use. As a reaction to the diminished use values of local ecosystem resources, citizen-workers in some locales mobilized in opposition to these waste disposal practices.

Throughout the 1980s, U.S. producers increasingly operated in a transnational economy marked by increased competitiveness, and shifting capital and natural resource flows (Lipietz 1987; O'Connor 1988). The Reagan and Bush administrations helped producers compete by allowing them to deflect the focus of the Resource Conservation and Recovery Act (RCRA) of 1976 from recycling *within* the production process (which was seen as too costly) to improved disposal of industrial *wastes* (which was seen as less costly), through landfills and incinerators.

This shift in RCRA interpretation led to a call from the Administration and major producers for more landfills and incinerators. Local communities reacted swiftly and defiantly against these proposals. To some extent, communities' fear stemmed from the coalescence of local pollution from existing landfills and the subsequent heightening of communities' consciousness about toxic waste pollution. National publicity about toxic hazards at Love Canal and other sites increased such local concerns (Szasz 1990, 1994; Brown and Mikkelson 1990; Schnaiberg 1992).[7] From this rising concern with toxic industrial wastes, local communities formed opposition groups, which joined forces with environmental organizations, to oppose *all* landfills and incinerators. This gave rise to the LULU movement (locally unwanted land uses), opposing such investments in their localities.[8]

As the LULU movement spread, a "landfill crisis" emerged. Existing landfills were "filling up" (e.g., Tackett 1987; Bukro 1989), while LULU groups stopped the construction of new ones and the expansion of existing ones. Simultaneously, LULU groups began to channel protests and fears toward locally elected officials, calling on them to control some portion of the land used for landfills and incinerators (Schnaiberg 1992). Consequently, local governments became focal points and mediators of these conflicts. While their response to these pressures varied widely, the dominant concerns were split between supporting constituencies and enhancing those dominant economic interests which, in turn, provide funds to the state and its transfer payments to constituents (as well as election support for legislators; Barlett and Steele 1992).[9]

Despite the ambivalence to act, local governments (municipalities) had to do something. First, they feared that constituents, fueled by these local LULU groups, would withdraw political support for those administrations that failed to adopt some type of palatable policy. Second, the Reagan-Bush administrations shifted responsibility into regional, state, and local arenas, making it *their* responsibility.[10] Third, industrial producers were placing pressure on local and other governments (Lowi, 1979) to maintain low-cost ("cost-effective") waste disposal, in order not to increase corporate costs in a time of rising transnational economic pressures (Szasz 1990; Blumberg 1980). Some local producers threatened to relocate production facilities if measures were not taken immediately (Gould 1991). Other producers refused to site new facilities in communities that could not provide long-term disposal options.

Despite the urgency, local governments were befuddled as to how to proceed. Building new landfills would increase costs for industrial producers, making this a politically unfeasible choice. Local officials could not afford to alienate powerful allies, shrink the tax base (as profits decreased), and lose jobs (again, as profits decreased and facilities relocated). Likewise, landfills had high social visibility (Schnaiberg 1993) and were, therefore, likely to draw LULU mobilization. Local government and industrial leaders managed these tensions by borrowing an old concept from the successful Keep America Beautiful campaign by using the principle of: "out of sight, out of mind" (Szasz 1990).[11] Garbage, landfills, and "resource conservation" became merged in a dramatically new program of "curbside recycling."

Typically, a curbside recycling program was envisioned to run as follows: A municipality would pick up wastes constructed of selected natural resources (most often paper, aluminum, steel, glass, and plastic). These wastes would be transported to a materials recovery facility (MRF), where the wastes would be sorted into recyclables and nonrecyclables (including wastes that were accidentally thrown into the recycling bin, and those that were too contaminated to be recycled). The end product was a recycled feedstock, comprised of discarded products made of natural resources that could be remanufactured into new products. The recycled feedstock was then sold to various producers, who used it to make new marketable products.

According to predictions by public policy experts, recycling could reduce local waste disposal costs, allowing communities to recapture some exchange value of this waste, as materials were sold to private sector organizations that would remanufacture new goods from these wastes.[12] Recycling would be the first stage in moving wastes into a more market-driven commodity than was the case for landfills or incinerators. It was the "solution" for the "landfill crisis" (Gutin 1992). Not only would recycling not generate local opposition, but it would win praise and votes for local officials. By reducing the waste stream, disposal costs would decrease, saving tax payers money. Finally, it would create jobs, as both the programs and remanufacturing process were labor-intense.[13] Thus, recycling was envisioned as a truly sustainable development practice that would balance environmental and economic costs, short- and long-term needs, and individual and communal interests.

By the early 1990s, communities across the United States were active in recycling. An estimated 5,400 cities and towns had curbside programs, and 41 states had official recycling goals (Consumer Reports

1994). Jerry Powell, the editor of Resource Recycling magazine and chair of the National Recycling Coalition, commented, "In the first week in November 1992, more adults took part in recycling than voted" (Consumer Reports 1994, p. 92). It was apparent that recycling had become institutionalized as a waste disposal practice. The industry was not going to dissolve. Too many municipalities, producers, and lenders had sunk too much capital into the industry. Likewise, too many politicians and policy planners had sunk too much political capital. As programs multiplied, however, the industry became less profitable. No organizations existed that were capable of "economically" recycling the wastes. In some cases, the wastes had become too commingled, and the physical-chemical separation necessary for the remanufacturing process was unavailable or very costly. Other times, there was not enough demand to warrant recycling. Mills underproduced. Finally, sometimes, physically and potentially recyclable goods were not remanufactured because the supply of wastes exceeded the remanufacturing capacity for that product. This was the case for certain types of steel and aluminum.

As insufficient demand grew for products remanufactured from recycled feedstock, markets became glutted and materials were either not marketable, or were sold for a small fraction of the costs of gathering and separating them. This discontinuity between supply and demand sent the price of recyclables plummeting, leaving municipal recycling programs and remanufacturers in financial trouble, and voters and lenders weary of future commitment. Prices for old newspapers in Chicago, for example, dropped from $42 a short ton in 1988 to $6 in 1992 (Apotheker 1993). Waste Age, a leading recycling industry journal, led off its "Year in Review" edition with, "For recyclers, 1992 was supposed to be the year of change as markets recovered from their 1991 slump. Instead, there were few glimpses of hope" (Rabasca 1992, p. 1). The industry was in danger of being scaled back, unless new markets could be developed.

Throughout the 1990-1992 period, a discourse emerged among recyclers, producers, state actors, and environmental organizations over how to develop markets. The consensus that emerged was that individuals and producers needed to "close the loop"—a strategy of balancing supply and demand by recyclers participating in both the collection of discarded materials (the supply) and the purchasing of remanufactured products (the demand).

"Closing the Loop": Focusing on Materials, the State, and/or Prices?

Choices of Materials

By 1993, nearly every actor involved in the recycling industry was preparing reports addressing the "closing the loop" problem. Representatives of industries with strong markets and municipal program operators favored a strategy of "getting the materials right." The logic of their argument was that "[l]ocal governments are being forced to recycle items that aren't economically feasible to recycle and businesses are being forced to absorb costs" (Rabasca 1993, p. 22). Recycling should be restricted to those goods that could be collected, sorted, and sold for a profit. All other goods should be disposed of through other waste disposal means.

This strategy was seen as politically favorable due to the invisibility of the action. Municipalities could still actively recycle, emphasizing the materials that were being collected, while downplaying those that were no longer collected (Bishop 1991; Morris and Dickey 1991). Ideologically, this argument was embedded in the logic of the treadmill, namely that the market should dictate. Protecting strong markets, while sacrificing weaker ones, was allowing the "free hand" to do its thing. Finally, the strategy was economically beneficial. It ensured profitable programs. This was especially important in locales where programs were coming under political attack from public officials who worried about increased costs of programs. Some officials voiced concern about recycling being used by opponents as an example of "liberal spending programs" run amuck. The best example of this is New York City, where the Democratic City Council went from passing an ambitious recycling plan 1989 to trying to scale back its program in 1992.

Environmentalists and representatives from industries with weak markets vehemently opposed this approach. Their response included an historical argument that markets always take time to develop. Furthermore, they remobilized the original LULU constituencies by arguing that "getting the material right" would not save landfill space by removing volume (like paper) or hazards (like batteries). Using comments like those of Karl Kamena of Dow Chemical who stated, "We need to look at what we can collect to get value rather than what we can collect to save our landfill space" (Rabasca 1993, p. 2), environmentalists were able to label this approach as anti-recycling. Despite the strength of these arguments, what eventually staved off these efforts was the ability of environmentalist and weak market recyclers to propose a myriad of alternative policy options which revolved around more proactive state actions.

Choices in State Actions

Environmentalists and weak market producers (what we could call weak social segments) were able to turn the problems of "closing the loop" back onto legislative bodies and regulatory agencies, arguing that they needed to get "the state right." The alternative policy option was to locate the right combination of proactive state actions needed to create financial incentives for producers to expand markets, thereby closing the loop. Policies would control at least the quantities, and occasionally the prices, of recyclable materials that were reutilized in remanufacturing operations (Morris and Dickey 1991; Beck and Grogan 1991; McCarthy 1991).

The most pervasive attempt to stimulate markets has been with minimum content guidelines that specify several criteria of minimal incorporation of both producer and post-consumer wastes in production. Initially, this idea arose with regard to newspapers. Environmentalists and recycled paper producers argued forcefully that technology made it easy and relatively inexpensive to produce recycled newspaper, while newspapers took up a large proportion of the landfill. In 1989, California and Connecticut passed laws that mandated that all newsprint consumed in the state by the year 2000 must have 50 percent recycled fiber (Beck and Grogan 1991). Using this precedent, environmentalists and weak market producers envisioned enacting similar legislation in other places to cover a range of materials and products. At the local, county, and state level, these efforts met with limited success. By 1991, eight states had passed minimum content laws relating to newsprint, directory stock, glass, plastics, high grade paper, and mixed grade papers (Beck and Grogan 1991).

Despite early success, many policies became embroiled in a political reaction by trade associations and individual treadmill agents, who transformed the discourse from an open one about social and environmental policy priorities to a "technical-economic" debate over the "feasibility" of meeting these standards. The political strategy has been to supersede public agency concerns about socio-environmental imbalances by introducing market-treadmill criteria for evaluating agency efficacy. Thus, representatives of the newspaper industry have argued that minimum content regulations are likely to drive up the costs of papers, driving many out of business. They have also resisted these efforts by undermining the enforcement of such laws. For example, they have manipulated "recycled content" more toward producer wastes (a traditional form of industrial economizing), and also toward complex schemes of measurement that rely heavily on producer reporting to state agencies, as the following statement from a plastics remanufacturer notes:

> The definition of the term "post-consumer" is a potential time bomb waiting to destroy residential plastics recycling initiatives. When we define post-consumer in terms of material that has "satisfied its intended use", we go nowhere far enough in providing a definition to help enhance post-consumer residential plastics recycling. It is easy for any of us who are actually in plastics recycling to come up with material that will meet some of the new definitions and offer twice the quality at half the price of material that *really* came out of household trash. If we really want to help recycle plastics from used beverage containers and other household plastic containers, we should *refine the definition of "post-consumer" by adding the words industrial-commercial (PCIC) or residential (PCR)*. If we begin to use the terms PCIC and PCR when it comes to recycling labels, we will better inform those who buy these products about the *actual origins* of the material.... It would be absolutely ludicrous to suggest that industrial or commercial high quality scrap should not be recycled, and this is not my intent. However, it would be equally foolish not to recognize the added costs that are necessary in collecting, sorting, and cleaning post-consumer residential plastics waste compared to post-consumer industrial-commercial materials. To merely use an arbitrary and somewhat capricious definition of "post-consumer" on a label describing content will actually prove to deter recycling (Forman 1991, pp. 103-104).

The current response by remanufacturers, which Forman decries, strongly echoes what Banner, Doctors, and Gordon (1975) and Olson (1986) have termed a *distorted indicators* model. Public policies are undermined by private treadmill actors, who produce an "epidemic of compliance *reports*," rather than a realistic report of an "epidemic of *noncompliance*." The consequence of this altered discourse has been a lack of national policies.

More recently, other recycling proponents have sought to recapture the discourse by supporting minimum content legislation. Chlorine-free pulp mills, for example, have pushed the EPA to specify guidelines for chlorine-free pulp in federal procurement of recycled paper (Woods 1993). In general, the debates over minimum content regulations mirror the vested interests of the various parties involved in the industry. There is a direct correlation between expressed policy preference and placement within the treadmill. Environmentalists and producers that make goods from recycled feedstock favor the guidelines. Consumers who purchase large quantities of an item (e.g., newspaper publishers) and producers who make goods from virgin feedstock disapprove of the guidelines.

A less contentious approach advocated by environmentalists and producers (from both strong and weak markets) has been increased state subsidies in the form of procurement. Local, county, state, and national state actors agree to purchase materials and supplies made from recycled feedstock. At first this appeared to be a responsible and palatable policy. The same fights over the policy implementation, however, ensued. Before state agencies could act on their commitments, debates emerged among producers over what actually constituted recycled feedstock. Some producers tried to scurry the intent of the commitment by arguing for low content of recycled feedstock, or for non-post-consumer waste to be considered recycled feedstock. These debates became fierce, mirroring the ones over minimum content regulations.

Simultaneously, some agencies that began to procure and use recycled supplies found the practice in direct conflict with other regulations. Alexander Battery Co., for example, developed a recycling program for batteries. The program was stopped, however, due to the illegality of shipping hazardous waste via the U.S. Postal Service (batteries are considered toxic waste). Another example is that of used tires, which were to be used as crumb rubber in asphalt. Support for this cheap method of recycling tires grew after initial testing demonstrated that adding tires to asphalt had numerous performance benefits for roads. The largest barrier was a regulation by the Federal Highway Administration that prohibited using federal funds to pay for experimental practices. Because crumb rubber asphalt was a new technique, it was classified as experimental. Without the federal highway funds, the process was too expensive for most states to use.

Changing these regulations also turned out to be more difficult than recycling advocates envisioned. Again, returning to the example of used tires, Senator John Chafee (R-RI) introduced a bill in 1991 that would have required recipients of federal highway money to use a 5 percent rubber crumb mix. Immediately the bill became politically charged. It was strongly supported by the Rubber Manufacturers Association, the National Tire Dealers and Retreaders Association, the Rubber

Pavements Association, and by environmental groups. It was staunchly opposed by the National Asphalt Pavement Association and the State Highway Transportation officials. The bill generated extraordinary debate and activity for such a small federal regulatory alteration, and lost by a 93-7 vote.

Across the board, recycling proponents faced staunch opposition to altering federal regulations. While the rhetoric of these debates has been technical and mechanistic, the motives have been political. Producer of virgin materials displaced by recycled goods derailed the program to protect their markets. Yet, the failure to implement these program must also be shared by advocates, who grossly underestimated the barriers to enacting and enforcing these policies. Time and again proponents of recycling were caught off guard by the fierce opposition to recycling initiatives from industries that stood to lose business. In one of the more recent public displays, President Clinton proposed that the federal procurement. guidelines be changed to allow agencies to purchase recycled paper. The administration believed that this was "sound environmental idea" and a "reasoned policy." The proposal became embroiled in an intense political conflict. Given the amount of fiscal outlays on paper, this is not surprising. What is worth noting is the extent to which the administration was caught off-guard.

We trace this blind spot to a fundamental misunderstanding of the motives and means by which the recycling industry emerged. The industry arose as an exchange-value-driven solution to a set of political and economic problems. Given how interests and power distribution emerge within the treadmill, it should not have been surprising that these types of barriers arose.

Choices in Pricing Policies

As a result of these earlier setbacks, recycling proponents have developed new, more market-oriented approaches to developing markets. These include tax credits or tax write-offs for MRFs and remanufacturing plants, which have become popular in less affluent communities as one way of attracting high-tech remanufacturing facilities. A variant of these approaches is Recycling Market Development Zones (RMDZ), which provide formal places where companies congregate to remanufacture goods. The state provide producers with assistance in obtaining permits, in technical and financial resources, and in marketing advice. In return producers agree to use recycled feedstock and to provide jobs in the community.[14] These policies have been less contentious, but the profits largely revert to treadmill producers, with community payoffs in the form of some employment and some small tax gains.[15] Additionally, the public support for recycling does have limits, and often severely restricts the breadth of these zones.

Tax benefits have served as a bridge between "getting the state right" and "getting the price right" approaches to closing-the-loop. Increasingly, this seems to have become the favored policy instrument of planners involved in the recycling industry.[16] The assumption behind this strategy is that recycling can be a market-driven industry, if true markets were operating. Proponents have gone as far as to argue that recycling is the most cost-effective mechanism of waste disposal. This fact, they argue, is distorted by historically outdated regulations that favor virgin materials (Hawken 1993).

Buttressed by an EPA study that identified one dozen federal guidelines that distort prices, recycling industry representatives have begun to identify specific federal regulations that should be removed. The most significant of these concern energy subsidies. Production processes that use virgin materials are more energy-intense than those that use recycled feedstock. Thus, energy subsidies favor virgin production processes. The example most often cited is aluminum. Tax code provisions subsidizing energy exploration and development costs amount to energy subsidies of 8.5 percent of the delivered cost of primary aluminum. Additionally, the federal government subsidizes energy production in terms of fuel extraction, processing, and transmission. This translates into energy cost savings of 17 percent of the delivered cost of the primary metal (Powell 1993). From this, the argument is easily made by recycling proponents that if energy were paid for at its true cost, virgin materials would increase in price much more than recycled goods, due to differences in the amount of energy used.

A variant on this theme has been the recent call for full-cost accounting. Here, government agencies that provide solid waste services are required to calculate the cost of providing that service, including future liabilities, opportunity costs, potential environmental costs, and avoided costs. For example, one study showed that when you purchase 100 screws in a plastic box for $2.99, the public picks up an additional invisible bill for $7.44 in environmental and health costs. If the same screws are purchased in a paperboard box, the invisible bill is 19 cents

(Hawken 1993). With a full cost accounting, the $7.44 would be factored into the price of the product. Recycling industry representatives argue that this would favor recycled goods, because they have far fewer health and environmental externalities.

Early attempts at "getting the price right" seem to suggest that these efforts will run into many of the same barriers as attempting to "get the state right." Retracting the regulations that distort prices has proven to be politically infeasible. The EPA had tremendous difficulties even issuing its report documenting that regulations distort prices. Internal fighting within the EPA almost shelved the report. At one point, the agency claimed that the only copy of the report was accidentally destroyed at the printers. Deciding what externalities need to be "fully accounted" for opens the industry to the same technical debates that have derailed minimum content laws. Finally, by centering the discourse around "prices," recyclers are forced onto unfavorable terrain.

Under the rubric of full-cost accounting, getting the price right has become the latest rallying cry from environmentalists and others trying to move recycling toward a sustainable development practice. Missing from this cry, however, is an understanding of the limitations of full-cost accounting within a treadmill of production. Regardless of the price, decision making will remain transaction based. That is, producers and state actors will base their actions on cost/benefit analyses with short-term growth as the criteria. Full-cost accounting would not ensure that sustainable development decisions would be made. Factoring the externalities would only induce producers to make some decisions that took into account social needs under particular circumstances. These include instances where there were exchange-value gains from this, or through lowering transaction costs of compliance with strong political regulations of the market (Walley and Whitehead 1994).

Interestingly, the present arguments for "better pricing" ignore the historical lessons of the 1970s in the United States. Attempts to calculate negative environmental externalities of production include proposals to assess the "natural resource units" embodied in each product (Westman and Gifford 1973). A similar argument was used for energy asessments, building on the theory of economist Georgescu-Roegen (1973) and the energy research of Pimentel and his colleagues (Pimentel et al. 1973 1975, 1976). Neither of these approaches was ever used in production practices, except where they pointed toward cost-savings in technological changes that could then be publicized as "greening" of the corporate innovators. Similarly, the "recycling" logic of RCRA was only practiced in the 1980s where corporations could recapture economically valuable toxic solvents, and thus lower their operating costs (Keefe 1993). Otherwise, producers would still engage in unsustainable practices. The central mistake made by many recent arguments is confusing *efficiency* with *sustainability*. Only where sustainability happens to tactically coexist with efficiency do such practices occur; and the strategic drive of treadmill producers is still short-term efficiency: "To assure sustainability, each generation must transfer sufficient assets to the next generation, so that the next generation is as well off as it is" (Norgaard 1995, p. 152).

Internalizing some negative environmental externalities can lead to greater efficiency, but not necessarily to long-term sustainability. Norgaard makes this point by deconstructing current models developed by environmental economists. He notes that even the most recent literature on sustainability draws on models and reasoning that largely ignore *inter*generational equity, paralelling our argument on *intra*generational equity. The emphasis in this literature is on institutions for internalizing externalities, institutions that move the economy from inefficient practices to more efficient ones. Daly and Cobb make a similar point in their discussion of chrematistic (treadmill) and oikonomia (communal) forms of capitalism:

> Whereas those chrematists who recognize externalities try to internalize them into the market and thus into the chrematistic system, oikonomia studies the community as a whole and locates market activity within it. Whereas chrematists, when they recognize that much market activity does not contribute to economic welfare and that some nonmarket activity does, propose to subtract the former and to add the latter, oikonomia, by contrast, suggests that no quantifiable features of the community can measure its actual health (1989, p. 141).

Most simply, those calling for full-cost accounting do not understand the dynamics which have driven the industry.

REVISIONING RECYCLING:
THE ROLES OF FOXES AND ROVERS

We initially stated that this paper is meant to be a sociological narrative on sustainable development. The first part of this narrative drew upon preexisting literatures and current contexts to suggest a missing piece of the current discourse, urging other analysts to rethink current social.

constructions of sustainability. We also indicated that our missing piece of interest was the importance of *intra*generational power distributions. In the rest of the paper, we address this point more directly.

For recycling to become a sustainable development practice, tough choices have to be made about how to close the loop. Choices need to be made about regulations, tax structures, and procurement policies. With each decision there will be benefits and costs, as well as a social distribution of them. Prices for some goods will decrease while they increase for others. Jobs will be lost in some locales in favor of others. Ecosystems will be preserved in some areas, and polluted in others. Crucial to our argument is that precisely those social segments *empowered* by their place within the treadmill to make decisions, are simply *incapable* of doing so in ways that will move the political economy toward a state of sustainable development.

When state and industry leaders make decisions about recycling, they act like foxes and/or rovers. Abstractly, the social structural problem is not one of *personal* intent or knowledge, but rather one of *social* placement within the treadmill. Like other actors, state and industry decision makers want abundant material goods and subsistence from ecosystem elements. The problem is that their placement within the treadmill requires them to achieve these ends only through the logic of treadmill of production organizations. Neither the state nor industry have the motive or means to shift toward sustainable development, given their placement within the treadmill. Primarily, this can be traced to the dominant relations that shape any emergent industry of the treadmill, including the recycling industry.

Emerging industries within a treadmill of production exist in fundamental tension with other preexisting industries. Mostly this is due to the existing treadmill's secondary effects on any emergent industry, which threatens to change procurement practices, regulations, and cultural norms for existing treadmill institutions. Emergence of this industry implies disruption of other industries, as old clients come to make new selections from within the newly expanded list of suppliers. Different types of producers, state actors, and communities have experienced this tension in differing ways, given their relationship to the larger political economy. For producers, the outcomes of the emerging recycling industry matter a great deal in terms of their future survivability in increasingly tight transnational markets. For producers that use recycled feedstock, profitability is a direct consequence of directions taken by the industry. Ideally, prices for recycled feedstock will decrease while demand for such products will increase (Holusha 1994). Each of the policies discussed will have dramatic impacts on the costs of recycled feedstock and the demand for products made from recycled feedstock. Conversely, producers that use virgin feedstock also have futures that are closely tied into the industry. The demand for recycled paper will reshape the demand for virgin paper and wood pulp. Furthermore, the success of one form of business within a sector of an industry increases intrasectoral competition by splitting revenues.[17]

For state actors, recycling embodies numerous challenges, opportunities, and tensions. Among local actors, it presents an opportunity to address landfill problems in a way that is politically expedient and financially beneficial. In the array of regional regulatory actors, recycling may redistribute power from some agencies to others, as regulatory programs are altered. Programs that bolster recycling do so at the expense of other programs, thereby reducing resources from other agencies. For example, the Department of Interior is likely to be a loser, relative to the Environmental Protection Agency and Small Business Administration. For elected state officials, recycling can reduce or elevate support for them. Decisions are likely to win the favor of some trade associations and the scorn of others. Developing successful programs is likely to gain an official some small measure of support, while a fiscally disruptive program is likely to reduce support. Importantly, the size of the industry may draw too many powerful producers into the area, making it impossible for most public officials above the local level to ignore emergent conflicts within the industry and between it and environmental activists. As we saw from congressional examples, elected officials then have to pick sides in redistributive conflicts (Lowi 1972).

For environmental organizations, recycling is a potential opportunity to push for more sound *ecological* use of natural resources. The emerging industry gives them an opportunity to diminish the economic importance of ecologically unsound practices. Likewise, it provides a growing public space to make arguments about the importance of ecosystem protection. The history of pushes and pulls is also one of congressional debates, media coverage, and local hearings. Each of these arenas provides visible venues to present ideas, and to introduce new ways of thinking.

From these social segmental analyses we can deduce that, given the relations that exist between different social segments and the political economy—what we have called each social segment's placement within the treadmill—recycling has become an important arena of action. The arena has become populated by a variety of participants, each of whom have a recognized stake in the outcomes. Each is willing to devote some resources (time, money, political influence) to shaping those outcomes, though different segments have different volumes of resources to allocate.

Given their placement within the treadmill, though, the relations among these potential decision makers are skewed. Producers and state actors exist in organizations that stockpile important resources. They have access to basic resources like money, time, and technical expertise. Their organizational affiliation and status as repeat players gives them easy access to information channels about important state decision-making processes. As one byproduct of these earlier actions, they have preestablished ties with other participants and decision makers. They have trained staff that can garner favorable frames for various conflicts. And they have the ability to sustain these efforts over time. Contrarily, for local community groups, resources are invariably scarce (Weinberg 1995; Pellow 1994).

Furthermore, the distribution among producers is also skewed. Larger and older firms often have a distinct advantage (Harrison 1994). They have stockpiled more resources, including political connections, legislative expertise, and public confidence. Bennett Harrison (1994) notes that in any competitive market, the better established firms are able to protect themselves. Innovative firms that challenge older ways of doing things directly (that is, in a zero-sum way) are likely to be bought and dismantled, or confronted with unfavorable regulatory and tax environments (Harrison 1994). This reflects precisely the motives and means within the emergent recycling arena. Established producers (who rely on virgin feedstock) and state actors are being challenged by smaller innovative firms (who rely on recycled feedstock). These smaller firms are at a distinct disadvantage. They do not have the resources to fight larger producers, whose production practices are threatened (Holusha 1994).[18]

Mostly, the problem of decision making is one of criteria. Given their motives and means, producers and state actors construct an agenda based around exchange-value interests, which in turn has patterned the industry around transaction-cost decisions (Williamson 1975, 1981). Decisions about how to develop minimum content laws, full-cost accounting, and other potential mechanisms of market expansion are talked about and adjudicated using primarily *market* criteria: price, quality, availability, convenience. In short, the industry is to be shaped, so that it can be attractive to investors, based on its reduction of total transaction costs of waste disposal.

As a transactionally driven practice, recycling is not sustainable. First, we note that there is little attention to the social relations of workers (and taxpayers) in both waste sorting and remanufacturing. Little attention is currently paid to the quality of labor inputs, including occupational hazards, other than to reduce transaction costs and increase profits by minimizing labor costs. Community development (a form of sustainable development) is rarely addressed in most governmental recycling programs in the United States. This limits the *social* sustainability of recycling programs. Typical of the transactional orientation is Bishop's summary:

> Three factors appear to contribute to most of the cost of [MRF] processing operations: *wage rates*, the level of capital investment, and the general level of productivity (which, of course, is closely associated with the investment in *equipment*).... *The faster the processing, the lower* [*the*] *cost.* Glass container processing is particularly sensitive to sorting rates because of the labor intensity of the process. *Relative sorting rates ... developed from time studies and estimates ... varied from 600 to 700 pounds per employee hour to over 2,000 pounds per hour* (1991, pp. 42-43; emphasis added).

Likewise, environmental protection hardly enters the current agenda for *remanufacturing* in the United States: "Of less impact to MRF operating costs, but still significant, is the overall level of residue generated" (Bishop 1991, p. 43).[19]

On the other hand, much of the existing remanufacturing processes and plants cannot operate with only recycled materials (Forman 1991). Physical, chemical, and/or biological criteria for remanufacturing require some balancing of feedstock attributes. In all such instances, therefore, virgin materials must be added to the remanufacturing process—a reality which many ardent recycling enthusiasts ignore, preferring to believe in recycling as a modern form of alchemy. The material requirements of remanufacturing often "open the loop," requiring extraction of feedstocks to provide virgin materials to mix with recyclables in remanufacturing. This intrinsic part of much of remanufacturing has potential implications for biodiversity, because the extraction of virgin materials has historically been associated with the destruction of habitat and/or species in the ecosystems where extraction takes place. Yet recycling debates about transactions rarely if ever incorporate issues of biodiversity and habitat protection in their encouragement of remanufacturing—focusing on the "re" rather than the "manufacturing."

Recycling that focused on both the "re" and the "manufacturing" would close the loop by requiring each producer and consumer to gather their wastes *and* to purchase back the remanufactured products generated from their own wastes. What we have lies mostly at the opposite extreme: sets of actors motivated by exchange-value interests, who dominate the entire process, including the sociopolitical citizen-worker inputs into legislation and gathering wastes.

These blind spots in current recycling programs limit the practice as an exemplar for a socio-environmentally sustainable form of development. Partially, these blind spots are self-imposed. They are a problem of foxes. Producers, state officials, and other recycling advocates have tremendous amounts of capital, both fiscal and political, sunk into the expectation of the success of recycling industries. Personal gain drives these segments to deliberately ignore the dissonances. Institutional and organizational blinders are also in place. In this regard, there is a problem of rovers. Recycling advocates do not understand the embeddedness of recycling in larger political and economic struggles. *De facto*, they have become passive agents operating within the treadmill's structuring of market-determined prices. Advocates of recycling as sustainable development have missed the consequence of how getting the material right represents a *de facto* historical shift from an environmentally *initiated* program to an economically *operating* system (Rabasca 1992, 1993). It is a major retreat from the *ecological* sustainability of development, defined here in terms of "closing the loop": repeatedly re-using virgin materials through remanufacturing and incorporating waste streams as their major feedstocks.

Recycling, like industrial ecology, inclines more toward transactions than toward expanding production and political relationships with citizen-workers. Dominant political and economic treadmill actors currently view citizen-workers much more as an economic *force* of production in the remanufacturing process than as a *relationship* that must be explored both socially and economically. The political use of citizen-workers by remanufacturing agents within the treadmill is largely restricted to encouraging their democratically elected representatives to use tax monies to subsidize remanufacturing (e.g., Rabasca 1993). Ironically, remanufacturers tend to promote *relationships* with citizen-workers in their consumer and worker roles, encouraging them to purchase recycled end-products at home and at work. Furthermore, they have given little thought as to what type of institutions and processes sustainable development practices, like recycling, could be successfully embedded within. *Therefore we can conclude that recycling proponents do not understand the process by which we move from the unsustainable treadmill toward sustainability. While they don't act like the foxes of the treadmill, it is because they only have a Rover-like understanding of the political-economic realities of the treadmill.*

TOWARD CITIZENSHIP AS SUSTAINABLE DEVELOPMENT: MARKETS, MEANS, AND SOCIAL MEMORY

Although recycling has had only limited success in challenging the unsustainable treadmill within the United States, we suggest that recycling might be a powerful force for sustainable development by redistributing decision making toward more decentralized citizen-worker groups. The best hope of moving toward sustainable development is to bring "the citizen" back in to the decision-making process. Social and political relations need to be rearranged and redistributed so that power lies with citizen-workers. They are the only social agents with an enduring *motive* for balancing use and exchange values over the short and long term, for both individual and community needs. But they currently lack the *means* to actualize these motives.

It is not our task here to develop a comprehensive sociopolitical program. However, we can envision a number of ways that this could be done that would move toward a state of sustainable development. Decision making, for example, could be relocated to local community organizations. Residences could be grouped into homeowners' associations, block associations, and buildings. These informal organizations would serve as small waste districts, each of which would be charged with devising solutions to their waste generation. Such practices already exist in other societies, such as Japan.

As social scientists, part of our contribution to social decision making about community wastes could be to collect data on historical and comparative narratives about the practices of other societies and other times, to systematically evaluate social and ecological consequences, and to disseminate these analyses to community groups through some form of "best practices" handbook (as corporate advisers are now doing in downsizing and re-engineering). Citizen-workers could then choose between recycling, landfilling, and incineration, but with a deeper and clearer understanding of the likely social and environmental consequences, as well as the economic consequences. States would then get out of the business of recycling, except to effectively price common goods, including raw materials and ecosystems used for disposal (including maintaining air and water quality). MRFs and landfills would be locally owned and operated by these local community groups, who could contract with private or community-based firms, both to pick up wastes and to operate the sorting and even remanufacturing facilities.

Essentially, we are talking about recreating a new type of more overtly politicized market (Lindblom 1977; Williamson 1975, 1981), shifting the nexus of where the competition takes place, and under what operating principles. In theory, an effective market works to keep prices as true indicators of *net* economic value added, it maintains the system at an efficient level, and it makes more choices "knowable." But such markets have become distorted when decision-making capacity increasingly falls under the influence of major treadmill producers. First, producers have every incentive to avoid true cost estimation. Once they evade a payment, the cost is diffused to the community and ignored in accounting. Local citizen-worker groups should be less resistant to full-cost accounting, because they have to pay all the costs, whether overtly through taxes or covertly through illness and loss of use values from local ecosystems. Treadmill producers in effect steal from others; citizen-workers would increasingly have to confront that they were stealing from other citizens and/or future generations of their own children and grandchildren (Norgaard 1995). Producers experience such social-environmental cost accounting as a burden, which can reduce their benefits from private transactions. Realistic cost accounting would matter more to citizen-workers who will experience a mix of use and exchange value costs and benefits. Such accounting would help locate choices that protect labor/wages and ecosystems.

A slightly different way to think about this is to consider what gets taken into account as part of the cost/benefit analysis. Producers and state actors do not have to deal with social and political externalities of waste disposal decisions. Producers are not concerned with the tax increases and social problems that arise from declining job bases. Likewise, they escape the political hostility and the internecine conflicts that arise as some groups are less impacted than others. A similar process occurs for state actors. A regulatory state is organized by areas of jurisdiction. Therefore, it has been outside the purview of the EPA or municipal sanitation departments to worry about or make decisions based on social needs. This is the purview of another agency. Again, this is different for local citizen-worker groups, who pay one local tax bill. Included in that bill are the local social, environmental, and economic costs incurred, as a by-product of past treadmill decisions, continuing through its current practices.

Second, producer-driven markets are not efficient over time. Winners and losers are more a product of past performance. Operating most efficiently in waste disposal has been determined by size and political power. By shifting power to local citizen-worker groups, the field would be opened for smaller firms to compete. For example, in one municipality we examined, scrap dealers have been chased out by a large waste management firm (Pellow et al. 1996). These dealers could not effectively handle the city's waste stream. If decisions were made by local citizen-worker groups that were balancing social, political, economic, and environmental issues, these firms could have continued to compete. They were capable of serving the community area. Furthermore, they were often more efficient at providing the *social* goods that are a part of the political criteria of citizen-workers, as opposed to the economic criteria of treadmill firms (Pellow et al. 1996).

Finally, there is the issue of information and market performance. Reaching a state of sustainable development requires making a multitude of decisions and compromises about practices in locales in terms of servicing those locales. Norgaard notes that classic economic theory requires that:

> resource owners not only be aware of the qualities of different resources but that they also know the total stock of resources, future demand and the prospects for new technologies (1995, p. 155).

Citizen-workers possess information about these choices and needs. In contrast, treadmill producers make decisions about compromises between jobs and environmental issues, and then only at an abstract level. Contrarily, citizen-workers have to live with the problem of job instability and local air, water, and land pollution, although they may also move farther from both types of problems (Schnaiberg 1986b). Markets are ideally suited to taking lots of information and using it to locate efficient practices. But markets must exist. There must be competition and choices at the dimension where information is held.

In sustainable development, this lived knowledge exists within citizen-workers' lives, not producers' or state actors' roles.

By reconstructing recycling around the enactment of citizenship practices, the criteria of policy decisions would not be primarily about solid waste disposal. The overall goal would be to create policies that relegated power to local groups, giving them the information to make decisions. Of course, producers and other actors would intervene at every step to distort this information. They would also work to capture these local groups. We do not argue that these problems would go away, only that they would be less pronounced. Currently, the only actor with an interest in preventing the distorted information in a given battle is another producer or state actor, who wants true information here, but distorted information in other situations. There is no interested party that really needs or cares about true information save one: The enactment of citizenship practices would empower the only group that really needs it. At most this policy would empower a group with the motives to move toward sustainability and the means to resist capture by treadmill proponents. At the very least, this policy would shift the question of sustainable development away from "how to get organizations to act against their interests" and toward "how to get people to act in their vested interest." This latter question seems to us to be more reasonable and realistic.

NOTES

1.   This approach is a self-reflective process that situates rigorously collected and analyzed data within preexisting literatures. It contextualizes past elements, through plot and setting, into a more analytic temporal ordering (Maines 1993). In doing so, it creates alternative versions, which challenge readers to examine their own belief structures. This debunking relies most heavily on the use of socially relevant concepts. This brings us back into everyday experience, and makes us look for differences between theoretical forms in the literature, and experiential substance in our daily lives (James 1907). In other words, these concepts offer alternative images, explanations, and arguments which probe the utility of our dominant symbols and theories. They reveal new versions of why things happen the way they do, and thus ultimately provide grounded assessments of many ramifications of our current social arrangements and practices.

2.   We could add a political dimension to this argument. This social and political space, although small, represents twenty-five years of modern environmental movement struggle (Gould, Weinberg, and Schnaiberg 1993). Thus, it should not be given up, as long as it can support a more grounded critique of present socioeconomic structures.

3.   The first principle of thermodynamics is referred to as the law of conservation and matter. Matter cannot be created or destroyed. Matter cycles through the global environment. It can be chemically or otherwise physically transformed, but all the original materials are preserved in some form, without any being lost or created. Unused matter does not disappear as it is changed or transformed within the production process. Instead, unused matter takes the form of additions to ecosystems. Pollution and solid waste are the societal labels assigned to this type of transformed matter.

4.   The second principle of thermodynamics is referred to as the law of entropy. As energy is altered from its potential energy form (e.g., coal or oil) to more socially useful forms of kinetic energy (e.g., combustion to drive turbines), there is a loss of organization, defined as an increase in entropy. Energy is reduced from organized chemical forms into randomized heat. This randomized heat is less readily usable in social production. In one sense, it is spent energy. It is still energy, but its form has been changed from a socially potential resource to a socially unavailable (i.e., disorganized) resource. All production processes rearrange matter in ways that decrease the amount of available ordered energy. Natural resource depletion is the common label given to the social problems that arise from this principle.

5.   For example, the 500 largest American producers failed to add any American jobs between 1975-1990 (Reich 1991).

6.   An interesting side note to this changing history is the beverage container industry. Over the last two decades manufacturers of beverage containers have taken three strong stands with regards to their containers. In the late 1960s and early 1970s, they helped to spawn an early "cosmetological" (Schnaiberg 1973) social movement that wanted to "Keep America Beautiful." From the mid-1970s to the mid-1980s they spent millions of dollars opposing container deposits ("bottle bills") and other legislation designed to facilitate container reuse. Starting the mid-1980s they became among the most enthusiastic industrial supporters of recycling (Schnaiberg 1993). This historical juxtaposition alone should challenge our assumption that recycling represents the imminent dominance of (environmental) politics over economic markets (Lindblom 1977).

7.   This was either an "epidemic of reports," as seen by conservative politicians, or a "report of an epidemic," as seen by activists (e.g., Brown and Mikkelsen 1990).

8.   Many critics have labeled these local movements as NIMBY (Not In My Back Yard) movements, attacking them as undemocratic. The NIMBY label implies that local activists are selfish, materialistic, and often naive and noncosmopolitan in their ethos. The local community values are portrayed as the very antithesis of national needs, because these local groups accept the various production organizations which increase local and national environmental risks. It often portrays the local groups as simple-minded defenders of the status quo, as opposed to the supposedly "progressive" advocates of economic opportunity. Our view of such attacks is that they blame the victims. Just as the concept of political correctness demeans the political objectives of those who want to defend social and political victims of discriminatory behavior by gross caricatures, so too does the NIMBY designation negate the strategies, tactics, and contexts of local citizens struggling to protect their citizen and worker rights.

9.   Modern structural theories of the state have moved well beyond the earlier academic consensus around a pluralistic model of mediation (Buttel 1985). Three major perspectives on the advanced industrial state have emerged in the past twenty years,

each of which has some relevance for this paper. Instrumentalist views (Miliband 1969) conceptualize the state as an agent of the interests of the capitalist class. The activities of the dominant class of capitalist producers are reflected by state actors and agencies. A revision of this perspective by Poulantzas (1973a, 1973b) envisioned the state as a reflection of the entire class structure of advanced industrial societies. This structural concept of the state theorized that the major goal of the state apparatus was to reproduce the capital logic of the society, with a broader and longer term perspective than that imposed by the immediate interests of any segment or fraction of the capitalist class itself. The newest reformulation of the state, most widely expressed in the work of Skocpol (1979) and her students (Evans, Rueschemeyer, and Skocpol 1985; Skocpol and Amenta 1986) offers a more complex and dynamic view of the state. State actors and agencies are conceptualized as having some autonomous interests of their own. This becomes an additional factor in determining state actions. As well, this concept of a state-logic argues that the state's policies are more volatile than suggested by the earlier conceptualizations. The state, embedded in national and world-systemic contexts, produces an historical and comparative variability across time and states. This is due to the opportunities and constraints offered to state actors, and to various classes and class segments in advanced industrial societies.

10. Technically, the provisions of the Resource Conservation and Recovery Act (RCRA) of 1976 gave the federal government the pretense for doing something. In contrast, the Reagan and Bush administrations chose to do nothing.

11. Many of the beverage container manufacturers who had collaborated on the Keep America Beautiful, Inc. campaigns of the 1960s and early 1970s (Schnaiberg 1973) successfully dealt with visible litter by distributing municipal containers widely enough to "keep litter in its place." They provided one model of successfully dealing with local social complainants (Spector and Kitsuse 1977). On the other hand, their efforts in the 1970s and 1980s against "bottle bills" strongly suggest that a *reusable* (refillable) container approach was deemed too cost-*in*effective for these beverage container industries.

12. Ironically, in many municipalities, such as Los Angeles, this was actually a reintroduction of much earlier programs of *garbage separation* that local citizens had eventually voted against because of their inconvenience (van Vliet 1990). These earlier programs predated most modern environmental movements, and were introduced to reduce waste disposal costs (thereby reducing local taxes for this purpose).

13. The logic here is that products are made close to the site of the natural resource. Thus, products made from virgin materials are often produced in remote areas, whereas remanufactured goods would be made in the vicinity of the waste stream. For example, paper mills tend to be located in remote places like the upper Northwest. Recycled paper mills could be located in metropolitan areas.

14. Again California appears to be the most advanced using this tool.

15. Ironically, many of these approaches to recycling are quite similar to community actions in support of waste incinerators, which require contractual commitments to keep the privately owned incinerators operating at a profitable way.

16. This can actually be stated more broadly for environmental issues, as evidenced by the National Commission on the Environment (1993, pp. 23-30).

17. Of course, there are exceptions to this rule. A firm may actually attract new customers. But even under this ideal condition they will still take some customers from other firms in the sector.

18. The only exception has been socially responsible recycling firms that are developed by entrepreneurs who want to get past "this way of doing things." Yet, given the relations of the industry even these firms have a choice: to play within a set of transaction-based rules, or to be pushed out by larger producers. A few smaller firms have been left alone, but this has mostly proven to be a reaction of their negligible impact. They are too small and isolated to matter.

19. Consider the actual linkage between recycling and remanufacturing, as noted in the technical media of the recycling industry. On the one hand, much remanufacturing involves some physical, chemical, and/or biological manipulation of recyclable materials. This produces both ecological additions or pollution, *and* energy and water inputs or withdrawals from ecosystems (Schnaiberg 1980, 1994). The example connecting the de-inking of newsprint with substantial pollution of local water sources is the best known but hardly the most pernicious (lead and mercury pollution in recycling batteries is a more toxic example).

REFERENCES

Anders, G. 1992. *Merchants of Debt: KKR and the Mortgaging of American Business.* New York: Basic Books.

Anderson, C.H. 1976. *The Sociology of Survival.* Homewood, IL: Dorsey Press.

Apotheker, S. 1993. "Curbside Recycling Collection Trends in the 40 Largest U.S. Cities." *Resource Recycling* (December): 27-33.

Ayres, R.U. 1989. "Industrial Metabolism and Global Change: Reconciling the Sociosphere and the Biosphere—Global Change, Industrial Metabolism, Sustainable Development, Vulnerability." *International Social Science Journal* 41(3): 363-374.

Banner, D.K., S.I. Doctors, and A.C. Gordon. 1975. *The Politics of Social Program Evaluation.* Cambridge, MA: Ballinger.

Barnet, R.J. and J. Cavanagh. 1994. *Global Dreams: Imperial Corporations and the New World Order.* New York: Simon & Schuster.

Barlett, D. and J. Steele. 1992. *America: What Went Wrong?* Kansas City: Andrews and McMeel.

Beck, P. and P. Grogan. 1991. "Minimum Content Legislation: An Effective Market Development Tool." *Resource Recycling* (September): 90-99.

Bishop, R.S. 1991. "Defining the MRF..." *Resource Recycling* (October): 36-43.

Blowers, A. and P. Glasbergen. 1994. "The Search For Sustainable Development." Paper presented at conference on The Politics of Sustainable Development Within the European Union, the University of Crete, October.

Blumberg, P. 1980. *Inequality in an Age of Decline.* New York: Oxford University Press.

Brown, P. and E.J. Mikkelsen. 1990. *No Safe Place: Toxic Waste, Leukemia, and Community Action.* Berkeley: University of California Press.

Bukro, C. 1989. "The True Greenhouse Effect." *Chicago Tribune* (December 31), p. 4.1.

Buttel, F.H. 1985. "Environmental Quality and the State." Pp. 167-188 in *Research in Political Sociology*, edited by R.G. Braungart and M.M. Braungart. Greenwich, CT: JAI Press.

Carter, N. 1994. "An Anthropocentric Defence of Sustainable Development." Paper presented at conference on The Politics of Sustainable Development Within the European Union, University of Crete, October.

Consumer Reports. 1994. "Recycling: Is it Worth the Effort?" February, pp. 92-98.

Coontz, S. 1992. *The Way We Never Were: American Families and the Nostalgia Trap.* New York: Basic Books.

Daly, H. and J. Cobb, Jr. 1989. *For the Common Good.* Boston: Beacon Press.

European Community. 1993. *Toward Sustainability: A European Community Programme of Policy and Action in Relation to the Environment and Sustainable Development.* Luxembourg: Commission of the European Communities, D-G XI.

Evans, P., D. Rueschemeyer, and T. Skocpol, eds. 1985. *Bringing the State Back In.* New York: Cambridge University Press.

Feshbach, M. and A. Friendly, Jr. 1991. *Ecocide in the USSR: Health and Nature Under Siege.* New York: Basic Books.

Forman, M. 1991. "In My Opinion ... Plastics Recycling: Let's Cut the Bull." *Resource Recycling* (May): 102-104.

Galbraith, J.K. 1992. *The Culture of Contentment.* Boston: Houghton Mifflin.

Georgescu-Roegen, N. 1973. "The Entropy Law and the Economic Problem." Pp. 37-49 in *Toward A Steady-State Economy*, edited by H.E. Daly. San Francisco, CA: W. H. Freeman.

Goodwin, R.N. 1992. *Promises to Keep: A Call for a New American Revolution.* New York: Times Books.

Gould, K.A. 1991. "The Sweet Smell of Money: Economic Dependency and Local Environmental Political Mobilization." *Society and Natural Resources* 4(2): 133-150.

Gould, K.A., A. Schnaiberg, and A.S. Weinberg. 1996. *Local Environmental Struggles: Citizen Activism in the Treadmill of Production.* New York: Cambridge University Press.

Gould, K.A., A.S. Weinberg, and A. Schnaiberg. 1993. "Legitimating Impotence: Pyrrhic Victories of the Modern Environmental Movement." *Qualitative Sociology* 16(3): 207-246.

————. 1995. "Natural Resource Use in a Transnational Treadmill: International Agreements, National Citizenship Practices, and Sustainable Development." *Humboldt Journal of Social Relations* 21(4): 61-93.

Gutin, J. 1992. "Plastics a Go-Go: The Joy of Making New Useless Junk Out of Old Useless Junk." *Mother Jones* (March/April): 56-59.

Hampden-Turner, C. and A. Trompenaars. 1993. *The Seven Cultures of Capitalism.* New York: Doubleday.

Harrison, B. 1994. *Lean and Mean: The Changing Landscape of Corporate Power in the Age of Flexibility.* New York: Basic Books.

Harrison, M. 1991. "Citizenship, Consumption, and Rights." *Sociology* 25: 209-213.

Hawken, P. 1993. *The Ecology of Commerce.* New York: HarperBusiness.

Holusha, J. 1994. "Rich Market for Business of Recycling." *New York Times* (October 8), p. 1.1.

Howe, J. 1994. "Facilitating Sustainability in Depressed Urban Areas." Paper presented at the conference on the Politics of Sustainable Development, University of Crete, October.

James, W. 1907. *Pragmatism: A New Name for Some Old Ways of Thinking.* New York: Longmans, Green and Co.

Keefe, J.M. 1993. "Pollution, Politics, and Policy: Implementation of Hazardous Waste Policy throughthe Resource Conservation and Recovery Act." Doctoral dissertation, Department of Political Science, Northwestern University, March.

Liberatore, A. 1994. "The Integration of Sustainable Development Policy Into Other Policy Fields: The Prospects and Barriers." Paper presented at the conference on the Politics of Sustainable Development, University of Crete, October.

Lindblom, C. 1977. *Politics and Markets.* New York: Basic Books.

Lipietz, A. 1987. *Mirages and Miracles: The Crises of Global Fordism.* Translated by D. Macey. London: Verso Books.

Lowi, T. 1972. "Four Systems of Policy, Politics, and Choice." *Public Administration Review* 32(4): 298-310.

————. 1979. *The End of Liberalism,* 2nd ed. New York: W.W. Norton.

McCarthy, J.E. 1991. "Waste Reduction and Packaging In Europe." *Resource Recycling* (July): 56-63.

Maines, D. 1993. "Narrative's Movement and Sociology's Phenomenon: Toward a Narrative Sociology." *The Sociological Quarterly* 34: 17-38.

March, J.G. 1987. "Theories of Choice and Making Decisions." Pp. 279-297 in *Strategies of Community Organization,* edited by F. Cox, J. Erlich, J. Rothman, and J. Tropman. Itasca, IL: F.E. Peacock Publishers, Inc.

Miliband, R. 1969. *The State in Capitalist Society.* New York: Basic Books.

Morris, J. and L.W. Dickey. 1991. "Three 80s for the 90s Will Cut Waste in Half." *Resource Recycling* (March): 111-117.

National Commission on the Environment. 1993. *Choosing a Sustainable Future: A Report of the National Commission on the Environment.* Washington, DC: Island Press.

Norgaard, R. 1995. "Intergenerational Commons, Globalization, Economics, and Unsustainable Development." Pp. 141-171 in *Advances in Human Ecology,* Vol. 4, edited by L. Freese. Greewnich, CT: JAI Press.

O'Connor, J. 1988. "Capitalism, Nature, Socialism: A Theoretical Introduction." *Capitalism, Nature, Socialism* 1(Fall): 11-38.

Olson, L.M. 1986. "Bureaucratic Control in Health Care: The Technology of Records." Unpublished doctoral dissertation, Sociology Department, Northwestern University, Evanston, IL.

Pakarinen, T. 1994. "The Politics of Sustainable Development: Theory, Policy, and Practice." Paper presented at conference on The Politics of Sustainable Development Within the European Union, University of Crete, October.

Pellow, D.N. 1994. "Environmental Justice and Popular Epidemiology: Grassroots Empowerment or Symbolic Politics?" Paper presented at annual meetings of the American Sociological Association, Los Angeles, August.

Pellow, D.N., A. Weinberg, and A. Schnaiberg. 1995. "Pragmatic Corporate Cultures: Insights from a Recycling Enterprise." *Green Management International* 12: 95-110.

Pimentel, D., L.E. Hurd, A.C. Belloti, M.J. Forster, I.N. Oka, O.D. Sholes, and R.J. Whitman. 1973. "Food Production and the Energy Crisis." *Science* 182(November 2): 443-449.

Pimental, D., W. Dritschilo, J. Krummel, and J. Kutzman. 1975. "Energy and Land Constraints in Food Protein Production." *Science* 190(November 21): 754-761.

Pimentel, D., E.C. Terhune, R. Dyson-Hudson, S. Rochereau, R. Samis, E.A. Smith, D. Denman, D. Reifschneider, and M. Shepard. 1976. "Land Degradation: Effects on Food and Energy Resources." *Science* 194 (October 8): 149-155.

Poulantzas, N. 1973a. "The Problem of the Capitalist State." Pp. 238-253 in *Ideology in Social Science*, edited by R. Blackburn. New York: Vintage Books.

_____. 1973b. *Political Power and Social Classes*. Translated by T. O'Hagan. London: New Left Books & Sheed and Ward.

Powell, J. 1993. "How Are We Doing? The 1992 Report." *Resource Recycling* (April): 38.

Rabasca, L. 1992. "Most Recycling Markets Remain Weak in 1992." *Waste Age's Recycling Times* (December 29), pp. 1-12.

_____. 1993. "Recycling in 1993 Ebbs And Flows." *Waste Age's Recycling Times* (December 28), pp. 1-12.

Redclift, M. 1984. *Development and the Environmental Crisis: Red or Green Alternatives?* New York: Methuen.

_____. 1986. "Redefining the Environmental 'Crisis' in the South." In *Red and Green: The New Politics of the Environment*, edited by J. Weston. London: Pluto Press.

_____. 1987. *Sustainable Development: Exploring the Contradictions*. New York: Methuen.

Reich, R. 1991. *The Work of Nations: Preparing Ourselves for 21st Century Capitalism*. New York: Alfred A. Knopf.

Richardson. D. 1994. "The Politics of Sustainable Development." Paper presented at conference on The Politics of Sustainable Development Within the European Union, University of Crete, October.

Schnaiberg, A. 1973. "Politics, Participation and Pollution: The 'Environmental Movement'." Pp. 605-627 in *Cities in Change: Studies on the Urban Condition*, edited by J. Walton and D.E. Carns. Boston: Allyn & Bacon.

_____. 1975. "Social Syntheses of the Societal-Environmental Dialectic: The Role of Distributional Impacts." *Social Science Quarterly* 56(June): 5-20.

_____. 1980. *The Environment: From Surplus to Scarcity*. New York: Oxford University Press.

_____. 1986a. "The Role of Experts and Mediators in the Channeling of Distributional Conflicts." Pp. 348-362 in *Distributional Conflicts in Environmental-Resource Policy*, edited by A. Schnaiberg, N. Watts, and K. Zimmermann. Aldershot, England: Gower Publishing.

_____. 1986b. "Reflections On Resistance To Rural Industrialization: Newcomers' Culture of Environmentalism." Pp. 229-258 in *Differential Social Impacts of Rural Resource Development*, edited by P.D. Elkind-Savatsky. Boulder, CO: Westview Press.

_____. 1992. "Recycling vs Remanufacturing." Working Paper. Center for Urban Affairs and Policy Research, Northwestern University, Evanston, IL.

————. 1993. "Paradoxes and Contradictions: A Conceptual Framework for 'How I Leanred to Reject Recycling.'" Paper presented at the Annual Meeting of the American Sociological Association, Miami, Beach, FL, August.

————. 1994. "The Political Economy of Environmental Problems: Consciousness, Coordination, and Conflict." Pp. 23-64 in *Advances in Human Ecology*, Vol. 3, edited by L. Freese. Greenwich, CT: JAI Press.

Schnaiberg, A. and K.A. Gould. 1994. *Environment and Society: The Enduring Conflict*. New York: St. Martin's Press.

Schor, J. 1991. *The Overworked American: The Unexpected Decline of Leisure*. New York: Basic Books.

Skocpol, T. 1979. *States and Social Revolutions*. New York: Cambridge University Press.

Skocpol, T. and E. Amenta. 1986. "States and Social Policies." *Annual Review of Sociology* 12: 131-157.

Somers, M. 1993. "Citizenship and the Place of Public Sphere: Law, Community, and Political Culture in the Transition To Democracy." *American Sociological Review* 58: 587-620.

————. 1994. "Rights, Rationality, and Membership: Rethinking the Making and Meaning of Citizenship." *Law and Social Inquiry* 19: 63-112.

Spector, M. and J. Kitsuse. 1977. *Constructing Social Problems*. New York: Aldine de Gruyter.

Stretton, H. 1976. *Capitalism, Socialism, and the Environment*. Cambridge: Cambridge University Press.

Szasz, A. 1990. "From Pollution Control to Pollution Prevention: How Does It Happen?" Paper presented at meetings of the American Sociological Association, Washington, DC, August.

————. 1994. *Ecopopulism: Toxic Waste and the Movement for Environmental Justice*. Minneapolis: University of Minnesota Press.

Tackett, M. 1987. "'Little Town that Roared' Savors Victory over Waste Dumper." *Chicago Tribune* (July 5), p. 1.4.

Tanzer, M. 1974. *The Energy Crises: World Struggle for Power and Wealth*. New York: Monthly Review Press.

Tibbs, H. 1993a. *Industrial Ecology: An Environmental Agenda for Industry*. Emeryville, CA: Global Business Network.

————. 1993b. "The Ethical Management of Global Technology." Paper prepared for the annual meetings of the American Sociological Association, Miami Beach, FL, August.

Turner, B. 1986. *Citizenship and Capitalism*. London: Allen and Unwin.

————, ed. 1993. *Citizenship and Social Theory*. London: Sage.

van Vliet, W. 1990. "Human Settlements in the U.S.: Questions of Even and Sustainable Development." Paper presented at colloquium on Human Settlements and Sustainable Development, University of Toronto, Toronto, Canada, June.

Walley, N. and B. Whitehead. 1994. "It's Not Easy Being Green." *Harvard Business Review* (May-June): 46-52.

Weinberg, A.S. 1994. "Environmental Sociology and the Environmental Movement: Towards a Theory of Pragmatic Relationships of Critical Inquiry." *The American Sociologist* 5(1): 31-57.

_____. 1995. "Citizenship and Natural Resources: Rights versus Practices." Working
    paper #94-26. Center for Urban Affairs and Policy Research, Northwestern
    University, Evanston, IL.
Weinberg, A.S. and K.A. Gould. 1993. "Public Participation in Environmental
    Regulatory Conflicts: Treading Through the Possibilities and Pitfalls." *Law and
    Policy* 15: 139-167.
Westman, W.E. and R.M. Gifford. 1973. "Environmental Impact: Controlling the
    Overall Level." *Science* 181(August 31): 819-825.
Williams, D.C. 1994. "Pragmatism and Faith: Selznick's Complex Commonwealth."
    Law and Social Inquiry 5: 775-801.
Williamson, O. 1975. *Markets and Hierarchies*. New York: Free Press.
_____. 1981. "The Economics of Organization: The Transaction Cost Approach."
    American Journal of Sociology 87(November): 548-577.
Woods, R. 1993. "Kraft Mill Asks EPA to Consider Chlorine-Free Paper Guidelines."
    Recycling Times (May 18), p. 3.
World Commission on Environment and Development. 1987. *Our Common Future*.
    New York: Oxford University Press.

AN ECOLOGICAL INVESTIGATION OF INTERSTATE MIGRATION IN THE UNITED STATES, 1985-1990

Dudley L. Poston and Michael Xinxiang Mao

ABSTRACT

Prior analyses of human migration have used demographic, psychological, political, sociological, economic, and ecological perspectives—each of which employs a more or less distinct set of independent variables. In this paper we endeavor to account for the variation in the size of interstate migration flows in the United States during the 1985-1990 period. Much of the prior research analyzing migration streams has relied heavily on spatial interaction models, with a heavy focus on economic approaches and variables. We ground our theoretical rationale and modeling in sociological human ecology. The data presented indicate that interstate migration is highly responsive to three classic gravity variables and six ecological variables, four of them pertaining to characteristics of the destination and two of them pertaining to characteristics of the origin. The findings suggest that ecological forces tend to be more effective as "pull" mechanisms than as "push" mechanisms.

Advances in Human Ecology, Volume 5, pages 303-342.
Copyright © 1996 by JAI Press Inc.
All rights of reproduction in any form reserved.
ISBN: 0-7623-0029-9

303

INTRODUCTION

A human ecological investigation of interstate migration flows is but one kind of study of migration behavior. Indeed, numerous analyses of human migration have been undertaken in past decades using many different approaches, including demographic, psychological, political, sociological, economic, and ecological perspectives. The distinguishing characteristic of each approach is its employment of a more or less distinct set of independent variables (for a review, see Frisbie and Poston 1978b, p. 6).

This paper endeavors to set forth a human ecological explanation of interstate migration flows in the United States during the 1985-1990 period. We base our theoretical rationale and modeling on prior work in sociological human ecology. Because so much of the prior work that has analyzed migration streams has used spatial interaction models with a heavy focus on economic approaches and variables (for reviews, see Greenwood 1975a and Jessadachatr 1989, among many others), one contribution of our paper is its articulation of the ecological approach for studying the phenomenon.

A major difference between sociological human ecology and economics is that human ecology, unlike economics, includes within its purview the entirety of collective life. Economics, for instance, does not "investigate the nonpecuniary aspects of economic relationships. Nor does it treat those subsidiary but contingent relationships which do not find expression in a pricing system, such as occur in the family and between nonprofit institutions" (Hawley 1950, p. 73). Or, as Gibbs and Martin (1959, p. 34) have noted, "whereas economists are ordinarily interested in the interrelationships of such variables as supply, demand, cost, and prices within a given sustenance organization, ecologists are concerned with the characteristics of the structure itself" (also see Poston, Hirschl, and Frisbie 1992).

THE ECOLOGICAL APPROACH AND PRIOR LITERATURE

This paper is an attempt to apply the ecological perspective to an analysis of migration streams. In the next few paragraphs, we focus in more detail on the ecological approach to migration. We then turn to a brief review of prior literature that has investigated migration flows and streams. Later sections will cover the data and methods of our analysis, its findings, and implications.

From the perspective of sociological human ecology, migration is the major mechanism of social change and adaptability for human populations. A knowledge of migration patterns tells us about how "populations ... maintain themselves in particular areas" (Hawley 1950, p. 149). The ecological approach asserts that human populations redistribute themselves in order to approach an equilibrium between their overall size and the life chances available to them. And as just noted, migration is seen as the principal mechanism for effecting this adjustment. It is a demographic response attempting to preserve or attain the best possible living standard by reestablishing a balance between population size and organization (Poston 1981, p. 138).

The theoretical foundation of sociological human ecology is based on the interdependence of the four conceptual rubrics of population, organization, environment, and technology. The interrelationships among and between these dimensions inform our understanding of migration patterns as follows: all populations must necessarily adapt to their environments, and these adaptations vary among populations on the basis of their social and sustenance organization, their technology, and the size, composition, and distribution of their population. The environment per se is comprised of both social and physical factors which tend to set constraints on the population and the form and characteristics of its organization. The technology that the population has at its disposal sets, in an important way, the boundaries for the form and type of environmental adaptation the population may assume. These may well change, however, as new or different technologies are introduced, allowing its relationship with the environment to change, and resulting also in changes or adjustments in the population's organization and size. Human ecology posits that, of the three demographic processes, migration is by far the most efficient agent for returning the human ecosystem to a state of equilibrium or balance between its size and organization.

The hypothesis typically investigated in ecological studies of migration (e.g., Sly 1972; Sly and Tayman 1977; Frisbie and Poston 1978a, 1978b; Poston 1980, 1981; London 1986, 1987; Ervin 1987; Saenz and Colberg 1988) is that that variability among human groups in their patterns of migration is a function of differences in their patterns of sustenance organization, technology, environment, and population.

We noted above that earlier analyses of migration streams in the United States and elsewhere have relied heavily on economic reasoning and models (for an exception, see Karp and Kelly 1971). These examinations have been tested within the framework of what has been referred to as spatial interaction. Spatial interaction models have been used to analyze migration streams in both developed and developing countries, including the United States (Blanco 1963; Greenwood and Sweetland 1972; Kau and Sirmans 1979), Sweden (Isbell 1944), India (Greenwood 1971a, 1971b), the United Kingdom (Flowerdew and Salt 1979; Fotheringham and O'Kelly 1989), Egypt (Greenwood 1969), and Thailand (Jessadachatr 1989), among several other countries.

The spatial interaction model has its genesis in the gravity model of the following form:

$$M_{ij} = P_i P_j / D_{ij},$$

where: M_{ij} = the total amount of migration between i and j;
          P_i = population size at i;
          P_j = population size at j; and
          D_{ij} = the distance between the two places, i and j.

The earliest application of this model to the study of migration flows is Ravenstein's (1885, 1889) work more than a century ago where he noted that "the great body of migrants only proceed a short distance," and that in estimating migration flows we "must take into account the number of natives of each county which furnishes the migrants, as also the population of the towns or districts which absorb them" (Ravenstein 1885, p. 12). In a later analysis, Zipf (1946) found that gross migration between two places varies positively with the product of their sizes, and negatively with the distance separating the two places. The spatial interaction model begins with the gravity model, but goes beyond it by introducing additional independent variables pertaining specifically to the positive and negative characteristics of the areas of origin and destination. These characteristics are often economic variables. That is, the factors at origin and destinations are typically operationalized with variables such as income levels, per capita government expenditures, employment rates, among others (for example, see Greenwood and Sweetland 1972).

The ecological modeling we undertake in this paper goes beyond these mainly economic considerations. A more broadly based set of independent variables will be introduced to represent the various dimensions of the ecological complex. We turn now to the variables of our paper and the hypotheses to be tested.

VARIABLES AND HYPOTHESES

Drawing on human ecological theory as well as prior studies using spatial interaction models in interregional migration studies, the following variables will be used.

The dependent variable is the total volume of migration between every pair of states. This will be operationalized in three ways, as we show below in the next section. The independent variables are the three gravity variables: population size at origin and at destination, and distance between origin and destination.

We now discuss the ecological variables we have selected as the remaining independent variables. These will be discussed according to each of the four ecological rubrics. Of the four rubrics, it is not an overstatement to note that organization is the most fundamental; indeed, a major aim of this paper is to ascertain how characteristics of a population's sustenance organization act as a catalyst for migration. We have thus selected the unemployment rate and the level of manufacturing wages as two of numerous possible independent variables to represent the sustenance organization of the population. Although these are patently economic in character, they are used here to represent aspects of the organizational capabilities of the populations, in this case, the states.

In sociological human ecology, the environment is defined as whatever is external to and potentially or actually influential on the phenomenon under investigation (Hawley 1968, p. 330). According to this definition, the environment includes not only the biotic or physical characteristics of an area, but also the influences that emanate from other organized populations in the same and in other areas; indeed, the latter may well acquire a more critical importance than the former (Hawley 1981, p. 9). Minority concentration and the crime rate are selected as independent variables to represent social aspects of the environment, and a climate variable is chosen to represent a physical aspect.

Technology has been argued by some scholars as very critical for the adaptation of human populations. It has been defined by Lenski (1970, p. 37) as the information, techniques, and tools by means of which people utilize the material resources of their environment. A problem with applying these dimensions to national subareas such as states is that, like the larger concept of technology of which they are a part, they have been conceived at the societal level of analysis. So one could argue that it is difficult to contend that the level of technology varies in any significant way at the subsocietal level. One way of getting beyond this quagmire is to focus on the information component of technology and to choose as an independent variable the educational level of the population, a variable that does indeed vary among subsocietal units. However, this is at best an imperfect solution.

Finally, we have chosen the independent variable of population density to represent the population rubric. Some may question the assignment of a density variable under the population rubric, noting that it may be more appropriately categorized as a gravity variable. We have not opted for such an assignment owing to the precedent in gravity model research to restrict gravity variables to population size at origin and destination, and distance. When one supplements these with others, such as density, one then begins to introduce theoretical meaning into the gravity model. Such is the task of our human ecological model, the results of which may be contrasted with the results of the "bare bones" gravity model.

All of the above independent variables have been shown to be important and significant predictors of migration in the ecological and spatial interaction studies cited previously.

The hypotheses may now be stated.

Hypothesis 1.   The larger the population size at both origin i and destination j, the larger the migration stream from i, and the larger the migration stream to j.

Hypothesis 2.   The shorter the distance between i and j, the larger the migration stream from i to j.

Hypothesis 3.   The higher the population density at i, the larger the migration stream from i; the higher the population density at j, the smaller the migration stream to j.

Hypothesis 4.   The higher the level of education at i, the smaller the migration flow from i; the higher the level of education at j, the larger the migration flow to j.

Hypothesis 5.   The higher the crime rate at i, the larger the migration flow from i; the higher the crime rate at j, the smaller the migration flow to j.

Hypothesis 6. The higher the concentration of nonwhites at i, the larger the migration stream from i; the higher the concentration of nonwhites at j, the smaller the migration flow to j.

Hypothesis 7. The higher the unemployment rate at i, the larger the migration flow from i; the higher the unemployment rate at j, the smaller the migration flow to j.

Hypothesis 8. The higher the wages at i, the smaller the migration flow from i; the lower the wages at j, the smaller the migration flow to j.

Hypothesis 9. The more favorable the climate at i, the smaller the migration flow from i; the more favorable the climate at j, the larger the migration flow to j.

The expected signs of the independent variables at origin and at destination with the dependent variable of migration flow are shown in Figure 1.

Independent Variables	Hypothesized Relationship of Origin Independent Variables	Hypothesized Relationship of Destination Independent Variable
Population Size	+	+
Distance between i and j	–	n.a.
Population Density	+	–
Education Level	–	+
Crime Rate	+	–
Nonwhite Concentration	+	–
Unemployment Rate	+	–
Manufacturing Wage	–	+
Climate	–	+

Figure 1. Independent Variables and Their Hypothesized Relationships at Origin and at Destination with the Dependent Variable of Migration Flow

DATA AND METHODS

The dependent variable in this analysis is the migration stream for the 1985-1990 period among and between each of the U.S. states, including the District of Columbia (these 51 units are hereafter referred to as states). Our use of the state as the unit of analysis is not without conceptual difficulty. One liability is that states are political, not ecological, units. Thus they do not possess the ecological integrity of geographical units such as metropolitan areas. States are also heterogeneous in composition and social characteristics such that the values of state-level variables are often averages of the values for the smaller ecological units that comprise them. These problems notwithstanding, we opted to use the state because migration streams for states include all the possible migration that may occur in the country. We also use the state as the unit of analysis because this is the smallest unit of analysis for which migration stream data are available for the 1985-1990 time period.

The dependent variable data are organized in a matrix of 51 by 50, or 2,550, migration streams among and between each of the U.S. states, including the District of Columbia. Because there were no migrants in 119 of these streams (as we note in more detail below), the zero-migrant streams have been dropped, leaving us with an N of 2,431 streams for analysis. These data have been taken from the One Percent Public Use Micro-data Sample of the 1990 U.S. Census of Population and Housing; the cases have been inflated to the 100 percent level using sampling weights developed by the Census Bureau. (To assess the coverage and validity of the 1 percent data files, we selected several census items and compared their inflated values across the U.S. states with values for them based on the 5 percent PUMS and the 100 percent tabulations; the 1 percent values across the states for these various items correlate very highly with the values based on the 5 percent PUMS and 100 percent tabulations, giving us reason to believe that there is no serious sampling problem in our use of migration data from the 1990 1 percent PUMS.)

The dependent variable is based on data enumerating the number of persons who moved from State$_i$ to State$_j$ during the period of 1985-1990. On the 1990 U.S. census questionnaire (long form), a person was asked if his/her residence on April 1, 1985 was in the same state as his/her residence on April 1, 1990, the reference date of the 1990 census. Persons answering in the negative are considered to be interstate migrants, and they comprise the data upon which our dependent variable is based.

Measures of the Dependent Variables

We now discuss the form of measurement of the dependent variable, the migration stream. Prior research indicates two main ways for measuring a migration stream between two areas: as an absolute number, and as a rate. Much of the early research used the absolute number of migrants (Zipf 1946; Stouffer 1940; Galle and Taeuber 1966; Greenwood 1969, 1971a; Haynes, Poston, and Schnirring 1973; Flowerdew and Salt 1979, among others). The use of rates is somewhat more prominent in work of this genre conducted in the past two or so decades (Karp and Kelly 1971; Greenwood 1971b; Greenwood and Sweetland 1972; Kau and Sirmans 1979; Jessadachatr 1989, among many others). Karp and Kelly (1971), Catton (1965), and others have criticized the use of absolute numbers for measuring migration streams, particularly when the population size of the area of origin, or of destination, is used on the right-hand side of the equation (as an independent variable). Karp and Kelly note that this amounts to saying that the larger the area, the greater the number of migrants there will be from it (1971, p. 12); this would be similar to saying that more crimes are committed in larger areas than in smaller ones (1971, p. 13). Karp and Kelly argue in favor of the use of rates, that is, the percentage of persons from the place of origin who leave and migrate to another location during a particular period of time.

There are assets and liabilities involved in the use of both kinds of measures. Absolute numbers in the migration streams allow the analyst to more easily associate push and pull characteristics of the origins and destinations with individuals and individual behavior. Policy decisions and adjustments may be better conceptualized if the outcome, that is, the dependent variable, is an absolute number of movers. Alternatively, migration rates necessarily move the level of analysis from the microscopic to the macroscopic; the volume of the migration stream is seen as a proportion of the population of the origin (or destination) area, and becomes recognized more so as a characteristic of the sending (or receiving) area.

We decided to operationalize the migration stream in terms of the absolute volume of the stream, and in terms of its proportion of the population of origin, and/or destination, that is, a rate. Moreover, following the precedent of Greenwood and Sweetland (1972) and others, we use two different rates for representing the migration stream, namely, migrants as a proportion of the population in the receiving area, and migrants as a proportion of the product of the populations in the sending and receiving areas. These three measures of the dependent variable may be represented as follows:

$$M_{ij},$$
$$M_{ij}/P_j,$$
$$M_{ij}/(P_i * P_j),$$

where: M_{ij} = the number of migrants moving between State$_i$ and State$_j$ in the 1985-1990 period; and

P_i and P_j = the population size of State$_i$, and State$_j$, respectively, in 1984.

The first of the three measures, M_{ij}, is the gross number of persons in each migration stream moving between State$_i$ and State$_j$ in the 1985-1990 period. Table 1 identifies and presents data for each of the ten largest interstate migration streams. The two largest 1985-1990 migration streams both originated in New York; the destination of the largest was Florida, and the second largest, New Jersey. The size of the New York-to-Florida stream is appreciably larger than the New York-to-New Jersey stream. The third largest stream originated in Texas with a destination in California; more than 200,000 persons comprised this stream during the 1985-1990 period. Alternatively, the counter-stream of California-to-Texas is the sixth largest stream with more than 144,000

Table 1.   The Ten Largest Interstate Migration Streams (M_{ij}), United States: 1985-1990

	Origin	Destination	Size of Stream
1	New York	Florida	377,724
2	New York	New Jersey	214,552
3	Texas	California	205,010
4	New Jersey	Florida	150,396
5	California	Washington	148,350
6	California	Texas	144,368
7	California	Arizona	131,924
8	New Jersey	Pennsylvania	129,078
9	California	Oregon	128,848
10	Ohio	Florida	119,652

persons. From viewing the 10 largest migration streams in Table 1, it can be inferred that: (1) most of the origin and destination states are those with the largest populations, namely, California, New York, Texas, and Florida; (2) several of the pairs of origin and destination states are neighbors, for example, New York and New Jersey, California and Arizona, California and Oregon; (3) three of the ten largest migration streams terminate in Florida, indicating very substantial in-migration flows to Florida. Florida's dominance in the resort and retirement industries, among other factors, is likely an instrumental factor "pulling" migrants from other states (Frey and Speare 1992).

We noted earlier that the units of analysis are the 2,550 migration streams between each of the 51 states (the 51 U.S. states and the District of Columbia); we also observed that 119 of these streams have no migrants in them, so they have been dropped from our analysis. Included among these 119 zero-migrant streams are New Mexico-to-Rhode Island, Nebraska-to-New Hampshire, the District of Columbia-to-South Dakota, Vermont-to-North and South Dakota, Hawaii-to-Wyoming, and so forth. Many of these origin and destination states have relatively small populations and, moreover, they are frequently far away from each other. Rather than listing each of these 119 zero-migrant streams, we summarize them by showing in Table 2 each of the 51 states according to the number of times each state has a zero-migrant stream at origin and at destination.

The top line of Table 2 indicates that Maine had six zero-migrant streams at origin, and one at destination; that is, of the 50 migration streams from Maine to the other states, six of them had no migrants; conversely, of the 50 migration streams from other states to Maine, one had no migrants. Three states had more than 10 zero-migrant streams at origin: Delaware with 15, Vermont with 14, and Rhode Island with 10. Two states had more than 10 zero-migrant streams at destination: Delaware had 18 and North Dakota had 13. The 14 states of New York, Pennsylvania, Ohio, Indiana, Illinois, Michigan, Virginia, North Carolina, South Carolina, Florida, Texas, Colorado, Arizona, and California had no zero-migrant streams at origin and no zero-migrant streams at destination.

The second of the migration stream measures, M_{ij}/P_j, is the first of the two rates to be used. It is the gross number of migrants moving between State$_i$ and State$_j$ in the 1985-1990 period, represented as a proportion of the population size in 1984 of the state of destination.

Table 2. U.S. States by Number of Zero-migrant
Streams, at Origin and at Destination, 1985-1990

| | *Number of Zero-migrant Streams* | |
State	*At Origin*	*At Destination*
Maine	6	1
New Hampshire	6	4
Vermont	14	6
Massachusetts	3	0
Rhode Island	10	6
Connecticut	2	0
New York	0	0
New Jersey	1	0
Pennsylvania	0	0
Ohio	0	0
Indiana	0	0
Illinois	0	0
Michigan	0	0
Wisconsin	0	1
Minnesota	2	0
Iowa	2	3
Missouri	1	1
North Dakota	2	13
South Dakota	6	9
Nebraska	3	5
Kansas	1	2
Delaware	15	18
Maryland	1	0
District of Columbia	5	3
Virginia	0	0
West Virginia	4	8
North Carolina	0	0
South Carolina	0	0
Georgia	1	1
Florida	0	0
Kentucky	3	2
Tennessee	1	0
Alabama	1	1
Mississippi	3	3
Arkansas	3	3
Louisiana	2	1
Oklahoma	1	4
Texas	0	0
Montana	2	4
Idaho	3	4
Wyoming	2	7
Colorado	0	0
New Mexico	1	1

(continued)

Table 2.   (Continued)

| State | Number of Zero-migrant Streams | |
	At Origin	At Destination
Arizona	0	0
Utah	2	4
Nevada	1	1
Washington	1	0
Oregon	2	0
California	0	0
Alaska	2	2
Hawaii	4	0
Total	119	119

Table 3 presents the 10 migration streams with the highest, and with the lowest, M_{ij}/P_j rates.

The migration stream between California and Nevada has an M_{ij}/P_j rate of .13, the largest of all of the 2,431 M_{ij}/P_j rates. This rate indicates that the volume of the migration stream between California and Nevada in the 1985-1990 time period is more than 13 percent of the 1984 population of Nevada. California is the origin state of five of the ten largest M_{ij}/P_j rates. Other things equal, this owes in part to the very large population size of California and the resulting large size of its migrant pool, as well as to the small populations of the five destination states of Nevada, Oregon, Hawaii, Arizona, and Washington, which comprise the denominators of the M_{ij}/P_j rates.

The migration stream between South Dakota and Massachusetts has an M_{ij}/P_j rate of .000005, the smallest of all 2,431 M_{ij}/P_j rates (see the bottom panel of Table 3). This rate indicates that the migration stream between the two states during the 1985-1990 period represents a very small proportion of the 1984 population of Massachusetts. To illustrate, the numerator of the rate, that is, the number of migrants between South Dakota and Massachusetts, is 26, and the denominator, that is, the 1984 population of Massachusetts, is 5,797,079. South Dakota is the origin state for three of the ten smallest M_{ij}/P_j rates. Moreover, several, but certainly not all, of the origin states with the lowest rates tend to have rather small populations.

The third migration stream measure, and the second migration rate, is $M_{ij}/(P_i * P_j)$. It is the gross number of migrants moving between State$_i$ and State$_j$ in the 1985-1990 period, represented as a.proportion of the

Table 3.   Ten Highest and Ten Lowest Interstate Migration Stream Rates
(M_{ij}/P_j), United States: 1985-1990

	Origin	*Destination*	*Rate*
	Highest Rates (M_{ij}/P_j)		
1	California	Nevada	.130340
2	Massachusetts	New Hampshire	.065500
3	California	Oregon	.048194
4	California	Hawaii	.047186
5	California	Arizona	.042927
6	Maryland	District of Columbia	.036887
7	Texas	New Mexico	.034459
8	New York	Florida	.034176
9	California	Washington	.034135
10	Massachusetts	Vermont	.031668
	Lowest Rates (M_{ij}/P_j)		
2431	South Dakota	Massachusetts	.000005
2430	Vermont	Ohio	.000009
2429	South Dakota	Ohio	.000010
2428	District of Columbia	Mississippi	.000012
2427	Connecticut	Mississippi	.000017
2426	Vermont	West Virginia	.000018
2425	Rhode Island	Michigan	.000019
2424	Delaware	Louisiana	.000020
2423	New Hampshire	Wisconsin	.000020
2422	South Dakota	Delaware	.000026

product of the population sizes in 1984 of the states of origin and destination.

Although the value of M_{ij} is found in all three measures, the three measures are not as highly related as one might expect. Among the 2,431 migration streams, the three measures are correlated as follows:

$$M_{ij} \text{ with } M_{ij}/P_j, .55$$
$$M_{ij} \text{ with } M_{ij}/(P_i * P_j), .18$$
$$M_{ij}/P_j \text{ with } M_{ij}/(P_i * P_j), .43.$$

The three correlations are positive, but far from perfect. Our decision to use three migration stream measures instead of one rests in part on their different conceptual bases, that is, a gross number versus a rate, as well as the lack of a high association between any of the pairs. One could also argue that we should have used a third rate, namely, M_{ij}/P_i, that is, migrants as a proportion of the population in the sending area. This rate is very similar to M_{ij}/P_j—the only difference being that one has a denominator representing the population at origin, and the other a denominator representing the population at destination. Given their similarity we chose the latter for conceptual reasons. Having described the three measures of the dependent variable, we turn now to a discussion of the independent variables.

Measures of the Independent Variables

The primary data source for the independent variables is the *1988 County and City Data Book* (U.S. Bureau of the Census 1989). Because our models predict the values of migration streams/rates that have as their reference point the 1985-1990 time period, all the independent variables should pertain to time periods prior to 1985. This strategy avoids the problem of simultaneity bias, that is, overlapping the time period of the independent variables with the period of occurrence of the dependent variable (Greenwood 1975b). We have just about met this objective with all our independent variables.

The independent variables are measured as follows.

1. Population Size is the actual number of people residing in a state in 1984.
2. Distance is the straight line distance in miles between the two centroids of every pair of states.
3. Minority Concentration is the percentage of the population in the state that is black and other races in 1984.
4. Crime Rate is the number of serious crimes known to police per 100,000 population in the state in 1985.
5. Education Level is the percentage of the population of the state that is 25 years of age and older that has completed 12 years or more education, 1980.
6. Unemployment Rate is the unemployment rate in the state in 1986 of the civilian labor force.
7. Wages refers to manufacturing wages in the state, in U.S. dollars, per production worker in 1982.
8. Climate Index is the average daily maximum temperature in January in the largest city in the state divided by the average daily minimum temperature in July in the largest city in the state (cf. Karp and Kelly 1971, p. 25).
9. Population density is the number of people residing in a state in 1984 per square mile of land in a state.

The above independent variables, with the exception of the Climate Index, are rather straightforward in their rationale and computation. The Climate Index is based on the assumption that most persons prefer to avoid exposure to bitter and cold winters, and excessively hot and humid summers. Hence, we have chosen as the elements of the Climate Index the average daily maximum temperature in January and the average daily minimum temperature in July; these temperatures, by the way, are based on 30-year averages for the period 1955-1985. The resulting index is lowered if it is cold during the day in winter or hot during the night in summer (Karp and Kelly 1971, p. 25).

The Climate Index is certainly an imperfect measure for at least two reasons. First, it does not include in its computation all important aspects of climate; for instance, rainfall is not included (Karp and Kelly 1971, p. 26). Second, we have based the value of the index for any one state on the value of the index in the largest city in the state. We opted for this strategy instead, say, of developing an index for all the cities and areas in the state and then calculating an average index (weighted by population size) across all the cities and areas of the state. Not only is this latter approach very cumbersome to compute but, detailed data for cities and areas of each state are not directly accessible. Indeed, for most states, 30-year average temperature data are available for only one or at best two cities.

Descriptive Statistics

Table 4 shows descriptive statistics for all the variables, expressed in their raw versions. When we use these variables later to test the hypotheses, they will all be transformed with natural logarithms. The averages and standard deviations for the predictor variables are reported for the variable as measured in the origin state (State$_i$). If all 2,550 possible streams were included in the analysis, then the mean and the standard deviation for each predictor variable would be identical because its mean and standard deviation in State$_i$ would be calculated for the same 51 states as would be the case for their calculation in State$_j$. But as we noted above, and indicated in Table 2, the flows between 119 certain pairs of states have no migrants in them, so these flows were excluded from the analysis. But the 119 origin states deleted from the analysis are not necessarily the same as the 119 destination states deleted (although, as one might surmise, many of the origin and destination states deleted are the same). Consequently, the means and standard

Table 4.   Descriptive Statistics for Dependent and Independent Variables:
                2,431 Migration Flows

Variable	Mean	Std. Dev.	Min.	Max.
Migration Flow	8,644	18,586	16	377,724
Population	4,783,606	4,996,701	487,299	25,797,834
Distance	1,216	909	30	5,110
Population Density	337	1,332	0.85	9,909
Education	67	8	53	83
Crime Rate	4,857	1,333	2,234	8,007
Nonwhite Concentration	15	14	0.73	72
Unemployment Rate	7	2	3	13
Manufacturing Wages	16,297	2,323	12,064	22,169
Climate Index	0.64	0.17	0.33	1.09

Note: See text for data sources and definitions of variables.

deviations of the origin- and destination-specific independent variables
are not identical; however, they are very similar. Thus our reporting
the values of the means and standard deviations of each independent
variable for State$_i$ does not detract in any serious way from our
understanding of their descriptions. The only independent variable for
which the above discussion does not apply is the distance variable,
because its value in each stream is based on two states.

The dependent variable—the migration flow between 2,431 pairs of
states—has an average value across the 2,431 flows of 8,644 persons,
with a standard deviation of over 18,500. The stream with the smallest
number of persons, 16, is that between Alabama and Delaware, and
between South Dakota and Delaware; the stream with the largest
number of persons, 377,724, is between New York and Florida.

Among the gravity variables, population size in 1984 ranges from a
low of 487,299 in Alaska to a high of 25,797,834 in California. The other
gravity variable, distance, has an average value among the migration
streams of 1,216 miles. The smallest value, a distance of only 30 miles,
is for the stream between the District of Columbia and Maryland. As
one might expect, many of the streams between the New England,
Middle Atlantic, and some of the South Atlantic states have relatively
short distances. The largest distance, 5,110 miles, is between Maine and
Hawaii.

The first ecological independent variable, population density, has an
average value among the 2,431 origins of 337 persons per square mile.
The highest population density, 9,909 persons per square mile, is in the

District of Columbia. Generally, many of the New England and Middle Atlantic states, along with Maryland and Delaware, have higher than average population densities. Alaska has the lowest population density, less than one person per square mile.

In terms of education, the average across the origin states is 67 percent (of those persons who are 25 years of age and older who have completed 12 or more years of schooling). The southern states tend to have values that are lower than the values of states in other regions; the ten states with the lowest educational levels are all located in the South. The state with the lowest value (53%) is Kentucky, and the state with the highest value (83%) is Alaska.

The crime rate, that is, the number of known crimes per 100,000 population, has a mean value across the origin states of 4,857 crimes, with a standard deviation of 1,333 crimes. The most dangerous state, that is, the state with the highest crime rate, is the District of Columbia with a rate of 8,007 crimes per 100,000 population; West Virginia has the lowest crime rate of all the origin states, namely, 2,234/100,000.

Nonwhite concentration, that is, the percentage of the population that is black or of other races, has an average value among the origin states of 14.5 percent. It is the highest in the District of Columbia, where 72.1 percent of the population is nonwhite; Hawaii has the second highest rate, a percentage value of 65.1. The state with the lowest value of the nonwhite concentration variable is Vermont, with a percentage score of 0.7.

The unemployment rate has a mean value across the origin states of 7 percent; the lowest value is 2.8 percent in New Hampshire, and the highest value is 13.1 percent in Louisiana. The ecological variable measuring annual manufacturing wages per worker in 1982 has an average value of $16,297; it ranges from a low of $12,064 in North Carolina to a high of $22,169 in Michigan.

Finally, the climate index has an average score among the origin states of 0.64; the lowest value, that is, the least favorable climate, is in Minnesota, with an index score of 0.3; the highest index value, or the most favorable climate, is in Hawaii, with a score of 1.1. In Minnesota, the average maximum January temperature is about one-third of the average minimum July temperature; whereas in Hawaii, the average maximum January temperature is about 1.1 times the average minimum July temperature. We turn now to the equations we estimate and their results.

Multivariate Equations

We use ecological variables within the framework of spatial interaction analysis to model interstate migration. We compare these results with those produced in a classic gravity model of interstate migration. In this section, we present and discuss the multivariate equations we will estimate. In the next section, we present the results of estimating the equations when the units of analysis are all 2,413 migration streams. And, in a later section, we present the results from estimating a series of state-specific ecological equations in which each equation has as its units of analysis the migration flows to, or from, a specific state.

Prior studies using spatial interaction and classic gravity models indicate that the relationships may be calibrated into a linear function by taking the natural logarithms of the variables on both sides of the equation. We have also transformed logarithmically all the variables used in the equations we estimate in this paper. These transformations are undertaken because many of the variables are skewed; moreover, inspection of their scatter-plots with the migration stream dependent variable informed us that the bivariate relationships were not always linear. The transformations correct these problems of nonlinearity and skewness, hence addressing important assumptions of ordinary least squares regression (Hanushek and Jackson 1977; Bradshaw and Fraser 1989).

The linear function for the classic gravity model that we will first estimate is as follows:

$$M_{ij} = (P_i * P_j) \: / \: D_{ij},$$

or using natural logarithms,

$$\ln M_{ij} = \ln P_i + \ln P_j - \ln D_{ij},$$

where: $\ln M_{ij}$ = the natural logarithm of the absolute value of the migration flow between State$_i$ and State$_j$; and

     $\ln P_i$ and $\ln P_i$ = the natural logarithms of population size in State$_i$ and State$_j$, respectively.

The ecological model of interstate migration will be tested with three different equations, each mainly differentiated with respect to the measurement of the dependent variable (see discussion above). The first ecological equation to be tested is the following:

$$\ln M_{ij} = \ln P_i + \ln P_j - \ln D_{ij} + \ln DEN_i + \ln DEN_j + \ln E_i + \ln E_j + \ln CR_i$$
$$+ \ln CR_j + \ln NW_i + \ln NW_j + \ln UN_i + \ln UN_j + \ln M_i + \ln M_j$$
$$+ \ln CL_i + \ln CL_j,$$

where: $\ln M_{ij}$ = the natural logarithm of the absolute value of the migration flow between State$_i$ and State$_j$;

$\ln P_i$ and $\ln P_j$ = the natural logarithms of population size in State$_i$ and State$_j$, respectively;

$\ln D_{ij}$ = the natural logarithm of the distance between State$_i$ and State$_j$;

$\ln DEN_i$ and $\ln DEN_j$ = the natural logarithms of population density in State$_i$ and State$_j$, respectively.

$\ln E_i$ and $\ln E_j$ = the natural logarithms of the level of education of State$_i$ and State$_j$, respectively;

$\ln CR_i$ and $\ln CR_j$ = the natural logarithms of the crime rate in State$_i$ and State$_j$, respectively;

$\ln NW_i$ and $\ln NW_j$ = the natural logarithms of the degree of nonwhite concentration in State$_i$ and State$_j$, respectively;

$\ln UN_i$ and $\ln UN_j$ = the natural logarithms of the unemployment rate in State$_i$ and State$_j$, respectively;

$\ln M_i$ and $\ln M_j$ = the natural logarithms of the per capita manufacturing wage in State$_i$ and State$_j$, respectively; and

$\ln CL_i$ and $\ln CL_j$ = the natural logarithms of the climate index for State$_i$ and State$_j$, respectively.

The second ecological equation is the same as the first, with two exceptions: (1) the dependent variable is M_{ij}/P_j, that is, we have divided the numerator by the size of the population of the state of destination; (2) because P_j is the denominator of the dependent variable in this equation, we have deleted this variable from the right-hand side of the equation.

The third ecological equation is also the same as the first, but with two exceptions: (1) the dependent variable is $M_{ij}/(P_i * P_j)$; here the numerator is divided by the product of the populations of the states of origin and destination; (2) because both P_i and P_j are in the denominator of the third equation's dependent variable, we have deleted both variables from the right-hand side of the equation.

As already noted, the units of analysis in this first section presenting the results of the paper are the 2,431 migration streams (of the 2,550 possible streams) with migrants in them; recall that 119 of the possible

2,550 streams had no migrants. Multiple regression analysis is used, and the regression coefficients (both *b* and *β*) will be used to gauge the importance of the independent variables. We now turn to the results of our analyses.

Results I: Analyses of All Migration Flows

The results from the multiple regression analysis estimating a classic gravity equation are shown in Table 5. As in prior research, the gravity equation contains only three independent variables, namely, the natural logarithms of population size at origin and destination, and the natural logarithm of distance between the origin and destination states. Their unstandardized regression coefficients (*b*), significance levels, and standardized regression coefficients (*β*) are presented.

The classic gravity model works precisely as hypothesized. Population size at both the origin and destination states is statistically associated with the volume of the interstate migration streams and, as predicted, its effects are positive. The independent variable measuring the distance between the origin and destination states is also statistically significant and, as expected, its association with interstate migration is negative. The shorter the distance between the origin and destination states, the larger the size of the migration flow from the origin to the destination. An examination of the standardized coefficients (*β*s) indicates that the two population size variables have greater effects on the volume of the migration stream than the distance variable. The three gravity variables in concert account for almost 56 percent of the variation in the dependent variable.

Table 5. Regression Coefficients from Gravity Model: 2,413 Interstate Migration Streams, United States, 1985-1990

Independent Variables	Metric Coefficient (b)	Significance	Standardized Coefficient
LnPopulation Size			
Origin	.715	0.000	.450
Destination	.804	0.000	.504
LnDistance	-.552	0.000	-.268
Constant	-10.986	0.000	
R^2 (adj.)	.559		

Table 6.   Regression Coefficients from Three Ecological Equations: 2,413 Interstate Migration Streams, United States, 1985-1990

Independent Variables	Regression 1 $(DV = \ln [M_{ij}])$			Regression 2 $(DV = \ln [M_{ij}/P_j])$			Regression 3 $(DV = \ln [M_{ij}/P_i * P_j])$		
	Coef.	sig.	Beta	Coef.	sig.	Beta	Coef.	sig.	Beta
Population									
Origin	.81	0.000	.51	.81	0.000	.59			
Destination	.89	0.000	.56						
Distance	-1.07	0.000	-.52	-1.07	0.000	-.59	-1.06	0.000	-.70
Density									
Origin	-.15	0.000	-.14	-.15	0.000	-.16	-.18	0.000	-.24
Destination	-.21	0.000	-.21	-.23	0.003	-.26	-.23	0.000	-.30
Education									
Origin	3.85	0.000	.27	3.85	0.000	.31	4.56	0.000	.44
Destination	2.57	0.000	.18	3.00	0.000	.24	2.96	0.000	.29
Crime									
Origin	.01	0.902	.00	.01	0.916	.00	-.16	0.091	-.04
Destination	.62	0.000	.11	.52	0.000	.11	.54	0.000	.13
Nonwhites									
Origin	.25	0.000	.14	.25	0.000	.17	.26	0.000	.21
Destination	.15	0.000	.09	.15	0.000	.11	.15	0.000	.12
Unemployment									
Origin	.01	0.869	.00	.01	0.869	.00	.03	0.718	.01
Destination	-.47	0.000	-.09	-.45	0.000	-.10	-.45	0.000	-.12
Wages									
Origin	-.43	0.024	-.04	-.44	0.025	-.05	-.78	0.000	-.10
Destination	-.76	0.000	-.07	-.98	0.000	-.10	-.97	0.000	-.12
Climate									
Origin	.78	0.000	.13	.78	0.000	.15	.70	0.000	.16
Destination	1.22	0.000	.20	1.17	0.000	.22	1.17	0.000	.26
Constant	-28.30	0.000		-28.89	0.000		-30.01	0.000	
R^2 (adj.)		0.76			0.68			0.53	

Note: All variables are expressed as natural logarithms; see text for definitions of variables.

We turn our attention now to the three ecological equations of interstate migration flows, and compare and contrast their results with those of the gravity equation. The regression coefficients for the ecological equations are shown in Table 6.

As already noted, the three ecological equations differ principally with regard to the measurement of the dependent variable of interstate migration flow. The first equation uses M_{ij}, that is, the actual volume of the interstate migration flow, as its dependent variable. This is the same dependent variable used in the gravity equation just discussed (Table 5). In this first ecological equation, the three gravity variables are by far the more influential of all the independent variables, and the direction of their effects is as expected. Regarding the ecological variables, ecological theory enabled us to expect that the population density variable at origin would be positively associated with the volume of the migration flow, but at destination it would be negatively associated with the volume of the stream. The regression results for the first ecological equation show that density is negatively associated at both origin and destination with the migration flow, although its effect at destination is considerably larger (about one-third larger) than that at origin. Regarding the effects of education, we expected a negative association at origin and a positive one at destination. The regression results for this variable support our expected positive effect at destination, however, at origin, education has a positive not a negative effect.

We expected the crime rate at origin to be positively associated with migration, and at destination to be negatively associated. The results indicate that the relationship at origin is positive as expected, but the coefficient is not statistically significant. At destination, the crime rate shows a positive, not the expected negative, effect. We hypothesized that the nonwhite concentration variable at origin would have a positive effect on the migration flow, but at destination its effect would be negative. The regression results support our hypothesis at origin, but not at destination. According to our hypotheses, the unemployment rate at origin should be positively associated with migration, and at destination the effect should be negative. The regression results support our hypothesis at destination. The coefficient of the unemployment rate at origin is positive, as expected, but it is not statistically significant. We hypothesized that manufacturing wages at origin would have a negative association with migration, and at destination its effect would be positive. The regression results show support for our hypothesis at origin, but not at destination. Finally, with regard to the climate variable, we anticipated that at origin, climate would be negatively associated with migration, but at destination, its effect would be positive. The regression results support our expectation of a positive association at destination, but do not show the expected negative association at origin. The total amount of variance explained with this first ecological equation is .76 (see bottom row of Table 6), a considerable improvement over the adjusted R^2 of .56 of the classic gravity model of interstate migration flows (see Table 5).

Before summarizing the results of this first ecological regression equation, we will inspect the results of the second and third ecological equations (see the middle and right panels of Table 6). Recall that these two equations differ from the first mainly with regard to (1) the measurement of the dependent variable, and (2) the inclusion or exclusion on the right-hand side of the equations of measures of population size at origin and destination. As we have already noted, the second equation measures the dependent variable as M_{ij}/P_j and excludes P_j from the right-hand side of the equation. The third ecological equation measures the dependent variable as $M_{ij}/(P_i * P_j)$ and deletes both P_i and P_j from the right-hand side of the equation. The results of the second and third regressions are not difficult to summarize because they are very similar to those of the first ecological equation. In fact, the results of these two equations not only support and reject the same hypotheses supported and rejected by the results of the first equation, they also produce coefficients with values extremely close to those of the coefficients in the first equation. The only major difference in the regression results of the three ecological equations has to do with the magnitude of the adjusted multiple coefficient of determination (R^2). In the second and third ecological equations, the adjusted R^2s are somewhat lower than the R^2 of the first: their scores are .76, .68, and .53, respectively. These differences are almost entirely due to the inclusion of P_i and P_j on the right-hand side of the first equation, the inclusion of only P_i on the right-hand side of the second equation, and the inclusion of neither as independent variables in the third equation. In the second and third equations, one or both of these indicators of population size are used as denominators on the left-hand side of the equation. Given their very high associations with the volume of the migration stream, it is understandable that their exclusion will decrease the value of the coefficient of determination.

Nevertheless, in our opinion it is most instructive to include the results of the three ecological equations. For one thing, a comparison of this type indicates that there is indeed a difference in the overall amount of variance explained (R^2) between a migration model measuring the dependent variable as a gross flow, and models that measure the dependent variable as a rate. However, as just noted, we know that this difference is mainly due to where the analyst places the values of P_i and

P_j, that is, on the right-hand side or on the left-hand side of the equation. The other reason it is instructive to include and compare the results of the three ecological equations is that, irrespective of whether the analyst measures the dependent variable of migration in absolute numbers or as a rate, the values of the regression coefficients are unchanged. This result, however, is due to the fact that in an important sense all three equations are the same equations, with the exception that the P_i and P_j values are used either as variables on the right-hand side of the equations, or as denominators on the left-hand side of the equations. When these varying strategies are followed, the values of the regression coefficients of the equations end up being similar to one another. (The reader is directed to a mathematical discussion of this issue by Greenwood and Sweetland [1972, p. 670].)

The three ecological regression models indicate that the most important and influential independent variables, in terms of those with the highest standardized coefficients (betas) as well as being signed in the directions hypothesized, are the gravity variables. It makes no difference if all three gravity variables are used, as in the first ecological equation, or if two are used, as in the second, or if only one is used, as in the third; they are consistently the most important of all the independent variables. The larger the size of the population at origin and at destination, and the shorter the distance between origin and destination, the larger the size of the migration stream between origin and destination, as measured by the absolute number of migrants, or as migration rates.

The next most important predictor variables are density at destination, education at destination, and climate at destination. In all three ecological equations, these three variables have betas of .20 or higher, except for the first equation where the beta for education at destination is .18. In three instances, their beta coefficients are above .30. The lower the population density at destination, and the higher the level of education at destination, and the more favorable the climate at destination, the larger the size of the migration stream between origin and destination.

There are three more ecological independent variables that in all three equations are both statistically significant and signed in the directions hypothesized. However, their values are lower than those of the gravity variables and the three ecological variables just mentioned. These are the nonwhite concentration at origin, the unemployment rate at destination, and manufacturing wages at origin. The larger the concentration of nonwhites at origin, and the lower the unemployment rate at destination, and the lower the manufacturing wages at origin, the larger the size of the migration stream between origin and destination.

Some of the ecological independent variables have no influence or effect on the size of the migration flow. That is, they have associations with the dependent variable that are either not statistically significant, or are not in the direction hypothesized, or both. To illustrate, in all three equations density at origin and education at origin are statistically significant, but they are not signed in the directions hypothesized. The crime rate at origin is not statistically significant, and the crime rate at destination is statistically significant, but in the incorrect direction. The unemployment rate at origin is not statistically significant. The nonwhite concentration index at destination is significant, but is signed in the incorrect direction. Finally, wages at destination and climate at origin are statistically significant, but do not have the signs hypothesized. We will address some of these issues in the "Implications" section. We turn now to our analyses of a series of state-specific investigations of the interstate migration flows.

Results II: Analyses of State-Specific Migration Flows

In the previous section, we estimated ecological models among 2,413 interstate migration flows, covering all the migration flows between every pair of the 51 states that had bona fide migration streams (i.e., streams with migrants in them) (see the results in Table 6). In this section, we estimate a series of state-specific analyses.

Our ecological models may be calibrated separately on a state-specific basis in two ways: (1) to examine the extent to which destination-specific ecological variables explain the volume of the out-migration flows from a specific state of origin, and (2) to examine the extent to which origin-specific ecological variables explain the volume of the in-migration flows to a specific state of destination. Because the 51 states differ in important ways from one another in their socioeconomic, economic, and related characteristics, it is likely that the independent variables that influence migration to or from each state may differ. We echo the comments in this regard of Greenwood and Sweetland (1972) that differences in industrial structure, income level, location, and a number of demographic factors may well result in migration elasticities that differ, perhaps appreciably, between states (p. 672). We have, therefore, disaggregated the 2,413 migration streams into a series of state-specific in-migration flows, and a series of state-specific out-migration flows. This permits us to treat each state separately, as both an origin location for out-migration flows to the other states, and as a destination location for in-migration flows from other states. We report on the results of such state-specific investigations in Table 7 where destination-specific variables are used to estimate 51 state-specific out-migration equations, and in Table 8 where origin-specific variables are used to estimate 51 state-specific in-migration equations.

The first row of Table 7 reports the degree to which destination-specific variables explain the size of the out-migration flows from the state of Maine. The second-to-last column indicates that there were 44 migration streams that originated in Maine and went to other states that had migrants in them, indicating that the Maine-specific equation has 44 units of analysis (i.e., it has 44 migration streams to study). All the independent variables in the equation, except for distance, refer to destination-specific attributes; that is, the independent variables are characteristics of the 44 states receiving out-migrants from Maine. The signs of the coefficients are shown in the table, and they are asterisked if they are both statistically significant and in the directions hypothesized.

In the case of Maine, there are four variables, out of ten in the equation, that are both significant and in the directions hypothesized: population size at destination, distance between Maine and the destination state, the nonwhite concentration index at destination, and the unemployment rate at destination. The results indicate that the larger the size of the population in the destination state, and the shorter the distance between Maine and the destination state, and the lower the percentage of nonwhites in the destination state, and the lower the unemployment rate in the destination state, the larger the size of the migration flow between Maine and the destination state. The table also indicates that these independent variables together account for 79 percent of the variation in the volume of the migration streams from Maine to the destination states. Variation in the magnitude of the out-migration flows between 1985 and 1990 from Maine to 44 other states is accounted for chiefly by the two gravity variables of population size at destination and the distance between Maine and the destination state, and the two ecological variables of the destination states pertaining to the concentration of nonwhites and the unemployment rate.

Table 7. The Significance of Destination-Specific Parameter Estimates for Each of 51 States: 50 (or Fewer) Migration Flows from Each Origin State, United States, 1985–1990

Origin	Pop_j	$Dist_{ij}$	$Dens_j$	Ed_j	Crm_j	$Nonwht_j$	$Unemp_j$	$Wages_j$	$Climate_j$	Constant	N	Adj. R^2
1. Maine	+*	−*	−	+	+	−*	−*	−	+	3.15	44	0.79
2. New Hampshire	+*	−*	−*	+*	+	+	−	−	+*	−5.86	44	0.72
3. Vermont	+*	−*	−	+	+	−	−	−	+	4.02	36	0.57
4. Massachusetts	+*	−*	+	+*	+	−	−	−	+	10.82	47	0.77
5. Rhode Island	+*	−*	+	+	+	−	−	−	+*	2.81	40	0.67
6. Connecticut	+*	−*	+	−	+	−*	−	−	+	5.24	48	0.77
7. New York	+*	−*	−	+*	+	+	−	−	+*	0.42	50	0.86
8. New Jersey	+*	−†	−	+*	+	−	−*	+	+*	3.47	49	0.83
9. Pennsylvania	+*	−*	−*	+	+	+	−	−	+*	−8.05	50	0.86
10. Ohio	+*	−*	−*	+	+	+	−	−	+*	−2.81	50	0.82
11. Indiana	+*	−*	−	+	+	+	+	−	+	−11.96	50	0.81
12. Illinois	+*	−*	−	+	+	+	+	−	+	−6.30	50	0.77
13. Michigan	+*	−*	−*	+*	+	+	+	+	+	−5.46	50	0.78
14. Wisconsin	+*	−*	−*	+*	+	+	+	−	+	−1.24	50	0.79
15. Minnesota	+*	−*	−*	+	+	+	−	−	−	−15.31	48	0.66
16. Iowa	+*	−*	−*	+	+	+	−	−	+	−12.05	48	0.71
17. Missouri	+*	−*	−*	+*	−	+	−	+	+*	−13.73	49	0.84
18. North Dakota	+*	−*	−	+	+	+	−	−	+	−8.65	48	0.65
19. South Dakota	+*	−*	−	+	+	+	+	−	+	13.82	44	0.57
20. Nebraska	+*	−*	−*	−	+	+	−	+	+	−20.03	47	0.65
21. Kansas	+*	−*	−*	+*	−	+	−	−	+*	−3.84	49	0.76
22. Delaware	+*	−*	−*	+*	−	+	+	−	+*	−1.20	35	0.63
23. Maryland	+*	−*	−	+	+	+	−	+	+*	−0.06	49	0.77
24. Washington, D.C.	+*	−*	−	+	+	+	−	+	+	−12.35	45	0.60
25. Virginia	+*	−*	−	+	+	+	−	−	+*	0.73	50	0.74

No.	State												
26.	West Virginia	+*	-*	-*	+	+	+	-*	-	+*	-0.95	46	0.84
27.	North Carolina	+*	-*	-	+	+	+	+	-	+	-5.21	50	0.71
28.	South Carolina	+*	-	+	+	+	+	+	-	+	4.98	50	0.65
29.	Georgia	+*	-	-	-	+	+	-	+	+	-0.71	49	0.81
30.	Florida	+*	-	-	-	+	-	-	-	+	5.19	50	0.78
31.	Kentucky	+*	-*	-*	+	-	+	-	+	+*	-16.91	47	0.79
32.	Tennessee	+*	-	-	-	+	+	-	-	+	8.78	49	0.84
33.	Alabama	+*	-*	-*	-	+	+	-	-	+	6.84	49	0.71
34.	Mississippi	+*	-*	-*	-	+	+	-	-	+*	4.18	47	0.80
35.	Arkansas	+*	-*	-*	-	+	+	-	-	+*	-8.96	47	0.83
36.	Louisiana	+*	-*	-*	+	+	+	-	+	+*	5.48	48	0.82
37.	Oklahoma	+*	-*	-*	+	+	+	-	-	+	-12.49	49	0.78
38.	Texas	+*	-	-	+	+	+	+	-	+	-1.09	50	0.79
39.	Montana	+*	-*	-	-	+	-	+	-	+	-4.23	48	0.70
40.	Idaho	+*	-*	-*	+*	+	+	+	-	+*	0.06	47	0.81
41.	Wyoming	+*	-*	-	+*	+	+	-	-	+*	-5.04	48	0.72
42.	Colorado	+*	-*	-*	+*	-	+	-*	+	+	-19.35	50	0.90
43.	New Mexico	+*	-*	-*	+*	+	+	-*	+	+*	-13.73	49	0.90
44.	Arizona	+*	-*	-*	+*	+	+	-	-	+*	-7.26	50	0.83
45.	Utah	+*	-*	-	+*	+	+	-	+	-	-21.87	48	0.78
46.	Nevada	+*	-*	-	-	+	-	+	-	+*	-3.18	49	0.79
47.	Washington	+*	-*	-	-	-	-	+	+	+*	-0.32	49	0.68
48.	Oregon	+*	-*	+	+*	+	+	+	-	+	-25.59	48	0.70
49.	California	+*	-*	-	+*	+	-	-	+	+*	-2.18	48	0.88
50.	Alaska	+*	-*	-*	-	+	+	-*	-	+*	26.68	50	0.66
51.	Hawaii	+*	-	-	+	+	+		+	+*	-5.90	46	0.83
	Total Number of Correct and Significant Coefficients	51	46	26	16	0	2	6	0	27			

Note: * Coefficient is statistically significant at .05, and is in the direction hypothesized (see Figure 1).

331

We direct attention next to the 38th row in Table 7—the equation for the state of Texas. The size of the migration streams from Texas to 50 other states (all 50 out-migration flows from Texas have migrants in them) may be explained chiefly by the two gravity variables of population at destination and distance between Texas and the destination, and the ecological variable of density at destination. These three variables explain the same amount of the variance in the out-migration flows, 79 percent, as four variables were shown (above) to explain the variance in out-migration flows in Maine.

A perusal of the other equations in Table 7 indicates that, among the states, many combinations of independent variables end up being the most influential predictors of out-migration flows. In most states, both gravity and ecological variables are among the most effective independent variables. The state of South Carolina, however, is an exception to this statement because in South Carolina there is only one significant predictor of the size of the out-migration flow, namely, the size of the population in the destination state.

The bottom row of Table 7 summarizes the results from the 51 state-specific analyses of the impact of destination-specific attributes on state-specific out-migration flows. Across the 51 state-specific equations, the most influential independent variable is the size of the population at destination. In all 51 equations, this independent variable is both statistically significant and in the (positive) direction hypothesized. Distance between the origin and destination is the next most important variable among the 51 state-specific equations; in all equations, except those for South Carolina, Georgia, Florida, Alabama, and Hawaii, the distance coefficient is statistically significant and negative.

Among the ecological variables, climate at destination is significant and positive in 27 of the 51 state-specific equations. Of interest is the fact that of the 24 remaining states, the ones where climate at destination is not an important predictor of out-migration flows are Maine, Vermont, Massachusetts, Connecticut, Illinois, Michigan, Wisconsin, Minnesota, Iowa, North Dakota, South Dakota, Nebraska, the District of Columbia, Montana, and Wyoming. These are states where average temperatures, especially in the winter months, are known to be particularly harsh. Yet, in the regression equations estimating out-migration from these states, the climate index in the destination states does not serve well as a predictor of the volume of their out-migration streams. As noted, the climate index, however, does work well as a predictor of out-migration in 27 state-specific equations, but these are typically states with mild climates. Climate thus appears to be an important predictor of out-migration from states with relatively mild climates, but not from states with relatively harsh climates. This finding seems to contradict common knowledge about the effects of climate on migration.

Of the other ecological independent variables, population density at destination is significant and signed in the negative direction in 26 of the state-specific equations, and the level of education at destination is significant and signed in the expected positive direction in 16 of the state-specific equations. The remaining ecological variables do not do anywhere near as well as those just discussed. The unemployment rate at destination is significant and in the expected negative direction in only six of the state equations. The nonwhite concentration index is significant and signed in the hypothesized negative direction in only two of the state-specific equations. And the independent variables representing the crime rate and manufacturing wages are significant and in the expected directions in none of the state-specific equations. We will discuss these results and their implications in the last section. We turn now to an examination of in-migration to each of the 51 states.

Table 8 presents the results of 51 regression equations that examine the significance of origin-specific variables in predicting in-migration flows into each of the 51 states. The first row of Table 8 presents the results of a regression equation of 49 in-migration streams (from 49 other states) into the state of Maine. Maine is the destination state, and the independent variables represent characteristics of the sending states, that is, the states providing in-migrants to Maine. The regression results indicate that only three independent variables are important in accounting for the variance in the volume of the in-migration streams from the 49 sending states, namely, the size of the population in the state of origin, the distance between the origin state and Maine, and the percentage of nonwhites in the population of the state of origin. The larger the size of the population of the origin state, and the shorter the distance between the origin state and Maine, and the higher the percentage of nonwhites in the origin state, the larger the size of the migration stream from the origin state to Maine. The independent variables account for 65 percent of the variance in the values of the migration flows into Maine.

The results of the Maine-specific equation are very similar to the results of the state-specific equations for 22 other states, namely, Pennsylvania, Illinois, Michigan, Wisconsin, Iowa, Missouri, Kansas,

Table 8. The Significance of Origin-Specific Parameter Estimates for Each of 51 States: 50 (or Fewer) Migration Flows Into Each Destination State, United States, 1985-1990

Origin	Pop_i	$Dist_{ij}$	$Dens_i$	Ed_i	Crm_i	$Nonwht_i$	$Unemp_i$	$Wages_i$	$Climate_i$	Constant	N	Adj. R^2
1. Maine	+*	-*	-	+	-	+*	-	-	+	-7.21	49	0.65
2. New Hampshire	+*	-*	-	+	+	-	+	-	+	-0.90	46	0.69
3. Vermont	+*	-*	-	+	-	+	-	-	+	-6.63	44	0.58
4. Massachusetts	+*	-*	+	+	+	-	+	-	+	-8.96	50	0.80
5. Rhode Island	+*	-*	-	+	-	+	+	-	+	1.86	44	0.70
6. Connecticut	+*	-*	+	+	+	-	+	-	+	-4.57	50	0.82
7. New York	+*	-*	-	+	+	+	+	-	+	-13.91	50	0.85
8. New Jersey	+*	-*	-	+	+	+	+*	-	+	-11.22	50	0.85
9. Pennsylvania	+*	-*	-	+	-	+*	-	+	+	-11.47	50	0.86
10. Ohio	+*	-*	-	+	-	+	+	+	-*	-16.01	50	0.84
11. Indiana	+*	-*	-	+	+	+	+	-	+	-14.22	50	0.81
12. Illinois	+*	-*	-	+	+	+*	+	-	+	-10.49	50	0.90
13. Michigan	+*	-*	-	+	+	+*	+	+	+	-17.88	50	0.84
14. Wisconsin	+*	-*	-	+	+	+*	+	-	-	-3.90	49	0.71
15. Minnesota	+*	-*	-	+	+	+	-	-	+	-9.05	50	0.70
16. Iowa	+*	-*	-	+	+	+*	-	-	+	-8.42	47	0.74
17. Missouri	+*	-*	-	+	-	+*	-	+	+	-10.68	49	0.85
18. North Dakota	+*	-*	-	-	+	+	-	+	+	-3.27	37	0.34
19. South Dakota	+*	-*	-	+	+	+	+	-	+	9.43	41	0.43
20. Nebraska	+*	-*	-	+	-	+	+	-	+	-6.61	45	0.59
21. Kansas	+*	-*	-	+	-	+*	-	+	+	-3.13	48	0.78
22. Delaware	+*	-*	-	-	-	+	+	-	+	-17.35	32	0.51
23. Maryland	+*	-*	+	+	+	+*	+	-	+	-9.90	50	0.82
24. Washington, D.C.	+*	-*	-	+	+	-	-	+	+	-21.18	47	0.73
25. Virginia	+*	-*	+	+	-	+*	+	-	+	-3.82	50	0.88

334

#	State	(1)	(2)	(3)	(4)	(5)	(6)	(7)	(8)	(9)	(10)			
26.	West Virginia	+*	−*	−	+	−	+	−	+	+	+	−20.72	42	0.77
27.	North Carolina	+*	−*	−	+	−	+*	−	+	+	+	−6.19	50	0.82
28.	South Carolina	+*	−*	+	+	+	+	−	−	+	−	−0.17	50	0.81
29.	Georgia	+*	−*	+	+	−	+*	−	−	+	+	−1.35	49	0.86
30.	Florida	+*	−	−	+	+	−	−	+	+	−	−2.75	50	0.84
31.	Kentucky	+*	−*	+	+	−	+*	−	+	+	−	−22.61	48	0.80
32.	Tennessee	+*	−*	−	+	+	+	−	−	+	+	5.17	50	0.86
33.	Alabama	+*	−*	−	+	−	+*	+	−	+	+	−1.78	49	0.89
34.	Mississippi	+*	−*	−	+	+	+*	+*	+	+	−	−6.30	47	0.75
35.	Arkansas	+*	−*	−	+	+	+*	+	−	+	−	−13.57	47	0.70
36.	Louisiana	+*	−*	−	+	−	+*	+*	−	+	+	12.86	49	0.71
37.	Oklahoma	+*	−*	−	+	−	+	+	+	+	+	−12.77	46	0.77
38.	Texas	+*	−*	−	+	+	+*	+	−	+	+	−3.84	50	0.90
39.	Montana	+*	−*	−	+	+	+*	−	−	+	+	−10.80	46	0.63
40.	Idaho	+*	−*	−	+	−	+	−	−	+	+	−21.39	46	0.68
41.	Wyoming	+	−*	−	+	−	−	−	+	+	+	5.19	43	0.56
42.	Colorado	+*	−*	+	+	−	+*	−	−	+	+	−13.96	50	0.86
43.	New Mexico	+*	−*	−	+	+	+*	−	−	−	−	−16.16	49	0.77
44.	Arizona	−	−*	−	+	+	+	+	−	+	+	−16.07	50	0.91
45.	Utah	+*	−*	−	+	−	+	−	−	−*	−	−16.58	46	0.72
46.	Nevada	+*	−*	−	+	−	+*	+	−	+	+	−11.54	49	0.85
47.	Washington	+*	−*	−	+	−	+*	+	−	+	+	−7.20	50	0.70
48.	Oregon	+*	−*	−	+	+	+*	+	−	+	+	−7.55	50	0.65
49.	California	+*	−*	+	+	+	+*	+	+	+	+	−13.49	50	0.89
50.	Alaska	+*	−*	+	+	+	+	−	+	+	+	10.72	48	0.51
51.	Hawaii	+	+	−	+	−	+	−	−	+	+	−23.29	50	0.68
	Total Number of Correct and Significant Coefficients	50	49	0	0	0	23	2	0	0	2			

Note: * Coefficient is statistically significant at .05, and is in the direction hypothesized (see Figure 1).

335

Maryland, Virginia, North Carolina, Georgia, Kentucky, Alabama, Mississippi, Arkansas, Oklahoma, Texas, Colorado, New Mexico, Nevada, Washington, and California. That is, the same three independent variables that were the only influential predictors of in-migration to Maine are the only influential predictors of in-migration flows in the state-specific equations of the 22 states just named.

Indeed, with the exception of the two gravity variables of population size at origin and distance between origin and destination, and the one ecological variable of nonwhite concentration, the other independent variables, representing characteristics of the sending states, are not very effective predictors of in-migration in any of the state-specific equations. The unemployment rate at origin is significant and signed in the expected positive direction in only the equations for the two states of New Jersey and Alabama. The climate index at origin is significant and signed in the hypothesized negative direction in only the equations for Ohio and Arizona. The coefficients of the other independent variables, namely, population density at origin, level of education at origin, the crime rate at origin, and the level of manufacturing wages at origin, are significant and in the hypothesized directions in none of the 51 state-specific equations.

Our investigations of the state-specific migration flows to and from the states indicate that the gravity variables are influential predictors in just about all of the 102 state-specific equations. The effects of the ecological variables are mixed and less consistent. They do appear to be more effective, however, when they represent characteristics of the destination states and are used to predict the amount of out-migration from a single state, than when they represent characteristics of origin states and are used to predict the amount of the flow of in-migration to a single state. A comparison of the numbers of significant coefficients in Table 7 with those in Table 8 provides support for this statement. We turn now to a discussion of the implications of our results.

DISCUSSION AND IMPLICATIONS

We have set forth and tested a human ecological explanation of interstate migration flows in the United States during the 1985-1990 period. We reasoned that because so many of the prior analyses of migration streams have used spatial interaction models with a heavy focus on gravity and economic variables, one contribution of our research would be its articulation and examination of the ecological approach.

The results of the several analyses we conducted indicate that gravity variables tend to out-perform ecological variables in their ability to explain variance in the volume of the migration flow. In all the equations we estimated, the gravity variables were shown to have higher standardized regression coefficients than the ecological variables. Therefore, on the surface, it would appear that the ecological approach as presented here has been surpassed by one dealing exclusively with gravity variables.

We are inclined to argue against this conclusion for several reasons. In the first place, the ecological variables add considerably to an explanation of interstate migration patterns based only on gravity variables. We have shown in this research that the three gravity variables—population size at origin and at destination, and distance between origin and destination—explain slightly more than one-half of the variance in the volume of the interstate migration flows. When ecological variables are added to the regression equation, the amount of explained variance increases to more than 75 percent. This indicates that a very substantial amount of the variance in the magnitude of the interstate migration streams is explained by the ecological variables, and this is an amount over and above that explained by the gravity variables.

Second, although the three gravity variables do indeed perform very well in influencing the magnitude of the migration flow, their performance should not come as that much of a surprise; and this is especially so with regard to gravity equations using gross flows as the dependent variable with population size at both origin and destination on the right-hand side as predictors. We observed earlier that in such a situation there will occur high associations of population size with gross migration flows. But as Karp and Kelly noted, this amounts to saying that the larger the area, the greater the number of migrants there will be from it (1971, p. 12), which is similar to saying that more crimes are committed in larger areas (1971, p. 13) than in smaller ones.

But there is still an additional question not raised directly, implied by Karp and Kelly, and it has to do with the theoretical meaning of these associations. What do these associations between population size and migration flows mean? How do these associations advance our understanding of the predictors of the volume of the migration flow? Other than telling us that the stream will be large (or small) if the populations at origin and destination are large (or small), such relationships tell us very little. Population size, especially at destination, has been referred to as the least pure, in a theoretical sense, of all the variables used to account for migration flows (Karp and Kelly 1971, p. 21). This is due to the fact that whereas "past studies of trends in migration show that the size of an (area) ... acts as a force of attraction for migrants, it is difficult to specify exactly what this attraction consists of" (Karp and Kelly 1971, p. 21). Despite their theoretical shortcomings, we used the gravity variables of population mainly because they have been included in virtually all prior gravity and spatial interaction investigations of migration flows.

This kind of critique, however, may not be leveled against the ecological variables. Indeed, the anticipated relationships of the ecological variables with migration flows are grounded in a rich body of theory that treats the occurrence of migration as a response to an imbalance in an equilibrium relationship between the population size of an area and its level of living. Therefore, we are of the opinion that the relationships reported in this research between the ecological variables and migration contribute considerably more to our understanding of the theoretical determinants of migration flows than do those between population size and migration.

What do our results have to say about the applicability of the ecological theory of migration? Before responding to this question, we should note that the ecological theory of migration is an extremely complex and subtle one. We have endeavored in this research to operationalize its main concepts in terms of only a few selected variables. In so doing, we have not done justice to its theoretical subtleties. Despite these obvious shortcomings in our operationalizations, the regression results, as already noted, indicate that the ecological variables are capable of increasing our understanding of the determinants of interstate migration. Let us explore in slightly more detail this issue and pay attention to the components of the theory.

The investigations of interstate migration streams in which we used all the migration flows as the units of analysis informed us that the three most important ecological variables are all characteristics of the destination areas: density, education, and climate. The next three most important ecological variables are the nonwhite concentration at origin, the unemployment rate at destination, and manufacturing wages at origin. Of the six most influential ecological variables, four of them are characteristics of the destinations. Similar results emerged in the state-specific analyses. One set of equations examined the importance of destination-specific ecological variables in accounting for out-migration flows from each of the states; another set of equations looked at the effectiveness of origin-specific ecological variables in explaining in-migration flows to each of the states. We found that several ecological variables at destination were very effective predictors of migration, namely, climate, density, and education. Conversely, we found that only one ecological variable at origin was a reasonably good predictor of out-migration flows from each of the states, namely, nonwhite concentration. These findings in concert suggest that the ecological theory of migration is much more relevant in explaining the variation in the volume of migration flows when its variables refer to characteristics of the destinations, rather than of the origins. That is, ecological forces tend to be more effective as "pull" mechanisms than as "push" mechanisms. Future investigations of the ecological theory of migration will need to pay closer attention to the different ways ecological factors effect the volume of the migration streams.

Several ecological variables were shown in our analyses to have little or no impact on the volume of the migration stream. A major factor is the crime rate, an indicator of the social environment. This variable, both at origin and at destination, and in the analyses of all migration streams and in the state-specific analyses, was never shown to be an influential predictor of migration behavior. The size of the migration flow is apparently not affected by the crime rate at origin or at destination. At least this is the conclusion when the crime rate is operationalized as the number of serious crimes known to the police per 100,000 population. The climate variable at destination was shown to be an important predictor of migration, but the climate variable at origin was shown to be an unimportant predictor. Our results indicate that climate, an indicator of the physical environment, has an impact on migration, but only at destination. Conversely, nonwhite concentration at origin, but not at destination, was shown to be a rather influential predictor of migration. This indicator of the social environment is apparently very important as a "push" factor, but not as a "pull."

In sum, among the major findings of this study is that interstate migration in the United States during the period of 1985-1990 is highly responsive to three gravity variables and selected ecological variables. However, our analysis measured migration in the general population, without specifying its sex, age, and race components. Further research on the determinants of interstate migration needs to disaggregate the dependent variable by sex, age, and race, once the full set of migration flow data from the 1990 U.S. census become available. Such strategies will enable the further and more specific examination of the ecological theory of migration than was possible in this paper.

ACKNOWLEDGMENTS

We are indebted to John M. Wardwell for insightful and very important comments on an earlier draft of this paper.

REFERENCES

Blanco, C. 1963. "The Determinants of Interstate Population Movements." *Journal of Regional Science* 5: 77-84.
Bradshaw, Y.W. and E. Fraser. 1989. "City Size, Economic Development, and Quality of Life in China: New Empirical Evidence." *American Sociological Review* 54: 986-1003.
Catton, W.R., Jr. 1965. "The Concept of 'Mass' in the Sociological Version of Gravitation." In *Mathematical Explorations in Behavioral Science*, edited by F. Massarik and P. Ratoosh. Homewood, IL: Irwin.
Ervin, D.J. 1987. "The Ecological Theory of Migration: Reconceptualizing Indigenous Labor Force." *Social Science Quarterly* 68: 866-875.
Flowerdew, R. and J. Salt. 1979. "Migration Between Labor Market Areas in Great Britain, 1970-1971." *Regional Studies* 13: 211-231.
Fotheringham, A.S. and M.E. O'Kelly. 1989. *Spatial Interaction Models: Formulations and Applications.* Dordrecht, The Netherlands: Kluwer Academic Publishers.
Frey, W.H. and A. Speare, Jr. 1992. "The Revival of Metropolitan Population Growth in the United States." *Population and Development Review* 18: 129-146.
Frisbie, W.P. and D.L. Poston, Jr. 1978a. "Sustenance Differentiation and Population Redistribution." *Social Forces* 57: 42-56.
_____. 1978b. *Sustenance Organization and Migration in Nonmetropolitan America.* Iowa City: University of Iowa, Iowa University Community Research Center.
Galle, O.R. and K.E. Taeuber. 1966. "Metropolitan Migration and Intervening Opportunities." *American Sociological Review* 31: 5-13.
Gibbs, J.P. and W.T. Martin. 1959. "Toward a Theoretical System of Human Ecology." *Pacific Sociological Review* 2: 29-36.
Greenwood, M.J. 1969. "The Determinants of Labor Migration in Egypt." *Journal of Regional Science* 9: 283-290.
_____. 1971a. "An Analysis of the Determinants of Internal Labor Mobility in India." *Annals of Regional Science* 5: 137-151.
_____. 1971b. "A Regression Analysis of Migration to Urban Areas of a Less-developed Country: The Case of India." *Journal of Regional Science* 11: 253-264.

————. 1975a. "Research on Internal Migration in the United States: A Survey." *Journal of Economic Literature* 13: 397-433.

————. 1975b. "Simultaneity Bias in Migration Models: An Empirical Examination." *Demography* 12: 519-536.

Greenwood, M.J. and D. Sweetland. 1972. "The Determinants of Migration Between Standard Metropolitan Statistical Areas." *Demography* 9: 665-681.

Hanushek, E.A. and J.E. Jackson. 1977. *Statistical Methods for Social Scientists.* New York: Academic Press.

Hawley, A.H. 1950. *Human Ecology: A Theory of Community Structure.* New York: Ronald Press.

————. 1968. "Human Ecology." Pp. 323-332 in *International Encyclopedia of the Social Sciences*, edited by D.L. Sills. New York: Crowell, Collier, and Macmillan.

————. 1981. *Urban Society*, rev. ed. New York: Ronald Press.

Haynes, K.E., D.L. Poston, Jr., and P. Schnirring. 1973. "Intermetropolitan Migration in High and Low Opportunity Areas: Indirect Tests of the Distance and Intervening Opportunities Hypotheses." *Economic Geography* 49: 68-73.

Isbell, E.C. 1944. "Internal Migration in Sweden and Intervening Opportunities." *American Sociological Review* 9: 627-639.

Jessadachatr, P. 1989. "An Economic Analysis of Interprovincial Migration in Thailand." Unpublished doctoral dissertation, University of Pittsburgh, Pittsburgh, PA.

Karp, H.H. and K.D. Kelly. 1971. *Toward an Ecological Analysis of Intermetropolitan Migration.* Chicago: Markham Publishing Company.

Kau, J.B. and C.F. Sirmans. 1979. "A Recursive Model of the Spatial Allocation of Migrants." *Journal of Regional Science* 19: 47-56.

Lenski, G.E. 1970. *Human Societies.* New York: McGraw-Hill.

London, B. 1986. "Ecological and Political-economic Analyses of Migration to a Primary City: Bangkok, Thailand, ca. 1970." *Urban Affairs Quarterly* 21: 501-526.

————. 1987. "Ending Ecology's Ethnocentrism: Thai Replication and Extensions of Ecological Research." *Rural Sociology* 52: 483-500.

Poston, D.L., Jr. 1980. "An Ecological Analysis of Migration in Metropolitan America, 1970-1975." *Social Science Quarterly* 61: 418-433.

————. 1981. "An Ecological Examination of Southern Population Redistribution, 1970-1975." Pp. 137-154 in *The Population of the South: Structure and Change in Social Demographic Context*, edited by D.L. Poston, Jr. and R.H. Weller. Austin: The University of Texas Press.

Poston, D.L., Jr., T. Hirschl, and W.P. Frisbie. 1992. "Sustenance Organization And Population Redistribution in New York State: A Human Ecological Analysis." In *Community, Society and Migration: Noneconomic Migration in America*, edited by P.C. Jobes, W.F. Stinner, and J.M. Wardwell. Lanham, Maryland: University Press of America.

Ravenstein, E.G. 1885. "The Laws of Migration." *Journal of the Royal Statistical Society* 48: 167-235.

————. 1889. "The Laws of Migration: Second Paper." *Journal of the Royal Statistical Society* 52: 241-305.

Saenz, R. and E. Colberg. 1988. "Sustenance Organization and Net Migration in Small Texas Nonmetropolitan Communities, 1960-1980." *Rural Sociology* 53: 334-345.

Sly, D.F. 1972. "Migration and the Ecological Complex." *American Sociological Review* 37: 615-628.

Sly, D.F. and J. Tayman. 1977. "Ecological Approach to Migration Re-examined." *American Sociological Review* 42: 783-795.

Stouffer, S.A. 1940. "Intervening Opportunities: A Theory Relating Mobility and Distance." *American Sociological Review* 5: 845-867.

U.S. Bureau of the Census. 1989. *1988 County and City Data Book*. Washington, DC: U.S. Government Printing Office.

Zipf, G.K. 1946. "The P1P2/D Hypothesis: On the Intercity Movement of Persons." *American Sociological Review* 11: 677-686.